DATE DUE

FUBARNOMICS

ROBERT E. WRIGHT

FUBARNOMICS

A LIGHTHEARTED, SERIOUS LOOK AT
AMERICA'S ECONOMIC ILLS

Prometheus Books

59 John Glenn Drive
Amherst, New York 14228–2119

Published 2010 by Prometheus Books

Inquiries should be addressed to
Prometheus Books
59 John Glenn Drive
Amherst, New York 14228–2119
VOICE: 716–691–0133
FAX: 716–691–0137
WWW.PROMETHEUSBOOKS.COM

14 13 12 11 10   5 4 3 2 1

Library of Congress Cataloging-in-Publication Data

Wright, Robert E. (Robert Eric), 1969–
    Fubarnomics : a lighthearted, serious look at America's economic ills / by Robert E. Wright.
        p. cm.
    Includes bibliographical references and index.
    ISBN 978–1–61614–191–2 (cloth : alk. paper)
    1. Financial crises—United States—History. 2. United States—Economic conditions. 3. Economics—Humor. I. Title.

HB3743.W75 2010
330.973—dc22

2010014736

Printed in the United States of America on acid-free paper

CONTENTS

Have we not suffered ourselves to be deceived by political demagogues and impostors, into this fatal thralldom, which without our timely and vigorous exertions, will terminate in the total destruction of our invaluable republican institutions?

—Anonymous, *Cause of, and Cure for, Hard Times: A Definition of the Attributes and Qualities Indispensable in Money as a Medium of Commerce*

Political realists may actually find comfort in the obvious futility of present policy. Who knows how many Americans may have learned salutary lessons from these depressing years?

—Rexford G. Tugwell, *Mr. Hoover's Economic Policy*

1

FUBAR, FUBAR EVERYWHERE

Ever wonder why so many college students spend more time working and partying than studying? Why we allow six guys in hardhats to stand around doing nothing while traffic snarls? Why you have to pay thousands of dollars for "title insurance" if you buy a house that's not located in Iowa? Why you can't refinance your home mortgage because *other* people stopped paying on theirs?[1] Why our forebears enslaved millions of people for a couple of centuries, then to end the institution fought a war so costly and bloody it would have been far cheaper to buy and free the slaves instead? How in the early 1930s one out of four adults went hungry as they searched for work while the government destroyed large quantities of food? Why ever since then young people in lousy jobs with small children are forced to pay a large percentage of their incomes to people who had decades to work and save? How healthcare and health insurance got so damn expensive? If you've asked yourself any of these or similar questions, or gotten queasy contemplating what passes for economic analysis in the media, this book is for you.

In terms of the actual value of stuff and services that the average American produces in a year (in the language of economists, real per capita gross domestic product), the US economy is among the best in the world and has been for two centuries. Since World War II, American labor productivity (the inflation-adjusted value of output per hour worked) has more than trebled.[2] It may seem strange to call such an economy FUBAR, an acronym apparently coined by the salty tongues of GIs during World War II that stands for fouled (ahem!) up beyond all recognition. Compared to most other national economies, the US economy is a clear winner. But its success is relative, not absolute, because even the American juggernaut finds itself weighted down by inefficient institutions and sagging sectors. This book discusses some of those ugly spots and, in the final chapter, proffers some tentative guidelines for their eradication or amelioration. If we bring lagging industries, such as construction, higher education, healthcare, and social insurance, up to speed, we will prosper as never before and free up resources to tackle other pressing problems, such as global climate change, predatory government, and terrorism.

Unfortunately, at present, the United States appears headed down a much less happy path. The late, great University of Maryland economist Mancur Olson argued that as nations age, their economies become inflexible due to the accumulated weight from special-interest legislation, from the ever-increasing number of laws enacted to aid the few at the expense of the many.[3] The American economy is no exception. From Washington, DC, Congressman John Murtha ensured that "pork," in the form of government contracts, poured into his district in western Pennsylvania. Many of the federal contracts that Murtha's favorite Johnstown-area firms won were "no-bid" deals. In other words, the companies faced no competition, virtually ensuring that they would reap large profits, ill-gotten gains sucked straight out of the taxpayers' pockets. And it gets worse, believe it or not. Many of those contracts were for goods or services that *no* branch of the military or government agency actually wanted or requested. If one of Murtha's favored firms made it, the government got it, whether it wanted it or not.[4]

Meanwhile, with the post-Katrina cleanup still far from finished, Senator Ted Stevens of Alaska tried to divert over $200 million to build a bridge to connect a small Alaskan town to a tiny island inhabited by about fifty people. The notorious "Bridge to Nowhere," as critics dubbed it, was snubbed even by locals who had gotten around quite well for generations by boat and airplane, thank you. (Small, private planes are ubiquitous in Alaska.)[5] If Murtha and Stevens were some sort of renegade exceptions to the rule, we would have little to worry about. Unfortunately, almost everyone in Congress relishes pork projects, or "earmarks" as they have come to be known.

Unelected bureaucrats, from the recalcitrant clerk at the department of motor vehicles to a GS-15 Step 10—the top of the federal government's "general schedule" of pay for bureaucrats—are also major contributors to FUBAR. Governments fail, or create FUBAR conditions, for a variety of reasons. Foremost, reality is a real bitch to understand. Only with considerable effort can the best and the brightest barely fathom its shadowy depths. Information about how the world works is scarce and imperfect, so trying to envision the future is daunting. Systems are chaotic, in the sense that small changes in initial conditions can lead to large differences in outcomes. (Watch *The Butterfly Effect* for an inkling.) A seemingly small policy change can ripple through the economy, destroying equilibrium the way a tossed pebble wreaks havoc on the surface of a placid pond. Unlike the pond, however, the economy doesn't necessarily return to its former state. Rather, like a human face, it may forever bear the scar created by the ill-conceived shock of a rock.[6]

Governments also fail because they are composed of fallible people. Sometimes their foibles induce them to make very well-intentioned mistakes. More often, though, their flaws lead them to satisfy their own wishes and purses, instead of those of the people they ostensibly serve. In some countries, including the United States, private interestedness is checked by elections or other parts of the government—you know, the three branches of government, the bicameral legislature, federalism, and all that. Self-interested behavior still pervades public life, but it is more muted than in Joe Stalin's Soviet Union or Bobby Mugabe's Zimbabwe. Instead of outright theft, American politicians and bureaucrats must engage in more oblique, and hence in some ways more insidious, self-serving activities. Earmarks, campaign contributions, vote swapping, work slowdowns, extra-long lunches, Luddite-like resistance to technology, and regulatory forbearance are only a few such behaviors.

I mean no disrespect to government employees who are, after all, only responding to incentives, or more usually the lack thereof. An anonymous author circa 1835 put it best: "I especially disclaim any allusion to the present incumbents; my business is with institutions, not individuals."[7] As Milton Friedman once pointed out, critics of government usually mean nothing personal. The savviest, most efficient private sector manager or worker will morph into a bumbling idiot soon after taking up employment in the public sector. If you've no idea what I mean, read some Kafka, or at least his Wikipedia entry. Visiting the government office nearest you usually will do the trick, too.

The root problem is that governments need not worry about output, or actual outcomes. Whether the government succeeds or fails, its tax-collecting minions are still going to knock on your door and take their due. In fact, if the government fails it may well ask for yet higher taxes! Johnny will be able to read or Mary won't get accosted or Widow Smith won't perish cold and hungry or al Qaeda will be defeated if only the taxman digs a little deeper into citizens' pockets, or so politicians often claim. There are limits, of course. A government that exacts high taxes and provides little in return faces a higher chance of a coup, rebellion, or revolution. But bad governments do not always face negative repercussions. Consider Cuba and North Korea, which for decades have groaned under authoritarian poverty but persist nevertheless.

Unlike for-profit enterprises, governments face no immediate sanctions for profligacy or inefficiency. George S. in accounts is deadwood, agency W hasn't served a purpose since World War I, bureaucracy Z is riddled with corruption, and X and Y do exactly the same thing, but it is easier to retain them than to rock the boat. (Some redundancies, like those built into the Constitution, are necessary to prevent the government from behaving in a predatory manner. Most redundancies, however, are just plain dumb.) The ship of state is therefore sinking, but its demise is so slow that its doomed passengers barely notice. We're like a colony of frogs in a big, old pot, resting quietly while the water around us slowly comes to a boil.

Also unlike private enterprises, parts of the government work at cross purposes with other parts of it for extended periods of time. Such discrepancies are usually unplanned, arising from conflicting special interests and the remnants of piecemeal policy prescriptions enacted over decades or centuries. For example, the US government long subsidized tobacco farmers and simultaneously tried to reduce cigarette consumption through taxes, bans, and public education. Government-sponsored agricultural R & D increased output and hence depressed prices at the same time that other government programs sought to increase agricultural prices. Programs that paid farmers not to grow crops decreased farm employment, forcing itinerant workers onto the dole or worse. Even more tragic, during the Depression some parts of the government burned crops (to raise agricultural prices to help farmers) while other parts struggled to obtain enough food to nourish the unemployed.[8] And you thought your boss sent mixed signals!

Because the government does not have to worry very much about outcomes, it provides employees with salaries based on their test scores, experience, and the like—not on how well they service taxpayers. Lifetime employment is almost guaranteed. (Only tenured college professors have a better deal.) Nobody receives a bonus for saving taxpayers' money. A bureaucrat who suggests radical changes will end up earning not laurels but a one-way ticket to a dead-end position in a cold, dangerous, or faraway post.

That is the way things are, but must they always remain so? The long-lived late-night comedy show *Saturday Night Live* once joked its way into an interesting idea. In 1991 and 1992, it relentlessly parodied presidential candidate Ross Perot. It was easy to do. Perot had an odd campaign strategy; strange mannerisms; big, comical ears; and a laughable running mate. His extensive business experience also made him suspect. In one skit, Perot, played by Dana Carvey, argued that his salary as president should be a function of the economy's rate of growth. Shy of 3 percent growth, Perot wanted no pay or even expenses because a "chimpanzee could run this country" and do as well, and Perot had "$3 billion back at home," the fruits of his business career. At 3 percent GDP growth, though, Perot wanted a payment of $1 billion. "Now, think about it," he implored, "that's a bargain! You're up $119 billion." At 4 percent, Perot's bonus jumped to $20 billion, another great deal, he argued, because "this isn't the President of G[eneral] M[otors] giving himself a big bonus when the company's losing money sending jobs to Mexico. I get my money *if* and *when* you get yours" [emphasis in original].[9]

Viewers laughed their asses off and commented on the absurdity of the notion. But why is performance-based pay for government officials absurd? Working out the details would be tricky—people generally do precisely what they are given incentives to do—but government would finally begin to concentrate on outcomes. Until that day, government inefficiencies and failures will persist because no one has an incentive to make the government more efficient, to maximize its output or minimize its input.

More is at stake here than just efficiency, though. When governments fail, the results are often spectacularly horrifying. Governments are among the leading causes of war, famine, and pestilence. (Organized religions are close behind, especially when they assume the trappings of government, as in medieval Europe and other theocracies.) Like any powerful tool, government can unleash great good but also great evil. It sometimes fixes the FUBAR parts of the economy, but more often it exacerbates existing problems and sows the seeds of future calamities.

***

If the government was the only cause of FUBAR, our course of action would be clear. Throw the bums out, reduce taxes, make it difficult for the government to borrow except in response to emergencies, deregulate everything, and stop redistributing so much wealth across classes and generations. Unfortunately, the world is not so simple, not by a long shot. Just as governments can fail, so too can markets.[10]

When the Creator cast us mere mortals out of paradise, It created two horrible devils, scarcity and asymmetric information. The former means that we cannot have our cake and eat it too. Doing A necessitates forgoing B. To buy guns (military protection) we must give up butter (consumer goods) and vice versa. Economists call that "opportunity costs." Scarcity makes markets possible, nay, necessary. We cannot have everything we desire, so we must have some way of rationing goods—physical things and services that people want.

In their purest form, as described in words by Adam Smith and in mathematics by Kenneth Arrow and others, markets are elegant ways of coping with scarcity. We still do not have everything that we want, but we do have ways of efficiently deciding what, where, when, and how much to produce and ways of distributing those goods in an ostensibly fair manner, with those who produce the most receiving the most in return. Were scarcity humanity's only punishment for our Fall, life would be pretty darn good indeed. Your relationship with your in-laws might still be FUBAR, but the economy would run like a fine Swiss watch.

But then the second devil, the true bane of our existence, blindsides us. Asymmetric information, the possession of superior information by one party to a contract or transaction, smashes Smith's words and Arrow's equations to bits. When people complain about markets, they are really almost always complaining about asymmetric information, or, to be more precise, its negative effects on the way the markets function. In the Smith-Arrow world, everyone knows everything, or at least everything he or she needs to know in order to avoid getting cheated by others. Markets, not firms, establish prices at just the point where businesses recoup their costs of production and earn enough profit to keep them producing. Consumers know what those prices are and can tell high-quality goods from low-quality ones. Workers' wages equal their marginal productivity, so no one is under- or overpaid and nobody shirks and gets away with it. As I said, if we had only to worry about scarcity, life would be pretty nice, not a paradise but not nearly as hellish as it is.

In the real world, the one suffused with asymmetric information, the pretty Smith-Arrow outcomes rarely occur. Consumers pay too much for crappy products, some workers earn more than they produce, others earn much less than they produce, and companies come to have market power—the ability to *make* prices rather than to *take* them from the market, as in perfectly competitive systems. With asymmetric information comes power, the ability to lie, cheat, and steal one's way to outsized profits. It's a two-way street, too. Sometimes businesses sucker investors into buying overpriced financial securities (stocks, bonds, mortgage-backed securities) or products (like eighty-five-dollar bottles of acai berry pills). Sometimes consumers trick banks into lending them money that they will never repay or insurers into paying fraudulent claims. Bob Seger was far too optimistic in his song "The Fire Down Below."[11] It's more like *everywhere* there ain't *nobody* treating *anybody* right. Just remember this isn't the fault of markets per se. If we are to fix all that is FUBAR, we must cast blame on the real culprit, the devilish asymmetric information. Like the hellhound Cerberus, asymmetric information has three ugly heads: adverse selection, moral hazard, and the principal-agent problem.

Adverse selection is asymmetric information before a contract. It occurs when one party knows more about a potential contract or exchange than the other party does. The classic case of adverse selection is the market for "lemons," which is to say automobiles that suffer from frequent mechanical problems. Information about cars is inherently asymmetric—owners/sellers know much more about their cars than potential buyers do. People who offer lemons for sale know that their cars stink. Most people looking to buy cars, though, can't tell that a car is prone to breakdown. They might kick the tires, take it for a short spin, look under the hood, and whatnot, all without discovering the truth. The seller has superior information and indeed has an incentive to increase the asymmetry by putting a bandage over any obvious problems. He might, for example, warm the car up thoroughly before showing it, put top-quality gasoline in the tank, clean up the oil spots in the driveway, and so forth. He may even lie about the automobile's history and provenance. The poor buyer offers the average price for used cars of the particular make, model, year, and mileage for sale. The seller accepts, with a smile. A day, week, month, or year later, the buyer learns that he has overpaid for his automotive lemon. He complains to his relatives, friends, and neighbors, many of whom tell similar horror stories. Apparently, they decide, all used cars are lemons.

Of course, some used cars are actually very reliable "peaches." A peach owner, however, cannot credibly inform potential buyers of the car's quality. He can tell the truth about the car, but how can the buyer be sure he isn't lying? So information about the car remains asymmetric, and the hapless buyer offers the average price for used cars of the particular make, model, year, and mileage for sale. But this time the seller declines, rendering the buyer's relatives, friends, and neighbors half right—not all used cars for sale are lemons, but those that are bought are!

The lemons story is a simple but powerful one. With appropriate changes, it applies to everything from horses to construction services to lemons (the fruit) to bonds. Suppose you have some money to lend, and the response to your advertisement is overwhelming because many borrowers are in the market. Information is asymmetric, so you can't really tell who the safest borrowers are. You then decide to ration the credit as if it were apples, by lowering the price you are willing to give for their bonds (raising the interest rate on the loan). Big mistake! As the interest rate increases (the sum that the borrower/securities seller will accept for his IOU decreases), the best borrowers drop out of the bidding. After all, they know that their projects are safe, that they are the equivalent of an automotive peach. People with riskier business projects continue bidding until they too find the cost of borrowing too high and bow out, leaving you to lend to some knave, to some human lemon, at a very high rate of interest that will never be paid. Adverse selection also afflicts the market for insurance. Safe businesses are not willing to pay much for insurance because they know that the likelihood that they will suffer a loss and make a claim is low. Risky businesses, by contrast, will pay very high rates for insurance because they know that they will probably suffer a loss. Anyone offering insurance on the basis of premium alone will end up with the stinky end of the stick, just as will the lender who rations on price alone.

Moral hazard is asymmetric information after the contract has been made. It occurs when one party to an already consummated contract or transaction knows more than the other party. The asymmetry allows a borrower or insured entity (not an applicant, as in the case of adverse selection, but an actual borrower or policyholder) to engage in behaviors that are not in the best interest of the lender or insurer. If a borrower uses a bank loan to buy lottery tickets instead of safe government bonds, as agreed upon with the lender, that's moral hazard. If an insured person leaves the door of his home or car unlocked or lets candles burn all night unattended, that's moral hazard. It's also moral hazard if a borrower fails to repay a loan if he has the wherewithal to do so, or if an insured driver fakes an accident.

We call such behavior "moral hazard" because it was long thought to indicate a lack of morals or character, and in a sense it does. But thinking about the problem in those terms does not help to mitigate it. Most of us have a price. How high that price is can't be easily determined and may indeed change, but offered enough money most human beings (except Gandhi, prophets, saints, and of course the reader) will engage in immoral activities for personal gain if given the chance. It's tempting indeed to put other people's money at risk. The higher the risk, after all, the higher the reward. Why not borrow money to put to risk? If the rewards come, the principal and interest are easily repaid. If rewards remain aloof, the borrower defaults and suffers but little; after all, we did away with debtors' prisons in the early nineteenth century.

The "principal-agent problem," as the name implies, is an important subcategory of moral hazard involving the tensions that arise between principals (owners) and agents (employees). Most of the time, owners must hire or appoint employees (or other types of agents) to conduct some or all of their business affairs on their behalf. Stockholders in joint-stock corporations, for example, hire professional executives to run their businesses. The executives hire middle managers who, in turn, hire supervisors who then hire employees, depending on how hierarchical the company is. The principal-agent problem arises when any of those agents does not act in the best interest of the principal, for example, when employees and/or managers steal, slack off, act rudely toward customers, or otherwise cheat the company's owners. If you've ever held a job, you've probably seen some, if not all, of these behaviors. If you've ever been a boss, or better yet an owner, you've probably been the victim of agency problems. I have been on this end, as a college professor occasionally saddled with lazy teaching and research assistants. One actually ended up in jail, but thankfully I was not the main victim of his perfidy.

Monitoring helps to mitigate the principal-agent problem. That's what supervisors, cameras, and corporate snitches are for. Another, often more powerful way of reducing agency problems is to try to align the incentives of employees with those of owners by paying efficiency wages (above market wages), commissions, bonuses, stock options, or other performance-based incentives. Caution is the watchword here, though, because, as mentioned above, people usually do *precisely* what they are rewarded for doing. Failure to recognize that apparently universal human trait has had adverse consequences for some organizations, a point most easily made through simple case stories. In one story, a major ice cream retailer decided to help out its employees by allowing them to consume, free of charge, any mistakes that they might make in the course of serving customers. What was meant to be an environmentally sensitive little perk turned into a major problem as employee waistlines bulged and profits shrank because hungry employees found it easy to make delicious frozen mistakes. "Oh, you said strawberry. I thought you said *my* favorite flavor. Excuse me, as I am now on break."

In another story, a debt collection agency almost destroyed itself by agreeing to change the way that it compensated its collectors. Initially, collectors received bonuses based on the dollars collected divided by the dollars assigned to be collected. So, for example, a collector who brought in $300,000 of the $1 million due on his accounts would receive a bigger bonus than a collector who collected only $100,000 of the same denominator ($300/1,000 = 0.30 > 100/1,000 = 0.10$). Collectors complained, however, that it was not fair to them if one or more of their accounts went bankrupt, rendering collection impossible. The managers of the collection agency agreed and began to deduct the value of bankrupt accounts from the collectors' denominators. Under the new incentive scheme, a collector who brought in $100,000 would receive a bigger bonus than his colleague if, say, $800,000 of his accounts claimed bankruptcy ($100/[1,000 - 800 = 200] = 0.5 > 300/1,000 = 0.30$). The collectors quickly transformed themselves into bankruptcy counselors because the new scheme inadvertently created a perverse incentive, that is, one diametrically opposed to the collection agency's interest, which was to collect as many dollars as possible, not to help debtors file for bankruptcy.

In a Smithian market, pressure from competitors and the incentives of managers would soon rectify such mishaps. But when the incentive structure of management is deranged, bigger and deeper problems often appear. For example, managers paid with stock options have the incentive to increase their companies' respective stock prices. They generally succeed in getting their companies' stock up, sometimes by making their companies more efficient but, as investors in the US stock market in the late 1990s and again more recently learned, sometimes through accounting legerdemain. Failures of corporate governance, we'll see, lay at the heart of much that is FUBAR.

Improperly aligned incentives like those described above also explain other market failures, including "collective-action problems" and "externalities." Collective-action problems occur when people can't figure out how to work together to solve a common problem. For example, sometimes people would be better off if they all contributed to some cause, like national defense. Rather than everybody pitching in, however, people have incentives to take a "free ride," to let others contribute while they pay nothing but still enjoy the protection of fighter jets, submarines, tanks, snipers, and the like. Because of rampant free riding, goods that are nonrivalrous and nonexcludable, goods that people can't be prevented from enjoying even if they haven't pitched in to pay for them, must be provided by the government if they are to be provided at all. For that reason, economists call them public goods.

Externalities are misalignments of individual and societal costs and benefits. They occur when the costs of producing a good or the benefits the good creates are not reflected in market prices. Pollution is the classic example of a negative externality, of costs imposed on society and not borne by the producer. Because factory owners do not have to pay for the problems their factories cause downstream, downwind, or later in time, they can sell their goods more cheaply. That means that people buy more units, encouraging additional production and yet more pollution. Education is the opposite case, the classic example of a positive externality. Society reaps *extra* benefits from educated people, benefits not reflected in graduates' lifetime earnings or the psychological benefits they gain from better understanding the world around them. Those extra benefits include better dinner guests, less crime, innovation spillovers, and so forth. Educated individuals do not personally gain from the extra benefits their education bestows on society. Whether a particular individual does or does not acquire an education will have no appreciable effect on the crime rate, the rate at which innovations spur additional innovations, or the number of dinner parties. So, the argument goes, individuals acquire less education than is socially optimal. The government should therefore subsidize education to ensure that individuals obtain more of it, not for their own sake but for society's.

***

If markets were the only problem we faced, our course of action would be clear. Do away with private property and prices. Have the government decide what, when, where, and how much to produce. Let it determine wages and other working conditions as well. Cheer Hugo Chavez, read Karl Marx or Edward Bellamy. To each according to his needs, from each according to his abilities. Huzzah! Huzzah! Huzzah! Unfortunately, as we learned above, the government's failures are as pervasive as the market's. Supplanting markets with governments, as communist countries have done, has led to nothing but economic disasters that killed millions of people and maimed the lives and limbs of millions more.

In case you haven't picked up on it yet, I'm no fan of partisan politics. Early in life I was a Marxist. In my midtwenties I switched to libertarianism, as if to lend credence to the old joke that if you are twenty and not a Marxist, you have no heart. If you are thirty and still a Marxist, you have no brain. Now, at forty-one, I'm a gung-ho fubaronomist. That means, basically, that I see the flaws inherent in both markets and governments. Rather than singing the praises of Friedman or Keynes, Hayek or Lenin, CEOs, or presidents, I want to find solutions to the problems that ail the economy, to root out and extirpate all that is FUBAR. And, unfortunately, many aspects of our material lives are indeed fouled up beyond all recognition.

Rather than analyzing problems bent on bashing governments or excoriating markets to score ideological points as I had as a babe, I began a few years ago to delve deeply into all the causes of our economy's numerous ills. What I found, time and again, were what I term "hybrid failures"—combinations of market and government failures. In fact, I've yet to encounter a major fouled-up portion of our economy that is not the product of a hybrid failure. Unfortunately, identifying a hybrid failure does not solve the problem. It does, however, put policy debates on a firmer footing. Once the hybrid nature of the FUBAR parts of our material existence is laid bare, real debate about reform becomes possible. Most of the time what emerges is a need to reregulate in a more intelligent manner, in a way that reduces asymmetric information or free riding rather than by arbitrarily hurting (or helping) businesses or consumers. I'll address that point in more detail later. Before that, though, we need to examine specific examples of hybrid failures causing economic foul-ups. So much of the economy is FUBAR that deciding what to discuss is not easy. I've chosen the topics covered herein based on my own interests and their intrinsic importance, which happily often coincide.

Up first, in chapter 2, "Death of a Salesman," the FUBAR processes by which we buy, sell, and insure the titles of our homes are described. Businesses naturally try to break free of the Smithian shackles of perfect competition, which almost inevitably tethers them to low profits. Governments should not let them stray very far from it—to get too close to monopoly, in other words. But out of laziness, incompetence, corruption, or some other failing, they often do. US governments allow not one but two cartels to distort the market for homes. As New York University economist Lawrence J. White has shown, real estate agents fix prices (their 6 percent commission) with impunity, while the government turns a blind eye.[12] An even more egregious cartel, recently exposed by New York University's press, sucks billions a year out of the pockets of homeowners under an elaborate scam known as "title insurance."[13]

As the world discovered to its monetary chagrin in 2007, the US home mortgage market is also FUBAR. Unsurprisingly, the hands of both businesses and governments are again drenched in blood—green, green blood. Traditionally, mortgage lenders decided who received mortgages and who did not. They were careful to lend to the best borrowers because if they did not, they would suffer for it later, when the borrower stopped repaying. To ensure that they had some cushion if prices decreased, they also insisted on down payments of 10, 15, 20, 25 percent, or even more. The government one day decided that too few Americans could buy homes on such terms, so it maintained the mortgage interest tax deduction and began guaranteeing mortgages for veterans and other political worthies. It also set up giant corporations that used the government's credit to sell scads of their bonds for a nifty premium. The corporations used the proceeds from the bond sales to buy mortgages from lenders who no longer wished to hold them, often because the government allowed their value to erode by letting inflation increase to dizzying heights. The lenders used the cash to make new loans, often at higher rates and always for a nice, fat fee.

By the early 1980s the government got its inflation problem under control, but the damage had been done. Many mortgage lenders had morphed into mortgage originators or brokers, companies in the business of arranging loans, not actually lending money. The loans themselves ultimately came from investors the world over. Superficially, the arrangement made some sense. Some companies specialized in arranging loans while others specialized in providing the funds, albeit in a circuitous fashion. The new system, however, was (and still is) rotten to the core because originators now made their money simply for arranging loans, the more and the higher value the better. They got paid no matter what happened to the mortgage, the house, or the homeowner in the future. They had ample incentives to ram big, complex mortgages—called subprime because everyone realized they were somewhat risky, although how risky no one really knew—down the gullets of people who had no idea what they were getting themselves into. Thanks to our FUBAR educational system, most buyers did not realize that the hot housing market of 2002–2006 was unsustainable. Heck, the fancy-smancies on Wall Street seemed oblivious too, as did their underpaid and overworked regulators. When housing prices stopped skyrocketing, and then had the temerity to reverse course, the subprime mortgages hit the proverbial fan, spewing their putrid insides hither and thither. Once again, both governments and markets were to blame for the stinky mess.

In chapter 3, "Bob the Builder," I argue that the custom construction industry is also a victim of large-scale hybrid failures. Some background is necessary here. Construction activity can be divided into three types: force account, speculative, and custom. Force account construction is the term for construction activities undertaken by an owner/contractor for the owner/contractor. Speculative construction is the term for construction activities undertaken by an owner/contractor for an arm's-length sale or long-term lease to a tenant. In those two types of construction, the incentives of the owner and the contractor are aligned because they are the same party. Although principal-agent problems within the firm can arise in force account construction, it is generally efficient. Speculative construction is somewhat less so because the owner/contractor builds with the intent to sell to a relatively uninformed third party. Nonetheless, a fairly efficient market for new buildings exists in many places in the United States, so the speculative owner/contractor cannot stray far from the prevailing price/quality equilibrium without suffering for it.[14]

Unfortunately, most of the $1+ trillion per year construction industry engages in custom building, where the owner and the contractor are different parties with vastly different incentives, information, and power. Contrary to conventional wisdom, the bidding process does not ensure efficient outcomes. Contractors regularly "game" bids, bidding strategically based on who they suspect is also bidding on the job and how much they think that the owner can pay. Most winning bidders have no intention of receiving only the amount bid. Instead, they intend to pad their bills through "change orders." Those extra charges that emanate from owner-initiated changes in the plan ought to be paid for by the owner, of course. Most change orders, however, are initiated by contractors who claim that the plans are flawed or concoct other justifications for their cash grab.

Owners often pay change orders because they do not know any better and because, after a job begins, the contractor is a near monopolist due to the time and expense it would take to engage a new firm. Owners sometimes employ attorneys or construction managers to protect their interests, but contractors stymied on change orders have other ways to make owners pay. One way is to reduce the quality of materials or workmanship. They can easily get away with such behavior because owners and their agents cannot be everywhere at once and because government inspectors merely ensure that materials and workmanship are up to code, not that those specified in the plans have been used. Contractors can also shift resources to more lucrative projects, making the owner who pushes back on change orders pay with delays.

Little wonder, then, that a large percentage of construction projects end up over budget or overdue. The percentage of projects where owners receive lower-quality materials or workmanship than they contracted for cannot be known with certainty but undoubtedly is also high. Once the incentive structure problem is clearly perceived, many of the traditional excuses for the construction industry's lagging productivity—unions, seasonality, cyclicality, the difficulties inherent in customization, general management backwardness—begin to look more like symptoms than root causes. Most construction companies are microsized; even big ones are not large, given the size of the industry. Construction firms remain small because companies do not have to be large to manipulate bids or to submit change orders, which is where most competition in custom construction occurs. It is not accidental that the largest, most innovative construction firms, from Levitt to Toll Brothers, have been speculative builders, not custom contractors.

Governments exacerbate the problems caused by asymmetric information in numerous ways. As noted above, government inspectors ensure that codes, not contracts, have been complied with. Unfortunately, building codes are often outdated, serving more to thwart innovation than to protect owners. Government-sponsored education does little to prepare owners to cope with contractors, engineers, or architects. Indeed, many observers and practitioners consider the training for all three professions as wholly inadequate. Many contractors, engineers, and architects lack even basic business skills.[15]

Governments have also wasted resources by bolstering unions. Unions are not at the root of the industry's woes—construction productivity in the South, where unions are weaker, is just as low as in the North, where they are stronger, and construction productivity has lagged while unions both North and South have flagged. Unions are not helpful, however, as they tend to give even more power to construction workers who hold captive their employers. Most construction workers are paid by the hour but determine their own work pace and procedures. In most other industries, hourly workers must do as management commands or lose their jobs. Typically only piece workers, who get paid according to how many units of work they successfully complete, have freedom of action at work, meaning they can do as they want as long as they meet their quotas.

Perhaps worst of all, government does not use its monopsony power (buyer "monopoly" power) to whip contractors into shape. Instead, many a marginal contractor has skimped along by suckling the sweet, sweet teat of overly fat government contracts. Governments could, and should, collect and disseminate information on contractors. That would create societal benefits by making information regarding contractor quality more cheaply and easily available to potential buyers. Alas, governments do not always, dare I say usually, do what they should.

Early US state governments, for example, had the power to end slavery. After the Revolution, those in the North successfully wielded that power, some ending slavery instantly, others opting for a more gradual approach. As chapter 4, "Uncle Tom's Cabin," shows, slavery was a very peculiar institution indeed. Regardless of race, religion, and so forth, slaves throughout history were not very good workers. The men, women, and children who our early governments allowed to remain in bondage were no exception. Ripped from their families and thrown into hardship, they feigned sickness and stupidity, broke tools, expropriated provisions, ran away, and, occasionally, arose in bloody retaliation. Only when worked in a closely monitored gang system did their efficiency levels approach those of free workers, an abomination felt to this day. Even then, most productivity gains in the antebellum South were due to the development of more easily picked forms of cotton rather than increases in worker efficiency. If Southern labor markets were like those described by classical economists, then planters voluntarily would have switched to a more efficient labor regime, like seasonal wage contracts. The market, though, was as enslaved as the slaves themselves.

The big slave and plantation owners did more than use their political power to keep slavery legal, they used it to keep slavery profitable and did so in a clever way, by tricking society into bearing the costs of their volatile labor force. By mixing illiberal doses of hatred, bigotry, fear, and the coercive power of the state, they were able to induce their poor neighbors to patrol the nighttime countryside to defend against insurrection, to force Northerners to return runaways, to cajole state governments into providing public whipping posts, and on and on. In short, the institution of slavery was nothing less than a form of pollution, the producer of a negative externality so large that it eventually led to America's bloodiest war to date. The Civil War itself was also FUBAR because its total costs far exceeded what would have been necessary to buy and manumit all the slaves. And nobody would have had to have died or hobbled through their adult lives missing one or more limbs, eyes, or ears.

The Great Depression was also FUBAR, as chapter 5, "The Grapes of Wrath," explains. Initially, most Americans considered the Great Depression, the massive downturn in economic activity between 1930 and 1933, a market failure. The stock market broke in late 1929 and soon thereafter banks began failing in droves. Franklin Delano Roosevelt (FDR) and his Democratic Party came to power, reformed the financial system, and the economy recovered, albeit slowly. Case closed, or so many believed.

In fact, though, the government was as much to blame for the Depression as market institutions, such as margin buying and the call market, were. America's central bank, the Federal Reserve, went into operation in 1914, just in time to help the United States become democracy's arsenal in the Great War. However, it helped to exacerbate a recession shortly after the war ended, but that was forgotten during the so-called Roaring Twenties. As stock prices spiraled ever upward, the Fed, as it came to be called, sat idly by instead of interceding with higher interest rates. After the crash, it reacted slowly and incompetently, ironic indeed, given that the institution had been formed to stop financial panic and contagion. Bank runs were also partly the government's fault, for insisting on unit, as opposed to branch, banking. States like California that had allowed intrastate branch banking suffered much less than those that had insisted that banks remain small, local, and branchless. The Hoover administration also exacerbated the dire economic situation by passing a high tariff, shutting off international trade just when the nation needed it most.

World War II did not get the United States out of the Depression, as many still believe. In fact, real per capita income turned upward in 1934, just as it did in all nations that jettisoned the gold standard, an international monetary system that caused the domestic money supply to drop to dangerously low levels. (High levels of unemployment persisted until the war buildup began in earnest, although in truth, odd government bean-counting rules were somewhat to blame.)[16] New Deal reforms did little other than redistribute income and cause a recession in 1937–1938, when the Fed again stumbled. Many New Deal financial sector reforms also accomplished little, other than creating new FUBAR conditions that later led to the savings and loan crisis and the corporate governance scandals of the early 2000s.

The New Deal also saddled America with Social Security, or the "Sacred Hoax" as I call it in chapter 6. Don't get me wrong, I think that a well-designed social safety net would be a very good policy indeed. No part of our current net, however, is well designed. In addition to gaping holes that do not catch anyone, our net often snares the wrong people. Social Security is a prime example. It effectively transfers wealth away from poorer folks, particularly ethnic-minority males, and gives it to white, middle-class females. Worse, the system is essentially a giant compulsory Ponzi scheme, and we're running out of enough new blood to keep the pyramid from toppling.

Theoretically, private insurance companies and mutual funds should be able to supply Americans with actuarially sound insurance and safe investment vehicles that would be superior to the life annuity, death benefit, and disability insurance provided by Social Security. The insurance companies in particular are so hampered by government regulations, however, that in reality they would be hard-pressed to do so. Of course, the regulations were put in place largely in response to market failures like asymmetric information. Still, rampant deregulation is not the answer. Clearly, more astute regulations are needed. Unfortunately, substantive regulatory reforms generally become politically palatable only in the aftermath of a crisis.

That, of course, is precisely the wrong time to implement reforms, a point also taken up in chapter 7, "House Scrubs." While in some ways America's healthcare system is the most advanced in the world, it is extremely costly and does not serve the median patient very well. This latest healthcare crisis is simply the most recent of a long series of crises. After World War I, the cost of healthcare exceeded the loss from wages forgone during illness for the first time, sparking calls for compulsory government programs. During the Great Depression, macroeconomic conditions stretched the system to the max, again eliciting calls for reform. After World War II, government tax laws cemented the employer-based model we remain stuck with to this day. Those, and additional crises in the 1960s, 1980s, 1990s, and 2000s, created a crazy hodgepodge of programs, perverse incentives, and other telltale signs of FUBAR. Again, governments and markets are to blame, both in spades. Nobody appears ready to tackle the root problem, which is that insurers pay for doctors to see patients rather than to make them well. Before rising healthcare costs can be tamed, let alone trimmed, patients will have to pay more out of pocket so they exert much more price discipline on healthcare providers. Additionally, insurers and patients will have to negotiate rates based more on results (outputs) and less on doctors' time (inputs).

Up next is our higher education boondoggle, the subject of chapter 8, "3rd Rock from the Sun." Higher education is a lagging industry where productivity, as far as we can tell, is stagnant. Tuition and other costs rise faster than inflation; complaints about low quality are numerous and for the most part well founded. American higher education is arguably the best in the world, but that does not mean that US universities and colleges are any good, only that foreign ones are even worse. Higher education has been in perpetual crisis for the last several decades. Tuition rates have soared in inflation-adjusted terms, forcing students to borrow or work instead of study. Standards have plummeted while grade "inflation" (actually compression) has led to ridiculous outcomes, like three-quarters of classes graduating with "honors." In the meantime, businesses have found that they've had to beef up corporate training to unprecedented levels.

The big problem with American colleges and universities—and this goes for private, public, and joint-stock schools like Phoenix and DeVry too—is that their professors are mere employees. The principal-agent problem therefore looms large and, of course, gets even worse when guaranteed lifetime employment, tenure, is added to the brew. But even when tenure is not available, professors often display the telltale signs of salaried employment status: lack of initiative, resistance to change, and detailed attention to the minutiae of the conditions of work life. Professors are not about to strain themselves to invent a new form of pedagogy in return for baubles and perhaps a fancy title. Like debt collectors and ice cream shop employees, they do precisely what they are rewarded for doing. That often means keeping their mouths shut and caving in to student —"customer"— demands to lighten the load.

What would happen if incentive structures within colleges and universities changed? What if instead of being owned by stockholders, state governments, or nobody at all, institutions of higher education were owned by their professors? What if professors, good ones, could become as rich as, say, partners in a big law firm (who, by the way, work just as hard as associates and clerks but often on higher-level problems)? Would their behavior change? Would they work longer, harder, smarter? Would new pedagogies arise and proliferate more often and more quickly than hitherto? Many think so and would like to give the experiment a fair shot. The problem, though, is that government-imposed startup costs are currently prohibitive. Many a bureaucratic hoop must be jumped through before a de novo school can begin operation. Governments and existing schools conspire to create yet another barrier, one that keeps information asymmetry high and hence virile. Currently, there are no good ways to rank schools' ability to teach undergraduates. Assumptions regarding quality must therefore suffice. Often, those assumptions are based merely on name recognition, which in turn often rests on little more than hoariness or a high-profile sports program.[17]

The government also adds to FUBAR by the way it subsidizes higher education. As noted above, many people believe that government should subsidize education because of the positive externalities that educated people create. They may well be right, and as a college professor I have a vested interest in believing them. But there is no reason that the government needs to pay most of the subsidies to schools rather than to students. And there is no reason in hell that government has to produce education itself via state-owned and state-operated schools. Instead, it should give the subsidy money to students and let them decide what to do with it. That's the way the GI Bill worked, and it was salubrious.

✱✱✱

Can FUBAR be fixed? Chapter 9, "Fighting FUBAR," offers hopeful proposals but no panaceas. When something is fouled up beyond all recognition, nothing is easy. Piecemeal reform over time usually leads to more FUBAR, not less. What is needed is bold political leadership informed by honest research. Too often, scholars and policymakers take sides in long-standing ideological debates that resemble little more than urination contests between five-year-olds. "Governments rule, markets drool," the little statists scream. "I'm rubber and you're glue, what you say bounces off me and sticks on you," the toddler libertarians scream back. "Time out!" I command. "You can come out of your rooms when you can analyze the dire problems facing our economy with if not perfect objectivity, then without partisan rage."

I'm under no illusion that policymakers will take up any, let alone all, of the recommendations I make. I do pray, however, that this book will elevate the level of policy discourse above hackneyed generalizations about the failures of governments and markets. Both are deeply flawed, leading to hybrid failures that hang like millstones around our economy's slowly breaking neck. Our most important policy questions, from healthcare to homecare and labor policy to old age security, stand in dire need of careful, nonpartisan analysis. A little levity in the process is necessary, if only to forestall uncontrollable sobbing. Of course none of the humorous faux pas, interpretative mistakes, or outright factual errors that may be found herein should be attributed to anyone except the author. Michael Bordo, David Cowen, Ed Knappman (my agent), Ron Michener, James Mueller, John Murray, Richard Sylla, Eugene White, and Deborah Vasta-Wright (my wife) helped me to refine portions of the manuscript, for which I heartily thank them.

2

DEATH OF A SALESMAN

Our Mortgage Mess and Financial Fiasco

Like Mick Jagger, Washington can't always get what it wants.[1] Despite trillions of dollars of bailout money thrown at the economy in 2008, 2009, and 2010, many Willy Lomans emerged in our midst. Loman was the troubled main character in Arthur Miller's acclaimed 1949 play, *Death of a Salesman.* Most critics and viewers concentrate on the sociological and psychological aspects of the play—Loman's affair and dysfunctional family life—and miss the economic causes of his troubles. Miller leaves enough clues scattered throughout the play, however, to reconstruct the outlines of Loman's economic backstory. They are eerily familiar. Poor Willy bought a house at the top of the market in the 1920s. Due to the Depression and the changes that his Brooklyn neighborhood underwent, Loman soon found himself "underwater" or "in the bucket." In other words, he owed more on his mortgage than his house was worth. Instead of moving to his new sales territory in New England, therefore, Loman had to commute back and forth. That led to his affair, the estrangement from his son, and other family problems. The mortgage, which he paid off the day he committed suicide, together with the real estate market, effectively killed him by driving him mad.

Death by mortgage is not as far-fetched as it sounds. Our real estate and mortgage markets are FUBAR and have been for a very long time. The bursting of the real estate bubble and the financial crisis of 2007–2009 have driven millions of homeowners underwater. Some have already killed themselves and sometimes have taken others with them. Untold others suffer lives of quiet desperation, stuck in dead-end jobs and with frustrated spouses because they can't sell their homes. Their best years spinning down the drain, they are becoming increasingly frustrated, desperate, and radicalized.

The suffering runs deep, suffusing every corner of how we build, trade, and insure the titles of our homes. Mortgages currently cause the most considerable consternation, reprising a role they have played repeatedly in the past. In fact, the subprime woes that began in 2007 were the seventh time in US history that a mortgage securitization scheme blew up.[2] The freaking seventh time. Fool me once, shame on you. Fool me twice, shame on me. Fool me seven times and...wow! Securitization—the bundling of mortgages for resale to investors—is not the only way that mortgages can cause problems. During the Depression, short-term unamortized mortgages wreaked havoc because many homeowners could not find refinancing as expected. Hit with huge balloon (principal) payments that they could not make, they defaulted en masse, necessitating massive government intervention. Even more dramatically, an earlier real estate bubble built on private callable mortgages initiated a series of events that ended with the American Revolution. The United States of America was born thanks, in large part, to a mortgage crisis!

*****

Every American schoolchild knows that the colonists of British North America declared their independence from Mother England because of tax disputes. What they don't know—because their teachers don't tell them, because most scholars have yet to realize it—is that the colonists were extremely sensitive about "taxation without representation" since they were already hurting economically. During the French and Indian War (1754–1763), a variety of circumstances, from low interest rates to high levels of trade, conspired to create a real estate bubble of massive proportions, especially in the colonies north and east of the Potomac River. After the war, however, interest rates increased and profits plummeted.

Land prices soon followed, dropping from 33 to 67 percent off their highs by the end of 1764. Lenders called in mortgages (most private ones were callable after just a few years), defaults soared, suits and judgments jumped, sheriff sales became ubiquitous, and prisons overflowed with debtors. Does any of this sound familiar?[3]

British policymakers responded to the crisis in precisely the wrong way, by increasing taxes, keeping a tight lid on colonial trade, and shrinking the money supply. The colonists therefore struggled not just against taxes but against a range of policies that threatened their very livelihood. They were so bloody angry about the Stamp Act because it came at a time when they were losing their homes, farms, and shops due to British macroeconomic policies, particularly the restrictions on paper money issuance and trade. Thus the bursting of an asset bubble, poorly handled, helped give rise to the independence movement. Before joining the Tea Party movement, think about how much worse our present government could be.

For the last forty years or so, historians of the American Revolution have studied what they know best, printed primary sources that elucidate the thought processes of elite colonists as they moved toward independence. More recently, some have attempted to add the voices of the downtrodden, primarily women, slaves, and Indians, to the mix. Their emphasis, though, remains on ideology, on quasi-coherent webs of ideas that historians call republicanism and liberalism. When confronted with economic issues, historians tend to retort that the Revolution must have been about ideology because the taxes and trade restrictions laid on the colonists were too small to induce rational people to rebel. With any proper accounting, the benefits of remaining in the British Empire far exceeded the costs, they claim. The Revolution, in their eyes, was therefore about taxation *without representation* rather than taxation per se, about *potential* threats to liberty rather than its actual diminution, about *ideas* rather than material reality.

Explicit taxes on the colonists *were* comparatively low, and the deadweight losses created by British trade policies *were* indeed small. But the empire imposed significant additional costs, and it was those costs that drove colonists to write the pamphlets and letters fleshing out their political ideology upon which most historians dwell. Without the macroeconomic disturbances of the 1760s, all the ideological musings in the world would not have turned the Stamp, Currency, Sugar, Townsend, Tea, and Quebec acts into the major turning points in imperial relations that they proved to be. "I must observe," a colonist argued in 1768, "that it is not the Stamp Act or New Duty Act alone that had put the Colonies so much out of humour tho the principal Clamour has been on that Head but *their distressed Situation had prepared them so generally to lay hold of these Occasions*."4 To fully understand the Revolution, therefore, one must understand how the colonial economy became so distressed. To understand that, a little economic background is necessary. And don't worry about the length, as the ground work laid here will help us to better understand the nation's most recent financial fiasco detailed in the second half of the chapter.

By the French and Indian War (1754–1763), most of the colonies in British North America were on what economists call fixed exchange rates. Prices were denominated in local pounds, shillings, and pence that, in turn, were tied to specific gold, silver, and copper coins. Pennsylvanians, for example, rated silver dollars coined in Mexico at 7 shillings and 6 pence Pennsylvania currency, while New Yorkers esteemed the same coins as 8 shillings New York currency. Obviously, a Pennsylvania shilling was worth a little more than a New York shilling. That made no real difference, just as it doesn't matter today that Canada or Britain or Japan use different units of account, by which I mean metaphorical measuring rods of value. All it meant was that a bottle of wine in Manhattan that sold for 8 shillings New York currency would sell for about 7 shillings, 6 pence Pennsylvania currency in Philadelphia. If it didn't, merchants would buy it where it was cheapest in real terms and sell it where it was most dear until the prices (plus transaction costs) equalized at about one Mexican silver dollar.

To say that the colonies were on fixed exchange rates does not mean that colonists could always buy foreign currencies, such as British pounds sterling, for the same local nominal price. To pay a debt in London or Liverpool, colonists could remit goods, coins, or a bill of exchange, a sort of international check, denominated in sterling. Prices of bills of exchange fluctuated with supply and demand but could not go too high because goods or coins could be sent instead. They could also not go too low because sellers of bills—people who held deposits in British banks or mercantile houses—would send for goods or coins instead of selling their deposits too cheaply. The range between the upper and lower bounds (the exchange rate band) was much larger in the eighteenth century than under the classical gold standard of the late nineteenth century because transaction costs (freightage, lost interest during time spent traveling, insurance) were much higher and because several metals were involved, not just gold. (The gold standard was an international monetary regime based on gold that reached its apex in the late nineteenth century. Under it, governments defined their local units of account [dollars, pounds, pesos, etc.] in terms of a specific amount of gold and promised to convert their currencies into gold at that rate upon demand. The gold standard brought domestic price stability but at the cost of periodic severe recessions. It began to lose favor during World War I, a process accelerated by the Great Depression. At the end of World War II, it was completely replaced by a new fixed exchange regime based on the US dollar known as Bretton Woods for the New Hampshire town where the initial plan was hashed out.)

No colonial central bank or treasury proclaimed or enforced the fixed rates, but nongovernmental institutions did, establishing and maintaining the fixed par of exchange between different currencies. In most of the British North American colonies, groups of merchants agreed on coin ratings, published them, and almost always adhered to them. Their actions were extralegal, so we know little of the actual proceedings. Still, the existence of coin ratings is well documented in colonial almanacs, however, and merchants' adherence to them is verified by references in their account books.

Complicating matters a little was the fact that colonial governments sometimes saw fit to issue fiat paper money, or "bills of credit" in the parlance of the day. (That's the same type of intrinsically worthless, crap paper—see the dust jacket!—that the Federal Reserve issues today.) Earlier in the century, South Carolina and the New England colonies had issued so many bills that they drove all of the gold and silver out of domestic circulation as people sent the precious stuff abroad to pay for imported goods, leaving behind only the bills of credit, which did not circulate overseas. A period of high inflation and floating exchange rates ensued. By the eve of the French and Indian War, however, all of the colonies had stopped issuing enough bills of credit to drive all the gold and silver out of domestic circulation, as in South Carolina, or were forbidden to issue bills anymore, as in New England. So the colonies were all on fixed exchange rates despite the circulation of some government paper money. That was possible because the quantity of bills in circulation remained less than what was needed for domestic transactions. That, in turn, allowed bills of credit and coins to mix promiscuously in circulation, as substitutes.

Although there were no government or even private banks, informal retail convertibility of bills of credit into gold and silver and vice versa was the norm. A 1780s retrospective by a writer calling himself Eugenio, possibly a reference to Eugenio Espejo (1747–1795), a pro-market Enlightenment thinker from South America, explained how it worked:

> Instant realization or immediate exchange of paper into coin at value was formerly practicable every moment. It is true that the government did not raise a sum of coin and deposit the same in the treasury to exchange the bills on demand, but the faith of the government, the opinion of the people, and the security of the fund formerly by well-timed and steady policy, went so hand in hand and so concurred to support each other, that the people voluntarily and without the least compulsion threw all their gold and silver, not locking up a shilling, into circulation concurrently with the bills.[5]

Some colonists believed that their governments could exert considerable control over the money supply by issuing new bills of credit. Others perceived that emissions of bills of credit merely displaced an equal amount of gold and silver, rendering the effects of paper money fleeting at best, kind of like shaky subprime mortgages. They realized that replacing expensive metals with cheap paper in domestic circulation created modest gains but feared the government could threaten the fixed par of exchange by emitting too much paper. Depreciation, inflation, chaos, and stagnation would follow. Those who doubted the government's ability to influence anything more than the composition of the money supply (the percentage made up of bills versus gold and silver coins) were closer to the truth. In other words, international trading conditions, not colonial governments, largely determined colonial money supplies, interest rates, and overall macroeconomic conditions. British trade regulations therefore had significant and palpable effects on colonists' well-being. Imperial taxes, payable only in gold, silver, or sterling bills, also weighed heavily on the colonies because they shrank the domestic money supply in addition to redistributing resources. British policymakers understood all this to some extent but didn't care, preferring instead to pander to special interests, like the absentee landlords of West Indian sugar plantations who thronged to both houses of Parliament. (That's right, the US Congress did not invent pandering. It merely perfected it.) Policymakers also sought to gain a final victory in a protracted power struggle with colonial legislatures over the power of the purse (control of the state's fiscal apparatus). When the worst financial crisis in North American history struck, the British tried to leverage it to regain control over their upstart colonies. Instead, they fomented rebellion.

After an initial period of adjustment, the colonial economy boomed during the French and Indian War. To help fight the war, colonial legislatures emitted large quantities of bills of credit. In support of His Majesty's troops, huge sums of gold, silver, and sterling bills of exchange flooded in. Simultaneously, colonial privateers (sort of like legal pirates, but from North America, not Somalia) plied the seas, seizing under the authority of the government's writ numerous French ships and cargoes, virtual manna from heaven. Colonial privateers also pretended to seize friendly merchant ships engaged in illegal commerce with the enemy, a ruse that protected smugglers from unfriendly privateers and the Royal Navy. Merchants also used flags of truce and falsified papers to penetrate lucrative but illegal foreign markets in the West Indies. The more things change…

Thanks to the wartime economic boom, the colonies were flush with foreign exchange. The price of bills of exchange dropped to the point of drooping and merchants temporarily reversed the usual flow of trade by paying for French sugar partly in gold and silver. By 1759, Lancaster, Pennsylvania, artisan John Frederick Koffler recognized all the signs of an asset bubble, including low interest and exchange rates, easy credit, high amounts of leverage, and ever-growing ranks of speculators:

> At the Commencement of this present War, the Number of Merchants in the City of Philadelphia might amount to about One Hundred, a few more or less.… Even now in the Month of August 1759, are there not two Hundred? Is it not likely that in a Year or two more, a third Hundred will be added to the Number? Pray how can such a number employed in the Mercantile trade, be supported at any Time?… The dealers in England, encourages them often to indulge us with large supplies of Goods, more than we have paid for, as well as long Credit, for the Payment of the same.[6]

Because the colonies were on fixed exchange rates and had plenty of foreign exchange, the prices of traded commodities such as sugar, molasses, flour, salted meats, and lumber, among others, remained tied to world markets and showed only a 20 to 30 percent increase during the war. Prices of nontraded goods like labor and real estate, by contrast, enjoyed no such tether and soared by 200 to 300 percent. In 1761, rents rose rapidly in New York, sparking a war of words in the local newspapers. Ledger entries verify the newspaper accounts. New York merchant James Beekman, for example, owned a house that he rented at £14 per year in 1757 and 1758. The rent rose steadily before settling at £24 a year in 1761, where it remained in 1762 and 1763.[7] Rent on a shop also rose, but by a more modest 40 percent. Returning to Philadelphia in 1763 after a sojourn in London, Benjamin Franklin reported that the "Rent of old Houses, and Value of Lands, . . . are trebled in the last Six Years."[8] About the same time, Franklin's son William, the newly appointed governor of New Jersey, noted a similar increase of "Threefold to what they were Seven Years ago."[9] A 1763 pamphlet also painted New Jersey's economy in glowing terms. "Your Lands are surprisingly advanced in Value," the author wrote, "and . . . the Province is in Fact richer in a great Degree than ever it was."[10] Bubble, bubble, toil, and trouble.

After the real estate bubble burst, colonists longed wistfully for the good old days, when their homes, farms, and shops could fetch a good price. In 1771, Stephen Crane of New Jersey reminisced that "the landed Property of this Province, is reduced to near one half, the Value it was, seven or eight Years past."[11] The following year, William Alexander of New York, aka Lord Stirling, was reduced to offering some of his considerable real estate holdings as prizes in a private lottery because of "the Sudden Change that took place in the Sale of Lands . . . after the last War render'd lands almost unsaleable."[12] Alexander was one of the lucky ones because he owned most of his real estate outright. Those who bought with short-term borrowed money, when prices were high, were met with doom.

Like Americans today, colonists regularly bought and sold real estate to have more room for their children, to move closer to friends and family, to take a new job, to build up a business, or simply to show off their prosperity. Also like today's Americans, colonists were enticed by rising real estate prices but could rarely afford to pay for their acquisitions with cash. In most parts of the continent, three types of mortgages were available, government ones that amortized over ten or so years, private ones callable by the lender after at most a few years, and private perpetual interest-only

(IO) mortgages called ground rents. Unlike more recent IO mortgages, ground rents were gilt-edged securities, as safe as British, and later US, government bonds because they had much lower loan-to-value (LTV) ratios, 10 to 80 percent generally, than today's subprime mortgages typically do (or rather did). Unlike today, lenders (called ground lords) had substantial recourse, including writs that empowered sheriffs to enter the property and take away and auction off goods to the value of the debt owed. If necessary, the ground lord could take title to the land and imprison the debtor until all debts and damages had been repaid. Few borrowers ever defaulted, however, because the contract was perpetual and noncallable. In other words, if the borrower kept up the interest payments, the ground lord could never insist upon repayment of the principal. (Instead, ground lords could sell the right to receive future ground rent payments to the borrower or a third party at a negotiated price.)

Those who borrowed from government loan offices were also protected from untimely calls. For forty-odd years, Pennsylvania's provincial government subsisted almost entirely on a liquor tax and the profits from its General Loan Office, which made 50 percent LTV amortized loans at 5 percent to thousands of safe Pennsylvania borrowers. Most other colonies enjoyed similar institutions. New Jersey's first loan office, for example, also lent at 5 percent and spread repayments of principal and interest into twelve equal annual installments. Its second and third loan offices increased the term to sixteen years. (Why we don't resurrect government loan offices is beyond me. Bankers might have something to do with it.) Government mortgages, however, were available to only a fraction of those who wished to borrow. Ground rents were generally available only in Pennsylvania, Delaware, and Maryland, and even there were usually limited to urban properties.

Short-term callable private mortgages supplied the balance of the demand for colonial real estate financing. In contrast to ground rents and amortized government mortgages, they were a disaster waiting to happen. If mortgages are not callable, as with ground rents, colonial government mortgages, and most mortgages today, borrowers cannot be evicted from their properties, no matter how low the market value sinks, as long as they continue to make scheduled payments. Similarly, those with long-term fixed-rate mortgages need not worry about facing higher payments if interest rates increase. But at that time colonists who borrowed on callable mortgages faced both risks. If real estate values fell, lenders could call for the principal on the grounds that their mortgages were undercollateralized, or, in other words, that the properties pledged to support the loans were no longer of sufficient value. If interest rates increased, lenders could also call simply to reinvest the principal at higher rates. (Usury laws or interest rate caps were in place, but they were about as effective as drug laws are today.)

Colonial prosperity, and with it the real estate boom, faded with the French and Indian War. The British army left for new battlegrounds, the lucrative privateering harvest faded into memory, and, thanks to unprecedented exertions by the British navy and customs officials, the lucrative trade with the foreign West Indies declined dramatically. The crackdown was so severe that even legitimate trade suffered. British naval vessels, one contemporary complained, "cramp Trade by stoping [*sic*] and detaining Merchants ships and pressing their Men."[13]

Due to that unfortunate confluence of events, the colonies suddenly found themselves running huge trade deficits, a topic Americans today know a little bit about. According to John Frederick Koffler, they may not have run surpluses even at the height of the conflict. "It will be found," he claimed in 1759, "that notwithstanding the Quantity of Specie left amongst us by the Army, the Ballance will be against us."[14] But exchange rates sank low enough to lure a "Number of young Men ... like the greedy Fish, [to] admire for a while the Bait, and then swallow it to their own Destruction."[15] In a few years, Koffler correctly predicted, exchange would rise back to normal, somewhat above the par of exchange, and the young adventurers would struggle briefly before failing.

Koffler was unusually prescient. Even as exchange rates rose and gold and silver began to flow out to make remittances in Britain, import levels remained elevated. Extravagant tastes newly acquired from British military officers were partly to blame for the miscalculation. As one colonist noted:

> Many Strangers principally belonging to the Army, being introduced among us, brought in Luxury and Extravagance like a Torrent, naturally hospitable and Ostentatious, they rivaled each other in Dress, Equipages and Entertainments, and Money being plenty in the Hands of all Ranks, those of inferior Fortunes imitated those of better. ... Thus the contagious Example of the Army and the Humour of entertaining them has been of more prejudice to the Colonies than any pecuniary Advantages they have received.[16]

While the balance of trade deteriorated, bills of credit were paid in as taxes and retired at a rapid rate, dropping in the Middle Colonies from about £2.50 sterling per capita in 1760 to £1.05 in 1763, the very year that a New Jersey pamphleteer predicted that the confluence of peace and the inability to print new bills of credit could create circumstances "when we may be exceedingly distressed for want of a Medium of Trade."[17] With gold and silver coins also fleeing the country, however, many colonists feared inflation more than deflation. In other words, they worried that their respective governments would not retire paper money rapidly enough to maintain fixed exchange rates. Some, including Pennsylvanian big wig William Allen and New Yorker Henry Lloyd, shifted into sterling or Massachusetts currency–denominated assets. As late as 1763, New York merchant John Watts warned friends not to invest in North America without safeguarding the principal against "the depretiation of our Paper Currencys," which he described as "an Evil likely to happen."[18]

Watts was almost on the mark. In late 1763 and early 1764 specie was so scarce that New York merchants began offering a 2.5 percent premium for it, and for a short time the value of the colony's currency floated. But with the paper component of the money supply decreasing at the same time and aggregate demand falling throughout the empire due to a postwar financial panic and recession, inflation quickly gave way to a nasty bout of deflation—a decrease in the average level of prices. The good news was that deflation returned New York to fixed exchange rates. The bad news was that colonial business conditions were dismal in 1764 and worse in 1765. As the monetary contraction continued, bills of credit became almost unattainable, even among wealthy merchants. In February 1764, Gerald Beekman reported that "all the money seems to be vanished out of our City and C[o]untry."[19] Despite having more than £12,000 due to him on bond, he confessed to being unable to raise even £500 at any rate of interest. Trade suffered as a consequence. "Commerce is so stagnated here," Watts reported, "that little or nothing sells."[20] "Trade in this part of the world," wrote another New Yorker, "is come to so wretched a pass that you would imagine the plague had been here, the grass growing in most trading streets; and the best traders so far from wanting assistance of a clerk, rather want employment for themselves."[21]

Despite poor business conditions in 1764, imports from Britain doubled, returning the quantity of goods imported to the same level as the war's boom years. The increase was due in part to merchants switching from smuggling to legal channels, but much of it was genuine, stemming from orders placed in 1763 when many merchants still anticipated bountiful prosperity. New York's imports from England fell by 26 percent in 1765, but that degree of retrenchment was insufficient in light of subsequent mild demand. Colonial merchants believed that the "first rigours" imposed by the "late dutys and restrictions... would be abated" due to the merchants' political pull in London.[22] They were sadly mistaken. Goods glutted the market, inventories swelled, and profit margins evaporated. Import merchants soon needed to sell goods nobody wanted, collect overdue accounts in an economy stripped of cash, and somehow make returns to England.

Throughout the colonies, tight money and depressed business conditions brought a wave of commercial bankruptcies. (If this doesn't sound familiar, go ask a loved one if you were in a coma in the autumn of 2008.) Watts reported in August 1765 that business in New York was "very languid, the weak must go to the Wall, frequent Bankruptcys & growing more frequent."[23] The war had created a bubble that was rapidly deflating. As one observer put it, "People were not afraid of entering into deep Engagements equivalent to our Circulation, which being since called in by Taxes or remitted for Goods occasioned a sudden Stagnation, and by calling upon and suing one another brought many to ruin."[24] The next year, John van Cortlandt reported that money was "scarce" or "very scarce." He also mentioned that New York merchants paid more for a bill of exchange drawn at thirty days sight than one drawn at sixty days sight, and that the difference was 2.5 percent (that is, £180 instead of £177.5 per £100 sterling). By selling a bill drawn at sixty days sight, then a month later making it good by purchasing one drawn at thirty days sight, a merchant could borrow money for thirty days. Van Cortlandt's comment permits us to infer the interest rate on such a loan, 1.4 percent for thirty days, or (with compounding) approximately an 18 percent annual rate.[25] (Legal interest in New York was capped at 7 percent per annum but, as noted above, such laws were easily evaded. And I'm not making this stuff up. The details have changed but Twain was right about history rhyming.)[26]

Commercial failures, the scarcity of money, and high interest rates drove real estate prices lower. In 1765, the editor of the *New York Gazette, or, Weekly Post-Boy* claimed that "there is such a general scarcity of Cash that nothing we have will Command it & Real Estates of Every kind are falling at least one half in Value."[27] In the Middle Colonies, per capita bills of credit balances decreased from £0.93 to £0.85 sterling from 1765 to 1766, and gold and silver coins remained difficult to come by. A gentleman in Trenton wrote his future wife in London that "Money is very scarce, and people were much mistaken who supposed that the Repeal of the Stamp Act would produce an immediate alteration in this respect."[28] In October 1766 printer James Parker wrote to Benjamin Franklin that "Money is really scarcer than ever I knew it here."[29] That same month David van Horne explained to a Rhode Island correspondent that obtaining more silver, gold, or bills of credit had been impossible because "it is so Exceedingly difficult to get money in even from the best people."[30] That was not surprising because "the best people" had deeply invested in real estate, the plummeting prices of which left them much poorer. By the end of 1766, the contraction of real estate prices had cost landholders approximately £2,000,000 sterling in New Jersey alone.

The crisis also made it more difficult to borrow. Anyone who tried to borrow in late 2008 or early 2009 can relate to that. "Debtors that were a year or two ago responsible for £1000 can not now Raise a fourth part of the sum," an observer noted, adding that "Men of the best Estates amongst us can Scarce Raise money enough to defray the Necessary Expences of their familys."[31] In the pamphlet *The Late Regulations*, John Dickinson painted a dire picture of the economic scene then unfolding: "Trade is decaying," he claimed, "and all credit is expiring. Money is become so extremely scarce," he continued, "that reputable freeholders find it impossible to pay debts which are trifling in comparison to their estates."[32] A vicious cycle took hold, one in which "the consumers break the shopkeepers; they break the merchants; and the shock must be felt as far as London."[33] William Donaldson summed up the situation in stark detail:

> The face of money is hardly to be seen in this Country, every man is suing his Neighbour which produces daily Bankrupts & the most pitiable scenes of distress; a Farm in this Neighbourhood was sold a few weeks agoe by the sheriff for £350 which the owner refused £1200 for 18 [months] agoe, which is the alteration of times here, owing chiefly to the scarcety of money & distress on Commerce.[34]

As the crisis deepened, such pitiable scenes became common. "I know of sundry Estates that has been taken by Execution," a New York merchant reported late in 1766, "and sold for not more than one third of their value owing to the scarcity of money."[35] By 1767, sheriff sales (similar to foreclosure auctions today) had increased thirteenfold from their 1760–1762 baseline in the Middle Colonies, and gold and silver were "well known not to be a third or fourth part" of what they had been when the colonies were in their most flourishing circumstances.[36] "It is indeed amazing," Benjamin Franklin ruminated, "that we had a Quantity sufficient before the War began, and that the War added immensely to that Quantity by the Sums spent among us by the Crown and the Paper struck and issued ... and now in so few Years all the Money spent by the Crown is gone away, and has carried with it all the Gold and Silver we had before, leaving us bare and empty, and at the same time more in debt to England than ever we were!"[37]

By 2010, I mean 1768, the crisis finally began to run out of steam, partly because few debtors were left to sue and partly because the futility of ruining one's debtors by forcing the sale of assets that no one could buy was apparent to all. Pamphleteer Stephen Sayre recounted an instance in New Jersey "of one merchant sueing seventy shopkeepers for debt; the seventy had lands, and their lands were sold at public auction for no more than the sum owing, by which means seventy families were deprived of their substance."[38] That story sounds exaggerated if not outright apocryphal, but private correspondence was replete with similar tales of woe. Many early third-millennium banks acted likewise.

Creditors stopped suing because it came to be seen as cruel to do so. Creditors did not recoup their full investments and had to suffer with the knowledge that they threw families out of their homes and husbands and fathers into horrid prisons. No Martha Stewart–like, modern white-collar-crime, pseudoprisons were these. Unlike today, the government did not provide imprisoned debtors with three squares and a cot (and a television, computer, etc.). All it did was keep the debtor confined, sometimes in the same cell with common criminals, brigands, and even violent felons. For food, water, clothing, bedding, and the other necessaries of life, debtors had to rely on family, friends, and charity. Conditions ranged from cramped to fetid. In Charleston, South Carolina, Anglican minister Charles Woodmason saw sixteen debtors crammed into twelve square feet of jail cell in 1767. "A person would be in a better Situation in the French Kings Gallies, or the Prisons of Turkey or Barbary," he opined, "than in this dismal place."[39] The jail in Worcester, Massachusetts, was not much better and even sported a dungeon for use on special occasions. In the parlance of the day, debtors were always depicted as "languishing" in prison.[40]

Conditions were so harsh in order to induce debtors to pay up. The assumption was that debtors could repay if they wanted to, with assets that they must have squirreled away. In other words, all defaults were believed to be due to moral hazard. By the late 1760s, even the dullest creditors came to understand that most borrowers could not repay due to macro-economic conditions well beyond their control. To punish them with imprisonment served no purpose. Lawsuits therefore began to taper off, but the economy remained far from robust.

By 1768 British vulture capitalists circled North America's economic carcass, but many of them feared the risk of landing. British traveler Alexander Mackraby wrote friends back home that there was "no time so proper as the present" to purchase lands in America; "They are to be had," he told them, "at a lower rate now than could have been at any period for years past, owing to the extreme scarcity of money."[41] Nevertheless, few wealthy foreigners swooped in to buy up land on the cheap because of the high political risk. Just as multinational corporations today avoid investing in places like Cuba, North Korea, Myanmar, and so on, few investors felt safe investing in a region in the throes of rebellion. Ironically, the increased political risk was directly related to British mishandling of their colonies' economic crisis.

Economic adjustment to the end of the French and Indian War should have come naturally to economies on fixed exchange rates. Falling per-capita money supplies and rising interest rates should have attracted gold and silver to the colonies like protesters to a World Trade Organization meeting. If left to their own devices, the colonies also could have established loan offices, as they had in the past, that would have increased the quantity of bills of credit in circulation and allowed at least some of those with private callable mortgages to refinance on reasonable terms. British authorities, however, blocked both avenues to recovery. First, the British stomped on any notion of the colonists emitting more bills of credit. Under the provisions of the Currency Act of 1764, existing legal tender issues in the colonies were to be retired as they came due, and after September 1764 any new emissions of legal tender bills, or extensions of the periods of existing bills, would be declared null and void. Small issues of paper money issued through a government loan office would have slowed or stopped the cycle of bankruptcies described above and restored some confidence in the book credit system, an important money substitute that also fell under pressure in the latter half of the 1760s. But it was not to be. In colony after colony, loan office acts were passed, only to be disallowed by imperial authorities. The hard line helped to keep the colonies on fixed exchange rates at the war's end but meant the economy was almost completely at the mercy of the trade winds, which rarely blew favorably in the 1760s, again due to British bungling.

British trade policies made it very costly for the colonists to obtain more gold and silver. Had British officials given the colonists some breathing room by loosening trade restrictions, many of the horrors of the 1760s might have been avoided, or at least mitigated, and the colonists would have been in much better humor when attempts were made to tax them. But the officials didn't. Instead, policymakers tightened their grip, forcing farmers who used the Hudson and Delaware rivers to get produce to domestic markets such as Manhattan and Philadelphia to clear customs. When they failed to comply, the British navy interceded. "The floating Custom Houses Not only Destress us in Our Trade," a New York merchant complained, "but go so far as Even to Empress Our Markit men and fisherman."[42] The British went so far as to establish a customs house in Albany that forced upper Hudson River traders one hundred fifty miles from the ocean to post bonds as if they were engaged in international trade.

Another remarkable instance of overbearing enforcement occurred in 1765. Hopeful of initiating trade with the new British possession of Pensacola, Florida, and the Spanish colonies, New York and Philadelphia merchants sent £100,000 in British manufactured goods there. When a Spanish vessel bearing $500,000 in coin arrived to buy from them, it seemed their expectations were fulfilled. The captain of a British naval ship, however, threatened to seize the vessel if a single dollar were landed, driving the Spaniards off. The merchants were "mortified with the loss of selling their Goods, and render'd unable to make remittances for them."[43] The captain's actions were almost lawful—it took lawyers a long time to condemn the action—but such strict enforcement was counterproductive economically, a point the colonists well understood. "All those dollars would in six Months time have been in England as Remittances," a merchant objected, "and what injury could that have been to the Nation?"[44] The cash-starved colonists remembered the incident for years. "It must not be forgot," a colonist later argued, "that our Trade to the Spanish and French West Indies was laid under the severest Restrictions, and the Spanish Ships were even prevented laying out their Money in our Ports."[45] That be FUBAR.

Passed at the behest of West Indian sugar interests, the Sugar Act of 1764 also impeded the speedy recovery of the colonial economy. The new law reduced the duty on foreign molasses but only to three pence per gallon, a levy that most colonial merchants considered prohibitively high if actually collected. (For decades, colonists bribed tax collectors for less than one pence per gallon.) The colonists needed foreign molasses to make rotgut rum, which they exchanged for other commodities and for slaves. Other provisions of the act were even more disruptive. Lumber and iron bound for Europe had to be transshipped through Britain, which reduced colonists' profits by forcing them to sell to British middlemen. New duties placed on the import of Madeira wine, the staple product of the wine islands, threatened to undermine the profitable trade of colonial provisions with those islands. Worst of all, those onerous restrictions struck just when the colonists most needed to acquire new sources of foreign exchange and specie.

The colonists responded by seeking out new markets in southern Europe. They made some minor inroads but ultimately found little basis for trade. A famine in Leghorn (now Livorno, Italy, detto Roma e Genova) in 1764 induced North American merchants to export wheat and other foodstuffs there. On the first day of 1765, however, a former New York merchant residing in the region reported that "the distress of this Country for want of Grain is certainly greatly abated."[46] He also noted that "no sort of Business" from North America would pay there, except for cod and salmon. The colonists tried anyway, only to find that their shipments tended to "clogg" a grain market "already too much stocked with said article."[47]

The Stamp Act and subsequent levies also posed grave threats to the colonists' material well-being because they required payment to Britain in specie. The sums involved were not large in absolute terms but with the colonists already struggling to make payments at home, much less the remittances abroad, they could not help looking upon the acts with horror. Watts doubted there was specie enough in the country to carry the Stamp Act into execution. Another colonist predicted that unless restrictions on colonial trade were lifted, the Stamp Act would "soon draw out all the little silver and gold we have or can procure, distress us to an Extremity and frustrate the very end of the Law."[48] Franklin testified before Parliament that in his opinion there was "not gold and silver enough in the colonies to pay the stamp duty for one year."[49] Since, in the end, no revenue was ever collected under the Stamp Act, and relatively little was collected under the other levies, asking whether colonists' fears were justified is an exercise in counterfactual history. Certainly, the apprehension of a new specie drain was real and constituted one of the major factors fueling colonial opposition to British tax acts.

British mismanagement of trade, money, and taxes, or rather their management for British interests first, is the proper context for the colonists' famous ideological ruminations on taxation, representation, and republican government. Macroeconomic policy-induced bankruptcies were just as predatory as outright property confiscation and thus raised the specter of John Locke and other constitutional thinkers. The Revolution, in other words, was about the real economic costs imposed by the empire as well as ideology. Without the rash of sheriff's sales and clear commercial distress, the colonists may have accepted the Stamp Act without agitation. The imperial crisis that followed the colonists' refusal to buy stamps would have been allayed and independence indefinitely delayed, as it was in Canada (which became a part of the British Empire during the French and Indian War) and the British West Indies.

***

A hybrid failure related to real estate and mortgages also lay at the heart of the financial crisis of 2007–2009. Just as in the 1760s, housing prices soared and people borrowed and bought, then they got into trouble when prices reversed. The real estate market experienced a bubble, or a rapid increase in value justified only by the expectation of yet higher prices to come. Bubbles originate in a soapy mixture of new technology and expected future demand of unprecedented proportions and are puffed up by cheap credit. By their very nature they are unstable, sparkling, and glistening as they magically float upward. Then they suddenly pop, leaving only toxins behind.

Low interest rates often give rise to bubbles by decreasing the total cost of assets. To borrow $10,000 for a year to buy a car at 10 percent simple interest will cost $1,000, raising the total cost of the car to $11,000. At 1 percent, the same loan will cost only $100, making the car's total cost (excluding taxes and so forth) only $10,100. Lower total cost, in turn, raises the quantity demanded. When the price of some good decreases, people buy more of it, sometimes a little more and sometimes a lot more. That is why stores hold "specials," auto manufacturers and dealers give "cash back," restaurants print coupons, and so forth.

Interest rates affect the total cost of some assets more than others. They have very little direct effect on toothpaste, food, and other inexpensive items, but they deeply influence the total cost of more expensive goods, things that people typically borrow to purchase. They have an especially powerful effect on real estate, which is relatively fixed in supply. Low rates bring down the total cost of owning land, increasing demand, but the supply does not change appreciably. That means prices can only go in one direction: up. The same analysis applies to real estate improvements, like houses and strip malls, although their supply will eventually increase as new construction projects are completed. Of course if interest rates increase, the process reverses, and real estate prices sag if all else is constant.

If investors believe that interest rates will remain low for an extended period, or if they think that some new technology or change in market conditions will make an asset permanently more valuable, they begin to get very excited. They will start to borrow money to buy the asset with the sole intention of reselling it soon afterward at a profit. In other words, they increase leverage (the degree of borrowing) to engage in speculation. Some people call this greed, but it is really just business, trying to buy low and sell high—or in the case of bubbles to buy high and sell yet higher. What makes speculation dangerous is the leverage or borrowing part. Playing with leverage is like playing with fire. If all goes well, fire is a great friend that helps us to stay warm, cook our food, and frighten away dangerous critters. If it gets out of control, however, it can burn both speculators and their lenders and, quite possibly, the entire economic forest.

Speculators employ leverage to increase their returns. Compare three investors, one who buys a house entirely with his own money, one who borrows half of the price of the house, and one who borrows 90 percent of the price of the house. Their returns (not including the cost of borrowing, which as noted above is usually low during bubbles) will be:

Period	House Price ($000)	Cumulative Return, No Leverage (%)	Cumulative Return, 50% Leverage (%)	Cumulative Return, 90% Leverage (%)
0	100	—	—	—
1	110	10	60	100
2	120	20	70	110
3	130	30	80	120

In this example, returns for the unleveraged investor are great, but not as high as for the investor who borrowed half the cash, in essence paying only $50,000 of her own money for the $100,000 asset at the outset. But even she looks like a chump compared to the investor who borrowed most of the money to finance the original purchase, putting up only $10,000 of his own money. In the first decade of the third millennium, speculators could borrow 125 percent of the value of the house that they were buying. That was extremely lucrative for both the borrower and the lender if housing prices continued to increase. But they didn't, and that touched off a panic.

When asset prices begin to slide, as they always eventually do, lenders get nervous and begin to call (ask for their money back) and restrict further lending. Most borrowers can repay only by selling the asset they borrowed to buy. They desperately try to unload, but buyers are few because prices are no longer soaring and easy loans are no longer to be had. That realization causes a panic, a moment when everybody must sell and few can or want to buy. Prices then plummet, triggering additional calls, and yet more selling. Speculators cannot sell assets quickly enough, or for a high enough price, to repay their loans, so banks and other lenders begin to suffer defaults. *Their* lenders (other banks, depositors, holders of commercial paper), in turn, begin to wonder if financial institutions are still creditworthy and call or restrict their lending. That is what brought down Bear Stearns, Lehman Brothers, AIG, and other seemingly invincible financial giants.

When a bubble bursts, the most highly leveraged speculators get burned the worst. As the price of the asset falls, the unleveraged investor suffers negative returns. The leveraged investors lose the same percentage and must now pay a high interest rate for their loans or put up the equity themselves, at a time when the cost of doing so is substantial. The higher the leverage, the larger the sum that must be borrowed at high rates. Also, the higher the leverage, the smaller the price change needs to be to trigger a call. At 50 percent leverage, a $100,000 asset could drop to $50,000 before the lender must call. At 90 percent leverage, a $100,000 asset need decrease only $10,000 to induce a call. At 100 (plus) percent leverage, any drop is enough to induce a call. Therefore, the leveraged speculator usually loses the asset, by voluntary or forced sale. The unleveraged investor, by contrast, can hold onto the asset if he wishes, in the expectation of higher prices in the future, or simply, in the case of a house, to have a place to live.

When in London, for example, that great sage Benjamin Franklin weathered the Panic of 1772 with no trouble. "Being out of debt myself," he later explained, "my credit could not be shaken by a run upon me: Out of debt, as the proverb says, was being out of danger."[50] Similarly, in China's Yunnan Province, a bubble in a special type of tea called Pu'er recently burst. The local farmers' aspirations were shattered and their cash flows crimped, but their balance sheets remained intact. They complained, for example, of owning fancy automobiles that they could not afford to put gasoline into and having to shift production to corn and rice. Because they were largely free of debt, however, they still had their farms, much improved during the boom, and could sell their fuel-less cars for cash. A lack of leverage will also save many Americans' retirement accounts. They sank dramatically in value due to the Panic of 2008 and the ensuing recession, but they did not have to be sold at a loss. They could be held onto until they increased. That is about the only bright spot in the whole mess.

Some financial economists of the rational expectations/efficient markets school of thought (those who believe that markets, financial ones anyway, are rational, efficient, incapable of going widely astray of fundamental values) argue that asset bubbles are impossible. In their models, which is to say in their minds, they are correct: speculators do not overpay for assets on the expectation of selling out to a bigger sucker, and sophisticated financial institutions do not make loans to such speculators. But in the real world, bubbles occur frequently. Another group of financial economists, the behavioralists, attribute them to human irrationality. People tend to launch themselves over cliffs like legendary lemmings and to make decisions based on emotions instead of cold, hard logic.[51] It is difficult to dispute the existence of excitable morons, even (especially?) on Wall Street. The efficient-markets proponents counter that the presence of irrational traders does not mean that markets, which aggregate the individual decisions of many participants, will be irrational. Just one rational trader can ensure proper prices, they believe, by exploiting the mistakes made by irrational traders.[52]

The sanguine expectations of the efficient-markets crowd, however, meet a difficult reception in many real-world markets. Central to their belief that one smart übertrader can drive prices to their rational value is the ability to "short" the asset or, in other words, to profit at the expense of investors who pay too much for it. That is done by borrowing from a broker, say, 1 million shares of a company's stock when it is trading at, for example, $100; selling the shares at that price; then in the future replacing the 1 million borrowed shares with newly purchased shares. If the stock price has increased in the interim, the speculator loses the difference. If the stock price has decreased, by contrast, the speculator earns the difference. If the stock price went down to $75, for example, the speculator's gross profits (that will be a double entendre for some readers) would be $25 million ($100 sale price − $75 purchase price = $25 × the 1 million shares).

In many markets regularly troubled by bubbles, including agricultural, real estate, and mortgage markets, shorting is impossible or at least very expensive. Proponents of efficient markets also fail to see that what is rational for corporations' stockholders may not be what is rational for their hired managers. Until the 1980s and 1990s, investment banks were partnerships, not publicly traded corporations. The partners paid themselves well enough to wear white shoes (a traditional sign of opulence on Wall Street due to the high cost of upkeep compared with black or brown shoes) with good heels (well-heeled, get it?), but, as owners rather than mere employees, they could not easily move to another bank. So salaries were kept in line and most profits were plowed back into their respective banks. With most of their wealth tied up in their banks, the principals did not take crazy risks themselves and watched the other partners closely to ensure that they were not driving the bank off the deep end. The system worked extremely well. Sometimes smaller or marginal investment banks went bankrupt but in the twentieth century few crashed and burned.[53]

Then the big investment banks went public and all hell broke loose. Instead of staid partners bent on ensuring a wealthy retirement, the key decision makers became mere employees. That changed their incentives in a very fundamental and dangerous way. Instead of working for real, long-term gains, investment bankers began to be rewarded for urgently seeking short-term accounting profits. Managers at investment banks began doing exactly what their incentives dictated, to maximize employee compensation. They were great at it, as employee compensation now amounted to fully half of profits. They tricked stockholders into this arrangement by arguing that the returns they received were very high relative to the low risks involved. They calculated the risks with models, called Value at Risk (VaR), that deliberately cut off the tails of the statistical risk distribution! In other words, the models did not account for unusual circumstances, the very time when risks would be highest. "This," says author and Wall Street critic David Einhorn, "is like an air bag that works all the time, except when you have a car accident."[54]

Fancy but flawed mathematics blinded more than Thomas Dolby with science.[55] Corporate monitors—from stockholders to the media to the rating agencies to business school finance professors to government regulators—all fell for the Gaussian copula formula of David X. Liu.[56] Like a mathematical Frankenstein, this hideous piece of technology turned out to be little more than a monster all dressed up in fancy Greek garb, a gross and dangerous approximation of reality rather than reality itself. Liu's formula hinged on the crucial assumption that correlations between financial variables were constant. When X goes up (down), Y does up (down). In reality, the relationships between financial variables are highly unstable, almost mercurial. Everybody knows what happens when you ass|u|me— you make an ass out of you and me. Instead of properly pricing risks, the formula grossly underpriced them.

The Frankenstein formula served one useful purpose, at least as far as investment bankers were concerned. It cowed corporate monitors with heavy-duty mathematics, freeing bankers to search out risky profits in what are, for them personally, one-sided bets. If a project paid off, at least in the short run, huge bonuses would be collected. If the project was a dog from the start, bonuses would be smaller but still large compared to what most chumps, like you and me, bring home. They pulled off that trick by threatening to leave for employment at competitors if their bonuses weren't kept up. When bailout recipient AIG paid $165 million in bonuses to executives responsible for the company's deep financial troubles, its CEO said that the "cold realities of competition" were to blame. If the bonuses were not paid, top employees would walk, further disrupting the company's operations. Or so was the claim.[57]

To be frank, I'm not certain why large financial services firms think that only a small portion of the population can perform for them. Whatever the reason, Wall Street firms seem to believe that the pool of talent is extremely limited, so instead of hiring from outside, they try to nab each other's employees, even weak ones. It's a fatal flaw because it makes one-sided betting possible, and such a bet was precisely why otherwise highly intelligent and trained people embraced a dumb idea like subprime mortgages. After all, even small children know that it is not a good idea to make 125 percent LTV loans to NINJAs (those with No Income, No Job or Assets), to lend huge sums to some liars ("no doc" loans made without documentation of their income, assets, and so forth were called "liar's loans"), or to entice weak borrowers with low teaser rates on adjustable-rate mortgages. And you don't need an MBA to realize that paying mortgage originators full commissions upon closing is as bad an idea as paying life insurance agents full commissions upon signing up a policyholder, an unprofitable practice that the insurance industry abandoned over a century ago. Of course, those types of loans looked much saner and more profitable when housing prices were surging upward. The banks' "pay big bonuses now, ask questions later" incentive system ensured that nobody much cared to ask if home prices could continue to climb so fast.

The perverse incentive of the one-sided bet is also what inspired the creation of the confusing array of instruments, markets, and institutions that suffused the news after the fall of Lehman Brothers in September 2009: CDOs (collateralized debt obligations), CMOs (collateralized mortgage obligations), credit default swaps (insurance against a company defaulting on its debt), hedge funds (unregulated mutual funds for rich people), MBS (mortgage-backed securities), SIVs (special investment vehicles), SPVs (special purpose vehicles), and all the other components of the so-called shadow banking system. The details of these are not necessary to delve into here because they were just so much smoke and mirrors designed to keep corporate monitors distracted and confused—about the true situation—that bankers were able to hide the huge risks they were taking with other people's money. When regulators started to catch on, financial institutions engaged in what economists euphemistically call "regulatory arbitrage" and changed their charters in order to fall under the scrutiny of new, more clueless regulators! That was easy to do, as by the 1980s ten federal agencies, more than fifty state bodies, and over twenty

SROs (self-regulating organizations) shared responsibility for the safety and soundness of the US financial sector.[58]

In any event, the fancy financial contraptions were ingenious but not works of genius. That is because, in the end, financiers weren't being paid to be smart, they were being paid to dive headfirst into the Next Big Thing. There was water and room in the pool at first, but soon all the frolicking made it increasingly dangerous to jump in. But they kept on coming until some necks and legs were broken. Then everyone in the pool was suspect, the liquid(ity) drained away, the proverbial party was over, and the government offered everybody CPR. Out of the woodwork ideologues oozed, fulminating about the end of capitalism and free markets. Don't listen to the hype! The crisis was a classic hybrid failure. Markets need lots of help to get so completely FUBAR.

***

To date, the US government has not implemented policies as outright fallacious as those of the British in the 1760s and 1770s. It may even succeed in returning the economy to prosperity, although as I will later discuss in the chapter on the Great Depression we should not hold our collective breath. Regardless of whether its bailout spurs a rapid recovery or not, the government's culpability in helping to cause the crisis is palpable and multifaceted. The government is at least as much to blame as the market for the real estate crash, the subprime mortgage fiasco, and the subsequent financial panic.

Since President Franklin Roosevelt's New Deal in the 1930s, a number of tried-and-true policies have eroded, creating perverse incentives. The most important was probably the gradual destruction of recourse, or the ability of lenders to go after borrowers' noncollateralized assets and future income for full repayment of mortgage loans. Recourse, as we saw in the opening section about the 1760s, was punitive (although not as punitive as being jailed!), but it served several important economic functions. Foremost, it made speculators pay for their mistakes, thus chastening them from chasing after every rainbow. It also encouraged them to work hard to keep their property because there was no easy out, no walk-away default. With the demise of recourse, those benefits were lost. The real estate bubble waxed large because people could get into the game with very little risk to themselves. If prices continued skyward, they would make a bundle. If prices sagged, they would lose the house(s) but little else because they had little or no money down on a nonrecourse loan. Nonspeculative borrowers also discovered that they could get out from an "underwater" mortgage by simply walking away. If lenders could garnish their income (current and future, from jobs, investments, or other sources) and attach their other property, borrowers would not be so quick to default.

Erosion of the doctrine of secret liens, which very sensibly held that if a borrower defaulted any so-called secret lenders (any creditor that for whatever reason hid its status from other creditors, not some sort of conspiracy) would be last in line to receive repayment, also exacerbated the bubble and ensuing crisis. The theory was that lenders that colluded with borrowers to hide their true leverage position disadvantaged other lenders. Courts devised the doctrine centuries ago to encourage transparency. As a Pennsylvania judge explained in *Clow v. Woods* (1819):

> [A] creditor ought not to be suffered to secure himself by means that may ultimately work an injury to third persons.... The law will impute it, at all events, because it would be dangerous to the public to countenance such transaction under any circumstances.... [It is] against sound policy to suffer a [debtor] to create a secret [e]ncumbrance on his personal property, when to the world he appears to be the absolute owner, and gains credit as such.[59]

By the second half of the twentieth century, the doctrine was under considerable stress due to subtle changes in the Uniform Commercial Code and emphasis on technicalities rather than substantive disclosure of prior liens. Investment banks and other large, complex financial institutions (LCFIs) exploited the weaknesses in the law to develop the fancy contraptions mentioned above that hid from their creditors, stockholders, and regulators the amount of leverage they were taking on in the mortgage, derivative, and other markets. That, in turn, allowed them to pay less to borrow than they would have if their true indebtedness were known. It also helped them to avoid the scrutiny of stockholders, including institutional investors, and regulators.

Relaxation of the old ways also led to the proliferation of piggyback and "silent second" mortgages, small loans used to finance down payments.

Even during the height of the housing bubble, many lenders remained conservative, only making loans with a loan-to-value (LTV) of 90 percent or lower and forcing riskier borrowers to pay private mortgage insurance (PMI). Many homeowners could not afford or, as we will see, did not want to make a down payment of 10 or more percent and did not want to pay PMI. To help out homeowners and pad their own pockets, mortgage brokers cooked up the silent second. Instead of plunking $50,000 or $100,000 down on a $500,000 house, the buyer obtained a $400,000 or $450,000 mortgage from a conservative lender and a second mortgage for most, all, or even more than the balance. Instead of making a safe 80 or 90 percent LTV loan, the conservative lender unwittingly made a very dangerous one and cheaply at that. The broker, meanwhile, pocketed two commissions.

In the previous section, I argued that when investment banks transformed themselves from partnerships to publicly traded corporations, the incentives of their managers changed radically. In one way, that was a market failure because stockholders paid too much for their shares given the risks they were unwittingly taking on. In another way, that was a government failure because regulators allowed the banks to go public without forcing them to create safeguards against excessive risk taking, such as basing bonuses on the creation of realized economic profit, not mere paper or accounting profits. Perhaps it is too much to ask regulators to see into the future, but they certainly should have responded more aggressively to the wave of naughty behavior that swept Wall Street in the aftermath of the bursting of the tech bubble in early 2000. In April of that year, the Securities and Exchange Commission (SEC) nabbed ten Wall Street and regional brokerage firms for "yield burning," that is, overcharging municipalities for government securities. Firms including Goldman Sachs, Morgan Stanley, PaineWebber, Prudential, Salomon Smith Barney, and Warburg Dillon Read agreed to pay more than $139 million in fines to the Treasury and municipal issuers. In a separate investigation, BT Alex Brown paid $15 million in disgorgement for yield burning.[60]

In September 2001, the SEC caught Chase Manhattan Bank for "recordkeeping and reporting violations" so serious that Chase agreed to a $1 million civil penalty, one of the largest fines ever for that type of violation.[61] That same year, Legg Mason coughed up $50,000 for failing to supervise one of its asset managers who defrauded investors by hiding problems at portfolio companies and materially overstating its High-Yield

Fund's net asset value.[62] At about the same time, ABN Ambro paid $200,000 because it allowed one of its managers to engage in "portfolio pumping," the purchase of portfolio securities near the end of a reporting period with the intent of increasing their market value.[63]

In 2002, the SEC forced Credit Suisse First Boston to pay $100 million for charging excessive brokerage fees (essentially kickbacks) in connection with "hot" IPOs. (It nailed Robertson Stephens Inc. of San Francisco for the same fraudulent activity the following year.)[64] It also caught Frank Gruttadauria, a branch manager for the Cleveland office of Lehman Brothers, for stealing at least $40 million from some fifty clients over a six-year period.[65] Datek Securities Corporation, later iCapital Markets, also paid $6.3 million for its illegal use of Nasdaq's Small Order Execution System.[66]

Conditions deteriorated yet further in 2003. Japanese regulators slapped Citibank, Goldman Sachs, JP Morgan Securities, Merrill Lynch, and Morgan Stanley with temporary trading suspensions for violating Japan's derivatives and short-selling laws.[67] Back at home, J.P. Morgan Chase and Citigroup paid $135 million and $101 million, respectively, for their respective roles in the Enron and Dynegy frauds. The SEC also got $80 million out of Merrill Lynch for its role in Enron's earnings manipulation.[68] But the biggest case involved a $1.4 billion settlement by ten of Wall Street's largest investment banks for allowing underwriters to corrupt the reports of their ostensibly independent research analysts. The companies included Bear Stearns, Credit Suisse First Boston, Goldman, Lehman, Morgan, Merrill, Citi, UBS Warburg, and US Bancorp.[69] (In connection with this settlement, Deutsche Bank agreed to pay $57.5 million in 2004.)[70] Prudential Securities paid $382,000 for failing to effectively monitor employees who defrauded investors by selling them shares in mutual funds without disclosing the existence of less expensive share classes in the same funds. American International Group (AIG) paid $10 million for helping to manipulate the earnings of Brightpoint Inc. by retroactively selling it an insurance policy that it used to cover up the losses of a foreign subsidiary.[71]

AIG ran into more serious problems in 2004, agreeing to pay a fine plus interest, and penalties totaling $126,366,000 for its Contributed Guaranteed Alternative Investment Trust Security (C-GAITS) product. AIG represented to clients that under generally accepted accounting principles (GAAP) the product would shield their income from "troubled or other potentially volatile assets." However, C-GAITS did not satisfy GAAP requirements.[72] Big regional bank Wachovia also felt the SEC's wrath in 2004, to the tune of $37 million, because it failed to disclose material information regarding its merger with First Union in a timely fashion.[73] Bank of America (and Fleet, its recent acquisition),[74] meanwhile, paid $675 million when the SEC and New York attorney general Eliot Spitzer implicated it in the mutual fund late trading and market timing scandals. Basically, in exchange for a fee, the banks allowed mutual funds to trade after the mandatory 4 p.m. closing time. That, in turn, allowed some big institutional investors, particularly hedge funds, to buy (or in a falling market sell) fund shares with knowledge of their net asset value (NAV) for the day, valuable information denied to the rest of humanity. Other practices—barely legal and highly unethical but thought necessary in the bear market of 2000 and 2001—encouraged frequent trading which drove up fund expenses and decreased fund returns, both to the detriment of long-term investors.[75]

All told, financial services firms paid an unprecedented $23 billion worth of penalties between 2000 and 2004. Regulators should have figured out that the sudden rash of wrongdoing was rooted in a massive misalignment of incentives between managers and stockholders. For the managers, crime in fact did pay. If the best-case scenario is you got filthy rich and the worst-case scenario is that you got caught and had to pay a fine *using somebody else's money*, why not go for it?

The credit rating agencies also missed the FUBAR-creating power of one-sided bets, but perhaps they should be forgiven because they constituted a hybrid failure themselves. From the late nineteenth century, when they first emerged, until the third quarter of the twentieth century, the agencies rated the quality of bonds and other securities and sold the ratings to investors, who used them to make investment decisions. The advent of cheap photocopying, however, hurt their business model by facilitating what economists call free riding. Ingenious but illegal entrepreneurs subscribed to the ratings in order to inexpensively copy and resell them to investors at prices far below what the agencies, which expended large sums to create the ratings, could afford to do.

To make up the lost revenue, the agencies began to charge the securities issuers for ratings. Regulators not only allowed this, they encouraged it by mandating that most types of institutional investors could invest only in investment-grade securities as defined by Moody's, Standard and Poor's, and a small handful of other agencies. Issuers therefore had to pony up or suffer a large loss of demand for their securities. At least two major problems arose from this arrangement. First, rating agencies had incentives to engage in grade inflation or compression. Rather than bite the hand that fed (paid) them, they naturally licked it. One thing led to another and soon the agencies and their corporate issuers were in bed together, having a grand old time making AAA-rated babies that in the good old days would have been rated BIG (below-investment grade, or junk).

Prime evidence of grade compression is that three AAA-rated bonds, one issued by a municipality, another by a corporation, and a third by an investment bank, would have different default probabilities! Unsurprisingly, such practices created confusion for investors. By law, rating agencies receive more and better information than other investors.[76] They are exempt, for example, from Regulation FD (full disclosure). Therefore, they can be leaked inside information before it hits the market. Ergo, argues David Einhorn, "the market perceives the rating agencies to be doing much more than they actually do" and that, of course, creates a false sense of security.[77] Much the same could be said of government regulators, including the SEC and even the mighty Federal Reserve.

Readers still enamored of the SEC after learning how it failed to respond to financiers' shenanigans (as if a few billions in fines every now and again would serve to chasten them) should read the letter that whistleblower Harry Markopolos sent to the SEC about Bernie Madoff's Ponzi scheme eight years before the fraud became public knowledge.[78] For a variety of reasons, none of them particularly good, the SEC ignored the warnings.[79] Also recommended reading is *Fooling Some of the People All of the Time*, which details Einhorn's failed attempts to induce the SEC to investigate Allied Capital, the nation's second-largest business development company (BDC). As a BDC, Allied makes equity investments in, and loans to, small businesses. According to Einhorn and the analysts in his Greenlight Capital hedge fund, Allied should be called ALL LIED because it hid information from investors and engaged in accounting practices that ranged from inappropriate to downright shady. For example, it recognized loan losses much more slowly than it should have according to SEC rules and paid dividends out of new capital, which most people would find a little Ponzi scheme-ish. Instead of immediately investigating Allied, however, the SEC first interrogated Einhorn because his fund stood to gain if Allied's share price sank, which it indeed did after Einhorn publicized his findings. Five years later, the SEC validated Einhorn's analysis, but it did not fine or otherwise penalize Allied.[80]

Apparently the SEC, like many naïve investors, believes that short sellers *cause* stock prices to decline when in fact all they do is predict a decline based on their analysis of a company's business model and prospects. In truth, the SEC and other regulators ought to *encourage* short sellers because they are bubble busters extraordinaire, unafraid to announce that the emperor has no clothes or the company has no earnings. Instead, regulators often make it difficult to short sell and thereby turn the markets over to the human lemmings responsible for asset bubbles.

The Federal Reserve System, America's central bank, is also a bungler. It has only two jobs, but they are whoppers: promote employment and maintain financial market stability. In 1792, Treasury secretary Alexander Hamilton and the nation's first central bank, the Bank of the United States, successfully met both goals by quickly squelching a financial panic without increasing moral hazard. They did so by following what would later be known as Bagehot's rule of lending to all comers who could post adequate collateral at a penalty rate. The collateral requirements ensured that the government aided safe companies caught up in the financial maelstrom but did not bail out risky ones. The penalty or above-market rate of interest ensured that nobody who could borrow privately went to the government for a loan.

Hamilton's rule was a brilliant policy, perhaps too brilliant. By the time America suffered from its next major peacetime financial panic, in 1819, it was all but forgotten. By the mid-1830s, the US government had given up on central banking, resigning itself to watch from the sidelines as financial panics in 1837–1839, 1857, 1873, 1884, 1893–1895, and 1907 played themselves out. On the eve of World War I, however, it again joined the central banking arena by creating the Federal Reserve System, or Fed as it is affectionately known. For a long time, however, the Fed was not very good. As we will see, it exacerbated the Depression and the Roosevelt Recession, became a mere tool of the Treasury during World War II, and caused the Great Inflation of the 1970s. But under Paul Volcker and Alan Greenspan the Fed started to get things right, or at least take credit for the halcyon days of the 1990s.

In retrospect, however, the Greenspan Fed made a fatal mistake by eschewing Hamilton née Bagehot's rule in favor of loose monetary policy.

Whenever the financial system appeared unstable, Greenspan responded by decreasing interest rates across the board. On the surface, lower interest rates work like a charm by shoring up asset prices (remember, as discussed above, as rates go down, the value of assets goes up) and hence balance sheets. Low interest rates also encourage businesses to expand investment and employment, which keeps people paying their mortgages and other loans.

As we have seen, however, low interest rates can puff up assets like a bubble. Moreover, by lowering interest rates in the face of danger, the Fed essentially rewarded risky behavior. In technical parlance, it increased moral hazard. Already rewarded to assume huge risks, managers of LCFIs came to believe that their institutions could not fail no matter how much risk they took on because good old Uncle Sam, in the form of the Fed and even taxpayers, would stand ready to rescue them. The precedents were certainly there. When the stock market tanked in 1987, Greenspan instantaneously responded with truckloads of cheap money. In 1990, the government began "resolving" insolvent savings and loans, a euphemism for paying off the banks' debts with taxpayer money. In 1997, 1998, 1999, 2000, and 2001, Greenspan's Fed responded to financial crises, ranging from the failure of a large hedge fund to potential problems following the Y2K conversion, with more cheap money.

Like a lab rat rewarded for pushing a lever, LCFI managers pushed away enthusiastically until the lever broke. They can hardly be blamed; the government explicitly told them that big, complex financial institutions, from Fannie Mae to Citigroup, would not be allowed to fail. Worse, the government set the price of this insurance, called Too Big to Fail (TBTF), at exactly zero. (The government does charge a premium for deposit insurance through the Federal Deposit Insurance Corporation [FDIC], but it is much too low in most cases and of course does not apply to insurers, investment banks, hedge funds, and the like.) In short, the government guaranteed the one-sided bets that financiers were being rewarded to make anyway. If told that all your gambling losses would be promptly reimbursed, wouldn't you go to Vegas or Atlantic City? I sure would, and I wouldn't play the nickel slots.

TBTF and the government's newfound proclivity for bailing out troubled institutions also weakened the monitoring that naturally takes place in credit markets. Investors believed, usually correctly as it turned out, that the government would keep them from losing money. So instead of denying funds to risky financial institutions or trying to induce them to reduce their leverage, investors joined the bandwagon. Some smaller financial institutions noticed and did everything they could to grow fast enough to get into the big leagues where, ironically, competition was cloistered.

***

The government also played an active, many would now say hyperactive, role in America's home mortgage and real estate markets. All else constant, owning is better than renting because the owner has more control over the property, lives rent free while making surefire investments (paying down the principal has a guaranteed positive return), and reaps the benefit of any price appreciation. From the government's standpoint, owners have a greater stake in society than renters do and hence have long been seen as an important source of political and fiscal stability. In 1893, for example, Seymour Dexter of the United States League of Building and Loan Associations commissioned a painting called *The American Home, Safeguard of American Liberties*.[81] While great for individuals and the government, homeownership has its drawbacks, too. High levels of it, for example, are associated with labor market rigidities (the inability of people to move to new geographical areas to work), higher rates of unemployment, and longer commutes, which of course spells more greenhouse gas emissions.[82] Nevertheless, the governments of many countries try to promote homeownership.[83] Unfortunately, the efforts of those governments tend to distort incentives and markets rather than to permanently increase the percentage of homeowners, which is only possible by increasing after-tax incomes or decreasing the cost of homeownership.

The mortgage-interest tax deduction, for example, is complete folly. It subsidizes the rich much more than the poor because the rich are much more likely to own homes, to take out bigger mortgages (and hence pay more interest), and to have higher effective marginal tax rates. The size of the subsidy has long swamped direct government housing aid to the poor, a fact known for decades although little has been done to correct it.[84] In the meantime, the unintended consequences of the policy have waxed to enormous proportions. Due to the deduction, which has grown in importance as income tax rates and nominal incomes have risen, Americans tend to stay heavily mortgaged rather than build equity in their homes as they did in the nineteenth and first half of the twentieth centuries. Favorable tax treatment of retirement savings has exacerbated the situation by rewarding Americans for investing in the stock market rather than paying down the principal on their mortgage. (For starters, employers generally match the former but not the latter.)

Ironically, tax policy almost turns homeowners into renters (with lenders as landlords) while simultaneously making them the absolute owners of insignificant slices of numerous corporations, including banks. Because they have little personal stake in any one corporation, and because the government prevents institutional investors such as mutual funds, insurance companies, and pensions from exerting much pressure on the companies they invest in, their ownership comes with precious little control. Managers can therefore run wild and leave the common taxpayer/ homeowner/retirement investor with nothing more than a hollowed-out shell, an Enron if you will.

Other tax policies also distort the markets for real estate and mortgages. Examples abound but are far too numerous, complex, and frankly boring to detail here.[85] The damage they do also pales as compared to that inflicted by the government-sponsored enterprises (GSEs) colloquially known as Fannie Mae and Freddie Mac. Founded as a government agency in 1938, the Federal National Mortgage Association (Fannie) for three decades provided liquidity to mortgage lenders by buying their safe (called "conforming" because they conformed to strict rules) mortgages, then packaging them together and selling them to investors. That was all well and good— between the Depression and 1970 the percentage of Americans who owned their own homes had jumped from about a third to about two-thirds, largely thanks to the availability of affordable financing.[86] In 1968, however, the government decided to sell off Fannie to private investors to get it off its own fanny (balance sheet), which was under pressure due to the budget deficits associated with the Vietnam War and President Lyndon B. Johnson's Great Society programs. Two years later, the government created a competitor, the Federal Home Loan Mortgage Corporation (Freddie).

The pair were tagged government-sponsored enterprises because the government implicitly guaranteed their debts. That allowed them to borrow much more cheaply than other corporations. By law, the GSEs were able to maintain a leverage ratio of forty to one ($40 in assets for every $1 in capital), the envy of even aggressive hedge funds. The GSEs were therefore very profitable, which gave them tremendous means and incentives to lobby Congress to leave them alone. That, in turn, led to the biggest irony of the entire financial fiasco of 2007–2009: the very institutions most clearly backed by the full faith of the US government's willingness to take money out of its citizens' pockets were among the least monitored in the whole system. Regulators could not chastise them, and their bondholders, lulled asleep by the government guarantees, had little incentive to pry. The GSEs' managers took their one-sided bets, diving into subprime and Alt-A mortgages in a big way. When these giants failed in September 2008, credit and derivative markets worldwide shuddered and stopped functioning.

Because the government guaranteed their bonds, Fannie and Freddie were an abomination of nature and in direct contradiction to the genius of American institutions. In his veto of the Bank of the United States (1816–1836), America's second central bank and an early GSE, Andrew Jackson noted that "the powers, privileges, and favors bestowed upon it in the original charter, by increasing the value of the stock far above its par value, operated as a gratuity of many millions to the stockholders."[87] Such a subsidy, he argued, was an unwarranted redistribution of wealth from taxpayers to stockholders. Moreover, the bank was unconstitutional because it was neither necessary nor proper. The same argument can, and in fact has, been made against Fannie and Freddie, which should be wound down and never reinstituted, except perhaps as a single government agency.[88]

The government also allowed corporate governance to shrivel up. In the nineteenth century, stockholders and bondholders took care of themselves for the most part.[89] Institutional intermediaries—such as investment banks, mutual savings banks, the forerunners of today's mutual funds, and trust companies, the ancestors of today's hedge funds—actively monitored managers, often by placing one or more representatives on their boards. The New Deal changed all that because some government officials somehow got it into their heads that institutional investors had caused the Depression. Debates in the House of Representatives, for example, made a direct connection:

> The failure of many of our great industrial corporations is due to investment-banker management.... Banker directors living remote from the properties operated have no understanding of the ... industry they

direct.... The deplorable situation of many of our great industrial corporations is directly due to their banker management.... Congress must
make it unlawful for any person to act as a director... who shall also be
an investment banker.[90]

Soon after, the SEC's William O. Douglas told a stunned audience of investment bankers that from then on they would be restricted to underwriting
and brokerage. "Insofar as management and formulation of industrial policies," Douglas said, "the banker will be superseded. The financial power
which he has exercised in the past over such processes will pass into other
hands." Since passage of the Investment Company Act of 1940, which
explicitly declared that "the national public interest is adversely affected
when investment companies have great size and have excessive influence in
the national economy," and the enactment of other regulations and codes
with similar effect, US financial institutions have found it extremely costly
and even impossible to acquire large ownership stakes in corporations.[91]

The alleged connection between large institutional investors and the
Depression, however, is tenuous at best. In 1953, law school professor
Horace Robbins argued that "there has been sufficient work done in the
analysis of money, credit, banking, profit rate and the expansion of markets,
to indicate that the causes of Depression lie elsewhere than in size"[92] and
subsequent studies have absolved the financial sector of most of the blame
for the Great Depression.[93] The restrictive policies have remained in place,
however, perpetuating a separation between ownership and control that has
led to a perverse outcome: strong managers and weak owners.[94]

***

Were that all! During the 1970s and early 1980s, high levels of inflation
pushed up total housing costs (house prices plus interest, insurance, taxes,
and repair costs) faster than many workers' wages, resulting in the perception that many Americans would soon not be able to afford to buy a
house.[95] As Gwendolyn Wright put it:

Americans in the 1980s are facing yet another housing crisis. It derives
from the rising cost of homes and financing for homeownership, the
shortage of rental units, the effects of an energy shortage, and severe

unemployment... The overwhelming majority of Americans cannot afford to buy a home today, whether it is a condominium, a townhouse, or a detached dwelling.[96]

As a result, political and ideological pressure was put on the government to enact policies designed to decrease the costs of homeownership, to make housing affordable for more Americans. Since 1977 one of those policies, the Community Reinvestment Act (CRA), has penalized banks that do not lend in the neighborhoods from which they take deposits. The presumption was that banks engaged in redlining, that is, refusing to lend to anyone who resided in lower-income or minority neighborhoods. To some, it seems patently unfair to accept somebody's deposit and then to refuse their loan applications, and automatically at that. Of course there is a huge difference between taking a deposit and making a loan. A deposit is essentially a loan *to* a bank, not from one. It would be silly to refuse a deposit, unless the depositor is a criminal bent on casing the joint or engaging in check kiting. But it is not silly to refuse to lend to somebody without a job or other income or any tangible assets. The government persisted, however, and the bankers became happy to oblige once they saw there were big bonuses for themselves in it.[97]

Meanwhile, in an Alanis Morissette–sized irony, the government missed several easy opportunities to make homeownership more affordable.[98] Housing costs thousands of dollars more than it has to due to two government-sanctioned cartels, one for title insurance and another for real estate sales. Title insurers can take advantage of homeowners because their product is arcane and often disclosed only during the closing process, where it appears as a $x,xxx line item. If questioned about the charge, the professional closers present (agents, attorneys, etc.) usually say that the policy protects the buyer from defects in the title, lenders insist upon it, and the price varies little from insurer to insurer. At that point, most people, eager to get into their new home, shut up and sign without shopping around for the best deal. Not that shopping would matter much, as five title insurers control 92 percent of the national market and at the state level the concentration is often even worse, with only two or three insurers dominating the market. Unsurprisingly, home buyers usually get a raw deal, a policy that costs far more than it is intrinsically worth. Equally unsurprisingly, title insurance companies are highly profitable yet extremely secretive. Only one state, Iowa, has done homeowners right, by copying Canada and supplying the equivalent of title insurance itself, at a far lower cost. All the US government has done to combat this expensive and pernicious cartel is to publish a report critical of it.[99] Big whoopity do!

The government has also let the residential real estate brokerage industry get away with financial murder. Although real estate brokers are numerous (there are literally millions of them), spread fairly evenly throughout the country, and entry barriers remain low, industry practices have the practical effect of enforcing set prices and not allowing competitive ones. Specifically, like Rudolph the red-nosed reindeer, maverick price cutters can be excluded from brokers' reindeer games, including access to the multiple listing service and choice prospects on the buy or sell side. It is better, most brokers conclude, to ask for the full 6 percent and take whatever business falls in their lap. The existence of a de facto cartel explains why most brokers have been able to charge 6 percent (7 percent in a few locales) for decades. It also explains why brokerage *rates* on more expensive homes are the same as those on less expensive homes when they should be lower because it takes about the same amount of work to sell any house, regardless of price. Little wonder that 15 to 20 percent of home sellers go the self-help FSBO (for sale by owner) route.[100]

Doing away with those two cartels would undoubtedly lower homeowners' costs by a nontrivial amount. Of course politicians prefer to dole out favors rather than take them away, and the status quo is not easily changed, especially when big chunks of cold cash are at stake. As H. Michael Manne points out, "a monopolist never gives up its position easily and will, if allowed, try to control, if not blunt, any change that portends an increase in competition."[101] Couple that with the fact that most people buy or sell only a few houses over their lifetimes, and the rationale for the government's lackadaisical attitude becomes clear. Houses and other parts of our "built environment" could also be rendered less expensive if the FUBAR construction industry were reformed, a topic to which we now turn.

3

BOB THE BUILDER
Deconstructing the Construction Industry

B ob the Builder is a delightful character on a stop motion "clayma-
tion" children's program created by British television writer and
producer Keith Chapman. Bob, his colleague Wendy, and their gang of
anthropomorphized construction equipment spend their days helping
people and learning valuable life lessons, like how to share and recycle.
When the safety glasses–wearing Bob asks "Can we fix it?" the other char-
acters always reply with a resounding "Yes we can!" Unfortunately, the
show does not teach the children of the thirty-odd countries where it airs
the most important lesson of all: the vast majority of construction contractors are nothing like Bob. They often can't fix it, don't show up on time,
and charge exorbitant prices. And oh yeah, Wendy may be the only female
in the entire industry.[1]

"We prop up a falling house with a cracked beam and put a broken
sleeper under the beam," an early nineteenth-century critic of monopoly
wrote, "without ever thinking of repairing the edifice itself."[2] The house
was a metaphor in that pamphlet, but in this chapter it is quite literal. The
US construction industry is the best in the world, but that isn't saying
much, as most of the world's nations remain dominated by predatory governments that offer few incentives for improvement of physical—let alone

human—capital.[3] In most places, therefore, traditional building materials and techniques prevail, and the benefits of newer, better ways of making homes, roads, and other built infrastructure are forgone. The construction industries of most developed nations produce at or near US levels; there is no superiority here as there is in many aspects of computer, bio-, nano-, and military technology. In fact, for large projects that are up for international bidding, US companies generally fare poorly because they usually face stiff competition from Asian and European rivals. In short, American construction firms can only brag about being less inefficient than the woefully inefficient companies elsewhere, which is akin to being the fastest of the slow, the brightest of the dull, or the slimmest of the obese.

Construction industry productivity in the United States has been flat or even perhaps slightly negative over the last five decades. In other words, a certain sum of real dollars (dollars adjusted for inflation) will buy an owner (individual, company, or government) the same quantity and quality of construction output (home repair, office building, or bridge) in 2010 as in 1960. If that sounds good to you, it shouldn't. A thousand bucks (in 2010 money) will buy you a much better laptop, cell phone, television, or other consumer electronics device than it would have in 1990 or even 2000. Go back to 1960, and laptops and cell phones didn't even exist, and most televisions had tiny black-and-white screens and pathetic speaker systems. And construction doesn't just pale compared to affordable 60-inch, color, HD flat screens with surround sound. Since 1960, nonfarm productivity, a broad swath of economic activity, has increased about two and a half times, despite being dragged down by lagging sectors, such as education, healthcare, and construction.

Abstract numbers aside, many people sense that something is seriously amiss in the construction business. Many custom projects take forever to complete or come in way over budget or suffer major quality problems. According to one study, nine out of ten transportation construction projects overshoot their budgets.[4] According to another study, commercial construction projects of all types are either late or over budget about half of the time.[5] Sometimes, as with Boston's "Big Dig" highway improvement program, projects are months or years late, cost millions or billions more than expected, and suffer from unbelievably poor quality. On a smaller scale, most people know a homeowner (or perhaps were themselves) somehow screwed by a construction contractor. The new bedroom ended up costing twice as much as initially projected, the renovation of the condo's only bathroom took a month instead of the promised week, or the hinges fell off the new kitchen cabinets just three months after their seriously crooked installation.

Of course everyone also knows of exceptions where a real-life version of Bob the Builder appeared and got the job done on time and on budget. In most of those instances, however, Bob was not doing custom work— special projects at the behest of the owner ranging from custom cabinetry to a billion-dollar office tower. Instead, he was working on "spec" or on "force account," meaning that Bob himself was the owner or the owner's *employee*, not a business firm contracted to do a specific job. Productivity in both of those noncustom parts of construction is relatively high because the owner and the builder are one and the same. Ergo, the shenanigans described above and below do not take place.[6] As a result, speculative and force account building is much more efficient than the custom variety as measured by average cost per square foot.[7] In other words, there is something to the old saying that if you want something done right, do it yourself. That is why, by the way, Lowe's and Home Depot exist and *This Old House* and similar do-it-yourself TV programs are so popular. People who wouldn't think of baking a cake or growing vegetables themselves, much less try to build their own automobiles or computers, will get out their paint brushes, hammers, and wood saws and do their own home improvements. That is because bakers, farmers, computer makers, and even automobile manufacturers (well, maybe not the US ones anymore) are much more efficient than our custom construction contractors.

The custom construction industry's productivity woes are a major problem for the economy because the United States will need some 100 billion square feet of new homes by 2030 due to population growth and replacement of old structures.[8] It will also need some $25 trillion (at current prices) in public buildings and transportation infrastructure repair, improvement, and expansion.[9] That's a lot of moolah to waste on an industry that in large measure remains wedded to nineteenth-century industrial structure and more recent but nevertheless obsolete technologies. (It's a myth that construction technology is centuries old. After a postwar burst, however, technological innovation in construction stagnated and lagged far behind manufacturing and most other areas of the economy.)[10]

***

Economic historian John Kenneth Galbraith once remarked that "capitalism has never anywhere provided good houses at moderate cost."[11] What is the construction industry's problem? It's FUBAR, of course, but why and how is it fouled up beyond all recognition? Agency problems and postcontractual monopoly powers are the main culprits. They render custom construction, the biggest portion of the industry, uncompetitive. In fact, construction management has been compared with the management of defense contractors, and not without reason—neither is much subject to competition.[12] Free entry without the salubrious effects of competition winnowing out inefficient practices and firms combine to produce an industry dominated by numerous small firms with weak management and little investment even in the adoption of existing technologies, much less R & D in the creation of new technological innovations.

Unions and workers more generally do not help the situation, but they also do not hurt it much. Productivity in union and nonunion areas of the country are about the same, and unions have lost their grip over time without corresponding improvements in construction productivity. Union workers get paid more than nonunion labor but also produce more per hour. There is no significant economic difference between paying a union carpenter $100 per hour and getting $150 worth of work out of him, and paying a nonunion guy $25 per hour and getting on average $75 worth of work from him. As John Fitzwater of Clarksburg, West Virginia, put it, "a union bricklayer can lay four times as many bricks [as a cheaper nonunion worker], and he does it properly."[13] Unions do more than increase wages and enforce seemingly arcane rules, they select and train workers to a degree that tiny construction companies never have, could, or would.

The behavior of construction workers is notoriously rude, crude, and socially unacceptable. The image of big burly guys in hardhats whistling cat calls, smoking, and telling their foreman to take a long walk off a short pier is a stereotype, but one tinged with truth. "If we have a slab to pour on Saturday morning, we do not pay the boys on Friday," one contractor confides, because "if we do, half of them will show up hung over and the other half won't show up at all."[14] (In most factories, by contrast, workers are always paid on the same day of the week regardless of overtime.) But it gets worse. Construction workers, union and open shop, have managed to obtain something that very few workers throughout history have been able: an hourly wage plus considerable discretion in when and how they do their jobs. Typically, hourly workers must do precisely as they are told or face immediate dismissal. In exchange for the certainty of their wages, hourly workers surrender their autonomy, even, in the bad old days, over their own bowels. Workers paid by the piece, by contrast, purchase their freedom by agreeing to receive a wage that corresponds to their output rather than their time on the job. Managers need not closely monitor those working on piece rates because if such workers have bad habits, like urinating twice a day, those workers will pay the price by receiving a smaller compensation. (In factory settings piece-rate workers may be fired if they don't meet or exceed their quotas consistently, but in most nonfactory situations managers or owners do not, and indeed usually cannot, provide even that level of monitoring.)

Makes sense, right? Logic ends, however, when it comes to construction workers, who generally receive an hourly wage but can do as they damn well please during that hour. Ostensibly, this is because construction is a much more dangerous job than making widgets in an indoor factory or stuffing envelops at home. Yes, apologists admit, twelve guys are standing around drinking coffee and shooting the bull for forty-five minutes, but that is only because weather conditions are not ideal. It is too hot, cold, windy, or sunny to undertake the next step in the construction process. That may be the case, but it doesn't explain why the workers still get paid. When safety or other conditions force work stoppages, factory workers are sent home without pay or are at least rescheduled. Why are construction workers compensated for standing around? The answer has little to nothing to do with the workers themselves and everything to do with the nature of their industries. Most factories function in extremely competitive environments. Most construction companies do not, so they have weak managers, typically former grunts themselves, with weak incentives to condition workers, invest in ways to work safely in a wider range of weather conditions, or do much of anything at all, in fact.[15]

Industry gurus like John McMahan note that "disputes between management and labor inevitably arise in every construction project."[16] Part of the problem may be a naturally recalcitrant labor force, but most of it is due to incompetent management. One study found that "more than half the time wasted during construction" was "attributable to poor management practices."[17] "Most residential construction projects today," writes contractor Dennis Rourke, "lack the strong management direction than can only be provided by an onsite professional."[18] As for strategic planning and research and development— fuggeddabout it!

Over the years, pundits, scholars, and industry apologists alike have come up with all sorts of excuses for the construction industry's poor performance.[19] They are all either complete baloney or, like the legend of construction worker unruliness just discussed, only symptoms of much more fundamental problems. The claim that seasonality is a major drag on the industry is belied by the fact that productivity in the sunny US South is about the same as in Canada and Sweden, where snow and cold weather can legitimately delay some types of projects. In the northern US, famous speculative builder Levitt and Sons worked eleven or twelve months per year while custom contractors often shut down for two or three months, especially, and unsurprisingly, if they could collect unemployment insurance.

Yes, every construction project is somewhat different, but the vast majority of projects are not nearly as unique as industry apologists would have you believe. Garages may be different sizes and have slightly different roofs, but they are all garages. Roads can be different lengths and widths and traverse different types of terrain, but they are almost all built the same way. Experienced contractors should be able to anticipate any difficulties but, as we will see, they have incentives to make owners believe that their projects present unusual challenges. All the better to bill you extra with, my dear owner.

Cyclicality—the extreme booms and busts that the industry experiences —is another specious bugaboo. One tip-off is that when cycles become less pronounced, construction productivity does not increase. Maybe any amount of cyclicality stymies growth of construction productivity through some unexplained or unexplainable mechanism. But other industries that face ups and downs are not FUBAR too. So is construction cyclicality due to some unstoppable force of nature or the nature of the industry itself? A bit of both, it turns out. The structure of the industry exacerbates the normal business cycle, making the highs higher and the lows lower than they would be otherwise.

In 1997, the construction industry was composed of over six hundred thousand tiny firms employing fewer than one hundred workers, a little over five thousand small ones with up to 999 employees, and four score or so medium-sized ones employing more than one thousand workers.[20] (Data from the 2007 census was not fully available at the time of writing, but the tables that were available were consistent with the 1997 statistics reported above.) Only about 10 percent of construction firms have assets greater than $250 million, a drop in the bucket for a trillion-dollar-a-year industry. Of major industries, only agriculture, forest, and fishing; education; and the catchall "other services" have so few big firms. Even the industry's hoariest companies—Bechtel, Brown and Root, KB Homes, Levitt and Sons, Pulte Homes, Ryan Homes, Toll Brothers—were small compared to industrial giants like GE, GM, or US Steel in their heydays.[21] What makes that fact even more surprising is that construction is a huge industry overall, employing some 5 percent of the national workforce and accounting for about 4 percent of the gross domestic product (GDP), and historically was even more prominent than that.

In good times, the number of construction companies expands due to the entry of mostly small or tiny firms splintering into several even teensier ones. In bad times, total construction activity declines with everything else, forcing the many marginal construction firms to fold. By contract, in most industries, non-FUBAR ones anyway, the number of companies shrinks during both boom and bust periods, during booms due to frenzied merger activity and during busts due to bankruptcies and the acquisition of struggling firms by larger, stronger ones. To stay competitive in most industries, companies must get ever larger and more efficient, hence the almost constant merger activity. Clearly this is not the case in construction, which rarely witnesses more than a few score mergers a year, and those are mostly small. It was no accident that *Fortune* once called construction "the Industry Capitalism Forgot."[22] The reason for this strange structure directs us straight into the industry's FUBAR heart.

***

Most owners, even presumably sophisticated corporate ones, mistakenly believe that soliciting three or more sealed bids will ensure competition and hence the best price, time, and quality available. That's a fatal assumption. Owners expect contractors to bid for free, but serious bids cost serious money (in proportion to the size of the project). Contractors cannot afford to expend such large sums for the mere chance of winning the business. As a result, contractors often "game" the bidding process. First, they divine a ballpark figure by making quick comparisons to other projects. Then, if they are flush with work, they'll bid high and happily take the job on the off chance they win. If they have little going they will bid low enough, with the ballpark figure as a benchmark, to be sure to win the contract. Rather than eat the loss, as commonsense and even some industry experts claim they do,[23] contractors will engage in what some call "change-order artistry," using their superior information to bilk the owner for everything they can. Asymmetric information rears its ugly head again.[24]

Making a change order stick is most easily accomplished if the owner is daft enough to make a change to the original plans. Inevitably, the change will create a host of unforeseen problems—the artistry is in coming up with plausible, expensive-sounding stories—that will end up costing the owner plenty. If the owner doesn't fall into that trap, the contractor begins to look for minor problems in the plans, then artistically turns them into major expenses. The same contractor who claimed that he has lots of experience with this type of job will suddenly act as though this particular project presents one-of-a-kind problems rarely seen in the annals of architecture or engineering. If that doesn't work, then problems with the construction site itself will crop up here, there, everywhere. Rocks will become boulders, clay is magically transformed into quicksand, and an eighth of an inch transmogrifies into a mile. Most owners cave in and pay the change order (extra charge) because they think their contractor is Bob the Builder or Bob Villa or because they simply do not know what the hell their contractor is talking about. Accelerator? Isn't that the gas pedal in my car? (No, it's material added to stucco, plaster, or mortar which speeds up the curing process.) Aggregate? That's the sum of some numbers, right? (No, it's crushed stone used to surface certain types of roofs.) Balloon framing? That's just silly. Balloons don't have frames. (No, it is a method for framing a house or other wood-frame structures.)[25]

Before some reader decides to club me over the head with a hammer, monkey wrench, or other blunt instrument, I should point out that I discovered change-order artistry by reading what contractors and analysts say about their own industry. Contractor David Gerstle writes that competitive bidding "often leads to the owner getting nailed during construction for numerous extra charges by a builder intent on making up for the too low price he had to submit to win the job in the first place."[26] Another notes that "it would be very easy to 'low-ball' a figure, get his [the owner's] name on the dotted line, and then start with the added costs."[27] If an owner pushes back on a dubious change order, that same contractor advises, "cheer up; maybe the owner will ask for a legitimate change order and you can get your money back."[28] Get *your* money *back* indeed! Industry analysts also note matter-of-factly that "some contractors may bid low with the intent of garnering profits from change orders."[29] "Contractors have intentionally submitted bids below fully loaded cost," wrote construction economist Julian Lange three decades ago, "in anticipation of recouping general overhead and profit through the price adjustments that result from design changes."[30]

In many other markets, sellers refrain from expropriating buyers because they realize that if they do so they are unlikely to get the buyers' business in the future. If the expected profits from repeated honest sales exceed the profits from a single scam, a seller will play nice. The most dramatic example of this is the foreign exchange business, where trillions of dollars of deals are struck without a written contract. In a world with only a few score major players, reneging on a contract would mean exclusion from a very lucrative club. Construction presents the opposite case: contractors know that repeat business is unlikely because contractors are so numerous and so small and because buildings last so long and are so expensive. Unless the owner credibly claims to have another project in the vicinity immediately on deck, and they rarely do (and when they do they usually put it out to bid), it is best to take as much advantage as possible. The possibility of referrals creates some incentive to play fair, but most referrals lead only to an invitation to bid (a cost) and not a contract, especially on bigger projects.

Even many owners are not very good stewards of their own projects. That is because most of the money comes from a bank. Owners know that if the worst comes they can default and walk away having only lost their initial equity. Due to the lack of de facto recourse against them, borrowers can exercise a sort of "put option" and leave the bank holding the bag, or rather the half-completed structure. Moreover, if the contractor gets the job done but in a costly manner, owners can spread the added cost over the life of the loan, which is certainly more palatable than coming up with it all at once. "The costs incurred," Martin Mayer explained, "can be loaded onto the mortgage and paid by the customer slowly."[31]

Sometimes owners hire construction managers to help them decide when a contractor is engaging in change-order artistry. Getting these guys to do a good job for the owner is, however, a tricky task. If the owner pays his construction manager a salary, the manager doesn't have much incentive to fight change orders. He is going to get big money no matter what. If the owner pays a percentage of the overall project, the manager likely will solemnly vow that all the change orders are valid and may even help the contractor come up with more! If the owner rewards the manager to fight all change orders tooth and nail, the contractor will stop showing up and/or begin to use inferior materials. That's possible because government inspectors only try to ensure that buildings are up to code or meet minimum standards. They do not, and indeed could not, police the quality standards in private contracts. As a result, shoddy building techniques like "splitting the difference" are widespread. As contractor Dennis Rourke explains:

> Splitting the difference is an excellent resolution for a number of construction problems resulting from missed measurements or a failure to maintain square, plumb, and level. By centering a wall-to-wall top that has been cut ½" short, the builder winds up with two ¼" gaps at each end which can be caulked or concealed with end splashes;... by splitting the difference in masonry joints to make up an out-of-level condition, the builder can sometimes accomplish the objective without affecting the aesthetics of the finished work.[32]

The contractor's postcontract monopoly power is another important component of his ability to hold up owners. As a practical matter, a contractor who has started a job is nearly impossible to replace. In most instances, it would cost too much and take too long (and time is money, especially when the owner has borrowed to complete the project) and both sides know it. So splitting the difference, tardiness, and change orders are countenanced.

Instead of designing a structure, then bidding it out, then building it, some owners opt for a "design-build" process whereby a building or other structure is designed as it is being built. The original notion was to speed up the construction process and keep runaway costs in line. In most instances, however, the design-build process, including its "fast-track" variant, leads to just as many changes and cost overruns as the traditional process because it does not address the industry's deepest and darkest problems, monopoly power and the gaming of bids.

The end result of both evils is that construction firms remain small. The competition on price and quality and the efficiencies of scale that force consolidation in other industries simply do not exist in custom construction— be it home improvements, commercial buildings, or transportation infrastructure. Contractor Dennis Rourke admitted as much in his textbook on residential building management when he wrote: "Many such builders are operating successfully with limited or no competition in markets of very limited absorption. In fact, the housing industry will always offer opportunities for small, specialized home builders in markets of limited competition."[33] A wave of consolidation and conglomeration in the late 1960s and early 1970s hit the skids for a number of reasons, including a dearth of true competition.[34] The most successful firms were and remain those that are best at "gaming" bids and engaging in change-order artistry, not those that are best at remodeling dens, building houses, putting up shopping malls, or carving tunnels out of mountains. Scale is therefore of little advantage. In fact, large size can be a major disadvantage in construction because an important method that contractors use to erase a bad reputation is to close shop and reopen under a new name. The larger the company, the more costly it is to use that technique to expunge a bad reputation.

Where is the government failure in all this? There are several government failures, in fact, most small but one whopper. Inefficient government regulations weigh heavily on an industry already crippled by the market failures described above. Outdated, ambiguous, and poorly understood inspection laws often do more harm than good. "One of the most pervasive problems in building-code enforcement," one study concluded, "is a widespread lack of qualifications among building officials at all levels," which leads to "delays and inconsistent enforcement."[35] Zoning can increase land values and cause other distortions, but it is not likely to go away because it provides "the main opportunity for local government corruption" according to UCLA law school professor Donald Hagman.[36] Perhaps worst of all, zoning, codes, mechanics' lien laws, and other rules and regulations impede construction industry consolidation. Expansion into even neighboring jurisdictions often requires a considerable expenditure of time and effort. Why bother when change-order artistry can be practiced close to home?

The Davis-Bacon Act and similar laws force contractors to increase compensation for workers on federal and most state construction projects. On public projects, those costs are passed on to taxpayers. When government construction activity crowds out private projects, forcing contractors to match government wages if they are to retain workers, owners ultimately foot the bill through higher bids and/or increased change-order artistry. And of course the artificially high wages do little or nothing to make workers faster or better. Similarly, Wick's law, which mandates the use of four different prime contractors on public contracts, adds an estimated thirty dollar per square foot to the cost of public buildings in New York City. "The legislators," builder Sam Lefrak once said, with some justice, "have legislated us into the ground."[37]

The Great Inflation of the 1970s, which most economists now agree was caused by the government's fiscal and especially monetary policies, caused a major, permanent increase in change-order artistry. Inflation hurt contractors by raising their costs unexpectedly. Unwilling and, due to their small size, unable to suffer any losses, they pushed increased costs onto owners and learned that it was pretty easy to do. Paul Volcker and Alan Greenspan eventually stomped out the fire of inflation, but contractors did not easily forget how to make change orders stick.[38]

The government's failure to eradicate organized crime also hurts construction productivity in some areas, like downstate New York and northern New Jersey. HBO's *The Sopranos* was of course fictional but not entirely fictitious. The greater New York area has long been known for corruption, graft, and grasping. As early as 1848, the author of a tract called *Frauds, Extortions, and Oppressions* noted that "so infamous a system would be tolerated in no place but Jersey."[39] Right now somebody like Paulie "Walnuts" Gaultieri is intimidating a construction manager or picking up an envelop for the big boss, money that came out of an owner's pocket one way or another. Even Tony Sopranos' haul is chump change, though, compared to the costs imposed by the government's most important failure.

Federal, state, and municipal (local) governments are the biggest buyers of custom contracting services in the nation. Public schools, government office buildings, military bases, and transportation infrastructure (roads, bridges, tunnels, etc.) constitute about 20 percent of the nation's built infrastructure by value, far more than any individual private company can claim.

If all three levels of government would work in concert, they could transform the industry for the better. To date, however, governments have been even bigger suckers than private owners, easily caving in to contractor change orders. It's not the government's money at stake, after all, but the taxpayers'. Why would a salaried government employee try to keep costs in line? Personal pride, perhaps, but that only goes so far.

***

The best proof that agency problems and postcontractual monopoly lay at the heart of the construction industry's unproductive ways is to examine the speculative building segment of the industry. Speculative builders, also called merchant builders, are construction firms that put up office buildings, strip malls, condominiums, and so forth on the hunch that somebody will pay a good price for them. They go bankrupt all of the time, but only because their business is highly competitive and they take big, leveraged risks.[40] (See chapter 2 for a discussion of leverage.) But that does not mean that they are inefficient. Their incentive is to put up buildings as quickly and inexpensively as possible, and they do just that. "Building a house is easy," one contractor noted, adding "building a deal is difficult."[41] When deals do not have to be struck, builders can build instead of searching out change-order opportunities. Dallas real estate developer Trammel Crow, for example, used to scratch out designs in the Texas dirt using his foot. Physical conditions like topography, subsoil issues, drainage, and weather; labor conditions like union work rules and subcontractor coordination problems; and political conditions like zoning and building codes that flummox custom builders are relatively easily surmounted by the better merchant builders.[42] Buildings go up fast and strong, and soon suitable tenants or owners appear, if the speculative builder has read market conditions correctly. If not, the builder goes under, and the community contains an empty new building, a small price to pay for avoiding the high costs of custom construction.[43] Speculative building is not a panacea. Demand for custom projects is likely to remain strong, and merchant builders tend to be extremely limited in scope, as evidenced by their failure to successfully enter new submarkets and their rocky relationships with their corporate conglomerate parents. So unfortunately there is little chance of them sweeping away the thousands of inefficient, tiny custom contractors.[44]

In the final chapter we'll explore ways to improve competition in the custom construction industry. Increased competition on price, quality, and time instead of bid gaming and change-order artistry will quickly transform the industry. Consolidation will allow contractors to tap economies of scale and scope, invest in R & D, gain control over their labor force, mute cyclicality, and drive out other undesirable elements, including Paulie and Tony. That, in turn, will bring tremendous gains in productivity. Imagine major roads and bridges costing millions instead of billions of dollars and large, comfortable, energy-efficient new homes that cost tens of thousands instead of hundreds of thousands of dollars to construct. That would free up resources for education, income redistribution, foreign aid, and myriad other worthy programs that we currently just can't afford.

4

UNCLE TOM'S CABIN
The Pollution of Slavery

Many people would agree that the most FUBAR institution in history is slavery. Too few, however, realize that slavery persists to this very day. It's an abomination of nature that needs to be rendered extinct. Before slavery can go the way of the dinosaur, however, we have to understand its hybrid causes. Slavery's horrors are not easily reconstructed in writing, but even if readers cannot trace their roots to slaves, they can empathize by examining the travails of other oppressed groups. Because my grandfather was a coal miner, for example, I'm haunted by Tennessee Ernie Ford's performance of Merle Travis's ballad "Sixteen Tons."[1] That's the song where Ford loaded sixteen tons of coal a day in exchange for sinking deeper into debt peonage to the company store. (Debt peons cannot lawfully leave their jobs or locales because they owe large debts to politically powerful creditors.) Songs also convey powerful images of the desperate lives of America's antebellum chattel slaves:

> Before I'd be a slave
> I'd be buried in my grave
> And go home to my Lord
> And be saved
>
> . . .

Got hard trial in my way
Heaven shall be my home
O when I talk, I talk with God
Heaven shall be my home
I don't know what people want of me
Heaven shall be my home.[2]

...

Timmy, Timmy, orphan boy.
Robert, Robert, orphan boy.
What shall I do for a hiding place? And a heaven, etc.?
I run to the sea, but the sea run dry.
I run to the gate, but the gate shut fast.[3]

Probably the best way to get a sense of slavery in the antebellum South, aside from perusing firsthand accounts for twenty or thirty years, is to read *Uncle Tom's Cabin*. Although strictly speaking a work of fiction, Harriet Beecher Stowe's classic bestseller certainly captures the general tenor of the times and the peculiarity of the institution of slavery, in much the same way that HBO's fictional series *The Corner* and *The Wire* exposed the realities of Baltimore's drug trade and dysfunctional government.

At the outset of the story, heavily indebted Kentucky slaveholder Arthur Shelby literally sold his most trusted man, Uncle Tom, down the river. By saving a damsel in distress, Tom managed to land safely with a good, if somewhat bigoted, family in New Orleans. After a few years, however, the death of the damsel and her father forced the family to sell Tom to Simon Legree, a vicious plantation owner. Contrary to the current stereotype of an "Uncle Tom" as a sellout to white interests, Stowe's Uncle Tom repeatedly stood up to Legree's cruel commands. "You must give up," another slave advised Tom, "or be killed by inches." "Well, then, I will die!" Tom responded.[4] And die he did, refusing to give up the location of several runaways. "'I know, Mas're; but I can't tell anything. *I can die!*' ... Legree, foaming with rage, smote his victim to the ground."[5]

Some contemporaries, usually slaveholders but occasionally others, claimed that slavery wasn't so bad because slaves were better fed and cared for than Northern day laborers. Their opinion was belied by the fact that thousands of slaves risked life and limb to become a Northern (or Canadian) day laborer, but very few wage workers, approximately zero, sold themselves into slavery. Benjamin Franklin had made the same point in his final public act, the authorship of a satirical newspaper piece, purportedly penned by Sidi Mehemet Ibrahim to the Divan of Algiers, justifying the enslavement of Christians. "While serving us, we take care to provide them with everything, and they are treated with humanity," Franklin wrote, just three weeks before his death. "The laborers in their own countries, are, I am well informed, worse fed, lodged and clothed."[6]

Why, then, did this most FUBAR of institutions arise and persist? And who should we blame for it? The market and the government are to blame, of course. Slavery was profitable, but only because the government allowed slaveholders to pass a good portion of the costs of slaveholding on to the rest of society. In other words, slavery created a negative externality, a type of pollution. If governments had taxed it appropriately, as they should have, slavery would not have been profitable for individual slaveholders and would have disappeared under its own immoral weight. Instead, governments decided whether or not to allow slavery within their borders, which in a democracy (more or less) meant that the institution was allowed to continue wherever slaves constituted a major form of investment. "Over the ages," Nobel laureate Robert Fogel tell us, "the incidence of slavery has waxed and waned."[7] Our purpose here is to explore the economic reasons why slavery appeared, why it disappeared in places, even some parts of otherwise staunch slave states like Virginia, and why in others it was stopped only by force of arms. It also explains why slavery still exists today in some forms in some places and how we can guard against its extension and maybe even rid our children and grandchildren of this scourge.

***

Upon my soul, I believe it to be a mere matter of dollars & cents. After all, slaves gradually recede from the approach of cheaper white labour, to latitude & products that white [laborers] cannot compete with.

—B. F. Stairley, slaveholder, 1855[8]

Pennsylvanians gave up their slaves with barely a whimper. Virginians, in contrast, fought a bloody four-year-long war over the mere intimation that the federal government might try to end human bondage. Philadelphia,

Pennsylvania's colonial river port capital, was a leading center of abolitionism. Williamsburg, Virginia's colonial river port capital, was a leading
center of proslavery ideology. Just a five-hour drive from each other today,
with deep ties to the Chesapeake basin, and with similar climates, flora,
and fauna, the two cities nevertheless diverged on the slavery issue. Why
did human bondage wane easily in Philadelphia and wax easily in
Williamsburg? More broadly, why did the North not only give up slavery
but go to great lengths to end it? Why did the South not only keep slavery
but go to great lengths to maintain it? Contemporaries and scholars have
debated those questions for well nigh two centuries.

In terms of per capita net worth (a stock) the antebellum South was
wealthy, by some accounts wealthier than the North. By some estimates,
specifically those that exclude slaves from the denominator, the South also
enjoyed a higher per capita income (a flow) than the North until the Civil
War. By all estimates it enjoyed more wealth and higher per capita income
than most other parts of the globe. (Originally, economists divided
Southern GDP only by the number of free persons, which made the South
appear extremely wealthy indeed. After the fallacy was exposed, economists
began to divide by the number of free and enslaved persons. The South's
per capita [total capita] income was of course lower but still relatively high
by the standards of the day.) But the South enjoyed wealth *without development*. Like Iraq, it grew rich by exploiting a comparative advantage arising
from a natural resource endowment. Prevent that endowment from being
marketed—as the North did with its blockade, and the US did with its
embargo—and the entire economic edifice came tumbling down.[9]

The South's lack of development was notorious. British traveler Joseph
John Gurney's description of the Mason-Dixon Line is just one of scores
of similar indictments of Southern underdevelopment:

> The distance between the two cities [Annapolis, Maryland, and Philadel-
> phia, Pennsylvania] is about one hundred miles, and one circumstance on
> the journey is well calculated to interest a stranger. It is the conspicuous-
> ness of the line, though without any natural division, which separates the
> slave-wrought lands of Maryland from the free territory of Pennsyl-
> vania. The sudden transit from inferior to superior cultivation, and from
> impoverished soil to fertility, is extremely striking—especially at the
> more advanced seasons of the year—and certainly it speaks volumes for

the instruction of statesmen, in proof of the utter impolicy of slavery. One can hardly imagine on what grounds this perpetual visible evidence can be long resisted.[10]

Slavery was both a cause and a result of the South's lack of development. The existence of slavery limited immigration into the region and also stymied the financial, transportation, and industrial revolutions that transformed the North. With urbanization thereby blocked, the slaveholding South was destined to remain rural and generally backward, the conditions under which slavery remained profitable to the individual investor. Slavery establishes and perpetuates itself where economic backwardness rules. If labor markets are underdeveloped, cash (physical exchange media) is in short supply, and contracts are difficult to enforce, then firms (plantations, farms, urban households, manufactories, and other business enterprises) will be more likely to decide that it is more profitable to own slaves rather than to rent wage laborers. As it becomes easier to find wage laborers, more convenient to pay them, and cheaper to enforce contracts with them (and they with employers), slavery becomes less attractive. But the presence of slavery impeded the development of the labor market and the financial system, trapping the South with its peculiar institution. The South, in short, was caught in a vicious cycle whereby economic backwardness led to slavery, which in turn perpetuated economic backwardness and hence further reliance on slave labor.[11]

Slavery thrived best where there were many slaves. If a firm was located in an area with a high density of slaves, it was more likely to choose slave over wage labor. Conversely, a firm that found itself in a low-density area was more likely to choose wage labor. There were several reasons for this. First, wage labor tended to eschew areas where slave labor predominated. Second, areas with high slave densities provided monitoring mechanisms as a public service (e.g., slave patrols and slave codes), thereby decreasing the control costs of individual slaveholders. Third, the proximity of other slaveholders decreased the transaction costs of owning slaves by creating a larger, more liquid, more efficient slave market. Fourth, the more slaves in an area, the more likely that slaveholding was seen as a socially acceptable institution. In fact, in areas with high densities of slaves, slaveholders may have exerted social pressures on firms to also adopt slave labor. In short, slavery was self-perpetuating.[12]

***

Given slavery's propensity to perpetuate itself, an understanding of its initial causes is therefore of prime importance. The reasons why slavery took hold in the South, and certain parts of the North, thus need to be explored in some detail. Climatic forces were at play, but given the fact that all three major types of labor were found in each section, other factors were involved as well. A fundamental variable in the labor decision facing firms in both the North and the South was the nature of specific firms and the type of labor that they required. In both sections, the ultimate decision of whether to use wage, indentured, or slave labor rested on the firm's assessment of the relative advantages and disadvantages of each labor type. Total productivity, availability/liquidity, and control and hypocrisy costs were the major variables of comparison.[13] Benjamin Franklin made one such comparison in 1760:

> The labour of slaves can never be so cheap here as the labour of working men is in Britain. Any one may compute it. Interest of money is in the colonies from 6 to 10 per Cent [total productivity]. Slaves one with another cost 30 l. Sterling per head [total productivity]. Reckon then the interest of the first purchase of a slave, the insurance or risque on his life, his cloathing and diet, expences in sickness and loss of time [total productivity], loss by his neglect of business (neglect is natural to the man who is not benefited by his own care or diligence) [control costs] expence of a driver to keep him at work [control costs], and his pilfering from time to time, almost every slave being from the nature of slavery a thief[14][control costs], and compare the whole amount of with the wages of a manufacturer of iron or wool in England, you will see that labour is much cheaper there than it ever can be by negroes here. Why then will Americans purchase slaves? Because slaves may be kept as long as a man pleases, or has occasion for their labour; while hired men are continually leaving their master (often in the midst of his business) and setting up for themselves [availability/liquidity].[15]

Comparing the relative advantages and disadvantages of slaves, servants, and wage laborers as Franklin did was a common practice among business firms. In the words of West Indian planter Richard Nisbet:

In the northern parts of America there are now, numbers of industrious white inhabitants [liquid wage labor markets], and when that is the case, the importation of Negroes will cease. No man who pays attention to his interest [total productivity] and peace of mind [costs of control and hypocrisy], will ever employ slaves to do his work, when he can get freemen at a moderate price [total productivity].[16]

There is a formula for understanding the economics and dynamics of slavery. By looking at this horrendous and dehumanizing institution through the prism of economics, we can understand the conditions under which some people decide to enslave others. Only by comprehending slavery from an economic perspective can we see how it came into being and therefore hopefully guard against its extension now and in the future. The formula operates this way:

$$S \approx (S_{prod} - W_{prod}) + (S_{liq} - W_{liq}) + (W_{hyp} - S_{hyp}) + (W_{con} - S_{con})$$

Where:

S = the prevalence of slavery at a given time, in a given area
$\approx$ = approximately equals
S = slave labor
W = wage labor
$f(x)$ = a function of x
S_{prod} = slave productivity = (output/total cost)
output = f(incentives, skills, firm size and organization, use of physical capital, suitability to climate and work)
total cost = present value (acquisition cost + depreciation + mortality + maintenance costs) + fertility
present value = the discounted present value of the costs (includes an interest rate variable)
acquisition cost = purchase price plus taxes or the cost of rearing
depreciation = loss of slave value due to aging, wear, and tear
mortality = cost of insuring slave lives or of bearing the economic risk of their death[17]
maintenance cost = cost of feeding, clothing, and otherwise maintaining slaves

fertility = number of live births

W_{prod} = wage labor productivity = output/wages

wages = the total pay of wage laborers, including cash and in-kind transfers

S_{liq} = slave liquidity = f(density of slave population; efficiency of slave markets)

density of slave population = number of slaves per square mile and slaves as a percentage of the population

efficiency of slave markets = transaction cost and ease of buying or selling slaves

W_{liq} = wage labor liquidity = f(density of wage laborers; efficiency of labor markets)

density of wage labor = number of wage laborers per square mile and wage laborers as a percentage of the population

efficiency of wage labor markets = cost and ease of hiring wage laborers

S_{hyp} = perceived hypocrisy of slaveholding

perceived hypocrisy of slaveholding = feelings stemming from the ownership of slaves, ranging from cognitive dissonance or unease (positive sign) to neutrality (zero) to feelings of social pride in the ownership of slaves (negative sign).

W_{hyp} = perceived hypocrisy of the use of wage labor

perceived hypocrisy of the use of wage labor = feelings stemming from the use of wage laborers, ranging from cognitive dissonance or unease (positive sign) to neutrality (zero) to feelings of social pride in the use of wage laborers (negative sign).

S_{con} = slave control

slave control = cost of controlling slaves *borne by individual slaveholders* (As discussed above, slaveholders shifted much of S_{con} onto society, thereby creating negative externalities.)

W_{con} = wage labor control

wage labor control = cost of controlling wage laborers *borne by individual employers*[18]

By rearranging the terms, we can examine the slavery issue from the standpoint of an individual firm. The decision whether to buy a slave (or machine) or rent a laborer is a variant of a question familiar to businesses.

In short, firms compared the net benefits (benefits − costs) of wage labor to the net benefits of slave labor:

$$W_{prod} + W_{liq} - W_{hyp} - W_{con} \equiv S_{prod} + S_{liq} - S_{hyp} - S_{con}$$

(Note that $\equiv$ is the symbol for comparison, not equality.)[19]

When the two sides of the equation were approximately equal, firms were indifferent whether they used free or slave labor. If in a given case $W > S$, firms chose wage labor over slave labor; if $W < S$, firms chose slave labor over wage labor. Slave and wage labor systems tended to self-perpetuate, so there was no reason to expect equilibrium ($W = S$), even in the long term. That is not to say, however, that the variables were immutable. The relative strength of both sides of the equation indeed changed, leading to changes in labor regimes. The model simply helps us to organize our thoughts regarding the economic reasons that slavery fluctuated. This discussion will be largely limited to the United States, but the model appears to hold in other places, including nineteenth-century Brazil and less-developed parts of the world today.[20]

When stated in mathematical terms, as above, the model is not easily tested because some of the variables, like those for hypocrisy, are well nigh impossible to quantify, while the others, like productivity statistics, are guesstimates at best. What the model allows us to do is to explain differences in slaveholding in two regions at the same time, or in one region over time, because it makes definite predictions about how changes in the direction (or sign) of variables will influence the prevalence of slavery.[21]

Although simple, the model rather effortlessly explains a great deal of the history of American slavery. It also helps us to grapple with counterfactuals like that posed by slaveholder B. F. Stairley in 1855. According to Stairley, if "all emigrating countries" were to "become republican" enough to stem the tide of new emigration to America and even coax "back thousands of her children," the North would soon "agitate reopening the slave trade with Africa!"[22] As the model and the historical narrative provided below show, matters were not even close to being that simple. Moreover, the model helps us to understand why slavery is not yet completely eradicated and perhaps never will be. It persists in poorly governed places and under certain conditions could make a comeback anywhere. That is an important reason why such formulas are necessary and require analysis— to stave off slavery rearing its ugly head again.

***

In the early colonial period, Southern firms were more likely to choose slave over wage labor because slaves were more available than wage laborers and probably as roughly productive. At first, slaves were cheaply controlled and slaveholding evoked few feelings of hypocrisy because bondage was still seen as a part of the human condition. Europe and Asia had a large number of serfs, Africa and the Middle East had slave markets, and historical texts from antiquity were rife with references to the institution. Moreover, in a world where economic growth appeared to many to be a zero-sum game, slavery seemed to some as no more exploitative than market exchange.[23]

At first, blacks were more akin to servants than to chattel. But whites soon came to own rather than rent (employ) black laborers for several reasons, some cultural, others economic. Economically, blacks did not come to the New World of their own accord and hence were closely monitored. Moreover, blacks newly imported from Africa did not have the necessary experience, language, numeracy, and cultural skills to engage in European free-market institutions, such as the labor market. Both characteristics made it cheaper to own (enslave) blacks rather than to employ (rent) them. By transmogrifying people into property, however, slavery took on a peculiar and immoral economic life of its own.[24]

Colonists attempted to enslave other groups too, namely, Indians and poor whites. Both attempts foundered. Indians were relatively unproductive and difficult to control because they succumbed easily to European diseases and found it relatively easy to escape captivity in the land of their birth. Hypocritical though it was, enslaving whites for life seemed ideologically repulsive as well as difficult to implement as a practical matter, so white bondage was generally limited to a term of years. The hypocrisy of owning white slaves seemed higher than the hypocrisy of using white wage laborers or white servants. In other words, pro–wage labor and antislavery ideology was stronger than anti–wage labor and proslavery ideology in the absence of racial or religious differences between master and slave.[25]

Early in the colonial period, the relative availability of slave laborers due to the transatlantic slave trade often tilted the firm's profitability calculation in favor of slaveholding. Slaves could be forced to migrate to any area and to stay and work there, but wage laborers could not. White indentured servants—mostly poor youths desperate to leave Europe to avoid repression or a life of crime—filled some of the labor gap. Indentured servitude flourished in the colonial period, but it was not a panacea. Servants were more costly to control than slaves because whites found it easier to escape bondage than blacks did, although both types ran away far too frequently for their masters' tastes. Even if they did not speak the prevailing language, servants looked and acted like freemen, and their presence was less likely to arouse suspicion or ire. Moreover, while masters could exact corporal punishment on servants, they were more strictly limited in the range and severity of punishments that they could inflict. In addition, servants, unlike slaves, could sue masters for breach of contract. So, *ceteris paribus*, other factors being equal, employers preferred slaves to indentured servants.[26]

In the colonial North, firms were more likely to choose wage over slave labor because wage laborers were both more available and more productive there. Moreover, wage labor evoked fewer feelings of hypocrisy than slaveholding did. Members of the upper class held those who did manual labor in contempt, but they did not find the institution of wage labor ideologically repulsive. Finally, wage laborers were relatively cheaply controlled because they could be dismissed and usually were their employers' creditors. (To this day, firms control wage earners by remaining constantly in debt to them for the last week's or month's pay.)[27]

In the North, black slaves were less productive than white wage laborers or indentured servants, or so most argued. Climatic differences may have played a role; regional differences in the nature of work and firms certainly did. Blacks were probably relatively more efficient than whites in warmer climes, and they certainly were less likely to succumb to tropical diseases. They were less efficient in colder climes and enjoyed no immunity advantage. So Northern firms were less likely to choose slaves in the first place, and they might sell them to the South if they did. In 1772, for example, Philadelphia merchant William Pollard returned "black Boy Jem" to the West Indies merchant from whence he came. Jem "might be a very good Servt. while with you," Pollard complained, "but I do apprehend as he grew up, a degree of Sullenness grew with him."[28] "During our Winter, which is very cold," Pollard explained, "he was not worth a Groat [a small silver coin worth 4 pence sterling, roughly 'a nickel' in today's terms] for he would be no where but in the Chimney Corner." "The difference in their Manner of living here, I apprehend is against Negroes,"

Pollard continued. "The Victuals go from our Table to theirs, & not having half employment in our Houses, they get fatt Indolent & Impudent, which was the Case with Jem." Other Northerners complained of the frequent illnesses, often respiratory, of their slaves.[29]

As West Indian planter Richard Nisbet noted, the North by the late colonial period had attracted large numbers of wage laborers. In most instances, wage laborers came to be preferred to indentured servants. For one, wage laborers were no more expensive to control. Moreover, they were more productive than servants because they had more incentive to work. As a general rule, servants did just enough to avoid the lash and to secure their freedom.[30]

The nature of firms was an important component of productivity, regardless of geographical location, because slaves and wage laborers represented two different types of costs. Slaves were considered chattel and hence capital goods. Like machines or cows, they could be bought or sold at will, but while owned they were "fixed" costs. In other words, they had to be maintained whether or not they were working. Employees, by contrast, were "variable" costs. In other words, the wage bill could be relatively quickly increased or decreased as needed.[31] Contractors were the ultimate variable costs, as they could be turned on or off cheaply and almost immediately. Today, firms, like universities, hire long-term workers, like tenured professors, to undertake essential, core activities. They hire shorter-term workers, like lecturers, to undertake activities for which there will likely be a need over a period of months or years. Very short-term workers, adjuncts, are also brought in and let go as needed.[32] Colonial firms were similar in that regard. Core activities were undertaken by the principals and long-term workers, like slaves, apprentices, and indentured servants. Journeymen and other types of employees handled some of the workload when needed. Occasional services were outsourced to other firms.[33]

So, for instance, plantation owners might hire wage laborers by the day during the harvest or by the task when they needed specific jobs completed, but the day-to-day work of the plantations fell to their slaves. Similarly, a cabinetmaker would employ a few slaves, indentured servants, and/or apprentices to help him with his core activity, building cabinets. In peak periods, he might hire a journeyman to help meet demand, but let him go after demand slackened. If he needed his wagon fixed, or his horses reshoed, he would outsource those functions to a cartwright and blacksmith, respectively. It would simply be too costly for a small cabinetmaker to employ a cartwright or blacksmith to do occasional work. Similarly, in the 1730s Philadelphia silversmith Joseph Richardson hired skilled help by the week for one pound, seven shillings, and six pence per week. He hired domestic help, by contrast, by the year at nine pounds per year. For occasional work, he hired artisans for the day or the task.[34]

Holding other factors constant, the larger the scale of an enterprise, the more likely it is to use long-term workers—tenured faculty, indentured servants, apprentices, or slaves—rather than mere at-will employees or outside contractors. So large plantations had their own slave blacksmiths and other artisans as well as slave field hands.[35] Few Northern farms achieved the scale of even modest Southern plantations. The nature of Northern agriculture largely determined the scale of farms. Most Northern crops, like wheat, were grown on a small scale just as efficiently as on a large scale. Where scale was important, as on iron "plantations," or Rhode Island's tobacco estates, some Northern firms employed slaves and indentured servants to carry out their core labor activities. The Martick Forge in Lancaster County, Pennsylvania, for example, owned two slaves, "one a Mulattoe man, a good forge man, the other, a Negroe man."[36]

Southern plantations, too, likely had scale economies, especially where crops amenable to the "gang system"—like rice, sugar, hemp, cotton, and to a lesser extent tobacco—were prevalent. In cultivating those crops, in other words, slaves could be forced to work together in groups called gangs where they could be more cheaply and easily monitored as they labored. Such plantations grew to be relatively large and hence were more likely to find long-term laborers like slaves less costly than wage laborers. Cliometric studies show that slaveholders accurately judged their labor needs and that they efficiently spread the workload out over the entire year. On average, plantation slaves worked about sixty hours per week in the spring, summer, and fall, and about forty hours per week in the winter.[37]

If free and allowed to flourish, blacks would of course be just as productive as whites. When enslaved, however, the productivity of blacks (or whites—or anyone for that matter) would be severely restricted. The crux of the problem was that the more skilled, learned, or otherwise productive that a slave became, the costlier he became to control and to keep in bondage. Generally, therefore, firms found it profitable to use slaves only in unskilled or semiskilled roles.

Slaves faced even weaker incentives than servants did. The servant, it was said, could look forward to his or her freedom. The slave could not. If the servant slacked off or ran away, he or she could be forced to make up the time, with damages. Slaves, needless to say, could not because they were enslaved for life and could not legally own property. It is not surprising, then, that slave productivity was low.[38]

In the words of Philadelphia doctor Benjamin Rush, "slavery is so foreign to the human mind, that the moral faculties, as well as those of the understanding are debased, and rendered torpid by it."[39] Throughout history, slaveholders have almost invariably considered their slaves, regardless of race, as dumb and lazy. That is not surprising since it is easier to debase and exploit the other by objectifying him. Also, slaves found it difficult to invest in their human capital (their skills and knowledge) and typically had little incentive to do so anyway. As Adam Smith so eloquently put it: "A person who can acquire no property, can have no other interest but to eat as much, and to labour as little as possible."[40] Fear of the lash—or worse— could induce slaves to move, but only laconically or while monitored closely. Moreover, some slaves apparently acted dumb—which could be considered a form of civil disobedience—simply to resist bondage and make their masters' lives "hard" ones.[41]

Those slaves who received education or training in a skill and who had an incentive to work were just as productive as whites. But they often also became "uppity," to wit, more prone to escape bondage, to foment rebellion, or to buy freedom. The rare slave that was hardworking, skilled, and *docile* was highly valued indeed. As early as 1703 slaveowner Jonathan Dickinson bragged to Isaac Norris that one of his slaves had been a "jobbing carpenter & wheelwright" for twenty years without ever "giving any occasion of offence or misbehavior." "For all which," he concluded, "he hath been very greatly Vallued."[42]

When owners allowed slaves private plots to work on their own account, they also became more "uppity" or, at the very least, reserved their most strenuous efforts for their own gardens. The owners of remarkable slaves, like the slave medical doctor James Derham, may have thought of themselves as good Christians when they manumitted their exceptional property (released their slaves from bondage), but just as likely the costs of control and hypocrisy grew too high for them to keep their charges enslaved. In short, slave productivity could not be significantly increased without simultaneously raising the cost of slave control and feelings of hypocrisy. That helps to explain why slaveholders were reluctant to allow their slaves to become literate or numerate, and why abolitionists fervently publicized the genius of poet Phillis Wheatley and other gifted Africans.[43]

Wage laborers, by contrast, had incentive to improve their human capital (their skills and knowledge) and to work diligently and productively. Moreover, wage laborers competed against each other while slaves largely found themselves cloistered from competition. It was no accident, Adam Smith noted, that slaves grew only the most profitable crops. Only "the planting of sugar and tobacco can afford the expence of slave cultivation," he argued. Smith concluded that "the work done by freemen comes cheaper in the end than that performed by slaves."[44]

Despite Smith's claim, slavery persisted in the world's most advanced economies for several centuries and is still rampant in some less-developed areas. So either many irrational firms existed, or slavery must have held certain economic advantages. As Franklin noted, one likely advantage was that in rural or undeveloped labor markets slaves were more easily obtained than wage laborers were (which gives us a major clue about where to look for slavery today). But in major cities like Boston, New York, and Philadelphia, wage laborers eventually became as easily acquired as slaves, tipping the equation away from slavery for many firms. In major colonial cities, however, the "wages of common labour [remained] so very high" that slaves continued to be favored for unskilled jobs, like domestic work.[45]

Moreover, Smith neglected to consider a crucial component of slaves' productivity, their fecundity. Slave children became the property of the mother's owner, so, in the words of William and Mary law professor St. George Tucker (yep, the guy's name was St. George), "the purchaser therefore calculated not upon the value of the labour of his slave only, but, if a female, he regarded her as 'the fruitful mother of a hundred more.'"[46] Sometimes the cost of the mother's lost productivity and the cost of rearing the child were too high for slaveholders to bear. So in 1733 one Connecticut slaveholder sold his female slave because she was too *good* of a "breeder." But where slave markets were well developed, slaveholders knew that slave children were an economic boon because they could be taken from their mothers and sold to other slaveholders for cash or cheaply raised to provide future labor, as needed.[47]

As noted above, the labor decision in colonial America hinged on factors like climate, region (North or South), firm size, firm type, control and hypocrisy costs, and the relative liquidity of the markets for slave, indentured, and wage labor. At the margin, that is, in cases where no clear answer to the labor decision emerged, major historical events played a crucial role. For example, various wars strengthened slavery in colonies like Pennsylvania that passed legislation allowing white indentured servants to join the armed forces without their masters' consent. As James Logan told John Penn in 1740, "no less than between 2 & 300 servants (tis affirm'd full 300)" joined Pennsylvania's armed services "to the very great loss of many of their masters divers of whom being poor Country men run in debt to purchase them, and now are ruined by that debt standing good against them while they are deprived of their Servants expected help to discharge it."[48] Lower duties on imported slaves also made slavery more prevalent by decreasing slave acquisition costs and thus increasing their relative productivity.

Similarly, the Revolution strengthened slavery by making wage laborers relatively scarce. It also bolstered slavery by touching off a mass exodus of small farmers from Virginia and other southern states. The stress of the war on small agriculturalists "occasioned the very great emigrations, which have been made, for several years past, from the adjacent States, to the settlement of Kentucke [sic], where the fertility of the country, and the smallness of their taxable possessions, render their subsistence more easy, and consequently their life more agreeable to them."[49] The small farmers sold out to planters, allowing plantations to grow large enough to achieve a scale of operations conducive to slave labor. In addition to the market for slaves, the market for additional land, be it near the home plantation or on the frontier, ensured that slaveholders did not run afoul of the law of diminishing returns. Slaveholders who knew their business never found themselves forced to add unprofitable amounts of labor to a fixed amount of land.[50]

But the Revolution also decreased the prevalence of slavery in two ways. First, it increased the cost of controlling slaves, who at least in the early years of the war were under the impression that the victorious British would emancipate them after the rebellion had been put down. Second, the Revolution made it more likely that firms would find hiring wage laborers preferable to buying slaves by increasing the perceived hypocrisy of slavery relative to wage labor. Through the bold efforts of Reverend Samuel Hopkins, and others, Americans North and South had to face the hypocrisy of freeing themselves from "slavery" while simultaneously enslaving Africans. It also created cognitive dissonance to secure the fruits of one's own labor while simultaneously stealing the fruits of another's. (Shame went a long way then and could also be employed today to make slavers as uncomfortable as possible with their labor force decisions.) Economic historians estimate that slaveholders appropriated over half of all the value created by the typical slave, a figure far higher than that generally appropriated from the average wage laborer. Benjamin Rush put the figure at 80 percent, but he seems to have neglected to include the cost of slaveholder-provided food and shelter. One of Rush's critics suggested that slaveholders "had rather support them at the yearly expence of half their worth, than by starving them," but he also suggested that slaveholders in fact usually provided slaves with only a portion of their subsistence.[51] Undoubtedly, the level of expropriation varied over time and place, but it was almost always high.

The effects of hypocrisy were strongest in the North. Philadelphia Quakers, who as a sect had countenanced slavery in the early colonial period, were among the first to denounce the immorality of the institution. Antislavery sentiment grew in the 1750s in the midst of the religious fervor known now as the First Great Awakening. In 1754, the Philadelphia Yearly Meeting published *An Epistle of Caution and Advice, concerning the Buying and Keeping of Slaves*, which reiterated its "Uneasiness and Disunity, with the Importation and Purchasing of *Negroes* and other *Slaves.*"[52] But not until near the height of the imperial crisis, in 1774, did the Philadelphia Yearly Meeting announce that it would disown Friends who trafficked in human chattel. Soon after, within days of the clash at Lexington and Concord, Anthony Benezet and other Philadelphians formed a small antislavery group. Although it disbanded, that group laid the groundwork for the significant reforms to come. Quakers from the "capital of conscience" literally had the least to lose economically and the most to gain psychologically and spiritually from abolition, so it was not surprising that the Yearly Meeting banned Quaker slaveholding altogether in 1776. The state of Pennsylvania followed with a gradual emancipation bill passed in 1780, after the availability of wage laborers rebounded off its wartime lows. The rest of the North followed Pennsylvania's lead as the liquidity of wage labor increased yet further after the war.[53] Also moral reservations must have played a role.

***

In 1774, the year for which the best data is available, slaves accounted for just 3.85 percent of the private physical wealth of colonists in the Middle Colonies, including Pennsylvania. In New England, where emancipation was easiest, slaves made up just .45 percent of all private physical wealth. In the South, by contrast, 33.59 percent of all private physical wealth took the form of slaves. It is not surprising, then, that most Northern states experienced little cultural, political, or economic difficulty ending slavery, although, from the slaves' perspective, they took their time about it. The last slave in Pennsylvania was freed in 1847; New Jersey's remaining slaves obtained their freedom in 1865, with the ratification of the Thirteenth Amendment. Politically, Northern states enjoyed a wide suffrage base, and nonslaveholders easily outnumbered slaveholders. Gradual manumission eased the economic pain. Moreover, very few Northerners had invested the bulk of their assets in slaves, so they did not possess a large incentive to fight the change, especially in the face of virulent antislavery republican ideology and the fact that they could recoup most of their losses in the liquid flesh markets of the South.[54] (The lesson for policymakers today is clear: best to nip the use of slaves in the bud, before it becomes too prevalent.)

For example, slaves in Bucks County, Pennsylvania, were few, numbering fewer than three hundred in 1790. Only 182 different Bucks residents registered their slaves as required by law. The vast bulk of Bucks slaveholders owned fewer than five slaves. Most of those who owned more than a few bondsmen were substantial farmers or merchants and members of the county's non-Quaker socioeconomic and political elite. The situation was similar just south in Philadelphia and elsewhere in the state. In 1790, 3,707 Pennsylvanians were enslaved. About one thousand Pennsylvania households owned a single slave each; almost seven hundred owned two, three, or four slaves; and fewer than two hundred owned five or more bondsmen. The loss of slaves hurt many of those households but devastated few of them. According to Philadelphia abolitionist Tench Coxe, by 1794 there were only 273 slaves in Philadelphia[55] "and not more than 3000 in the state of Pennsylvania."[56] By 1798, only 1,100 persons in the entire state remained enslaved. Even if valued at one thousand dollars apiece, far above the prevailing market price, slaves would have accounted for only 1.08 percent of Pennsylvania's total physical assets that year.[57] (Of course that was little consolation to those remaining in bondage.)

Other Northern economic ties to slavery were weak, too. In the late colonial period even abolitionists admitted that in the "northern provinces there [were] not very many, who [were] immediately concerned in the trade to Africa for slaves."[58] Although by the early national period some Northern firms had grown rich in the slave trade, emancipation in the North was not a threat to their profits because Southerners continued to buy slaves from Northern slavers in significant numbers. In fact, almost as many Africans were imported into the United States between 1780 and abolition of the external slave trade in 1808 as had been imported into the country during the previous century and a half. Finally, the capital assets used in the slave trade, mostly ships, could be outfitted to undertake other types of trade.[59]

The continued development of wage labor markets in Northern cities also eased the passage and implementation of the North's gradual manumission laws. As early as 1804, foreign travelers noted that white domestics in the North were plentiful and generally docile. Early national Pennsylvania's wage labor market was especially liquid. According to George Washington, Philadelphia was "the general recepticle [sic] of foreigners from all countries, and of all descriptions."[60] Further, most of those immigrants stayed in Philadelphia or its environs because they found Pennsylvania's government liberal, its lands fertile and well improved, and slavery on the wane. As the immigrants poured in, the liquidity of wage labor soared, tilting the balance yet further away from slavery.

Employees of all types had good reason for cheer. Thanks to banks—new institutions that were much more prevalent in the North than in the South before the Civil War—Northern employers found it easier than ever before to meet payroll in cash. Historians sometimes chastise powerful financial institutions, like both Banks of the United States, for making large loans to the rich, forgetting that the proceeds from those loans were often destined for the pockets of common laborers. The rich of course borrowed to pay their workers and to buy goods from businesses, which was then divided between the owners, the owners' suppliers, and the owners' workers.[61]

By 1804, due to the changed circumstances, many Northern slaveholders found it "for their advantage to promise their slaves liberty on condition of serving a few years under indenture."[62] The costs of controlling slaves and suffering the hypocrisy of the institution were simply too high to bear when wage laborers were quickly found, cheaply contracted with, and, perhaps with the aid of a bank, easily paid in cash for their efforts.

Soon, in most parts of the North, slavery was scotched, if not quite finished. For similar reasons, indentured servitude also waned and by 1830 was rarely encountered. High white birth rates and massive immigration from overseas and the South eradicated both forms of servitude in a sea of liquid wage labor.[63] The early national North provides a clear prescription for those seeking to reduce slavery today: promote immigration, if possible, enhance the efficiency of wage labor and financial markets, and ostracize slavers socially as well as legally.

Unfortunately, in 1793 the trend away from indentured labor was not yet discernible. Northern states therefore consented to passage of the Fugitive Slave Act by Congress in that year. The act decreased the cost of controlling slaves for the remaining Northern slaveholders and also reduced the costs of controlling indentured servants. After passage of the act, runaway Pennsylvania indentured servants had to do more than cross the Delaware or the Mason-Dixon Line in order to secure their freedom.

The situation in the South in the early republic was vastly different. For starters, immigrants generally eschewed the South; many poor, white Southerners emigrated north to flee the opprobrium and downward pressure that slaves put on wages. Kentuckian Richard Oglesby fled to Illinois, where he later was elected governor. According to Oglesby:

> I came myself from a slave State. Poor white girls washed there all day over a hot and steaming tub, and under a blazing sun, for ten cents a day. ...And why was this? Simply because a negro wench, equally strong, could be hired for that price. In Kentucky I was a laboring man. I hired out for six dollars a month. Why couldn't I get more? Because a negro man, of... equal physical strength, could be hired for seventy-five dollars per year.[64]

Moreover, Oglesby added, the Negro "would be submissive," that is, easily controlled.[65] Ogelsby was far from alone. White wage laborers in the South received low, irregular wages and would not do, or be asked to do, a range of menial work considered suitable only for slaves. Greatly oppressed, many wage laborers were unreliable, often worked drunk, and were a serious threat to abscond if their pay was advanced to them in cash. "Slaves were the only reliable laborers," many Southern employers concluded, because "you could command them and *make* them do what was right."[66]

That was probably an overly optimistic view, as slaves apparently regularly feigned sickness to avoid work, but slaves on balance must have been much more pliable than the uppity white laborers.[67]

Partly due to the relative dearth of white inhabitants, nonslaveholders simply did not have the political clout that they enjoyed in the North. Poor whites, already called "white trash"[68] by antebellum antislavery polemicist Hinton Helper, outnumbered slaveholders, but slaveowners generally cowed them into political submission, making a mockery of elections and the other trappings of democracy. Professor St. George Tucker and the perceptive French traveler Alexis de Tocqueville also argued that democracy, peace, and slavery were antithetical.[69]

Many Southern slaveholders had invested a significant portion of their assets in slaves. Even gradual emancipation would cost them dearly. In fact, according to some estimates, slaveholders had more invested in slaves in 1860 than Northerners had invested in banks, railroads, and factories *combined.* (If true in 1860, it was likely true for 1790 and 1830, too.) Finally, in many places slaves were so numerous that their eventual emancipation raised the specter of racial warfare or black political dominance. Imbued with the notion that blacks were intellectually inferior to whites, ironically enough after the South had prohibited the teaching of reading and writing to slaves, most Southerners saw free blacks as living oxymorons. Rampant racism of course had decreased the perceived hypocrisy of owning other human beings.[70] (For policymakers today, antiracism programs and education can be more than feel-good projects, they can create a bulwark against an evil, FUBAR institution.)

In terms of the relative productivity of slave and wage labor, little had changed from the colonial period. *Ceteris paribus,* wage laborers had more incentives than slaves did and hence they worked more efficiently. Here is how the *North American and United States Gazette* put it:

> In the very nature of things, the freeman must produce more than the slave. There is no conclusion of science more certain. Under a system which gives to a laboring man the fruit of his toil, there is every motive to render him diligent and assiduous. If he relies on being employed by others, his wages rise with his reputation for industry, skill, and faithfulness. And as owner of the soil, there is every assurance that he will do what he can to cultivate it to the best advantage, and develop its latent

wealth. Self-interest will call forth what powers of intellect and invention has to aid him in his work.... How different it is with slave labor! The slave toils for another, and not for himself. Whether he does little or much, whether his work is well or ill performed, he has a subsistence, nothing less, nothing more; and why should he toil beyond necessity? He cannot accumulate any property for the decline of his years, or to leave to his children when he is departed.... It is common for even the advocates of slavery to declare that one freeman is worth half a dozen slaves.[71]

But, as in the colonial period, not all factors were equal. For one thing, slaves were much more likely to toil for large firms that enjoyed significant scale economies. Although the average Southern plantation in the early republic was not as large as it would be in the antebellum period, in both periods it was considerably larger than the average Northern farm. In 1860, only 467 Northern farms contained over one thousand acres, but the South boasted 4,571 plantations that size or larger. And while the North had 2,472 farms larger than five hundred acres, the South was home to over 16,800. Conversely, the North contained 413,917 farms between fifty and ninety-nine acres, compared to only 181,395 in the South. The larger Southern firms were those that used slaves, usually in highly efficient, production line–like groups, as noted earlier, called gangs. Moreover, plantation owners in the early Republic saw slaves as a sound investment since they would increase their productivity by reproducing themselves faster than they died. The slave population grew even after importation from abroad was outlawed in 1808.[72]

As in the colonial period, slaveholders continued to face a trade-off between the quality of slave human capital and slave docility. The more skilled that slaves became, the higher their productivity and efficiency, but also the more they felt, both objectively and subjectively, the injustice of their situation, and the more likely and capable they became of causing major production disruptions. James Hammond of South Carolina, for instance, argued that "whenever a slave is made a mechanic, he is more than half freed, and soon becomes, as we too well know, and all history attests, with rare exceptions, the most corrupt and turbulent of his class."[73]

In addition, slave productivity was limited because slaves had a reputation for damaging expensive capital equipment. When Southerners tried to use slaves in heavy manufacturing, for example, the results were mixed because the principal-agent problem inherent in the master-slave relationship loomed even larger in the factory. In the words of historian John Ash-worth: "Many slaves did not wish to be slaves, did not wish to see the fruits of their labor appropriated by another and therefore attempted, in various ways to resist this exploitation."[74] Antebellum Americans and contemporary scholars agree that slaves, North or South, East or West, broke far more tools than wage laborers did. Slaveholders conveniently attributed that fact to the slaves' racial inferiority; one Southern doctor went so far as to label it a disease, *Dysaesthesia Aethiopica*.[75] Most such "accidents" were likely quite deliberate attempts to get a break, to exact revenge on the master, or simply to validate the slave's humanity through a form of what most observers today would consider justified civil disobedience. Slaves employed in industry were even more destructive. Moreover, owners never had legal recourse for "any losses which may result from the carelessness or malevolence of the slave."[76] Little wonder, then, that the average slave employed much less physical capital per person than the average Northern wage laborer did.[77]

One solution to the slave incentive and agency problems was to allow slaves to "hire" themselves. Under that arrangement, a slave paid his (or her) master a flat stipend or an annual percentage of his earnings. The slave then hired himself out by the task or period, paid his dues to his master, and retained any surplus. Such arrangements, critics have been quick to point out, replaced the master-slave relationship with a partnership (if a percentage) or debtor-creditor relationship (if a flat fee). Although technically illegal, self-hire became common in the older, urban areas like Charleston, South Carolina.[78]

The fact that people demanded occasional services from slaves and that many masters were willing to supply the self-hire market strongly suggests that Southern wage labor markets were stunted. The Richmond tobacco industry is a telling case. Tobacco factories *employed* a large number of slaves. In other words, the tobacco manufacturers paid the slaves' masters a fee for the use of their slaves and paid the slaves a small living stipend and, increasingly, cash bonuses for meeting production quotas. The undeveloped nature of Richmond's white labor market clearly explains the tobacco industry's unusual decision to create one of the few institutions more peculiar than the peculiar institution itself.[79]

All factors considered, the productivity of slaves and wage labors were roughly the same and slave masters and their apologists knew it. To prevent ideology from urging the switch to wage labor, Southerners attempted, largely successfully, to both lower the perceived hypocrisy of slaveholding and to increase the perceived hypocrisy of using wage labor. Slavery apologist George Fitzhugh, for instance, argued that slaves were better off than wage laborers because their masters buffered them from the vagaries of the marketplace. A good number of persons, North and South, equated the condition of Northern workers with that of Southern slaves. Clearly, such claims did not convince Northern abolitionists, who were quick to note:

> Poverty is not Slavery, and bears no resemblance to Slavery; bad as it is, where is the poor man who would exchange his destitution for the condition of the sleekest and fattest slave in the country, deprived as the latter is, of the right to himself, and to his family and earnings.[80]

Lowell mill "girl" Clementine Averill also eloquently rejected Southern apologists' claims that chattel slaves were better off than Northern workers. "Can the slaves leave when they please, and go where they please? Are they allowed to attend school, or travel for pleasure, and sit at the same table with any gentleman or lady?" she asked, rhetorically.[81] Of course claims of the moral superiority of slavers were not made to sway abolitionists but rather to convince fence-sitters to stay put. The rhetoric apparently worked for decades. We must never allow it to gain so much credibility ever again.[82]

The hypocrisy of slavery was ultimately a personal issue, so it is not surprising that some Southerners found the cost of hypocrisy too much to bear and released their bondsmen. In the 1790s, Tucker noted that Virginians had manumitted more slaves than had the residents of the New England states. (Of course the percentage was much lower in Virginia.) Frederick Law Olmsted encountered one such Southerner who explicitly argued that "he was first led to disuse slave-labor, not from any economical considerations, but because he had become convinced that there was an essential wrong in holding men in forced servitude ... and because he was not willing to allow his own children to be educated as slave-masters."[83]

Many Southern legislatures outlawed manumission, however, because free blacks threatened slavery on several fronts. First, free blacks increased the cost of controlling slaves by aiding and abetting them and creating confusion over the race/caste boundary line. Second, they increased the liquidity of wage labor by selling their services by the time or task. Third, the existence of free blacks increased the perceived hypocrisy of slave-holding by reducing, although not eliminating, confidence in proslavery racial inferiority theories.[84]

Slaveholders in the early Republic also sought to reduce their indi-vidual cost of controlling slaves by shifting as much of the cost as possible onto society through the extension of slave codes, patrols, and other insti-tutions of repression. After Gabriel Prosser's conspiracy in 1800[85] threat-ened Richmond, for instance, the state of Virginia thought it prudent to maintain a company of about one hundred full-time soldiers in the capital district. And, as we have seen, slaveholders in 1793 reduced the cost of controlling slaves by trying to force Northerners to return slave runaways. Again in the antebellum period, slaveholders imposed some of the costs of slaveholding onto nonslaveholders both North and South of the Mason-Dixon Line.[86]

***

By 1830 or so, it was clear that the North and South had chosen different paths. The South grew moderately rich by exploiting its natural resources, especially its rich cotton lands. The North grew extremely rich by devel-oping a modern, urban, industrial economy. Since the Old South's best soil was exhausted by monoculture, it sold slaves and their progeny to the newly opened, fertile West. Southern agricultural firms became either huge, commercial plantations or small, subsistence or semisubsistence farms, with precious little in between. Meanwhile, in the North, the com-mercialization of even the smallest farms ensured that crop yields per acre increased nearly every year. Intense competition drove the less-efficient farmers out of business, helping to create a wage labor supply for the region's burgeoning factories.[87]

By the antebellum period, the Northeast was highly urban compared to the South. In 1830, more than one in three denizens of New England and the Middle Atlantic states lived in cities, compared to about one in ten Southerners. Tellingly, Southern cities, as relatively few and unpopulated as they were, were hotbeds of abolitionism. But there was precious little Southern abolitionists could do because political power lay outside the cities. "Slavery impoverishes Virginia," Horace Greeley argued, "but it enriches the Johnny Tylers, Johnny Masons, and Billy Smiths, that govern Virginia."[88] He almost had it right. Slavery did not impoverish the South, but it certainly prevented it from developing.[89]

"The evidence is quite clear," write economic historians Fred Bateman and Thomas Weiss, "that the South had not attained its full industrial and economic potential, nor does it seem to have been laying an adequate foundation for postbellum transformation and industrialization."[90] Where slavery waned, as in Maryland and Northern Virginia, some development ensued. But even border states like Kentucky paled as compared to the North, especially after completion of the Erie Canal tied Manhattan's fine deep water port to the vast expanses of the Great Lakes. That narrow ditch lowered the cost of transportation enough to allow hordes of wage laborers to flow West, and the produce of the West to flow to the Northeast's rapidly growing cities. Funded by the North's modern financial system, additional canals and railroads also sprang up, tying distant marketplaces together into regional markets. Philadelphia, for example, was connected to Pittsburgh, and hence the interior of the continent, via canal, turnpike, and rail. Well before the Civil War, the North enjoyed an integrated, liquid market for wage labor and an entrepreneurial *esprit* unmatched, if not in the world, at least anywhere that slavery held sway.[91]

Why did the South maintain an institution that slowed its economic development? Recall the second part of Greeley's comment, to wit that slavery enriched *some* Southerners. Economic decisions are made at the level of the individual firm, not the aggregate level, so although slavery injured the South's economy, the institution profited the individual slaveholder. How is it possible that individuals gained while the entire economy suffered? Quite simply, slavery created negative externalities, that is, costs borne by society rather than by individual slaveholders.[92] Most forms of individual investment made in the North, by contrast, created positive externalities,[93] that is, benefits that accrued to society rather than individual investors.[94] The distinction can be seen by examining the effects of two thousand-dollar investments, one made in equities and bonds by a Pennsylvanian and one made in slaves by a Virginian. Financial investments ultimately fund physical activities as much as direct investment in a capital "good," such as a slave, does. Moreover, slaves served many of the functions of financial instruments. In fact, they even served as collateral for much of the lending that took place in the South. And, as we have seen, they were considered liquid assets that could be leased out to generate a stream of revenue analogous to stock dividends or bond interest payments. The Pennsylvanian may have chosen to invest in financial securities due to the dearth of scale economies in Northern agriculture and the relative liquidity of Northern financial markets. The Virginian, facing the relatively illiquidity of the Richmond securities market and the scale economies available in agriculture, chose to buy a slave. After all, the net returns to each *investor* were likely much the same. If they were not, investors would have put their money where it was expected to reap the higher return until any substantial differential was eliminated.[95]

The point here, though, is that the *social* return on each type of investment was vastly in favor of the Pennsylvanian's choice because his or her funds helped to create productive networks of banks, turnpikes, and manufacturing and commercial enterprises. Such networks created immense positive externalities. Turnpikes, for instance, lowered transportation costs and hence made markets for agricultural and manufactured goods both larger and more efficient. Larger markets, in turn, allowed more firms in more industries to achieve efficient scale. Such firms often financed their expansions by making use of the North's money and capital markets, networks that efficiently linked entrepreneurs to savers.[96]

The Virginian's investment, in contrast, although personally lucrative, imposed a huge cost on society. For starters, the cruel nature of chattel slavery deeply affected the psychology of both the enslaved and the enslaver. Moreover, we have already seen that slaves were less efficient than they would have been if free. Those inefficiencies were embedded in slave prices and hence slaveholders' returns, so they mattered little to slaveholders and in fact may have aided them psychologically by making it easier to believe that slaves were lesser than whites, if not less than human. But the economy still bore the immense opportunity costs of supporting millions of individuals who were, for lack of a better term, underemployed and underutilized. As Adam Smith noted, "slaves... are very seldom inventive; and all the most important improvements... have been the discovery of freemen."[97] (Note that race played no role in the difference; Smith's example referred to Hungarian and Turkish miners.) And society at large, or more precisely those individuals who knew that racial inferiority theories were factually incorrect, suffered the bulk of the psychological distress that the continued existence of the immoral institution engendered. Other social costs or "negative externalities" included the cost of the institutions of repression. Southern ladies, for instance, could send indolent slaves to a public guardhouse to be whipped.[98]

Nonslaveholding Southern whites bore the brunt of the social costs of slavery in the form of lower literacy rates, fewer economic opportunities, and political subjugation to slaveholders. Southerners like "Aristides" argued persuasively that Southern states were oligarchies, ruled by aristocratic slaveholders, for aristocratic slaveholders. South Carolina, he claimed, was ruled:

> entirely and completely by about 32,000 aristocrats.... They make your Legislatures, your judges, your magistrates, your governor. And do these, your lords and masters, the slaveholding nobility, ever do anything for the prosperity of the whole State? No, never, never!... What, for instance, have they done for the education of your children?... In the northern free States, they have schools at the public expense all over the country, supplied with good teachers, and rich and poor all send their children to these schools. Hence, in New-England, you can seldom find a man who cannot read and write; but in our State, one-fifth part of the adult whites cannot read.[99]

It was in the interest of slaveholders, he continued, "that those who do not own slaves should be kept in ignorance, or otherwise they would know how our interests are neglected, and our rights have been craftily stolen from us."[100]

It could be argued that Northern employers threw off the costs of controlling wage laborers onto society at large, too. But there were three major differences. First, the costs imposed on society were lower. Wage laborers sometimes rioted and were quelled by force at public expense. But such outbursts were rare because, unlike slaves, wage laborers were not at constant war with their employers and society. Second, wage laborers were citizens, not chattel, so the cost of controlling them outside of the workplace indeed *should* have fallen on society. Finally, the costs were localized. Labor riots in Philadelphia for the most part cost Philadelphians, not Southerners or even other Pennsylvanians.

The negative externalities created by slavery, in contrast, were not only borne by the South. Since the South's poor showing during the Revolution, many Northerners believed, correctly as it turned out, that the South could not wage war successfully because, as a Virginia abolitionist put it in 1785, "the Negroes will always in time of war, prove injurious to the country wherein they live; for being naturally inimical to those who are their oppressors, they will avail themselves of every opportunity which may offer, of liberating themselves."[101] Were America to be invaded, the South would be easy pickings, making it more difficult for the North to defend itself. The Fugitive Slave Act, particularly the new and improved version passed in the antebellum period, was another salient example because it forced Northerners to actively support the capture of runaway slaves.[102]

Another negative externality was that slavery stunted the development of the North as well as that of the South. By 1860, the Northeast was, in per capita terms, the most financially and economically advanced region in the world, with the possible exception of some parts of England. Moreover, by the Civil War, decades of Northern economic development had created major differences between the sections. The South was not poor by contemporary standards but clearly, as Hinton Helper delighted in detailing, it lagged the North developmentally.[103]

Unlike the South, the North's prosperity rested on a wide variety of economic activities. Verily, it suffered temporary, cyclical economic setbacks, such as the recessions of 1818–1822, 1837–1843, and 1857–1858. Barring an act of God, however, the North's diversified economy could not be derailed. The South's income, by contrast, rested on King Cotton. If cotton were dethroned, the South would have suffered immensely. The North would not have been hurt as badly, but, as it discovered after worldwide demand for cotton slacked off after the Civil War, it would not have been immune. Moreover, the slave rebellions and/or mass manumissions, followed by mass migrations, that likely would have occurred had the cotton crop or market failed would have shaken the Republic to its liberal core, perhaps more violently than the Civil War itself did. In short, Jefferson was only half right when he said that slaveholders had a wolf by the ears. He should have also mentioned that Northerners held the beast's tail.[104]

Many Northerners came to see the South's peculiar institution as a great millstone that slowed the economic development of the entire nation. As Frederick Law Olmsted noted, productivity was the key to wealth, and slavery kept Southern efficiency low. But it took a Southerner, Hinton Helper, to elucidate the full implications of Southern backwardness:

Nature has been kind to us in all things. The strata and substrata of the South are profusely enriched with gold and silver, and precious stones, and from the natural orifices and aqueducts in Virginia and North Carolina, flow the purest healing waters in the world. But of what avail is all this latent wealth? Of what avail will it ever be, so long as slavery is permitted to play the dog in the manger? To these queries there can be but one reply. Slavery must be suppressed; the South, so great and so glorious by nature, must be reclaimed from her infamy and degradation...the various and ample resources of our vast domain, subterraneous as well as superficial, must be developed, and made to contribute to our pleasures and to the necessities of the world.[105]

In short, ending slavery would allow free migrants and immigrants to flow into the South, alleviating downward wage pressures in the North and opening up new vistas for Northern capitalists. Both in fact occurred after the Civil War. One thing seems clear: between 1854 and 1856, Northern laborers were hurting, and they quickly jumped on the abolitionist bandwagon once antislavery rhetoric grounded itself in economics as well as in morality and religion.[106]

At the same time that Northerners saw the South wasting the nation's resources and degrading wage labor, Southerners saw even the slightest attempt to undermine slavery as damaging. They may have been so sensitive because the value of their property was at risk. The economic profitability of slavery (had society not borne much of the control costs) may have approximated zero in many places in the South by the late antebellum period, especially on smaller plantations. (Indeed, the amount of Southern households that owned at least one slave decreased from 36 percent in 1830 to 25 percent by 1860.) On the eve of the Civil War, many believed that one good Northern worker produced as much in a day as four slaves typically did. Slaves could be driven to produce at higher rates but only for short periods. If pushed too hard for too long, tools began to snap, ill-defined "sicknesses" cropped up, slaves took flight, and barns mysteriously caught fire.[107]

Why, then, did slave prices skyrocket in the 1850s? It was not because of higher output per slave, which was largely stagnant. Rather, high cotton prices led to increased demand for slave labor at the same time that prohibition against the international slave trade restricted supply. More demand and less supply of course both put upward pressure on prices, a point that contemporaries readily grasped. "Prohibition against importation from Africa" led to the high prices, even in depressed areas.[108] "A young woman worth $1,000," slaveholder B. F. Stairley explained to H. C. Carey in 1856, "in two years will hire for $120 at least and raise a child that will be worth $250 or $300. Her hire will cancel nearly the interest on her investment— the increase is profits."[109] Because contemporaries viewed slaves as capital, high prices were interpreted as signals of the institution's strength. But if slaves were substitutes for wage labor, as they are considered in this chapter, their high price lowered the profitability of the institution by decreasing both slave productivity and liquidity vis-à-vis wage labor. Indeed, according to some contemporaries, slavery was under pressure by 1860 because slave prices were very high and some Irish immigration "made free white laborers more easy to be procured"[110] in some places, including New Orleans.[111]

Abolitionism may have significantly increased the cost of controlling slaves. As early as 1740, slaveholders feared that abolitionist sentiments were "dangerous to the publick Safety."[112] By the 1860s, many South-erners, like South Carolina widow Keziah Brevard, were convinced that abolitionism increased slave control costs. "We are attached to our slaves," she wrote, adding "they are as our own family & would to day have been a happy people if Northern fanaticism had not warred against us."[113] Per-haps then only the internal slave trade and scale economies on new, large plantations that used the gang labor system maintained the viability of the peculiar institution. That would explain why slaveholders saw the exten-sion of slavery into the territories as such a crucial issue.[114]

On September 18, 1860, Brevard told her diary that she wished that she "was prepared to die & could go" to her God. But she was not prepared to meet Him because she treated her slaves harshly and for some strange reason she received nothing but "impudence" in return. "I cannot think," she confided, "of imposing such servants on any one of my heirs."[115] She would not have to. An uncivil war between the states that sent slave pro-ductivity spiraling downward and the hypocrisy of owning and the costs of controlling slaves surging upward would see to that.

The North and South would have been better off if they had ended slavery with diplomacy and finance rather than wasting millions of lives and some four years kicking the bejesus out of each other on battlefields from Antietam to Gettysburg to Vicksburg. The war also deranged the US monetary system for several decades and impoverished the South for a full century. In retrospect, it would have been far cheaper for the government to buy all the slaves and free them. (Back of the proverbial envelop: 4 million slaves in 1860 times $1,000 on average, a generous sum, equals $4 billion. According to an official study completed in 1879, the North alone expended over $6 billion on the war by that time. Pension payments to veterans and their families added another $3.3 billion to costs by 1906. The South also spent over $2 billion on its war effort. And none of the aforementioned sums account for the value of lost lives or the opportunity costs associated with the destruction of the South's economy and financial system.)[116] Perhaps learning from the horrors of the US Civil War, Brazil did just that—bought and then freed its slaves—in 1888. In so doing, the Brazilians deranged their economy, permanently, some would say, but the US government would have done a better job financing an emancipation scheme because its financial system was far superior to that of Brazil.[117] So why then did the war occur? Here, the simplest answer is probably the best: nobody realized how long, bloody, and expensive the war would be, and once shots were fired, no compromise seemed possible.

***

According to nonprofit organization Free the Slaves, more people today are enslaved than ever before. This is plausible because, although the percentage of all humans who are enslaved is low by historical standards, the current world population is much higher than in any previous period. Slaves today sell for a pittance, less in nominal terms (and hence much less in real terms) than the slaves in antebellum America did. That is because, legally speaking, most are actually debt peons, people forced by their creditors and prevailing law to remain in dreary jobs, like the coal miners in Ford's song mentioned at the beginning of this chapter. In terms of the model presented here, debt peons are less productive than slaves because their children are not as surely appropriated by the owner and the market for peons is not as liquid as that for slaves. Moreover, control costs are higher because peons are not as easily identifiable as slaves, at least those based on race. Often, peons are prevented from fleeing to freedom only by armed guards. The same goes for the unfortunate young girls forced into prostitution in China, Moldova, and elsewhere.

Other parts of our FUBAR past long thought eradicated also haunt us from time to time. In particular, the specter of global economic depression overshadows the rest. To understand what can be done to avoid that, we need to examine the Great Depression, yet another hybrid failure of massive proportions.

5

THE GRAPES OF WRATH
Failed Bailouts and the Great Depression

John Steinbeck's *The Grapes of Wrath* is one of the most powerful American novels of all time. Written and largely set in California in the late 1930s, the novel follows the trials and tribulations of the Joad family of Oklahoma. Like thousands of other families displaced from their farms by a combination of the Great Depression, ecological disaster (the so-called Dust Bowl), and the increasingly widespread mechanization of agriculture, the Joads were forcibly evicted from their farms by banks and landlords. They joined in the mass exodus along Route 66 to California but found their new state largely inhospitable. The migrants fought among themselves, making it nearly impossible to work together to unionize and battle oppressive employers and venal government officials. Several members of the Joad family passed away due to the stress, but the remainder pushed on in search of work, bumping along between ramshackle Hoovervilles and government camps. An in-law abandoned his wife, who bore the unlikely name of Rose of Sharon, and an unborn child. In the book's final scene, Rose of Sharon suckled a starving man with the full breast of milk that nature intended for her stillborn baby.

Like all great moments in literature, *The Grapes of Wrath*'s final scene can be interpreted in a variety of ways. Many contemporaries saw it as a call for communism, so the ending was dramatically changed in the 1940 movie version starring Henry Fonda, which was produced and directed by Darryl Zanuck and John Ford, respectively, both of whom were political conservatives. I see the final scene as clear evidence that the Great Depression was a hybrid failure. The Joads' story was America's. Both capitalists and the government were to blame for the Joad family's many misfortunes. Market forces drove the Joads out of Oklahoma and kept them down in California, where the government tried to help them but failed and ultimately made matters worse. The book is, of course, fictional but, like *Uncle Tom's Cabin*, it's depressingly realistic. The economic downturn of the 1930s did displace millions of Americans, some of whom perished due to malnutrition, exposure, or accidents while stowing away on trucks, ships, and trains.[1] The Great Depression did cause massive unemployment, up to 25 percent, which brought out the best and worst in people while simultaneously exposing the weaknesses of many local and state governments.[2] Due to the crash and subsequent economic recession, the longest and steepest in recorded history, thousands lost millions, due mostly to stock speculation, and millions lost thousands, due mostly to joblessness and failed banks. Most important, the Great Depression showed beyond all shadow of a doubt that markets could fail in a major way when they had considerable help from the government.

***

The first thing to understand about the Great Depression is that it was really a "double dip" recession, not a single, sustained downturn in economic activity. The Depression proper lasted from August 1929 until March 1933, although in common folklore it is remembered as encompassing the entire 1930s, ending only with the massive mobilization required to fight World War II. From that misunderstanding stems the bizarre claim that Hitler (or Hitler and Tojo) "saved us from the Depression."[3] In fact, by 1937 real per capita output had almost recovered to pre-Depression levels before plunging into darkness again until the middle of 1938. Getting the chronology right helps to disentangle the causes of the first recession, the effects of the government's sundry bailout attempts, and the causes of the so-called Roosevelt recession of 1937–1938.[4]

The second thing to understand is that the stock market crash in late

October 1929—unimaginatively tagged Black Thursday (the 24th), Black Monday (the 28th), and Black Tuesday (the 29th)—did not cause the Great Depression. As noted above, the recession that lasted until March 1933 had begun in August 1929, at least according to the official bean counters at the National Bureau of Economic Research. The economy showed significant signs of softness before then, however, as we will see. The myth that the stock market crash touched off the Depression originated with the New Deal. "Only later," wrote business historian Robert Sobel, "when a nation deep in depression had to find a scapegoat, did the businessman go into eclipse, and did the Great Crash become the symbol of a nation's entrapment by the forces of Wall Street."[5]

What caused the recession, then? This will sound eerily familiar, but the economy turned south due to the bursting of a real estate bubble coupled with deep structural problems that policymakers allowed to fester. Oft depicted as "roaring," the economy of the 1920s was anything but. It started out in recession, in reaction to the end of World War I and the influenza pandemic that took more lives worldwide than the war itself had. Unlike most flu epidemics, the 1918–1919 influenza killed mostly vigorous young adults rather than infants and the elderly, thus magnifying its economic shock. Real per capita income began growing again by 1922, largely due to tremendous growth in new technology sectors. Other sectors were not nearly as buoyant, leading to flat real wages and palpably increasing disparities of wealth. The agricultural sector in particular experienced significant pain, as mechanization and consolidation drove many marginal farmers off the land and into precarious new occupations. Such profound structural change caused thousands of tiny rural banks to fail. Like the canary in the coal mine, they portended future disaster. Few paid attention, however, as people looked agog at technology companies and fretted about Prohibition, which banned the production, distribution, and sale of alcohol throughout the United States. Like our own never-ending War on Drugs, Prohibition did little to stop drunkenness and much to drain valuable public resources, both money and brainpower, into the bottomless barrel of enforcing the unenforceable.

Despite these significant structural problems, the real estate and stock markets boomed, lulling many people to nap in a bed of alleged cash. I say alleged because people for some strange reason view the prices of a few stocks, especially those composing the Dow Jones Industrial Average (DJIA or Dow), as a barometer for the economy. They certainly are at times, but they need not be. For starters, quoted stock prices are just marginal prices. If a few shares of a company with 1 million outstanding shares trade at $25 per share, people take that to mean that the market values the company at ($25 × 1 million equals) $25 million when in fact perhaps most of the million shares could not be sold for more than $20 each, or $15, or whatever. This problem looms even larger for infrequently traded stocks and real estate.

Many market participants assume prices increase because expected business profits or rents increase, both signs of a vibrant economy. In fact, the prices of stocks, real estate, and other assets can increase simply because interest rates decrease. And interest rates could decrease for numerous reasons, including recession! Instead of analyzing cause and effect carefully, investors sometimes interpret rising prices as a signal to leverage up, to borrow and buy in the expectation of soon selling out for a profit. As we saw in chapter 2, this reaction is especially likely in a low interest rate environment and will create a bubble of large proportions if a seemingly compelling story about future productivity drowns out the voices of critics and a large influx of new traders cancels out the efforts of short sellers.[6]

The economy of the 1920s appeared to roar because bubbles in real estate and corporate equities (stocks) ballooned upward, driving up marginal asset prices and making people feel richer than they actually were, or should have been. The conditions for bubble formation were just right. The 1920s witnessed "the greatest bull bond market" in American history. Interest rates, in other words, dropped almost continuously from May 1920 to January 1928, from well over 5 to just over 4 percent for corporate bonds, on average. Yields on high-grade municipal bonds and treasuries also dropped by about the same amount. In what one central banker called "one of the most costly errors" in central banking history, the Federal Reserve kept its own discount rate low as well, largely to assuage the fears of America's European allies that all of their gold was bound for the New World.[7] At the same time, the quantity of commercial bank loans soared—from $25 billion in 1922 to $36.1 billion in 1929.[8]

It also became a little cheaper and a whole lot easier to obtain a mortgage. Total mortgage lending jumped from less than $1 billion in 1920 to over $3 billion per year in the mid-1920s. Cheap financing, combined with the inability to short the market, touched off a real estate bubble. The situation in Florida was the most outright outrageous. Prices for completed buildings, improved tracts (with streets and lampposts, etc.), city lots, and completely virgin land ticked upward almost daily, as new speculators with fresh cash arrived by train. To fleece the newbies as quickly and thoroughly as possible, so-called binder boys, come-on girls, and bird dogs plied their shady trades. Their efforts paid off as even swamps and scrub wastelands went from virtually worthless to valuable in just a few years as housing developments, miles from nowhere, sprang up like mushrooms. A mellowing followed by the September 1926 hurricane washed all the exuberance away.[9]

Although Florida's infamous boom has attracted the most attention, the phenomenon was actually a national one. The story elsewhere was less dramatic but no less dangerous for economic and financial stability. New residential construction nationwide increased from about $2 billion in 1922 to $5 billion in 1925, a figure matched the following year. In 1927, new construction dropped to about $4.5 billion and in 1928 to about $4 billion. In 1929, the market dropped to just $3 billion. Total construction (residential, commercial, and government) followed a similar trajectory. An index of single-family house prices did as well, starting at about 80 on the scale in 1920, topping out at 110 in 1925, and dropping to 100 by 1929.[10]

The bust in construction activity and real estate prices did little directly to dampen the effervescence of the stock market and arguably added to the froth by concentrating speculative activity on it. In fact, stock prices did not begin to inflate in a convincingly bubbly fashion until early 1927, just after the Florida lands lost their luster.[11] The fall in real estate values, however, indirectly popped the stock market bubble by helping to bring on recession. The story is a disturbingly familiar one. As prices dropped, defaults increased, especially for the 80 or so percent of mortgages that were short term and nonamortizing. When the loan principal fell due, many borrowers found it difficult to refinance because the sums they owed were greater than the current market value of their homes. Unsurprisingly, foreclosure rates increased, injuring banks, life insurance companies, and other lenders to the point that some failed and others had to restrict new lending. That, in turn, crimped businesses that sought to expand, which of course eventually had adverse effects on employment and output.[12]

That process, however, took a few years to play out, giving the stock market plenty of time to puff up. Interestingly, the government had helped to embolden many new investors to enter the securities markets. For decades, securities salesmen, some shadier than a big elm on a summer afternoon, had tried to lure the poorer citizens into the stock market. They occasionally succeeded but found their task much easier after World War I because many people had learned the nuts and bolts of buying, holding, and selling financial securities during the government's wartime Liberty Loan bond drives. By 1929, the number of stock market investors had sky-rocketed to between 1.5 and 3 million. Nobody is certain of the exact figure, but everyone agrees that growth in the number of stockholders was exceedingly rapid, especially in 1928 and 1929.[13]

Many of those new to the stock market in the 1920s were women. That had less to do with the Nineteenth Amendment and flapperism than with the fact that wealthier women had long played a role in American capital markets. As early as the 1790s, women were on the lists of corporate stock-holders and US government bondholders. By the 1880s, women had begun to move into careers in the financial services sector as insurance agents and stockbrokers who specifically targeted female investors.[14] Nevertheless, old stereotypes died hard, inducing some brokers "to discourage women customers on the grounds that women, as a rule, did not understand stock market operations and wouldn't take the trouble to learn, and because a woman always felt, somehow, that she had been cheated if she lost any-thing in the stock market."[15] As it turned out, female investors new to trading in the 1920s were no bigger stooges than their male counterparts.

Not everyone was in the stock market, of course, but people from all walks of life dove in, as was typical during earlier US bubbles. In early 1792, for example, oystermen and prostitutes had purchased bank stocks and government bonds. In the late 1920s, barbers, beauticians, chauffeurs, shoeshine boys, valets, window cleaners, and even Wyoming cattlemen entered the markets.[16] The *Saturday Evening Post* nicely summed up the sit-uation with a bit of doggerel:

> Oh, hush thee, my babe, granny's bought some more shares
> Daddy's gone out to play with the bulls and the bears,
> Mother's buying on tips, and she simply can't lose,
> And baby shall have some expensive new shoes![17]

Rich industrialists, whose experience was in engineering, construction, or manufacturing rather than finance, also joined the party. The influx of inexperienced investors, rich, poor, and in between, exacerbated the bubble because the new money they brought into the market prevented short sellers, both experienced ones and the shrewder newbies, from bidding stock prices down to more rational levels. "The orthodox market players of the East, meaning mainly conservative bears on the Stock Exchange and plenty of plungers too," the *New York Times* reported in September 1928, "have dropped millions of dollars in an ineffectual attempt to stop the tidal wave of stock buying."[18] The influx also convinced shrewd, experienced traders that prices already irrationally high could go higher still. Unsurprisingly, trading volume soared to unheard-of levels and speculators took on ever more leverage by buying on margin through their brokers. In other words, they did not pay for their stock outright but rather put a little money down on each share and borrowed the rest. The volume of call loans, as loans on margin were termed because they could be called for at any time, increased from about $1 billion in the early 1920s to almost $6 billion by the end of 1928. The loans allowed speculators to put just a small percentage of their own money down but reap all of the profits of any upswing in prices. Of course that also meant that they suffered the full brunt of any losses, plus interest.[19]

Some investors were willing to take the risk because they believed prices would continue to rise even after they moved above fundamental levels. As long as new money kept flowing in, the stock market was little more than a giant Ponzi or pyramid scheme. Instead of being tied to economic fundamentals, like expected future profits, stock prices floated on public sentiment. For years, that sentiment was largely bullish—a penchant for buying and also for bullshit. Many of the turds came from on high. Treasury secretary Andrew Mellon (1855–1937) told investors that "there is no cause for worry. The high tide of prosperity will continue."[20] In December 1928 President Calvin Coolidge informed Congress that the country should "regard the present with satisfaction and anticipate the future with optimism."[21] Just before turning the reigns of executive power over to Herbert Hoover, Cool Cal again opined that stocks were cheap and the economy sound.[22]

Through printed periodicals and radio broadcasts, businessmen also pinched out steaming loaves of optimism. In 1928, Roger Babson (1875–1967), a well-known entrepreneur and business theorist, warned that the election of Democratic presidential candidate Al Smith would bring on recession while the "election of Hoover and a Republican Congress should result in continued prosperity."[23] (To his credit, he later recanted.)[24] On New Year's Day 1929, Charles Mitchell of National City Bank said that "business is entering the New Year upon a high level of activity and with confidence in the continuation of prosperity."[25] Later in 1929, IBM's Thomas Watson, automaker Walter P. Chrysler, and Lewis Pierson of the Irving Trust Company, among others, also spread the bull, thick and stinky.[26] Most infamously of all, DuPont and GM financier John J. Raskob (1879–1950) told readers of *Ladies' Home Journal* "Everybody Ought to Be Rich."[27]

Numerous economists, including Joseph Stagg Lawrence, Edwin Kemmerer, Charles Dice, Joseph Davis, and Edmund Day, were also inveterate bulls, and slingers of bull.[28] Their voices drowned out those of critics like *New York Times* financial editor Alexander Dana Noyes, who called it a bubble and reminded readers that it was bound to burst.[29] They derided as "obsolete" investment banker Paul Warburg's warning that the "orgy of unrestrained speculation" had reached "a saturation point" and must soon give way to reality.[30]

Bullish economist Irving Fisher (1867–1947) may have inadvertently triggered the bursting. Probably the greatest US economist between the death of Alexander Hamilton and World War II, Fisher knew the economy was bound to pull back if only because of the deadweight loss caused by Prohibition and the massive restructuring occurring in agriculture, which was still important in terms of labor, if not output. At the same time, he believed that the technological breakthroughs of the decade were real. So just two weeks before the black days at the end of October he made a statement that haunted him to the end of his life and that probably haunts his ghost to this day: "stock prices have reached what looks like a permanently high plateau."[31] Soon after, he recanted and argued that prices would continue to climb, but his initial comment probably crystallized what many investors had in the back of their minds, that recession meant at least a leveling off in prices and hence an end to the party. As we have seen, bubbles must rise consistently or die. To be maintained, highly leveraged positions need gains. When prices stagnate, or worse yet, slip, stocks purchased on margin and other leveraged assets must be sold. When everyone must sell, marginal prices drop quickly, forcing yet more selling, eventually turning the day "black."

The recession, then, precipitated the crash by bursting the stock market bubble. Of course, the crash also exacerbated the recession, lengthening and deepening it. That, however, is hardly the whole story. A full year after the crash, the Dow was a little below 200, the same level it had closed at on its nadir on November 13, 1929. Real estate prices were also well off their 1920s highs but not yet in the pits. Nobody was yet calling the downturn a depression, much less "the Great Depression." Clearly, asset bubbles in corporate equities and real estate had deflated and the economy was soft, but a turnaround could have come at any time. In fact, James Farrell of US Steel believed that "after the turn of the year operations in the steel industry will substantially improve." Met Life executive Frederick Ecker was also optimistic. Even the typically bearish Noyes was hopeful, as were many respected economists.[32] In January 1930, for example, the Harvard Economic Society said that "the severest phase of the recession is over." In March it claimed that manufacturing was "definitely on the road to recovery." In May it prognosticated that business would "turn for the better this month or next, recover vigorously in the third quarter and end the year at levels substantially above normal." As late as November 1930 it claimed that the end of the downturn was near.[33]

Why was the so-called smart money so far wrong? Banks began to fail en masse and the government implemented the most dangerous bailout in history. Combined, they turned the economy to toast slathered in FUBAR-flavored jam. Due to the recession, borrowers began to default on loans. Depositors fretted for the safety of their money, and rightly so. Most banks were extremely small and hence highly dependent on the economic health of their local communities. If a major company went bankrupt or if several big employers had layoffs, such banks could be quickly inundated with non-performing loans (NPLs). Few deposits were insured, by the government or anyone else for that matter, so depositors usually reacted to such news by pulling out their deposits en masse, just as in the bank-run scene in *It's a Wonderful Life*. Unlike Bailey's Building and Loan, however, most banks were not headed by Jimmy Stewart and did not have the community goodwill or the timely cash infusion from Donna Reed necessary to save them from a concerted bank run. They therefore went bankrupt, often taking some of their depositors with them. Their borrowers, by contrast, still had to pay up.[34]

Fearful that their banks would be next, depositors of safe banks also panicked, ruining many solvent institutions. "The failure of one bank caused distrust to rage around others, and to bring down banks that were really solid," economist Alfred Marshall once wrote, "as a fire spreads from one wooden house to another, till even nearly fireproof buildings succumb in the blaze of a great conflagration."[35] Understandably, the remaining banks became hyperconservative. They restricted their lending to businesses and invested heavily in government bonds, the safest and most liquid asset around, and also kept massive reserves of cash on hand. The reserves made them less likely to fail because they would have plenty of money to meet depositors' withdrawal demands, but it also decreased the money supply. That, in turn, led to deflation, the opposite of inflation. In other words, the price level actually decreased. That made it more difficult to repay loans because borrowers' revenues of course declined right along with the prices that their products could command. Delinquent loans hurt yet further both banks and their borrowers. Businesses also found it difficult to expand operations when the prices of their output would be some unknowable percentage lower in the future. Prices of physical inputs (raw materials like cotton, iron, foodstuffs, and so forth) declined but, given the laws of the day and prevailing attitudes, it was nearly impossible to force or even induce workers to accept nominal wage cuts. When a desperate coal company tried to cut workers' nominal wages 10 percent in 1931, for example, furious workers retaliated by killing a sheriff and a worker who chose not to strike.[36] Workers' real wages, the amount of stuff that they could buy with their paychecks, increased as prices sank. High real wages hurt employers, however, which responded with mass layoffs. High levels of unemployment created yet more NPLs for banks and further cut consumption, hurting businesses yet more. The Depression was a cycle as vicious as a pit bull with rabies.[37]

Was any of that rabid cycle the government's fault? Arguably, all of it was. Both the federal and state governments badly bungled bank regulation. The number of commercial banks climbed sharply in the first few decades of the twentieth century, from about nine thousand in 1900 to some thirty thousand in 1921.[38] The vast majority of those banks, however, were small and vulnerable because most state governments prevented them from branching even across the street, much less across state lines. Canada and California weathered the Depression comparably well because they allowed branching, so their banks were bigger, more diversified, more robust, and much less likely to fail.[39]

American governments were so daft because they feared concentrated financial power, a major American bugaboo since the early days of the Republic and the debates over the first and second Bank of the United States. In 1831, for example, Missouri senator Thomas Hart Benton complained that the second Bank of the United States (1816–1836) "tends to aggravate the inequality of fortunes; to make the rich richer, and the poor poorer; to multiply nabobs and paupers."[40] By the late nineteenth century, many Americans feared that a handful of powerful investment bankers, working in conjunction with the commercial banks, trusts, and life insurance companies that they controlled, were the most powerful men in the land. Repeated government and muckraker probes of the "Money Trust" certainly exposed rampant conflicts of interest and other governance problems. The assertion that investment bankers enjoyed some market power was also a solid one; the investment banking industry was dominated by a dozen or fewer institutions.[41] But Louis Brandeis's claim in his almost hysterical exposé, *Other People's Money and How the Bankers Use It*, that "investment bankers and their associates... control the people through the people's own money" was never substantiated[42] and in fact other observers noted that the largest US banks were "not particularly large when judged by English or European standards, and none is in a position, either, because of its dimensions or its privileges to exert an effective control over the rest."[43]

J. P. Morgan and his associates sat on the boards of many companies, "interlocking" their directorates and giving Morgan and his moneyed minions some control of their operations. But such activity was hardly unusual and in fact was long the norm in places like Japan and Germany. Moreover, the investment bankers did not consolidate the many companies that they influenced but usually kept them separate. So the $22 billion of assets that Morgan allegedly controlled, a massive sum for the early twentieth century, was split into many distinct companies, the assets of which were walled off from each other. What Morgan and other investment bankers did was more akin to networking than concentrating: it was closer to zaibatsu, keiretsu, chaebols, or cartels[44] than to what J. P. Morgan Chase has done in recent years.

The federal government's banking policies failed as well, in two ways. First, during the Civil War it began to allow bankers to obtain federal charters instead of restricting them to state charters (or no charter at all), as it had in the antebellum era. At first, the government forbade national banks to branch. Later, it told bankers they had to follow the branching rules of the state that they decided to locate within. So even America's many national banks were national in name only and in reality were severely limited in scope and hence stability.[45]

Banking regulation was quite weak, largely due to regulatory arbitrage, the eternal search for riskless profits garnered by ensuring one's company fell under the jurisdiction of the most hapless government authorities possible. Each state decided how much equity capital its banks had to hold; national banks had to hold a 20 percent reserve fund in addition to a minimum capitalization based on the size of the community it served.[46] Asset restrictions on state banks also varied by state but were generally weak. They were quite stringent for national banks, especially when it came to mortgage lending.[47] The National Banking Acts also imposed reserve requirements on bank notes and deposits, but state regulations were much more lax. In fact, as late as 1887 only three states imposed reserve requirements on their banks. By 1909, however, all but thirteen states had imposed some sort of requirement, probably due to numerous state bank failures in the wake of financial panics in 1893 and 1907. State-run deposit insurance also spread over the period, but then receded as their large costs became evident.[48] Supervision and examination of the national banks fell to the Comptroller of the Currency. The states were slow to implement examination of their banks, but by 1914 all required some type of annual exam. The quality of examiners was, however, notoriously low. Unsurprisingly, most banks were state chartered, not part of the national system.[49]

Second, the Federal Reserve did nothing to save distressed banks or keep the money supply from shrinking. "The Federal Reserve Board in those times," economic historian John Kenneth Galbraith wrote, "was a body of startling incompetence."[50] As people nationwide resorted to barter, municipal bills of credit, private chits, and—more embarrassingly—Mexican pesos,[51] and as the deflation-unemployment spiral described above set in, the Fed resigned itself to defending the gold standard. Its policies kept real interest rates, nominal interest rates adjusted *upward* due to expected deflation, through the roof. With interest rates and wages high, businesses would not invest because few projects showed any hope of returning a profit under those conditions. The Fed's intransigence was as ironic as it was tragic since the major reason for its creation was to prevent the money supply from shrinking during periods of economic distress.[52]

***

Compared to the New Deal that would follow, the administration of Herbert Hoover (1929–1933) did relatively little to try to reverse the economic downturn.[53] After the stock market break in October 1929, for example, Hoover refused to try to "talk up" stock prices with encouraging comments.[54] His rhetorical views on the importance of individualism and his generally pro-business attitude, particularly his reluctance to blame the Depression on the financial industry or to use antitrust laws like the Sherman Act to break up large industrial corporations, seemed to cast Hoover in the same mold as nineteenth-century advocates of the minimalist state, as the provider of national defense, courts of justice, and little else.[55] The commonly held notion that Hoover believed in laissez-faire, or complete government noninterference with the economy, is, however, clearly a myth. The Hoover administration interfered with market mechanisms enough in the early 1930s to prompt FDR to claim that Hoover was "leading the country down the path to socialism."[56] Despite being painted as a man of inaction, Hoover implemented several important economic reforms before leaving the Oval Office. The problem was that they all failed to stimulate recovery—but only in that sense was Hoover a stick-in-the-mud, do nothing kinda guy.

Hoover's first responses to the crisis, in late 1929 and 1930, were minor and piecemeal. He sped up federal construction projects and urged governors to do likewise on state and local projects. Hoover also met with business leaders and encouraged them to increase or at least keep up capital spending on repairs, equipment, new construction, and so forth. He cajoled labor union officials into forgoing strikes and demands for wage increases. He also tried to convince the press to refrain from making dark predictions about economic collapse and concentrate on the facts. Finally, Hoover implemented a tax cut, but a very small one. Although generally greeted with an enthusiastic response, Hoover's meager early efforts to shore up confidence, demand, and employment had little discernible positive effect on the economy.[57]

The first major Hoover bailout attempt was called the Smoot-Hawley Tariff Act after the two jokers who concocted it, who happened to be US legislators. Enacted in June 1930, the act imposed the highest tariffs, or taxes on imported goods, in US history. Republican Willis Hawley (1864–

1941) hailed from Oregon's First Congressional District, for which he had served in the House of Representatives since 1907. Ironically, before turning to politics Hawley had taught history and economics at Willamette for about sixteen years. Apparently, he knew little of either subject because his bill flew in the face of both economic theory and historical reality. Ridiculously persistent myths to the contrary notwithstanding, America's industrial revolution began late in the eighteenth century, not after the Civil War, and owed little to tariff protection. Reed Smoot (1862–1941) was a Republican from Utah and, judging from the photographs I've seen of him, a total nerd. By the 1930s, however, he was a powerful nerd, having served in the Senate since 1903. He almost wasn't allowed his seat because he was a Mormon, and an apostle of the Latter-day Saints at that. He was eventually allowed in, however, because he had only one wife and purportedly did not take the Mormon "oath of vengeance" against the US government (which had treated Mormons rather roughly in the 1840s and 1850s). Whether or not he took the oath, the tariff he cosponsored did take a terrible toll on America. Not that he was solely responsible for the economic carnage that followed. It was the entire Republican government's call, and it made the wrong one.

The government's thinking was clear—clearly oversimplified, that is. Aggregate output (Y), they knew, equals consumption (C) plus investment (I) plus government expenditure net of taxes (G) plus net exports (exports minus imports, or NX). Administration officials couldn't figure out how to influence C or I and were ideologically opposed to increasing G by much, but they thought they could rig NX. By increasing tariffs, they would reduce imports. If exports held up, NX and hence Y would increase. In the process, they would win many votes from business interests and protectionist stooges. Or so they hoped. Instead of fixing the economy, however, Smoot-Hawley made matters worse by starting a trade war. Instead of beggaring our neighbors, we all beggared each other, and came darn close to buggering each other in the process. Our literal neighbor and largest trading partner, Canada, began a counterattack quickly joined by Australia, France, Italy, India, and Switzerland.[58] By 1933, foreign trade had dropped by over 60 percent, far more than the drop in overall economic output. Smoot and Hawley got their just deserts in 1932, when they both lost reelection bids. Although many Americans thought the act would be beneficial, 1,028 economists had opposed it,[59] as had Henry Ford, who called it "an economic stupidity," GM director Graeme Howard, who predicted it would cause the "most severe depression ever experienced," and investment banker Thomas W. Lamont, who termed it "asinine."[60]

Throughout most of 1931, the Hoover administration stayed the course by continuing the so-called stabilization program, which, as we have seen, attempted to stimulate the economy with public works projects. The problem was that many state and local governments, although still onboard in principle, were no longer able to continue large-scale spending because their tax bases had shriveled from grapes into raisins. Unlike the federal government, most could not borrow enough cheaply enough to take up the slack. The same dynamic hurt railroads and utilities as well. As a result, capital spending dropped over 20 percent from the previous year, which obviously was not very economically stimulating. For a variety of reasons, the federal government did not understand the full extent of the problem until well into 1932 and even then refused to rectify the situation by using its good credit and borrowing capacity to aid nonfederal projects, like the facilities in Muscle Shoals, Alabama, later known as the Tennessee Valley Authority. Hoover's administration also steadfastly refused to provide any form of direct public assistance, insisting that all aid must come from strapped local governments or private charities. In 1931, Congress allowed World War I veterans to borrow up to half of their government pension payments (due in 1945) but only over Hoover's emphatic veto. "We cannot further the restoration of prosperity by borrowing from some of our people, pledging the credit of all of the people, to loan to some of our people who are not in need of the money," he wrote. About 18 percent of veterans were unemployed at that time, inviting many to question Hoover's grasp of reality.[61]

Late in 1931, Hoover tried to reform the banking system by creating a voluntary association called the National Credit Corporation (NCC). It soon foundered, however, because it was too small to handle the magnitude of the banking crisis, which included the failure or severe impairment of thousands of banks nationwide.[62] The NCC was a bit like trying to save a limb amputee with a Band-Aid and aspirin. The following year, 1932, Hoover again attempted to bail out distressed banks by creating a larger and more ambitious institution, the Reconstruction Finance Corporation (RFC). Unlike the tariff hike, the RFC was not outright destructive and after a rocky start may have marginally helped the recovery by speeding up the resolution of failed banks. Nevertheless, it did not stem the waves of bank failures that repeatedly shocked the economy and further decreased the all-important money supply.[63]

Hoover's biggest blunder was keeping the United States on the gold standard. By the end of his administration only America and France remained wedded to the stuff.[64] By staying on gold, the United States and France prevented the reexpansion of the money supply that was lifting other major economies out of dark depression. Instead of monetary reform, Hoover offered only watered-down palliatives, like the anti-hoarding campaign of early 1932. An attempt to cajole hordes of people into not hoarding money and returning it to the banking system, the campaign soon petered out after some initial success.

Also in 1932, Hoover tried to reactivate the economy with a modest government stimulus program made possible by redefining the term "balanced budget" so as not to include the borrowings of the RFC and several other parts of the government. That gave the administration some leeway to expand spending, which it did on so-called income-producing projects, like toll bridges and tunnels, docks, and other revenue-generating public works. So-called unproductive works, like freeways, were eschewed because they did not "prime the motor" of economic growth. Needless to say, the new initiatives fell far short of the mark.[65]

In the end, the public's views of Hoover's economic policies were mixed and heavily dependent on the observer's side of the political aisle. Many on the Right thought he did the best that could be done, while many on the Left castigated him for doing too little, or in the case of the tariff and RFC, far too much. In an election year pamphlet, for example, college professor and soon-to-be member of the Roosevelt administration Rexford Tugwell mocked Hoover as a tragic figure with a "series of fixed ideas, inherited from a vanished past," a man with a "mania for facts and an obsession for acting on them—if only they will behave!"[66] He also painted Hoover as "a humorless man who is both clumsy and earnest," a victim of a "psychological ordeal," a "disease" of his own making.[67] Few independents were likely swayed by such vituperation, but most figured that whatever Hoover and his fellow Republicans were doing simply wasn't working. Here Tugwell was closer to the mark: "What was done was invariably done too late to be of any use or else the measures were too feeble to have any effect."[68] In the end, many swing voters, almost all Democrats, and a number of disillusioned Republicans voted for the Democrats and their charismatic New York governor Franklin Delano Roosevelt in 1932. FDR's victory rendered Hoover a lame duck afraid of his own shadow. For five months, the federal government embarked on no new initiatives and simply bided time.

***

Professional opinions about the Roosevelt administration's bailouts, generally termed "the New Deal," were also mixed and largely, but not wholly, a function of political ideology. Some economists and businesses opposed all or most of them, but others, followers of John Maynard Keynes and kindred spirits, supported them. The basic notion was that the government could increase G almost at will by borrowing and spending. All else constant, that would drive up Y and hopefully stop the cycle of unemployment, default, and bank failure that plagued the economy in the early 1930s. Did the rash of government spending programs cooked up by the Roosevelt administration pull the economy out of recession? The timing was right: Roosevelt took office in late March 1933, and in his first hundred days he induced Congress to pass numerous spending measures. Even more spending came in subsequent years. Government deficit spending (G), however, was simply too small to have had much effect. The economy recovered because the money supply grew after Roosevelt devalued the dollar. That decreased real wages and real interest rates, which increased investment (I) by making some businesses profitable again.[69]

Some economists argue that increasing G cannot really help the economy, Keynes and his many minions to the contrary notwithstanding. Remember the tax rebate checks the government sent you in 2001 and 2008? What did they do for the economy (as opposed to your wallet)? Exactly zero. Oh, I was happy to cash both checks and spend the manna, as I am sure you were, too. And businesses were happy to serve us meals, sell us televisions, and so forth. Knowing that the windfall was temporary, however, none of them invested in new facilities or hired new employees. And most people realized that government borrowing today means higher taxes tomorrow, which of course mutes the effects of the stimulus. The rebate checks were therefore little more than a fart in a bottle. They didn't last very long or smell very good.

Little Orphan Annie was right: the New Deal was more political bunk than economic funk.[70] Rather than depicting the New Deal as the economy's savior in the mid-1930s, it's more accurate to say that the economy managed to bounce back despite the bungling interference of the Roosevelt—and Hoover—administrations.[71] That is not to say, of course, that the New Deal's *relief* programs should not have been implemented. If anything, they should have been extended so that Rose of Sharon would have gotten the nutrition and healthcare that could have saved her baby. Relief redistributes resources rather than increasing the size of the economy, but it is the right thing to do during systemic downturns, when people are laid low through no fault of their own. Too bad the government botched many of its relief efforts by waging turf and ideology wars against state and private relief organizations like the Fraternal Order of Eagles and the nation's schools of philanthropy.[72]

New Deal programs that created public goods also should be immune from imputation. As discussed in the first chapter, public goods are things of value that the government must produce if society is to enjoy them because no individual or business would have an incentive to create them. Technically, pure public goods are nonexcludable and nonrivalrous, meaning that no one can be excluded from using the good and consumption of the good by one person does not reduce its availability for others. National defense is the classic example, as is protection of life, liberty, and property more generally. Public goods are very different critters than private goods, like hamburgers and automobiles, which are both excludable and rivalrous. Nonrivalrous but excludable goods, like cable television, are called club goods because free riders (nonmembers) can be kept out but viewers do not use up the signal. (Broadband is a different story!) Common goods, like clean air and water, are nonexcludable but rivalrous. Such goods are often quickly degraded due to what economists call the tragedy of the commons. Since nobody owns them, nobody takes care of them.

Not all examples of goods, however, can be so easily or neatly categorized. Take, for example, the YMCA or other fitness *clubs* or country *clubs*. The name suggests that they provide club goods, but anyone who has tried to find an open Stairmaster at 5 p.m. on the first Monday after New Year's knows that congestion has the same effect as rivalry. The other members don't use up the machines or cart them home (well, usually, anyway), but if they are on them when you want to be, they may as well have. Or consider the Dust Bowl. It was not quite a "tragedy of the commons" story because the farms were private goods. It was more of a collective-action problem because cutting down trees and plowing every foot of ground is only a problem when everyone does it. (Even the Dust Bowl was a hybrid failure, by the way, because farmers' predilection to farm every available inch was rooted in the government's policy of selling land only in small parcels in arid areas where larger farms would have been more appropriate.)

Likewise, many goods provided by the government are quasi-public goods at best. Fire departments, for example, are almost always public today. In the past, however, they were entirely private. Some believe that governments took them over in order to create more patronage positions for politicians to dole out to the faithful. Similarly, long-distance roads were almost all privately owned before the Civil War. Their transition to public, or quasi-public, control was justified by the claim that turnpike companies were unprofitable. My research shows, however, that many turnpike companies were profitable and would have been even more so if the government had made it easier for them to collect tolls (i.e., had allowed them to exclude literal free riders, people using so-called shun-pikes to circumvent toll collection booths. If you ever tried to sneak onto the New York Thruway or other well-managed toll road, you know that it is possible to prevent most people from using long-distance roads for free).

Most New Deal programs, however, did not supply public goods. Worse, they hurt the economy by unwisely allocating resources. Some of the New Deal dollars that did not merely redistribute wealth, in other words, may have actually destroyed wealth by using real resources to create goods that nobody at the time wanted. Of course that is only to argue that the programs were suboptimal compared to a smoothly func-tioning, non-FUBAR economy. To the extent that the programs used resources that would have been wasted due to the uncertain business cli-mate, they were better than nothing. The government itself helped to create, perpetuate, and even amplify the uncertainty that plagued the busi-ness environment because business leaders could not reliably predict politicians' actions or bureaucratic interpretations of new regulations.

The Federal Deposit Insurance Corporation (FDIC), a New Deal pro-gram that insured the retail deposits of solvent banks beginning in 1934, was a great boon even before it began operations because its mere announcement induced depositors to stop running on their banks. That helped to keep the money supply from disintegrating, which, as we have seen, was crucial to the recovery that lasted from March 1933 until May 1937. Ever since, the FDIC and similar funds have effectively prevented classic bank runs, like that in *It's a Wonderful Life*. It has not, however, stemmed the tide of so-called silent bank runs, where creditors simply refuse to roll over short-term loans to banks. It also lulls depositors to sleep, which allows bankers to take on additional risks without fearing the wrath of depositors. The FDIC's twin, the Federal Savings and Loan Insurance Corporation (FSLIC), was one of the key causes of the savings and loan crisis of the 1980s for precisely that reason. Most economists agree that aside from its initial success in stabilizing the banking system in 1933, the FDIC's net contribution to the economy has been approximately zero. Due to the existence of insurance, bank runs are less likely but bank risk taking is higher.[73] (It is not the case that banks would not be able to attract deposits without some sort of insurance. History shows that in economically peaceful times uninsured banks attract deposits with little trouble. When a crisis hits, however, panic sets in and depositors literally run to pull their money out before it's all gone.)

Given the initial effectiveness of the FDIC, it is ironic that the Roosevelt administration opposed its creation. Its intransigence led to a great compromise of dubious merit. The advocates of deposit insurance, led by Henry B. Steagall (1873–1943), a Democratic congressman from Alabama, joined forces with advocates of the separation of commercial from investment banking, led by Virginia Democratic senator Carter Glass (1858–1946). The compromise, officially known as the Banking Act of 1933, created the FDIC and also, in a section colloquially known as Glass-Steagall, forbade banks from engaging in both investment banking activities (e.g., issuing securities) and commercial banking activities (e.g., accepting deposits and making loans).[74] The major fear was that risky investment banking activities endangered the safety of deposits and hence the solvency of the insurance fund. Of course, that potential problem would have been mitigated if the FDIC had charged risk-based premiums, to wit, if it charged riskier banks proportionally more to insure their deposits.[75] It would later do so but not effectively, likely because the intricacies involved boggled its staff. For a variety of reasons, government regulators have been slow to use market-based signals of financial institution risk taking.[76]

The Gramm-Leach-Bliley Act of 1999 officially repealed the Glass-

Steagall prohibition, about a decade after the Federal Reserve had rendered it a dead letter by allowing bank-holding companies to acquire investment-bank subsidiaries and about four decades after financial innovations and regulatory arbitrage had greatly weakened the "Chinese Wall" separating the two types of banking activity. The law never made much sense because commercial bankers who want to take big risks can do so in numerous ways (e.g., derivatives or speculative loans) regardless of their (in)ability to underwrite securities.[77] Glass-Steagall was thus akin to trying to reduce the murder rate by banning baseball bats but allowing an open trade in assault rifles. Tellingly, few other countries adopted similar prohibitions, and many actually encouraged the development of so-called universal banks that engaged in securities underwriting, loan making, and deposit taking. Some commentators blamed the Panic of 2008 on the repeal of Glass-Steagall, but when pressed most admitted that they invoked the law merely as an example of the need for reregulation. In other words, they did not know what they were talking about.

The new Securities and Exchange Commission (SEC) also had a dubious impact on the US financial system and economy. In order to garner support to create the SEC, politicians greatly exaggerated many of the abuses alleged to have caused the crash and Great Depression. The notorious stock pools, for example, did try to manipulate prices but were only modestly successful in doing so in the short term and completely unsuccessful in the long term.[78] A famous three-hundred-year-old description of the Amsterdam stock market by Joseph de La Vega suggests why:

> The bulls are like the giraffe which is scared by nothing.... They love everything, they praise everything, they exaggerate everything.... The bulls make the public believe that their tricks signify wealth and that crops grow on graves. When attacked by serpents, they ... regard them as both a delicate and a delicious meal.... They are not impressed by a fire nor perturbed by a debacle.... The bears, on the contrary, are completely ruled by fear, trepidation, and nervousness. Rabbits become elephants, brawls in a tavern become rebellions, faint shadows appear to them as signs of chaos.... What is there miraculous about the likelihood that every dwarf will become a giant in the eyes of the bears?[79]

He then detailed a dozen ways in which bears and bulls tried to influence securities prices. The net effect of their machinations, however, was cloudy. Sometimes the bulls won, sometimes the bears won, but their activities often canceled out each other. "Numerous brokers are inexhaustible in inventing involved maneuvers," de La Vega explained, "but for just this reason do not achieve their purposes." Systematic manipulation of the market was impossible, he explained, because the bulls and bears competed against each other, each tugging at the price but ultimately in vain. Also, as rational investors learned the tricks of trading, they came to expect hyperbole, false rumors, sham sales, and the like. Indeed, one of the first popular guides to financial investment, Thomas Mortimer's *Every Man His Own Broker*, explicitly warned British investors to avoid taking advice from professional traders.[80] By the 1730s, if not earlier, many close observers of the markets believed that more or less rational investor expectations of future profits drove most changes in stock prices in the London market.[81] Adam Smith himself argued that "stock-jobbing tricks" would work only "sometimes"[82] and recent econometric research suggests that securities prices in eighteenth-century Britain followed a "random walk," meaning it was impossible to predict when they would increase and when they would decrease.[83] So unless early twentieth-century Americans were a good deal dumber than their ancestors, they too would have quickly learned to avoid market manipulations.

Moreover, early attempts to regulate securities markets in the United States fell afoul of some special interests, such as small banks. In particular, the so-called Blue Sky laws hid a private agenda behind a façade of proconsumer rhetoric. Many unsophisticated investors were fleeced by fast-talking securities sales reps. In the early twentieth century, the US Secret Service estimated that securities swindles amounted to some $75 to $100 million per year.[84] Some companies, like the Aetna Express Company, were outright scams. The officers sold stock directly to the public or used vagrants as brokers, collected the cash, then disappeared. As investors grew warier, scams grew more sophisticated. Some invested in real assets and proudly displayed titles, neglecting only to mention that the lands were barren hilltops in Arkansas worth $5 in total.[85]

Other companies were bona fide endeavors but functioned on the fringes of the law. "Wildcat" insurance and guaranty companies that accepted premiums but didn't pay claims abounded, taking advantage of lax enforcement of the postal fraud laws. As one Chicago police officer put it: "That crime of so despicable a type as the cowardly robbery of the poor through the United States mails should flourish as do the schemes at present overrunning the whole country is a sad commentary on our laws and the machinery of the government for their enforcement."[86] But as the nation's thousand or so "bucket shops" showed, investors could be fleeced in person, too. In such shops, investors could place bets on the movement of commodities and securities prices. If legitimate, the shops provided farmers and other businessmen with an inexpensive way to hedge risks. But many proprietors fled town rather than make big payoffs to their clients.[87]

Other securities were merely "hyped" or "puffed." In other words, their advertising was filled with hyperbole that led investors to overestimate their value.[88] By 1900, quaint old notions about trusting other people and being kind to strangers were giving way under the exploitative weight of "grifters." Advice books warned readers: "Don't take it for granted the stock offered will turn out a great money maker and dividend payer because the promoter tells you so."[89] Investors did learn, but so too did the grifters.

To protect the innocent from security scams and flimflams, the government had to regulate securities issuance, or so politicians claimed. Some states did so simply by mandating minimal acceptable levels of disclosure. A good argument can be made that such laws, if well designed and adequately monitored, could benefit market efficiency by reducing asymmetric information. Other states, however, went even further and allowed government regulators to decide whether or not specific individual securities could be issued in their respective states. The more numerous small banks in a state (vis-à-vis stockbrokers), the more likely that state was to pass the more restrictive type of legislation and the more likely state regulators were to deny issuance applications. Unsurprisingly, the profitability of banks increased in states where Blue Sky regulations severely restricted new issuance. Put another way, state governments allowed banks to limit competition for business loans and consumer deposits under the guise of protecting widows and orphans![90]

Despite that ominous precedent, someone had to take the fall for the Depression and the government was not about to blame itself or the Fed.[91] Securities market participants were the best scapegoats because few people understood what they did and most maintained hoary and deep prejudices against them.[92] Americans, nay, all human beings, innately distrust and envy great wealth. Likely a residue of life in poor, zero-sum economies, where the rich truly became so at the expense of their neighbors,[93] our instinctive repulsion has largely been overcome by education in the rich, positive-sum economies of North America, Western Europe, and East Asia. People in those places, in other words, realize that wealthy individuals and large corporations usually create new wealth, not steal existing property. In a crisis, however, people often revert to emotion or instinct and back politicians and policies that they wouldn't under normal circumstances.[94]

Thus emboldened, the administration forged ahead. Interestingly, Roosevelt placed Joseph Kennedy in charge of the SEC. The first businessman to back Roosevelt for president, Kennedy had made a fortune in unsavory ways, including rum running and bear stock market pools, where groups of wealthy investors engaged in short selling. That made him perfect, Roosevelt argued, because he knew the tricks of the trade and where the proverbial bodies were buried.[95] Maybe so, but Kennedy did not turn the SEC into a very potent regulator. Chronically short of funds, the SEC was a nearsighted and nearly toothless securities market policeman. Unfortunately, investors believed the SEC was bigger, stronger, and smarter than it actually was. So much like the FDIC, the SEC's biggest effect was to reduce private monitoring. Investors began to act like people who leave their doors unlocked when they vacation because they believe the town cop will watch their house and automobile as if they were his own. When they returned home to all of their property, they attributed it to police vigilance rather than blind luck. If robbed, they were shocked and wondered how anything like that could ever happen.

Like the Blue Sky laws before it, the Securities Act of 1933 and its progeny, the SEC, were supposed to reduce asymmetric information between the buyers and sellers of financial securities, like stocks and bonds, by forcing issuers and their investment bankers to register numerous items with the SEC, including:

1. a copy of the issuer's articles of incorporation
2. the use to which the funds will be put
3. the offering price to the public
4. the offering price to special groups
5. the fees offered to promoters
6. the underwriters' fees
7. the net proceeds to the issuer
8. information about the issuer's products, history, and location

9. detailed balance sheets and income and expense statements for the last three years
10. details about pending litigation and legal opinions related to the issue

The financial statements had to be audited by an independent accountant. The issuer was held unconditionally liable for material misstatements or omissions, while its underwriters were held conditionally liable unless they could show that they did "due diligence." Unlike some of the state Blue Sky laws, the SEC did not pass judgment on the worth of the issue, but merely worked to ensure that potential investors had ample and accurate information on which to base their decisions.[96]

Econometric analysis of prices, volumes, and bid-ask spreads (essentially broker-dealer markups), however, reveals that disclosure rules initially did not reduce information asymmetries.[97] Instead, the main effect of the hastily composed and enacted legislation was to aid large, established investment banks, like Morgan Stanley, that relied on the old syndicate system of separate wholesale and retail banks. Newcomers that utilized an innovative integrated (wholesale and retail) structure were effectively shunted aside. The act also mandated that new securities be marketed solely to institutional investors, which also favored the old-line companies over new entrants. In addition, the code's prohibition of discounting was clearly anticompetitive. Most strangely of all, the law actually prohibited the dissemination of information about securities during certain critical windows. In addition to being full disclosure legislation, says Paul Mahoney, the dean of the University of Virginia's School of Law, the Securities Act of 1933 was "equally a secrecy statute."[98] Unsurprisingly, investment banking grew highly concentrated in the 1930s. The largest twenty banks controlled over 80 percent of the new issues market in the latter part of the 1930s. Regional investment banks handled the securities issues of small, regional companies, but once those clients grew to any size, they lost them to New York firms, which managed some 90 percent of the national market.[99]

In sum, on net the SEC did not increase disclosure and may have injured investors by creating a false sense of security. Moreover, it reduced competition in securities underwriting. Glass-Steagall of course did likewise by barring participation by commercial banks. Ironically, then, the market power of investment banks, the so-called bulge bracket ones that earned obese 6 percent underwriting fees for decades and almost ruined the American financial system and economy in 2007 and 2008, stemmed directly from New Deal policies.[100] Roosevelt talked a good game, but when it came to financial regulation he and his so-called Brain Trust were either duplicitous or dupes.

Equally telling, the Roosevelt administration did little to reform abuses in the financial media, like the pump-and-dump schemes perpetrated by trader John Levinson and *New York Daily News* columnist Raleigh Curtis. Levinson bought stock X at $y, then Curtis mentioned the stock favorably in his column, causing its price to leap to $y plus $z, where z was a nontrivial positive number. It was always illegal to lie about a security, and it became illegal to trade on inside information, but anyone can opine about prices with minimal disclosure of his or her own interests. Almost completely unchecked, pump-and-dump schemes and similar shenanigans helped to inflate the dot-com bubble of the 1990s and the mortgage and real estate bubbles of the 2000s.[101]

The motivation of financier Bernard Baruch (1870–1964), who purportedly sold his stocks for gold before the crash on the advice of a beggar but continued to speak favorably of the markets' prospects, remains unclear.[102] Interestingly, however, Baruch later became a member of Roosevelt's Brain Trust and was a major mover behind the ill-fated National Recovery Administration, which I'll discuss below. Even more interestingly, Roosevelt himself had been governor of New York during the final phase of the great bubble and hence was in an eminent position to do something about any wrongdoing. Yet he did nothing.[103]

***

In short, some New Deal bailout programs used up durable resources like land on suboptimal projects. Others did not create clear public goods. Others temporarily stabilized the economy but destabilized it later. Some distorted the financial system for vindictive or self-interested reasons. Perhaps even more destabilizing were clearly deficient programs that were simply wrongheaded, attacking the wrong problems in the right way, or methodologically flawed, attacking the right problems in the wrong way. One doesn't kill zombies with a stake to the heart or sunlight (except *I Am*

Legend zombies) or destroy vamps with a bullet to the brain. But that didn't stop the government from trying to support farm prices, which had dropped precipitously in the latter half of the 1920s, from $1.30 to $0.44 per bushel of wheat and $113 to $29 per bale of cotton.[104] Initially, the government's policy was the height of economic and political folly, destroying crops in the field and six million young pigs fattening for market.[105] The correct policy, of course, would have been for the government to buy the food with borrowed or new money and distribute it to the needy. In subsequent years, US agricultural policy was made only slightly less destructive by paying farmers not to grow crops or raise livestock in the first place. Farmers gladly took animals and acres out of production, cashed their government checks, and increased yields per acre on the rest of their farms by investing more heavily in tractors, fertilizer, better seeds, and so forth. That kept output high and prices low, a fact that even cocksure AAA (not a battery or a rating but the Agricultural Adjustment Administration) bureaucrats eventually conceded. Soon, farmers captured the AAA, turning their ostensible regulators into prisoners who did their bidding in Congress. [106] Unsurprisingly, agricultural subsidies remain with us to this very day, although comedians regularly deride them. My favorite is the following fictional letter to the "Honorable Secretary of Agriculture" from a wannabe nonfarmer:

My friend, Bud, over in Texas, received a check for $1,000 from the government for not raising hogs. So, I want to go into the "not raising hogs" business next year. What I want to know is, in your opinion, what is the best kind of farm not to raise hogs on, and what is the best breed of hogs not to raise?... I want to be sure that I approach this endeavor in keeping with all governmental policies.... I would prefer not to raise razorbacks, but if that is not a good breed not to raise, then I will just as gladly not raise Yorkshires or Durocs. As I see it, the hardest part of this program will be in keeping an accurate inventory of how many hogs I haven't raised.... [My friend, Bud, is very joyful about the future of the business. He has been raising hogs for twenty years or so, and the best he ever made on them was $422 in 1968, until this year when he got your check for $1,000 for not raising hogs.]... Now another thing, these hogs I will not raise will not eat 100,000 bushels of corn. I understand that you also pay farmers for not raising corn and wheat. Will I qualify for payments for not raising wheat and corn not to feed the 4,000 hogs I am not going to raise?... Also, I am considering the "not milking cows" business, so send me any information you have on that, too.[107]

Perhaps the worst of the New Deal's bailouts was the National Industrial Recovery Act. In July 1933, Roosevelt announced the new program, noting that it was designed to increase hourly wages and keep prices up by means of the collusion of government-sanctioned cartels. To induce companies and consumers to join the effort, the administration created a Blue Eagle emblem, a spread-winged raptor clutching an industrial cog in one claw and three lightening bolts in the other, over the phrase "We Do Our Part." Roosevelt explained that "in war in the gloom of attack, soldiers wear a bright badge to be sure that comrades do not fire on comrades. Those who cooperate in this program must know each other at a glance. That bright badge is the Blue Eagle."[108] After the beloved president's speech, the Blue Eagle emblem quickly gained notoriety. Hollywood hotties Martha Virginia "Toby" Wing (1915–2001) and Frances Drake (1912–2000), for example, sunburned the emblem onto their backs, although of course not in blue.

Due to the government's call for consumers to boycott firms that refused to join the NIRA, companies at first clamored to join to enjoy the right to put the eagle on their advertising and products and thus avoid their customers' wrath. The government, however, announced the program before enough emblems were available, so it had to outsource their printing to private companies. It also had to allow exempt companies, like sole proprietorships, to display the emblem so they would not be mistakenly boycotted. It allowed companies that were noncompliant to join and at first did not have a compliance division. Even after its establishment, the compliance division took only 564 cases to court out of the 155,102 complaints it received. Soon, the Lincoln, Nebraska, compliance board quit in disgust. Only about a third of the businesses under its jurisdiction sporting the Blue Eagle faced complaints, but it lacked the resources to force the businesses to comply or to give up their emblems. Soon after, most of the Lowell, Massachusetts, board quit for the same reasons.

The NIRA's laughable execution was surpassed only by the inanely insane economic theory underlying the program. The poor little eagle and the program it symbolized were doomed from the start. As noted above, the biggest problem facing the economy was that wages were already too high. Driving them higher would simply create more unemployment, a far cry from Roosevelt's claim that the Blue Eagle was a "badge of honor... in the great summer offensive against unemployment."[109] The government's reasoning was backward. It believed that high wages created prosperity but in reality, as banker Albert Wiggin noted, "it is not true that high wages make for prosperity. Instead, prosperity makes high wages."[110] Moreover, the price level was almost entirely a function of the money supply, not of market structure. Instead of supporting prices across the board, the NIRA's cartels, in other words, merely caused relative prices to change. They also injured consumers dull-witted or patriotic enough to shop only where the Blue Eagle kept prices of specific goods artificially high. Thankfully, most American consumers and businesses were not so daft. Especially given the program's well-known enforcement difficulties, the public felt justified ignoring emblems and seeking the best bargains. After the initial flurry of activity, the Blue Eagle died quickly and painlessly, at least relative to other government programs, like the seemingly immortal agricultural subsidies mocked above. The Supreme Court drove the final nails into its little coffin by declaring it unconstitutional. The compliance office took up the wrong case and lost big time in the most important court in the land.[111]

Auto manufacturer Henry Ford was the first major public critic of the NIRA, refusing to sign the industry code in August although his company had long since far exceeded the guidelines. Ford was an advocate of efficiency wages, or paying workers extremely well but expecting much from them in return, so he already paid much more than the guideline minimum wage. Apparently, however, he disliked the code's recognition of workers' right to unionize. He called the eagle a "Roosevelt buzzard" and ignored a cartoon showing him cutting off his own nose with a pair of scissors labeled "nonparticipation."[112] Tellingly, the government continued to buy his company's automobiles anyway. American citizens must have followed their Uncle Sam because Ford lost no market share during the Blue Eagle's brief life. Smaller fries began to take heart and stand up to the big blue buzzard, too. In Hagerstown, Maryland, for example, gasoline station–owner Herman Mills publicly fought the NIRA, vowing to take his case all the way to the Supreme Court on the grounds that it eliminated legitimate competition. The government was astute enough to sidestep Mr. Mills but soon fell afoul of the Schechter Brothers, purveyors of kosher chickens in Brooklyn. They bought the birds wholesale, alive, and kept them alive until a customer picked one for dinner, at which point a shochtim would ritually slaughter it if he believed it fit for human consumption. The brothers were also fierce competitors, eager to hold their own against larger rivals by cutting prices when necessary. Those practices, however, ran contrary to the NIRA codes and unusually vigilant inspectors let the Schechters know it. Eventually, the NIRA dragged them into court. Fearful that their very Jewishness was on trial, the chicken men fought like the dickens. They made it to the Supreme Court and won by showing the codes were as un-American as they were unconstitutional.[113]

***

Were it not bad enough that the administration's bailout policies slowed the economic recovery after 1933, its fiscal and monetary policies outright caused the recession of 1937–1938. First, the government weakened the recovery by raising taxes on the rich to extraordinary levels, inducing many of them to join a "strike" of capital, to stop investing.[114] On the fiscal side, Roosevelt insisted on balancing the federal budget. I'm all for fiscal responsibility, but 1937 was probably too soon to reduce government borrowing because businesses, still reeling from ridiculous policies like the NIRA, were not yet ready to fill the void. But probably the biggest shock was the Federal Reserve's reduction of the money supply. The bumbling central bank thought that banks were being too conservative, that they were holding too many reserves and making too few loans. In one of the most tragic non sequiturs in US history, it capriciously raised mandatory bank reserves not once, not twice, but thrice.[115] That, of course, sent the money supply into another nosedive, raised real interest rates, and caused great uncertainty among banks and businesses alike. Unemployment rates soared yet again. (Despite the economic recovery of the mid-1930s, employment levels had yet to recover because businesses retained their most productive workers and had not needed to hire back the dead wood. Also, structural changes in the economy had permanently displaced millions of workers, mostly marginal farmers like the Joads of *The Grapes of Wrath*.) Another depression seemed inevitable.

Fortunately, it never came, and not because of Hitler's insistence on invading Poland. Well before World War II began in Europe and years before Pearl Harbor dragged the United States into the global fracas, the economy righted itself and began to grow once again.[116] The government in a sense "caused" the turnaround by doing the one thing that was sure to help: nothing at all. That's right, nothing at all. Economies blessed with nonpredatory governments, modern financial systems, open-access entrepreneurship, effective corporate management, and appropriately educated workforces naturally thrive. As Glasgow University economist Adam Smith put it in one of his lectures some two hundred and fifty years ago, "Little else is requisite to carry a state to the highest degree of opulence from the lowest barbarism, but peace, easy taxes, and a tolerable administration of justice; all the rest being brought by the natural course of things."[117] Alas, governments these days are rarely content to leave well enough alone. The US federal government's intrusion into retirement and healthcare, which began in a major way during the 1930s and 1940s, turned minor market failures into major hybrid ones. As we will see in the next two chapters, both essentially suffer from a form of Depression depression.

6

SACRED HOAX

Social Security and the
Distortion of Retirement Savings

S ocial Security has often been described as the "third rail" of American politics. (For those unaccustomed to the murky depths of subway systems, the third rail is the electrified one that powers the trains. Touch it and you die.) That is because most Americans now see Social Security as a sacred entitlement.[1] It was here when they started working and paying in and they expect it to be around when they retire. It may have helped out their parents or other close relatives along the way. Or so it may have seemed. What is now a hoary, sacred entitlement was once a newborn, cruel hoax.[2] Social Security became law, as we will see, because of political forces stirred up by the Great Depression. Once in place, it grew to massive proportions, as bureaucracies are wont to do. Ironically, Social Security's sacrosanct status could cause another depression, right about the time of the program's hundredth birthday.[3]

For several generations, the Social Security Administration (SSA) has provided working Americans and their families four types of benefits: death insurance, disability insurance (added in 1956), survivorship payments, and life annuities upon attainment of retirement age. At the program's inception, the two-hundred-fifty-dollar death benefit was enough to ensure a proper, if not elaborate, burial. Today, it is economically insignificant for both the government and the vast majority of recipients, and it would have been eliminated long ago if the government behaved efficiently. It doesn't, so those payments continue to flow. Survivorship benefits go to deceased workers' spouses and their minor children. The retirement annuity is where most of the political action dwells and is what most people associate with Social Security.

At first glance, Social Security seems like a wonderful program designed to help widows and orphans, the old and the infirm. In actuality, it most assuredly is not. It certainly makes payments to those groups but does so at a very high social and individual cost. In fact, were the government subject to its own truth-in-advertising laws, Social Security would be known as Social Screwity because it systematically injures the poor, minority groups with lower-than-average life expectancy, and men, and *it is well known to do so.* For all those reasons, I call the program a sacred hoax, a FUBAR oxymoron if there ever was one. As usual, layers of market and government failures compose the heart of the problem. Other observers have almost picked up on this. For example, law school professors Michael Graetz and Jerry Mashaw write that "for reasons of history, politics, inertia, and simple error, we have constructed a social insurance regime that is riddled with gaps, overlaps, inefficiencies, and inequities. That is how," they add, "programs come to be simultaneously inadequate and unaffordable," or in other words royally FUBAR.[4]

✷✷✷

First came market failure, or at least the perception of market failure. Indubitably, the Great Depression created the economic pressures that led ultimately to Social Security's enactment. As we saw in chapter 5, however, a hybrid failure fomented the Depression. What we have here, then, is a hybrid failure setting in motion events that led to the creation of yet another hybrid failure.

Some authors creatively divine the emergence of Social Security in the United States from social and demographic trends. My erstwhile boss, Thomas Cooley, for example, argues that Social Security arose out of increased life expectancy, a shift from "rural to urban social structures," and industrial productivity increases.[5] Tom was a great dean, but I disagree with him. What mattered was not the location or type of economic activity but rather the composition of business firms. Prior to 1900 or so, most farms and other small businesses were family affairs that responded flexibly to changes in worker status (e.g., lighter or more appropriate duties for the aged or disabled) and economic conditions (e.g., everyone's consumption was cut during recessions).[6] The elderly were protected by law because they tended to own the family firm (e.g., farm, shop, home). In short, security became shakier as people transitioned from being owners or family members of owners to being arm's-length employees.[7]

More important, Tom's and similar models fail to explain why Social Security was a better alternative than private security, perhaps not the private security of the nineteenth century (work until you drop; have the chillun' care for you if you are unlucky enough to have to stop working before you die),[8] but the private security that financial intermediaries began developing in the late nineteenth and early twentieth centuries before the government crushed their efforts: life, health, and disability insurance; annuities; pensions; and mutual funds. Tom and his tribe are in good company. None other than Nobel laureate Joseph Stiglitz claims that the US government had to enact Social Security programs because "private markets for annuities did not work well."[9] In other words, Social Security was necessary because markets failed to provide citizens with essential financial products like life and disability insurance and old-age pensions.

Professor Stiglitz's claim, though oft repeated,[10] is more assertion than fact. By the 1920s, private businesses like life insurance companies and other financial intermediaries provided the major components of economic security, including life annuities, life insurance, and disability insurance. Calls for European-style government pension plans were ignored because they were essentially not needed. Aid to dependent children and workers' compensation, by contrast, did require government intervention, and they were given starting in the 1910s.[11] Ironically, government tax and regulatory policies were to blame for most of the shortcomings and inefficiencies in the private markets for security products.

Before passage of the Social Security Act in 1935, fewer than 4 percent of America's senior citizens received public pensions. The federal government's successful pension program for veterans of the Civil War had largely run its course, although one widow lived until 1998. (Apparently she married an old Civil War veteran when she was very young.)[12] State government programs, although ubiquitous, were niggardly. Most were means tested and required forfeiture of pensioners' estates to the government upon their deaths. Long residency requirements and stingy payments, usually less than ten dollars per month, further limited their impact.[13] In terms of public support for the aged, America lagged behind Germany and other advanced economies but only because America possessed a much more effective system of private security.

The cornerstone of private security was the family. People tried to take care of their own. If they couldn't or wouldn't, their aged or disabled parents, aunts, uncles, nephews, nieces, and cousins ended up as charity cases or in an almshouse or poor farm, where conditions were deliberately depressing.[14] Since the dawn of human history, similar systems had worked tolerably well. Relatives had the greatest incentive to aid the downtrodden and also had the best information about who had fallen on hard times due to bad luck and who was down due to vices like drinking and gambling. By tearing families apart and spreading them far and wide, urbanization and modernization somewhat decreased the availability of information about who was a drunk and who was hit by a tram on the way to church. But they hardly eliminated those incentives and information.

Moreover, those with limited, distant, or unreliable relatives could readily supplement family aid with savings and insurance. As early as the 1820s, surprisingly large sums accumulated in mutual savings banks (MSBs) and building and loan associations, which provided the poor with safe returns, generally between 4 and 6 percent. Many saw as a positive characteristic the necessarily illiquid nature of such accounts because it prevented withdrawals for light and transient causes.[15] MSBs and building and loans generally invested in mortgages and bonds but not stocks. In the 1920s, increasing numbers of workers began to supplement their savings with the direct purchase of equities or investments in nascent mutual funds or investment companies.

Also beginning in the 1820s, Americans could purchase low-cost annuities for a term of years or life from insurance and trust companies. In wasn't until after the Civil War, however, that life insurance became widely available at rates affordable to most American families. Whole-life policies contained a savings component that could be used to fund an annuity if the insured lived to retirement age. Term policies were cheaper but expired with no value if the insured lived through the contract term. By 1900 even society's poorest strata could afford small amounts of so-called industrial insurance at a nickel or two per week provided by huge corporate life insurers or numerous small assessment and fraternal insurance companies. Affordable term group life policies appeared in the 1910s and proliferated widely in the 1920s, when disability riders also became common. At first limited to commutation of premiums, disability riders soon came to include income maintenance clauses.[16]

In the nineteenth century, companies often made ad hoc payments to loyal but superannuated former employees. By the early twentieth century, some companies, especially railroads, public utilities, and metal firms, began to provide workers with formal retirement pensions, some self-administered and others run by life insurers. They proved a good way of attracting and retaining talent, of reducing stealing and other forms of moral hazard, of providing managers with a convenient slush fund, and of combating unions.[17]

Undoubtedly, untoward government regulations hampered the growth of the private security system, especially the insurance component of it. For decades, life insurers had been attacked by the more sensational parts of the mass media, which complained about the allegedly excessive commissions companies paid to insurers' sales agents, the huge assets that the bigger companies amassed (said to be more than entire nations), and humungous salaries that dwarfed those of the president of the United States himself. Particularly galling was the cozy relationship that developed between the big insurers and investment bankers like J. P. Morgan. An in-house power struggle at one of those insurers, the Equitable, garnered enough negative press by 1905 to induce the New York legislature to investigate. Known as the Armstrong Investigation after William H. Armstrong, the chairman of the investigation committee, the real-life force behind the inquiry was Charles Evans Hughes (1862–1948). Later New York's governor and the US Supreme Court's chief justice, Hughes put in a masterfully zealous performance. His probing questions revealed accounting irregularities, repeated attempts to bribe public officials, rampant nepotism, almost dictatorial control of proxy votes, unconscionable levels of risk taking, deceitful sales practices, and outrageously costly marketing methods.

The government's response was terrible and swift. In addition to squelching risky and illegitimate activities (which of course it should have), New York regulators—the country's de facto insurance regulator because its pronouncements were soon widely imitated nationwide—directly killed off innovative policies like tontines (policies that paid windfall profits to the longest-lived policyholders) and strongly advised that stock companies convert to the mutual form. While mutuality (i.e., being owned by policyholders rather than stockholders) reduced abuses and increased public confidence in life insurance contracts, it also turned the industry into a bed of giant sloths. Although some mutuals manage to remain vibrant due to the incentives of their general agents, many remain content to grow larger rather than more efficient. Had joint-stock insurers not been eviscerated by Armstrong and if regulators had put more emphasis on insurer solvency and less on keeping premiums low, disability, group life insurance, and other private security contracts would doubtless have advanced far more rapidly than they did.[18]

The Depression also ravished the private security system. Family structures and private charity broke down just as thousands of banks folded, paying pennies on the dollar to depositors. After the crash, companies abandoned 45 of the 418 pension plans in existence.[19] With help from a loosening of accounting rules most life insurers were able to stand firm. Almost all, however, had to cut back on disability riders due to their abuse by policyholders feigning infirmity in order to receive premium commutations and monthly checks. One claimant, for example, at first claimed to have tuberculosis. When a medical examination proved otherwise, he switched his story, claiming that he either had an undiagnosed throat ailment or neurosis. Similar attempts to scam insurers abounded, and many were successful, at least for a time, which greatly strained insurers' finances. In short, regulatory pressures and intense competition had induced many insurers to grossly underestimate (and hence undercharge for) moral hazard.[20]

The Depression also hurt stock prices and hence stockholders, many of whom (by percentage of all stockholders, not the value of their holdings) were working folk. Ironically, the New Deal exacerbated the situation. FDR won election to the presidency in 1932 based partly on his promise to clean up the US securities industry.[21] He used his inaugural address, the famous one about having to fear only fear itself, to bash financiers:[22]

> Plenty is at our doorstep, but a generous use of it languishes in the very sight of the supply. Primarily this is because the rulers of the exchange of mankind's goods have failed, through their own stubbornness and their

own incompetence, have admitted their failure, and abdicated. Practices of the unscrupulous money changers stand indicted in the court of public opinion, rejected by the hearts and minds of men. True they have tried, but their efforts have been cast in the pattern of an outworn tradition. Faced by failure of credit they have proposed only the lending of more money. Stripped of the lure of profit by which to induce our people to follow their false leadership, they have resorted to exhortations, pleading tearfully for restored confidence. They know only the rules of a generation of self-seekers. They have no vision, and when there is no vision the people perish. The money changers have fled from their high seats in the temple of our civilization.... There must be an end to a conduct in banking and in business which too often has given to a sacred trust the likeness of callous and selfish wrongdoing... There must be an end to speculation with other people's money, and there must be provision for an adequate but sound currency.[23]

And, as we learned in chapter 5, New Deal reforms like the SEC and NIRA negatively impacted the business environment. By attacking financiers and industrial interests, the Roosevelt administration beat down already badly battered stocks. At least one female retiree wrote to Eleanor Roosevelt to complain about the negative impact of her husband's policies on the retiree's remaining net worth. "I had my savings so invested," she wrote, "that I would have had a satisfactory provision of old age. Now thanks to his [FDR's] desire to 'get' the utilities I cannot be sure of anything, being a stockholder, as after business has survived his merciless attacks (if it does) insurance will probably be no good either." The distressed writer was not some rich widow, either, but "an ordinary white collar worker at $1600 per [year]."[24]

The Depression decimated private security, but, had it desired, the government could have aided the industry with tax breaks, improved regulation, and progrowth policies. Republican congressman Charles Eaton of New Jersey stated the choice clearly. "We stand today in this country," he bellowed, "at the crossroads of a great decision... whether we are going to choose American organized industry as the instrument for the solution of these tremendous, far-reaching problems, or whether we are going to... attempt to solve these problems by government."[25] Instead of fixing the private system's problems, however, the government opted to create a ticking time bomb. Social Security was not the worst of all worlds, but in the long run it proved itself badly designed.[26] Even staunch Social Security advocate Grace Abbott admitted that "in attempting to evaluate the Social Security Act, even those of us who are its best friends must admit at once that it did not come into existence as a perfect piece of legislation."[27] Of course what matters to politicians is the short term, and in that regard Social Security was indeed "the bomb"—the good kind.[28]

***

Social Security's origins are dirty. Basically, the government enacted it only to stave off even more destructive legislation. The Depression radicalized some Americans and provided far more with too much time on their hands. The result was a movement that could have destroyed the American economy. The initial perpetrator was an unassuming sixty-seven-year-old physician from Long Beach, California. His name was Francis E. Townsend and his radical plan—which called for the government to pay two hundred dollars per month (about seven thousand five hundred dollars in 2010 dollars)[29] to Americans sixty or older—bore his surname. Born in Illinois in 1867, Townsend moved to California as a young man to farm. Frustrated with the farm life, he turned to medical school, where he fell under the sway of a professor who was an ardent socialist. Townsend led a somewhat interesting life. He served in the US Army medical corps during World War I but stayed in the States. Several entrepreneurial attempts, including a dry ice factory and real estate ventures, failed before the sickly Townsend settled into a cushy government job. In June 1933, however, he was laid off.[30]

The economic motivation of Townsend's plan was to stimulate aggregate demand. To receive the next month's check, seniors had to spend all of their previous stipend within the United States. Saving and employment were forbidden. In addition to rewarding seniors for decades of service to the nation as workers, parents, and homemakers, the payments would create jobs at restaurants, theaters, automobile dealerships, and so forth. The people thus employed would then have money to buy things, putting yet more people to work by inducing businesses to produce more by adding a third shift or building new factories. That would turn depression into elation, by gum! So far, so good, or at least so much better than the NIRA's Blue Eagle. But where would the money come from? Nobody wanted to just print it, as they knew that would eventually lead to inflation and new economic problems. Borrowing would not work either because the sums involved seemed too vast. Besides, borrowing today meant paying taxes tomorrow.

Why not just get the money from taxation then? Ay, there is the mighty rub. How would taking two hundred dollars from a young person and giving it to an old person to spend help the economy? Many intuited that it wouldn't, but then there was some vague talk of a "multiplier," by which it was meant that money changing hands in exchange for valuable goods was better than money sitting idle. It still wasn't clear, however, how taking money from the young person to give to the old one was fair. If giving pensions was such a good idea, the *New York Times* jibed, why not give everyone a pension?[31] Public discourse was confused enough, however, that some people bought into the multiplier idea as well as the notion that employing fewer and less-experienced workers—the direct result of the incentives created by the plan—would somehow be better for the economy.

The question then became what sort of tax to enact. Townsend's answer was preposterous. Don't get me wrong. While there are plenty of goods that governments can provide, including national defense, funding them is problematic because there is no such thing as a good tax. In addition to their redistributive effects, taxes create deadweight loss, a loss to one or more parties that no other party gains, by driving a wedge between sellers and buyers. Taxes can also distort economic activities by creating perverse incentives. (We've already encountered that idea in chapter 2 when discussing the effects of mortgage interest deductions and so forth.) Newspaper pages are so large because at one time newspapers were taxed based on the number of pages, not words or inches. Because of taxes, some architectural styles stress inner courtyards as to minimize the number of windows visible from the street. Households in Czarist Russia were huge because individuals were not taxed, households were. And on and on.

Nevertheless, some taxes are better than others by being less bad. The Holy Grail of optimal tax theory is called the "least bad tax" (LBT), the tax that minimizes deadweight losses and least distorts economic incentives. What Townsend had in mind was more of a "most bad tax." He wanted a national tax on business transactions. Theory and historical experience with a similar tax, the Spanish Empire's infamous alcabala, confirm that such a tax would have created large deadweight losses. It also would have been highly distortionary, leading to massive vertical integration as companies sought to minimize the number of taxable transactions along the value chain. In other words, farmers would have merged with super-markets, food processors, and restaurants; coal and iron miners with steel-makers, automakers, knife manufacturers, and so forth. Already fearful of large companies, New Dealers could not get behind that. Roosevelt, it should be said, denounced Townsend's and similar schemes as "shortcuts to utopia."[32] The force of public opinion, however, could have foisted the Townsend Plan upon the nation anyway.

Townsend was not the only member of the so-called lunatic fringe. Huey Long, Gerald L. K. Smith, Father Charles Coughlin, Father Divine, Aimee Semple McPherson, Upton Sinclair, and thousands of lesser-known lights harbored radical ideas and claimed numerous vociferous followers. Long's Share Our Wealth (SOW) proposal was probably the most dangerous if only because Long, who called himself the Kingfish, was a first-class populist demagogue with almost total control of the resources of Louisiana. Like a giant pig, SOW would eat the wealthy and suckle the common folk with five thousand dollars for a house, car, and radio (although not yet a radio for the car). Townsend was more successful, however, because he added a very strong ally to his side, the almighty dollar. Unlike most social movements, which relied on the time and donations of do-gooders and fanatics, Townsend appealed to his organizers' wallets. The results were nothing short of stunning. At its height, the Townsend Plan, as both the plan and the organization supporting it were known, claimed 2 million members and raised money faster than even the Democratic Party!

Townsend's campaign began in September 1933, just months after he became unemployed, with a letter to the editor of the *Long Beach Press-Telegram* outlining his plan. Legend has it that the sight of three old women sifting through his garbage for scraps of food touched him off. Perhaps he knew he would soon have to do likewise if he didn't act. In any event, the letter was soon followed by an advertisement soliciting support and a barrage of kudos and knocks. Momentum began to pick up when real estate agent Robert Earl Clements began to help Townsend with marketing and organization. The shrewd Clements, who had made and lost a fortune by 1933, was not the social activist type, but his fiancée was and she pressed him, teasing that he would never regain his fortune as long as the economy was in the shit can. As soon as Clements learned that California law allowed nonprofit organizations to earn a profit, as long as profit making was not its main purpose (we would call this a not-for-profit today), he was hooked.

Townsend was the public face of the organization, but Clements was the moving force. In early 1934, Clements hired the plan's first canvasser, a man who went door-to-door soliciting signatures and cash contributions and selling Townsend pamphlets. Additional canvassers were easily culled from the ranks of unemployed salesmen. Paid a commission, they worked long and hard. (I know from personal experience how enticing such a job can be. As a canvasser for NYPIRG circa 1990, I earned 40 percent of my haul plus the satisfaction of feeling as though I was helping consumers and mother New York.) In March, Townsend and Clements started paying themselves two hundred dollars per month out of the canvasser's collections. Townsend had created his own private Townsend stipend, albeit one he had to work a little for. By mid-1934, the organization had divided California into sales territories, hired two commissioned managers to run them, and published the *Modern Crusader* (later *Townsend Weekly*) newsletter. The managers received 2.5 cents per member and 1 cent per booklet. All told, they cleared about five thousand dollars before being forced out because their sales staff hit upon the lucrative expedient of creating local Townsend clubs led by energetic volunteers who did most of the recruiting and dues collection. In exchange for their dues, members received the right to attend weekly meetings, to worship the increasingly famous Dr. Townsend and his plan, and to dream of fat government checks arriving each month.

With those strong financial incentives in place, Townsend, Clements, and their commissioned minions created some very compelling marketing ideas. The Townsend Plan astutely wrapped itself in Christianity, nationalism, and optimism. Modern machines, they argued, made twenty- to sixty-year-olds so productive that it was now possible for children to study and train instead of work and for seniors to retire in comfort. That resonated well with seniors, of course, who Townsend Plan literature referred to as "prosperity agents," but also was music to the ears of advocates of education and working people worried that they might die at their drill presses or with shovels in hand. The Townsendites also avoided alienating anyone by bashing only one group, "habitual criminals." As the stipends would not be means tested, even the wealthy met equal treatment at their hands. Perhaps most important of all, the plan (although not the tax on which it depended) was so simple that it could be grasped by all, even the dullards in Washington.

In January 1935, a bill based on his plan, the McGroarty bill, was introduced in Congress, landing Townsend on the cover of *Newsweek* and touching off a flurry of activity, including a massive petition- and letter-writing campaign on behalf of the bill. To stop Townsend and the rest of the lunatic fringe, Roosevelt's cronies drew up talking points with titles like "Why the Townsend Old-Age Revolving Pension Plan Is Impossible." The plan, they said, was "fantastic," "cock-eyed," and likely to cause hyperinflation à la Weimar Germany. When summoned before Congress to testify, Townsend and even his actuarial experts wilted. Their figures simply did not add up, and the language of the McGroarty bill was exposed as hopelessly vague on key points. Undaunted, Townsend and his crew redoubled their efforts, and in April 1935 they brought in a new bill with tighter definitions, some means testing, and benefits, estimated at forty to sixty dollars per month, tied to the tax haul.

The new Townsend bill posed a palpable threat to the administration's economic security bill. Served a Southern California lemon, the Roosevelt administration made lemonade, whispering into the ears of fiscal conservatives in Congress on both sides of the aisle that a compromise measure must be supported lest something far worse gain traction. Townsend's popularity made clear that the electorate wanted some form of government old-age relief and pensions. Many Americans found Townsend's plan too extravagant, however, so a stingier plan would likely meet the approbation of most voters. That stingier plan, the Social Security Act of 1935, had numerous major provisions including unemployment insurance, aid to families with dependent children (AFDC), and aid for the blind. The two of interest here were Old Age Assistance (OAA), and a retirement annuity that would soon expand to Old Age and Survivorship Insurance (OASI).[33] The assistance began immediately but amounted to less than twenty dollars per month on average and varied greatly from state to state. The annuity program exempted a large portion of the workforce, including agricultural and domestic workers, sailors, and bank employees, and would not be fully implemented until 1942. Until then, it paid only tiny lump-sum death and retirement benefits equal to the worker's contributions plus interest. The program was funded by a 1 percent payroll tax on wages (called the Federal Insurance Contributions Act or FICA since 1939) under three thousand dollars per year with a 1 percent employer match. Designed to accumulate reserves in the Treasury, the tax was initially set to increase to 3 percent in 1940.[34]

Due to the low level of the benefits provided under the act, the Townsendites found themselves down but far from out. Their claim that the aged deserved government pensions vindicated by the passage of the Social Security Act, they continued to press their crazy plan. In 1936, the Townsend Plan merited 402 articles in the *New York Times*, the eighth-most publicity the Gray Lady bestowed upon a social movement organization in a single year during the entire twentieth century. (Only the Black Panthers, the NAACP, the KKK, the AFL, the CIO, the Congress of Racial Equality, and the Anti-Saloon League ever had a more publicity-filled year.) The good doctor's plan was also plugged in theaters throughout the nation. More national radio advertising and the relocation of the plan's headquarters to Washington, DC, also fueled the new wave of enthusiasm. A nationwide push to form new clubs and the creation of a more elite type of club eligible for inclusion in the new Townsend National Legion kept the coffers full. Polls taken in March 1936 suggested that between 42 and 55 percent of Americans favored the Townsend Plan.

Critics counterattacked again, however, by pointing to the large sums earned by Townsend and other top leaders. Clements resigned, as did many organizers when Townsend tried to shift them from commissions to salaries. Townsend then fell in with Gerald L. K. Smith, an outstanding orator laden with considerable baggage, including an alleged quest to become America's dictator. Roosevelt's landslide reelection in 1936, which Townsend had vigorously opposed, spelled additional trouble for the organization. Congress convicted Townsend of contempt, fined him, and sentenced him to thirty days in prison! Townsend's influenced waned, but he leveraged his impending martyrdom astutely enough to receive Roosevelt's executive pardon.

In 1939, continued pressure from Townsend and newer old-age pension advocates, including a Townsend splinter group that went by the name "Ham and Eggs," induced the government to significantly amend the Social Security program. The Supreme Court upheld the program's constitutionality but said nothing about its efficacy, let alone its political appeal or lack thereof. Since its inception, the program had come under attack from the Left, which thought it too stingy, the Right, which deprecated the payroll taxes that funded it, and the Center, which noted that excess payroll taxes inevitably would be spent, and possibly wasted, on *other* government programs.[35] Some feared the fiscal power that the government was amassing. Michigan Republican senator Arthur Vandenburg found it "scarcely conceivable that rational men should propose such an unmanageable accumulation of funds in one place in a democracy."[36] Worst of all, some employers remained noncompliant.[37]

Those criticisms, combined with a desire to restart the economic expansion throttled by the Roosevelt recession, created momentum for reform. In open congressional hearings, numerous proposals were advocated, including a revised Townsend bill that was shot down due to Townsendite bungling. Thanks to its influence, however, Congress ignored calls for disability and health insurance, placing emphasis instead on liberalizing retirement and survivorship benefits, or OASI. Specifically, a sixty-five-year-old wife became eligible to receive half of her husband's benefit, a major increase over the initial allotment. In addition, the spouses and minor children of deceased workers became entitled to monthly stipends and a two-hundred-fifty-dollar lump sum. The resulting legislation was a boon to workers because it delayed the planned payroll tax hike and made them eligible for payments in 1940 instead of 1942. Benefit levels remained far below that advocated by Townsend and other groups, but overall the reforms affected something miraculous, increased benefits and decreased taxes. The miracle worker was the shift to a pay-as-you-go system from the more fiscally conservative, original one. Everyone except the unborn got what he or she wanted.[38]

Following the 1939 Social Security reforms, the Townsend Plan renewed itself yet again and enjoyed some success in the 1940 elections. The horror of Pearl Harbor, however, effectively ended its quest. By 1943, Congress had turned conservative and the economy boomed along with the bombs going off in Europe and the Pacific. Like an old general, the Townsend Plan simply faded away before finally perishing, a mere shadow of its former self, in 1980. With or without Townsend, Social Security would have grown eventually anyway. As a quasi-pyramid scheme, it had to.

***

A pyramid, Ponzi, or chain letter scheme is a hoary type of financial scam wherein the perpetrator pays returns to early investors solely (or mostly in more sophisticated versions) out of the principal payments made by later investors. Any rapidly growing financial intermediary can resemble a pyramid scheme, but only superficially. Bona fide investment companies use their customers' principal to purchase assets like stocks, bonds, and real estate and make payouts based on earned returns. The Ponzis and Madoffs of the world, by contrast, don't invest; they just redistribute and steal. As it evolved, Social Security took a position halfway between a legitimate financial intermediary and a pyramid. Unlike a true pyramid scheme, Social Security is not a fraud designed to enrich the person at the top. Like a pyramid scheme or intergenerational chain letter, however, Social Security was a great boon to the first workers it included, not so lucrative for later workers, and may end up impoverishing millions.[39]

Fraudulent pyramid schemes are generally short-lived, so their mortality is not a big issue. Social Security, by contrast, will soon be an octogenarian. The people at the top of the pyramid have died and no longer receive payments. (Well, except in cases of fraud, but that need not detain us here.) What that means is that instead of terminating at a relatively narrow apex, the top of the pyramid is now quite broad. The pyramid continues to grow at its base but due to the baby boom and large increases in life expectancy, the top of the pyramid waxes ever larger relative to the base. One way to see this is through the so-called inverse dependency ratio, the number of workers (base) divided by the number of beneficiaries (top). In 1940, the ratio was 159 to 1.[40] By the 1990s it had fallen to 3.3 to 1 and will probably sink to fewer than 2 to 1.[41] That's more like an isosceles trapezoid than a pyramid! Another way to track the flattening of the pyramid is to calculate average annual returns, which have fallen to 2.18 percent for women and a mere 0.78 percent for men.[42]

Unlike financial intermediaries, Social Security was founded, continued, and expanded for ideological reasons, not for profit. From its inception, Social Security has rallied those on the Left and disappointed many on the Right. By the 1950s, technical critiques of the system had largely given way to partisan polemics with conservatives like Herbert Hoover arguing that the nation could not afford to expand the program during the Cold War and liberals like union leader Walter Reuther countering that the nation could not afford to *not* fund the program liberally. "In the Cold War," he said in 1950, "we are judged by the peoples of the world on our social performance on behalf of our mothers, our young, our infirm, and our aged.... I urge you not to pass ammunition to our totalitarian foes" by skimping on Social Security.[43] Today, the same partisan rage continues to infect public and even scholarly discourse on the subject, although of course nobody nearing retirement wants to see his or her benefit levels cut.

Also unlike financial intermediaries, Social Security does not really earn investment returns. Surplus funds go into the government's general revenue hopper with the Social Security Trust Fund taking nonnegotiable bonds in exchange. The trust fund is part of the same government that issued the bonds, so even though the bonds nominally pay interest into the fund, the practice is more akin to an accounting shell game than a bona fide investment. The bonds are essentially the government's promise to take money out of taxpayers' right pockets to put into their left pockets.[44] Of course, Social Security does not always run a surplus. It did initially because it taxed all covered workers but paid benefits to very few of them. Over time, however, the ratio between the taxpayers and the beneficiaries deteriorated as taxpayers died or retired more rapidly than new workers started paying into the system. That demographic inevitability required raising the tax rate, which unsurprisingly was politically unpalatable, or finding new workers to cover. In 1950, reforms extended OASI by about 10 million workers, to about 75 percent of the labor force.[45] Benefits were also increased, by almost 80 percent, and payroll taxes increased.[46] By 1953, OASI finally surpassed OAA (Old Age Assistance) recipients in terms of importance.[47] In 1954, however, bean counters foresaw a solvency crisis looming and pressed to broaden coverage again. By the end of Eisenhower's second administration, 90 percent of workers were covered.[48]

The political pressures to expand Social Security after the war were enormous and multidirectional. Tens of millions of workers who paid into Social Security during the war as industrial workers saw their coverage vanish when they returned to uncovered occupations after the war. Southern politicians warmed to Social Security because many young workers, some white but many black, fled the South's increasingly mechanized farms after the war, leaving the region with fewer workers to support the young and the old. That, of course, put stress on Southern families and state coffers that Southern politicians were eager to alleviate with federal programs, such as Social Security. Throughout the land, politicians eager to please veterans without increasing general taxes also saw salvation in Social Security. Finally, inflation put constant pressure on real benefit levels, inducing recipients to lobby for increases. Having abandoned the gold standard to get out of the Depression, the nation had to contend with almost yearly increases in the cost of living, which burdened those on fixed incomes like bondholders and Social Security recipients.[49]

Between its inception in 1935 and the end of the century, Social Security was tweaked, updated, and reformed almost fifty times. By the Nixon administration, Social Security had expanded to its limits.[50] To maintain program solvency or keep up with inflation, taxes had to be raised some twenty times.[51] Unsurprisingly, extensions of the program were generally made in election years while tax increases and retrenchments passed in off-election (odd) years.[52]

The final major program expansion came in 1972. The creeping inflation that had plagued the economy since World War II became more virulent in the late 1960s and early 1970s, severely injuring those on fixed incomes, including retirees, many of whom slipped below official poverty levels. President Nixon opposed benefit increases because he believed that they helped to fuel inflation. Wilbur Mills (1909–1992), chairman of the House Ways and Means Committee and not coincidentally a Democratic candidate for president, countered that a 20 percent increase was in order and that future increases should track inflation via automatic cost of living adjustments (COLA). Mills's proposal passed, but ironically he lost his nomination bid. The 1972 amendments also included Supplemental Security Income (SSI), a form of assistance for the indigent aged, disabled, and blind. It also provided men, like women, the option to retire at age sixty-two in exchange for lower monthly payments.[53]

Combined with stagflation (high unemployment and high inflation), the 1972 legislation caused major fiscal problems. Benefits automatically rose every year due to COLA at the same time that unemployment spelled lower payroll tax receipts. In addition, older workers who received pink slips chose to retire at the earlier ages, further stressing the system. In 1975, the program ran its first deficit. The government responded by threatening to force the final remaining uncovered groups, employees at all levels of government and at nonprofits, to join the system.[54] At that point, something had to give. The pyramid could not grow larger, not without annexing Mexico anyhow, and if the movie *Red Dawn* (1984) is any indication, the fear was that the tanks would be running north rather than south. In 1977, taxes were raised and benefits delayed. President Jimmy Carter claimed that the reforms would put Social Security on a sound financial basis until 2030, but they soon proved insufficient. In 1983, on the recommendation of an independent commission chaired by Republican economist Alan Greenspan (yes, the same fellow who later ran the Fed), the government increased the payroll taxes and the full retirement age, made benefits subject to federal income taxation, and mandated universal coverage. In addition, the amendments meant that those who retired early received less per month than previously and those who retired later would get more than hitherto.[55] Those changes were supposed to fix the program until 2063, but by the 1990s the short-term future of Social Security was again in doubt.[56]

According to some, spending on "entitlement" programs like Social Security and Medicare will nearly bankrupt the federal government, driving the ratings of its bonds to junk status by 2020, or necessitate massive tax increases (on the order of 50 percent higher than their current level) that will push "tax freedom"—the day by which you've paid your annual taxes—from early May to Independence Day![57] In other words, federal spending as a share of GDP will increase to about 50 percent. The Social Security surplus will soon turn to a deficit, so the Treasury will have to start repaying the IOUs it has been handing the Trust Fund for the last several decades. Instead of decreasing federal budget deficits, in other words, Social Security will begin to add to them. To paraphrase policy analyst Charles Schultze (1924–), it's not the wolf at the door, it's the termites in the woodwork.[58]

Tweaking the system, however, threatens massive retaliation on the part of vested interests.[59] Moreover, some argue that "if it ain't broke, don't fix it!" Robert Eisner, for example, says flat out that "Social Security is not broke. It is not going bankrupt. It faces no crisis."[60] Oddly, he later admits that "projections three decades and more ahead are, to use a gentle word, dubious."[61] He is closer to the truth here. Fact is, nobody knows, or can know, what will happen to Social Security in the future. Projections depend upon birth, interest, inflation, labor force participation, and unemployment rates, longevity, age at retirement decisions, and, most crucially of all, productivity growth. If future workers can produce significantly more than earlier ones, the dependency ratio of 2 workers to 1 retiree need not frighten us. Those 2 workers will be able to produce so much that they can support the retiree without working longer hours or cutting into their own consumption.[62]

If productivity does not improve quickly enough, and if current benefit levels are to be maintained, a higher percentage of workers' (ostensibly higher) income will have to go to taxes, with the payroll tax topping out perhaps as high as 20 percent.[63] Since the early 1980s, however, tax increases have run into major political roadblocks and tapping into general revenues would fool only fools.[64] Benefit reductions are equally anathema.[65] The expected inflation-adjusted return on Social Security for the taxpayer is already so pathetically low that any combination of tax increases or benefit cuts threatens a negative average return (i.e., the average worker will get back less than one dollar for every one dollar contributed in taxes).[66] Americans already receive less than they would have if they had invested all their contributions in Treasury bonds, the most conservative investment possible![67]

***

The mere existence of Social Security crowds out private alternatives. Astute insurance agents and investment advisers use Social Security's low benefits base to get a foot in the proverbial door when talking up prospects.[68] Nevertheless, the payroll tax limits what people are able and willing to spend on private coverage and how much they are able to save.[69] After World War II, continued bungling by government regulators also stymied the development of private security. Private annuities, disability and life insurance, pensions, and savings products would all be more highly developed if regulators would have nurtured them instead of treating them as if they were all frauds. Knowledge of investment basics would also be far more advanced than at present.[70]

Spurred by favorable tax treatment for employers and high-wage employees, pension plans and other fringe benefits grew rapidly during and after World War II. Linking retirement savings to employment, however, was a bad policy because employers regularly used pensions to control workers and reduce legitimate turnover.[71] Instead of giving businesses tax breaks for pensions, the government should have given individuals tax breaks for saving for retirement (including paying down the principal on a home mortgage). It eventually did so, with Keough, Roth, and similar plans, but not many people can afford to invest in them after paying into Social Security and employer pension plans. Instead of learning the ins and outs of investing for themselves, many people came to rely on employers or their far-from-unbiased investment advisers. The results have been disastrous at times, especially when employees, usually with employer prompting, have invested too heavily in the stocks of shaky employers like Enron.

Even when properly invested, company pension plans are cagey. There are two main types: defined benefit and defined contribution. Defined benefit plans promise to make specific payments to workers upon retirement and can be administered by insurance companies or trustees. The former are safer but more expensive. The latter is more subject to abuse and often underfunded, enabling the employer to default on its promises if it fails or runs into financial difficulties. In its infinitesimal wisdom, the government from 1942 until 1961 favored the establishment of trustee-administered defined benefit pension plans with its tax policies. During the economic troubles of the 1970s, many of those plans succumbed to self-dealing (e.g., mob union boss Jimmy Hoffa) or company failure (e.g., ugly automobile manufacturer Studebaker). Claiming market failure, the government responded in 1974 with the Employee Retirement Income Security Act (ERISA) and the Pension Benefit Guaranty Corporation (PBGC), a sort of FDIC for private pensions.[72]

Many shrewd employers saw PBGC as a way of dumping their pension plans onto the government while simultaneously aiding their own balance sheets. An explosion of claims, most caused by the government's insurance scheme, resulted. By the early 1980s the government caught on, closed loopholes, and raised premiums and regulatory compliance costs, inducing employers to switch en masse to defined contribution pensions like 401(k)s and 403(b)s. Employers also liked defined contribution plans because they helped minimize pesky problems like rate-of-return risks, accounting uncertainty, administrative costs, weak workers, and long-term employment contracts.

Defined contribution plans, however, are more portable than defined benefit plans. Moreover, they cannot fail because they make no promises. Employees and/or employers contribute to the plan, employees choose how to invest, within parameters chosen by the employer, and employees get whatever their contributions earn. Millions of Americans learned the downside of defined contribution pensions in 2008, when the stock market plummeted, taking their investment portfolios with it. Truth is, those not near retirement age will not suffer due to the bear market, as it will almost certainly be followed by a strong bull market. Those close to retirement should not have had much of their nest egg invested in equities. This is just one of many reasons why we need to improve investment education in the United States. Other ugly aspects of defined contribution plans include hidden fees and kickbacks to employers. Better (though not necessarily more) regulation would help here.[73] (I reject the claims of elitists that most Americans are too dumb, rather than too ignorant, to invest rationally.)[74]

Unfortunately, the government is more adroit at creating additional regulations than at improving existing ones. As anyone who has ever lived in a house with a septic tank knows, more is not always better. Regulation of life insurance, for example, has generally meant more crap. In the 1950s and 1960s, regulators' refusal to allow life insurers to invest in equities stymied the industry's growth.[75] Regulators also saddled insurers with high administrative costs. Some insurers have to keep four sets of books, one for the IRS, one for rating agencies, one for their own planning and incentive compensation purposes, and one for state regulators.[76] In 1988, New York again changed its preferences and began to encourage mutuals, which controlled about half of the industry's assets, to demutualize (become stockholder-owned companies). In 2003, when the demutualization wave finally crested, only three of the ten largest life insurers remained mutuals, and stock insurers dominated the industry. Insurers that demutualized proffered a number of reasons for the change but most stressed the need for improved access to capital markets to support merger and acquisitions activities and product and distribution development. Demutualizing companies also argued that the joint stock form would better allow them to attract, motivate, and retain the best insurance professionals. Critics countered that most demutualizations provide windfalls for managers while on net do little or nothing for policyholders. Moreover, stock companies are rightly considered less trustworthy than mutuals because they have more incentive to engage in sharp business practices.[77]

Unlike businesses in some industries, insurers have not systematically "captured" or co-opted their regulators. That is largely because different types of insurers (stock v. mutual; large v. small; geographically concentrated v. dispersed; and so forth) have different interests. Rather than uniformly aiding insurance companies, insurance regulations also aid (or injure) other stakeholders, including consumers, noninsurance companies, political elites, and the regulators themselves. In addition, insurance regulation is usually complex, relegating consumers and most politicians to the sidelines.[78]

Although some regulations, like the untaxed inside buildup of life insurance, aided insurers, numerous other regulations injured them. Many regulations made little economic sense, forcing insurers to incur costs greater than the benefits the regulations provided. For example, the government-mandated unisex rating is extremely problematic because women live longer than men, men are more likely to be involved in an automobile accident, and so forth. Far from being fair, forcing insurers to charge the same rate for different risk classes injures both the companies and their policyholders, both directly by the implied subsidy and indirectly by weakening the insurer. (Insurance is still regulated by states so some readers may live in states that no longer have unisex ratings.) Regulations also induce insurers to avoid new lines of business, such as banking, for fear of increasing their regulatory burdens yet further. Life insurers long faced regulations mandating investment of their assets in specific categories and even within certain geographical boundaries. Ostensibly enacted to ensure the solvency of the companies and hence their policies, such regulations did not demonstrably increase policyholder safety. Perversely, the tax code subsidized the smallest life insurers, to wit, those with the highest costs and, more important, the highest probability of failing.[79]

Beginning in the 1950s, and worsening in the 1960s and 1970s, life insurers faced disintermediation (removal of funds by customers) pressure on two fronts, reduced sales and increased policy loans. Instead of buying individual whole-life insurance, postwar workers increasingly obtained term coverage through employers' inexpensive group policies. Although coverage was lost when a worker left a job, group policies quickly supplanted industrial insurance. Other Americans bought individual term policies and invested the rest in high-yielding mutual funds. Life insurers, the equity holdings of which were limited by law, found it difficult to compete in an era of unprecedented and persistent inflation. Also, existing whole-life policyholders took out policy loans, the interest rates on which were capped at 5 or 6 percent, invested their borrowings in higher-yielding money market mutual funds, and pocketed the difference. Others lapsed or surrendered their policies for cash. In the group arena, large employers increasingly self-insured simply because it was cheaper to do so than to buy insurance. The Great Inflation also hurt the asset side of insurers' balance sheets because regulation and custom had left them saddled with huge portfolios of long-term fixed income assets that earned little compared to new, short-term investments that better reflected the increasingly inflationary environment.

Life insurers responded to the disintermediation process described above by morphing into financial services firms. They introduced a number of new products like mutual funds into the mix, created interest-sensitive life insurance products (including universal-, variable-, and flexible-premium variable life and variable annuities), changed their investment strategies to increase liquidity in the face of outflows, and cut expenses in myriad ways. Some of them also took on more risk, on both the asset and the liability sides of their balances sheets, hoping that increased returns would keep investors interested in their shares, policies, and guaranteed-investment contracts (GICs). For example, two new life insurers that grew aggressively in the 1980s only to fail in the early 1990s, First Capital and Executive Life, invested heavily in junk bonds financed by the sale of GICs. Others, including Monarch, took different poisons, commercial real estate mortgages and bank loans, but suffered the same melancholy fate.

The government tried to help, too, but inconsistently. For example, ERISA strengthened insurer-provided pension funds by imposing a stringent fiduciary responsibility upon fund managers. But a decade later, the government allowed banks to issue fixed and variable-rate annuities and thus compete against insurers. The SEC and the courts also forced insurers to register some of their newer and more innovative products, like variable annuities, on the grounds that they were not insurance under the Securities Act of 1933. (Unlike a standard annuity, which pays a fixed rate [say ten thousand dollars per year], a variable annuity pays a base rate times some measure of inflation, like the consumer price index. So instead of receiving only ten thousand dollars when inflation is at 10 percent [0.1], a variable annuity holder would receive eleven thousand dollars—$10,000 + $10,000 × 0.1—which of course protects purchasing power.)

Tax treatment of life insurance was uneven, variable, and extremely complicated, even for experts. Generally, tax policy favored group over individual policies because the former, like fringe benefits generally, were untaxed. Millions of individuals bought term and invested the rest, specifically in individual retirement accounts (IRAs), because the tax code ordained it. For various arcane reasons too mind-numbing to detail here, however, some wealthy individuals benefited from purchasing whole-life policies rather than investing in tax-sheltered funds. Due to a variety of technical rules, like the "Menge 10-for-1 adjustment," tax policies hit life insurers particularly hard when inflation and nominal interest rates were high. Companies that sold participating policies were hit particularly hard because tax authorities considered part of their premiums, that part which represented an equity stake in the insurer, a taxable security.

In the end, life insurer responses to disintermediation were only partially successful. Industry assets and insurance in force continued to grow in nominal terms, but life insurers' relative share of savings eroded. Several high-profile scandals (vanishing premium policies; policy twisting; investment churning)[80] and failures in the late 1980s and early 1990s injured the industry's prospects further, both at home and abroad. Since the late nineteenth century, US life insurers had been major players in the world's most important markets, but due to the stresses of the 1970s and 1980s they began to lose ground.[81]

Given the proper regulatory regime, private security—the life, health, disability, and other insurance policies described here, as well as prudent investments in certificates of deposit, stocks, and bonds—can clearly replace Social Security. Private businesses might be able to replace other portions of the government's social safety net as well and even redefine traditional entitlements in more socially optimal ways. It may be possible, for example, to protect people from the risk of having an unsuccessful career. Some are skeptical,[82] but brilliant Yale economist Robert Shiller, the dude who predicted the two most recent financial crashes, notes that more people would take career risks if they could hedge their future income against failure. That, in turn, would endow the world with more rocket scientists, brain surgeons, social scientists, high-quality artists, musicians, and the like. Shiller admits that strong adverse selection and moral hazard would work against private provision of such insurance. In other words, people who knew themselves to be weak and dumb would opt for the insurance while the best and the brightest would not. And people on the margin with a small probability of making it big only if they worked extremely hard would find it tempting to slack and collect the insurance.[83] Shiller, however, believes those problems could be overcome, if only regulators would allow the proper policies to be written. But what if he is wrong for a change? Certainly the government could directly redistribute income from the successful to the poor, allowing the latter to afford the purchase of private security products.[84]

Some scholars and the SSA itself claim that Social Security is America's "most popular and successful social program."[85] (To put the qualifier "most" into perspective, each year since 1977 fewer than half of all Americans polled were "confident" in the system.[86] At the same time, 90 percent "approved" of it.[87] Go figure.) Proponents of Social Security note that in 1959, 35 percent of the elderly "lived in poverty" compared to only 12 percent today, less than the 14 percent rate for the overall population.[88] One problem here, however, is the way poverty is measured. In 1959, the family part of the private security net was still strong in places. Elderly persons who received financial aid from siblings, children, and so forth could well show very little taxable income, making them appear poor. Likewise, "poverty level" measurements rarely consider that retired persons have lower expenses than working-age ones. (Healthcare, the big exception, will be taken up in the next chapter.) They no longer need to buy or maintain work clothes, suffer commuting or lunch expenses, and the like. Moreover, in 1959 many owned their own homes and thus could get by on much less income. The claim that without Social Security "almost half the elderly today would fall below the poverty line"[89] is preposterous because it fails to account for the fact that without Social Security, people could have had much higher levels of savings and that Social Security induces people to retire earlier than they otherwise would.[90]

I do not doubt that Social Security checks have saved some people from extreme want. Before judging Social Security a success, however, we have to ask if those folks could have been saved from want in a less costly manner. None other than Arthur Altmeyer, "Mr. Social Security" himself, argued in 1945 that it would be inequitable to compel workers to participate in a system that costs them more than it would to obtain similar benefits on their own.[91] Proponents note that Social Security's overhead costs amount to only 0.6 to 0.8 percent of taxes collected, far less than the insurance industry's 12 to 14 percent expense ratio.[92] But such a comparison is far from fair. For starters, Social Security is compulsory, so it has no significant advertising, marketing, or sales costs. Moreover, collections are handled through the Internal Revenue Service and disbursements through the Treasury. Most important of all, the quality of Social Security's benefits is extremely low. In fact, about the only advantage it has over private security is COLA.[93] Of course, cost of living adjustments are necessary only because the government has decided to institutionalize inflation.

For starters, the percentage of earnings that OASDI replaces for retired workers has varied considerably over time. In 1940, the average beneficiary received 27 percent of his preretirement income from Social Security. By 1949, that figure had fallen to 16 percent before rebounding to about 35, where it held relatively steady until 1970. Due to the effects of inflation and COLA, the percentage grew rapidly in the 1970s to a high of 54 percent in 1981. Since then, the percentage has fallen back below 40 and is projected to reach a mere 28 percent in 2030.[94] These swings make it difficult for working people to predict their future retirement income and suggest why many younger Americans think the figure might drop to insignificant levels or even zero by the time they retire.[95]

Despite numerous failed attempts to incorporate disability insurance (DI) into Social Security in the 1930s and 1940s, Congress in 1956 forced the Republican administration of Dwight Eisenhower to implement a program. The political story of DI's emergence is almost as sordid as that of Social Security itself but far less colorful. Our lawmaking process is often akin to that of sausage, to wit, something you might want to consume with onions and peppers on a hard roll but never witness being manufactured from sundry pig parts.[96]

Social Security's DI program was weak in two major ways. First, decisions about who was disabled or not were left to state-level bureaucrats beholden to state political interests. The likelihood of receiving benefits therefore varied greatly over place and time. Some states were more liberal than others; all were more liberal when state coffers were flush. Yet payments were uniform throughout the country, despite significant differences in the cost of living. Second, Social Security's disability coverage was of the extremely limited "any occ[upation]" variety, rather than the much more valuable "own occ[upation]" type offered by private insurers, many of which took valuable lessons away from the beating they had taken during the Depression.[97] Any occ policies pay off only if the injured worker cannot perform any occupation, while an own occ policy pays if the worker cannot perform his or her previous occupation. A surgeon who lost one hand in an automobile accident, for example, would not receive payment under an any occ policy because she could still do other work, but she would receive compensation under an own occ policy.[98]

Initially, payments to children of dead, disabled, or retired parents stopped at age sixteen, or eighteen if enrolled in school full-time. In 1965 the age was extended to twenty-one for full-time students, but in the early 1980s was rolled back to eighteen.[99] That was fine in an era when most people did not go to college but is woefully inadequate today and points to one of Social Security's biggest weaknesses, that it does not create assets that can be bequeathed to heirs. Term life insurance, by contrast, can be used to fund a payment stream that will see children through college, graduate school, and indeed their entire lives, not just high school. Unlike Social Security payments, which have been indexed to inflation since 1972,[100] money invested in stocks and bonds can lose market value. When their owner dies, however, the investments persist and can be given to a spouse, children, and grandchildren, or charity. When a Social Security recipient dies or attains age eighteen, as the case may be, his or her benefits cease. That serves to keep the poor impoverished, and here is why. Social Security payroll taxes now (2009) amount to 15.3 percent of wages up to $106,800.[101] (Technically, that is the self-employment rate. Employees pay half of that, with a full employer match. Economists agree, however, that in most situations employees pay the full amount of the tax, half through the explicit deductions that appear on their pay stubs and half through a lower wage.)[102] That is a very regressive tax, meaning one that falls more heavily on the poor than the wealthy. And there is no way to reduce it via tax deductions. For many, having such a large amount of their paycheck taken away means that they cannot afford any private security, including retirement savings or life or disability insurance. When they die, they have little or nothing to pass on to the next generation.[103]

Were that not bad enough, Social Security is not actuarially sound. Everyone pays the same tax, or "contribution," even though each individual represents very different risks. That sounds fair, but is as far from fairness as one can get because payouts are based on longevity, fertility, marital status, and the pattern and length of lifetime earnings.[104] Basically, individuals more likely to die young (e.g., poor, sickly, male, black) in effect subsidize those who are more likely to die old (e.g., rich, healthy, female, white). Married or single, individuals pay the same sum into Social Security, but the married workers get much more out of it, in the form of survivors' insurance and spousal benefits. Social Security also favors couples who have children later in life, when mortality and morbidity rates are higher for all groups of people. Were it not for disability insurance and, especially, the progressive nature of the benefit formula, which ensures that the poor receive a higher percentage of their contributions than the rich do, the intragenerational redistribution would be even greater.[105] The intergenerational "fiscal child abuse" features of the program have already been noted above (the stuff about the quasi-pyramid scheme aspects of the program).[106]

Unfortunately, few people have studied these important distributional issues. Advocates of Social Security generally ignore them completely, preferring instead platitudes about Social Security being "social insurance ... meant to provide at least a minimum standard of support for all, regardless of initial station or life's vicissitudes."[107] But how can a program that systematically takes from the poor to give to the middle class be considered social insurance? After all, social insurance is supposed to provide "income security" and "insurance for people who could not otherwise afford it."[108] Social Security is not "social" in that sense nor is it "insurance" in any meaningful sense of the word.[109] Our retirement system is almost as FUBAR as our healthcare system!

7

HOUSE SCRUBS
Hypercostly Healthcare and Insurance

Is the healthcare industry more like *House* or *Scrubs*? In the Fox medical drama *House, MD*, Hugh Laurie portrays Dr. Gregory House, a cynical, drug-addicted, and nearly friendless medical genius. In a typical episode, House and his team must diagnose and treat a critically ill patient. They err at first, causing complications that nearly kill the patient. But then, in a brilliant leap of insight, House discerns the real problem and swiftly and surely restores the patient to health. Everybody lives happily ever after, or rather until the next episode again demonstrates the power of modern American medicine to cure even the strangest maladies.

Scrubs, by contrast, is a medical drama-comedy. The title is a double entendre: scrubs refers to the distinctive clothing donned by medical professionals as well as substandard individuals (who, I've repeatedly heard, find it difficult to get any love). The long-running show stars Zach Braff as John Dorian (J. D.), an intern at Sacred Heart Hospital whose mental observations/narrated voiceovers provide the show with most of its funny moments. Braff and his fellow interns do not kill many patients—that would not be very funny—but their incompetence is often apparent. In episode 3 of the first season, for example, J. D. feared that a fellow intern accidentally left a surgical instrument in a patient struggling with a post-op infection. It turned out, however, that J. D. was at fault for giving the diabetic patient insulin before he ate, causing a dangerously large drop in his blood sugar. The series also pokes fun at doctors' so-called bedside manners, which can be atrocious. That is an important issue, as numerous studies show that the manner of care is an important component of outcomes.[1] For example, a close family friend in intensive care recently burst into tears when two thoughtless doctors discussed his low probability of survival within easy earshot. Maybe they thought he was too drugged to understand or maybe they just didn't care. Either way, they were both right and wrong, right that the family friend was doomed but still in the wrong.

The US healthcare industry, it turns out, is just like those doctors and a combination of both shows, often technically astute but overall deeply flawed. Brilliant, if somewhat eccentric, doctors have concocted seemingly miraculous cures for a wide variety of ailments. At the same time, however, many doctors and other healthcare professionals behave like clownish scrubs who render indifferent service at high prices. The world's fanciest medical technology is available, but only to some. America's medical system has put the kibosh on AIDS, rendered many types of cancer survivable, and helped highly premature babies not only to stay alive but to thrive. Yet Americans still die of simple infections, myocardial infarctions that could have been prevented with aspirin, and routine diseases discovered too late because people hesitate to visit doctors. "Just how good is American medical care?" three researchers recently asked. "Sometimes excellent," they concluded, "but much more uneven and unexceptional than many once thought."[2] Like the chapter title says, House Scrubs.

An episode from my own life exemplifies these paradoxes. On April 14, 2008, I was at a book talk and reception in Manhattan. At around 7 p.m., my lower abdomen didn't feel so good, kind of bloated and tight. Thinking I had scarfed down some bad sushi, I excused myself and headed home to Philadelphia, only to get stuck in a massive construction-related traffic jam. (Surprise, surprise.) By the time that I got home, my wife, an RN, was already dozing. Exhausted, I mentioned my stomach ailment and slipped into bed. Over the course of that tortuous night it dawned on me that my growing pain was more than a little fishy. I waited until the kids were off to school before telling my wife I had appendicitis. She agreed and whisked me off to my GP, who quickly concurred.

So far, so good. The emergency room was next. I was quickly admitted.

Then something horrible happened: the hospital discovered that I had too much insurance. That's right, too much insurance, the opposite of having not enough. When a patient doesn't have enough insurance, hospitals and other providers can refuse treatment (except in life-threatening situations). When a patient has too much insurance, hospitals are happy to treat and treat and treat, and that is exactly what happened to me. Specialist (ka-ching!) after specialist (ka-ching!) came in, prodded my abdomen, and asked me more or less the same set of questions. I didn't complain because I was all hopped up on dilaudid (ka-ching! but worth every penny). Somebody got the bright idea (ka-ching!) that I might be suffering from diverticulitis instead of appendicitis. Before the surgeon could operate, therefore, I would need a CAT scan (ka-ching! ka-ching! ka-ching!). My appendix, however, had other ideas. It decided to burst while I was in the scanner. I started foaming at the mouth and suffered febrile convulsions, but luckily the local version of House arrived and took command. He stabilized my condition, removed what was left of my appendix through three tiny incisions, and gave me some drugs that prevented infection. A few days later I was out of the hospital and a week or so after that I returned to my regular teaching schedule.

Getting fixed up so fast was great, but almost dying due to a surfeit of insurance and the seemingly endless parade of scrubbish specialists was indicative of the FUBAR that has long pervaded the US medical establishment. The growth of so-called medical tourism—uninsured or under-insured Americans traveling abroad to have major medical procedures to save money—is rampant and hence far more troubling. Nobody knows how many Americans are going to India and similar destinations for healthcare services, but estimates vary from an eye-popping seven hundred fifty thousand to a still disturbing sixty thousand at the conservative, McKinsey-end of the spectrum. Yes, both figures are per year. Some of the tourism remains internal, to low-cost areas like Sioux Falls, South Dakota. The main reason that places like Sioux Falls and India prevail is that competition for limited patient dollars keeps efficiency high without eroding quality. In such environments the benefits of new technologies, procedures, and business forms are constantly weighed against costs. In much of America, however, benefits consistently trump cost considerations, driving prices ever upward.[3]

The decline of American healthcare is a hoary, hybrid history intimately intertwined with insurance. Before the twentieth century, doctors were little more than quacks who probably killed as many people as they helped by randomly employing time-tested techniques like bloodletting and mercury purges. Understandably, most people self-medicated with sundry snake oils, patent medicines, or just straight booze. Medical expenses were incurred infrequently and were rather low (you get what you pay for). Wages lost during bouts of sickness were approximately four times higher than hospitalization and other medical costs. Health insurance as we think of it today was therefore a distant concern. Before about 1920 or so, what most working people craved was insurance for lost wages, not for their medical treatment.

In the late nineteenth and early twentieth centuries, however, medicine advanced by leaps and bounds due to the use of new drugs and surgical techniques. For the first time in history, boasted Harvard biochemist Lawrence Henderson in 1910, a random patient with a random ailment meeting with a random doctor enjoyed "a better than fifty-fifty chance of profiting from the encounter."[4] Demand for medical services therefore increased. At the same time, the American Medical Association (AMA) limited the available supply of medical services. Formed in 1847 but not formally incorporated until 1897, the AMA sought strenuously to professionalize doctors, which meant raising the average quality of those practicing medicine above the level of barbers while simultaneously restricting their supply. Restricted supply plus increased demand of course spelled higher prices. By 1935, medical expenses outstripped lost wages by about $1.75 to $1.00 and today vastly overshadow them.[5]

Americans responded to those higher prices in a variety of ways, including self-help, charity, mutual cooperation, and formal private insurance. Combined, they worked quite well until government policies suffocated the first three and badly mutilated the fourth. The Great Depression pushed healthcare and health insurance toward FUBAR. But World War II, or rather the Stabilization Act of 1942, which froze wages but gave employers large tax breaks for offering employees fringe benefits like pensions and health insurance, shoved it down the slippery slope.[6] Aside from Hitler's refusal to retreat from Stalingrad (thankfully!), the tax deduction was the biggest bungle of 1942. The persistence of the deduction was perhaps the biggest mistake of the second half of the twentieth century, after the communist experiment. Simply put, employer-based insurance decouples cost and treatment. In other words, those who use healthcare do not have to pay much for it, or for their insurance, either. That, among other factors, allowed costs to run amok at 7 or 8 percent per year. Employer-based insurance is also the leading reason why millions have been living without any insurance at all. Insurers partially combat adverse selection, the fact that sick people seek insurance more readily than healthy people, by excluding preexisting conditions. That tactic, combined with the tremendous amount of job churning that occurs in the United States, means many were doomed to lose coverage.

Today, the United States spends far more on healthcare than any other nation, over $2.25 trillion or some 17 percent of GDP. Americans spend as much on pet healthcare today as they spent on themselves just fifty years ago, adjusted for inflation! Americans are on average less satisfied with their healthcare, however, than people in scores of other countries. Tellingly, those who are currently satisfied with the level of care they currently receive expect to be much less satisfied in the future. The best US medical practices are the best in the world, but the average level of care is surprisingly low, with fewer than half of patients receiving world standard "best practices" treatment.[7]

Meanwhile, almost everyone is paying more than ever before for basic care. "Health security" has long been in decline: by 2009, some 50 million Americans had no insurance coverage at all, tens of millions more fretted about losing their coverage, which was only as secure as their insecure jobs, and millions more were inadequately covered.[8] Healthcare costs loomed large in personal bankruptcies, imposing high costs on everyone by raising lending risks and hence borrowing costs for a huge segment of the American population.[9] Even more disturbingly, life expectancy lagged behind that of Japan by almost half a decade and that of most other rich nations by several years. Yet Americans spend more and more on healthcare each year; the average of $6,200 in 2000 jumped to $9,100 just five years later. Worst of all, the huge Health Care Reform Act of 2010 will probably allow costs to continue to spiral upward. To tame the ravenous beast of medical care inflation, we must track it back to its birth lair.[10]

✳✳✳

Before government, there was charity, self-help, mutual cooperation, and private insurance. By the 1920s, America's cities were home to over one thousand free health clinics, called dispensaries, many of which were largely funded by charities.[11] Prudent workers maintained savings accounts large enough to see them through short periods of illness. Employers and co-workers voluntarily aided those who missed weeks of work but recovered before they became eligible for long-term disability. As companies grew larger and more impersonal and direct medical costs began to exceed the opportunity cost of lost wages, mutual cooperation became more organized. It took two major forms, fraternal organizations and industrial sickness funds, some of which were mutual benefit associations or establishment funds associated with particular employers and some of which were sponsored by labor unions.[12]

Circa 1900, more Americans belonged to fraternal associations than any other type of voluntary association, with the possible exception of churches. In addition to coordinating social functions like drinking, fraternals provided sickness insurance to between 10 and 30 percent of adult males. Both types of industrial sickness funds combined to cover another 15 to 25 percent of the workforce. Uncovered workers tended to be poor, nonunionized, and either very young and healthy or very old and sickly. (In recent decades, by contrast, many of the uninsured simply did not have jobs that offered an insurance benefit. They also tended to get less and lower-quality medical attention than insured persons.)[13] While not covered by formal insurance, all were protected to some degree by personal savings, aid from friends and family, and formal charity networks. They were, in other words, self-insured.[14]

Far from being a quaint vestige of simpler times long gone by, mutual cooperation provided powerful mechanisms for solving the two key economic problems of insuring health, adverse selection and moral hazard. Adverse selection occurs when only sick or sickly people purchase health insurance. Moral hazard takes place when healthy people claim to be sick in order to collect insurance benefits. Mutuals mitigated both forms of asymmetric information by exploiting the social and informational cohesiveness of various community, social, and work groups. They minimized administrative costs and adverse selection by recruiting new members and handling paperwork themselves. By personally tending to sick members, they could provide in kind kindnesses while simultaneously discouraging shirking. People who would think nothing of defrauding a distant, faceless insurer (be it a for-profit corporation or a government) would never even consider taking advantage of their friends, neighbors, and co-workers, partly from respect for them and partly from the knowledge that they would be relatively easily caught and severely punished, if only socially. Moreover, the benefits that mutuals paid were admittedly "modest." That reduced the temptation to shirk and minimized losses when the inevitable scoundrel slipped through the cracks here and there.[15]

The greatest strength of mutual health insurance, however, was also its greatest weakness. Small size allowed fraternal associations to mitigate asymmetric information but left them vulnerable to local shocks, including contagious diseases, natural disasters, and the like. Even in the best of times, most appeared financially shaky because they were pay-as-you-go schemes with dues assessed and paid as needed. Much like Social Security, they were essentially quasi-pyramid schemes that did not accumulate significant financial reserves. Unlike Social Security, however, the schemes were purely voluntary, so membership could quickly collapse if calamity struck or the average age of the group frightened away potential young newcomers. By the Great Depression, increased regulatory scrutiny led directly to their relatively rapid demise.

Union sickness funds and mutual benefit associations proved more robust. Beginning in the Civil War, industrial sickness funds relieved workers of the uncertainties, unfairness, and free riding associated with informal "pass the hat" assessments. At first, most were run entirely for and by workers, but over time management began to pitch in with cash contributions and administrative assistance. The funds, many businesses learned, improved worker productivity, reduced workplace accidents, and slowed turnover without creating dreaded "job-lock" or insufficient turnover. Like their workers, moreover, managers preferred making a single contribution to an association "rather than to respond to a series of small solicitations" for aid from employees.[16]

Compelling workers to join was either illegal or imprudent, so the key to success was to set the benefit level just right. If too low, workers saw little point in joining. If too high, workers could not afford to join. Benefits at 50 to 67 percent of pay were typically in the right range, especially if the fund kept costs down by denying benefits for the first month of membership, limiting benefits to a duration of thirteen weeks, and withholding benefits for the first week in case of sickness (but not for accidents, which were much more difficult to fake). Those restrictions of course limited adverse selection and moral hazard, as did the practice of hiring association doctors to verify the claims of workers' and their doctors. Like other people (and canines), doctors tend not to bite the hand that pays (feeds) them. By 1890, sickness funds numbered over five hundred nationwide, mostly in the industrial belt of the Northeast and Midwest, precisely where they were most needed.

Recognition that medical care reduced the length of disability increasingly drew industrial sickness funds into providing medical benefits, too, including well visits, vaccinations, inoculations, and other prophylactic health services. Mutual aid societies continued to thrive into the 1920s. By the 1930s, hundreds of sickness funds, most in companies with one hundred or more employees, provided benefits to millions of employee-members. The institution faded during the 1930s and 1940s, however, due primarily to the emergence of sick leave, a fringe benefit paid directly by employers to sick workers, and improvements in commercial insurers' group health insurance actuarial tables. More accurate tables meant that premiums could be slashed without endangering the insurer's solvency or profits.

For-profit health insurers have been around in various forms since the mid-nineteenth century but initially found it difficult to compete against mutuals at the low end of the market because they could not as cheaply mitigate runaway adverse selection and moral hazard. The advent of group policies, so-called because they covered groups of workers, helped them to combat adverse selection and decrease administrative costs while simultaneously building impressive-looking actuarially calculated reserves. That brought them into favor with regulators during the Depression, which otherwise hurt for-profit insurers by causing high lapse rates. A game similar to cutthroat euchre broke out. Typically, the card game euchre, a faster and dumbed-down version of bridge and pinochle, is played by two teams of two players. In the cutthroat version, it is every player for herself, but that usually means the two players with the lowest points temporarily team up against the player then in the lead. So it was with health insurance. Socialists (yes, there was once a thriving Socialist movement in America) and other proponents of government-based systems and for-profit insurers bashed mutuals (fraternals and industrial sickness funds) for being inexperienced rubes. The mutuals and Socialists, however, joined forces against the greedy for-profit insurers. In the same breath, the private mutuals and for-profit insurers deprecated the notion of government healthcare. Compulsory or universal government plans were rife with moral hazard, but voluntary ones, for-profit or mutual, suffered from adverse selection. With the main players thus preoccupied, a fourth player joined the game and won a few hands but lost the match.

With industrial sickness funds waning, insurers stagnating, and government-based medicine stuck in the mud, prepaid hospitalization and physicians' plans found fertile ground. For patients, prepaid plans served primarily as a hedge against rising medical costs while for the medical providers they reduced price competition and provided steady income. Had the government not interceded, prepaid hospitalization and physicians' plans could have created a system where the incentives of patients/insureds and medical providers would have been very closely aligned. The biggest problem with healthcare is that patients pay to be seen, not to be made well, so doctors have incentives to keep patients coming back for additional treatment. Every American probably knows some poor soul like my father, who has been under the care of various doctors for over three decades. The better ones alleviate his pain, but nobody has set him right for any extended period. Why would they want to?[17]

The system that most closely approximates a pay-for-health plan is, not coincidentally, among the best in the world. The Veterans Health Administration (VHA) should not be confused with the Department of Defense, which was in charge of the scandalously awful Walter Reed Medical Center exposed by the *Washington Post* in 2007. Although a government entity, the VHA runs fairly efficiently and, most important for the argument here, provides a much higher level of care than elsewhere in the United States or, indeed, the world.[18] The key, I contend, is its budgeting process. If it fixes up a vet lickety split, the ex-soldier puts less strain on its resources, which makes life easier for VHA administrators and staff. The incentive is not as strong as direct cash payments would be so the VHA is still far from perfect, but unlike most medical care providers it's not in the business of, well, ensuring future business. (The big downside is that if the VHA's budget becomes seriously underfunded, a real threat given the politics surrounding it, the quality and quantity of its care could depreciate rapidly.)

When doctors and hospitals turn insurers, as they did with prepayment plans, they suddenly want to cure patients as quickly and inexpensively as possible. If the contract is such that patients get to stop making payments when they are sick, the medical community will strive to keep them from falling ill in the first place! Under such a contract, doctors and hospitals would essentially guarantee their own work, decreasing the need for potential patients to uncover information about who the "good" ones are. Under prepaid plans, any doctor or hospital in business for any length of time must be good. Prepayment plans would also decrease the need for medical malpractice (medmal) insurance. High medmal premiums of course increase medical costs directly by raising doctors' costs, but they also do so indirectly by inducing doctors to order tests of dubious necessity simply to cover their exposed posteriors. The people ultimately reamed by America's hyperactive medmal system are the patients.[19]

Unfortunately, an incentive-compatible prepayment system was not in the cards in the 1930s (or in 2010). Bolstered by tax and regulation exemptions, prepaid plans instead became the famous Blue Cross and Blue Shield system.[20] Blue Cross and Blue Shield carried the day in the 1930s, but after World War II for-profit health insurers, armed with new tax breaks and improved actuarial tables, counterattacked. Enjoined to charge the same premium within a given community, the nonprofit Blue Cross and Blue Shield plans faced significant adverse selection after commercial insurers began to offer low premiums to actuarially healthier segments of the population. Essentially the for-profits siphoned off those most likely to remain healthy, leaving those most likely to file big claims with the Blues. Although the Blues dominated some local markets into the 1990s, commercial insurers at the national level outstripped them in terms of the total number of people insured by the early 1950s. The Blues suffered yet more in the 1970s and 1980s because they adapted too slowly to inflation and other rapidly evolving market conditions.[21]

As noted above, World War II provided a tremendous boost to employer-provided health insurance because it was not subject to wartime wage controls and was a boon to both employers, who could deduct insurance premiums as business expenses, and employees, who did not have to pay taxes on the benefits received. Also recognized was the fact that employer-provided insurance limited adverse selection by pooling risks by employer, many of which employed workers with a broad range of ages and with a wide variety of healthcare needs but few extremely unhealthy individuals. After the war, the tax exemptions were strengthened and unions won the right to negotiate benefit packages on behalf of their members.

Private insurance waxed further as the Murray-Wagner-Dingell bill of

1949, a measure that would have provided all Americans with nationalized health insurance, waned. By 1958, 75 percent of Americans had some form of private health insurance, much of it provided via employers. Many of the uninsured were elderly or poor, leading to the passage of Medicare and Medicaid legislation in the 1960s. Insurers could hardly complain about the government serving a market that they neglected. Later extensions of Medicaid competed with private insurance, however, with each dollar of government aid shrinking private markets by an estimated fifty cents. The awkward combination of employer-provided group insurance and government social insurance remains in place to this day, even after passage of the Obama administration's reform bill in March 2010.[22]

***

Before healthcare can improve (higher-quality care at the same cost or the same level of care at lower cost), health insurance must be reformed. The FUBAR nature of healthcare is directly linked to the perverse incentives created by employer-provided insurance. Instead of shopping around for the best medical values available in their area, insured people tend to visit those offering the highest level of care. Their cost, often just a $5 or $10 co-payment, is the same whether they see a Dr. House or a Dr. Value, so they see whichever Dr. House accepts their insurance, even for a case of the sniffles. That induces most Dr. Value types to try to look more like House, very expensive and hence ostensibly highly skilled. (Although as noted above many do not actually provide anything close to House-level service.)[23] Because of that dynamic, insurance premiums continually rise faster than inflation. Nobody, however, has an incentive to change his or her behavior unless everyone changes. In other words, a classic free-rider problem exists: premiums will increase whether or not any given individual decides to search out the best value rather than the best treatment. By shielding people from the ultimate costs of their decisions, both employer-provided group insurance and social insurance fuel rising healthcare costs.[24]

The big question, therefore, is how should health insurance be restructured? Should the government become more involved or less? Or rather how should the government's role in health insurance change? Unfortunately, government bureaucracies tend to rely on the so-called garbage-can method of decision making. When faced with a crisis, whether a real one or one concocted for political purposes, government agencies leaf through years and sometimes decades' worth of previously rejected plans submitted by sundry professors, think tanks, special interest groups, utopians, and other do-gooders. By mysterious processes that may include the study of chicken entrails and random selection, they push one or more proposals forward for legislative consideration. Unsurprisingly, the results are almost invariably unsatisfactory.[25]

"Major reform of American health insurance has once again risen to the top of the political agenda," wrote healthcare policy guru Jacob S. Hacker in the introduction to his 2008 volume, *Health at Risk*.[26] He was right. One of the first major initiatives of the Obama administration was to proffer a major healthcare reform bill. Unfortunately, the proposal was shrouded in misinformation. From the Right came shrill and, frankly, crazed claims of death panels, Nazism, and the like. From the Left emanated the much more reasonable-sounding claim that Obama's plan was designed to create a dual system based on a government insurance option. The problem with that claim, of course, was that the government option would have offered subsidies as well as insurance. Private insurers therefore complained that they would not be able to compete because the government would undercut their premiums by taking some of the costs of the program from the tax till.

The overall level of the public discourse remained pitifully banal, but after many harrowing twists and turns, including the demise of the public option, reforms were finally passed into law. The legislation, however, is the bastard child of sundry sordid political compromises and maneuvers. As such, it is loved by few and loathed by many, Right and Left. The fact that many of its provisions will not take effect for years isn't helping to win over those of us who are happy to accept anything that actually reduces costs or raises quality.

Many Americans still want some form of government-provided universal healthcare. The forces of history, however, remain arrayed against them. Five times in American history, just after World War I, during the Great Depression, after World War II, in the 1960s and 1970s, and again in the 1990s, politicians from the Left (and once even "Tricky Dick" Nixon) pushed for the establishment of a compulsory, publicly funded national healthcare system. Five times they failed.[27] National healthcare plans were rebuked each time by a coalition of politicians ideologically opposed to the extension of government powers (Republicans and conservative Democrats from the South), doctors fearful of losing their power to price discriminate (to charge those with higher incomes more for the same services), insurers threatened with extinction of major lines of business, unions that fretted loss of prestige and control over workers, profit-minded business managers, workers satisfied with the status quo, and the almighty AMA.[28] The AMA was so adamant in its opposition that it reportedly blocked passage of the Social Security Act due to a single sentence calling for the SSA Board to examine the healthcare system. Rather than tangle with the powerful doctors' lobby, Congress deleted the offending sentence.

America's failure to implement a national healthcare system similar to those in Britain and Germany, however, ran deeper than the AMA, which was not a monolith. Doctors suffering due to the Depression saw some virtue to a steady government salary. Moreover, the issue was salient. The 1935 *Report of the Committee on Economic Security*, for example, stressed the importance of insuring against sickness, which it called "one of the major causes of economic insecurity which threaten people of small means in good times as in bad."[29] The problem during the New Deal was simple overload. With so much aid from so many new programs going to so many different groups it was easy to put healthcare on the back burner.[30] Ever since, Americans' mixed feelings about various New Deal programs and big government in general have served as a powerful impediment to both state- and federal-level initiatives. At the heart of the issue is power. Under a market system, consumers have the power because insurers and doctors have to provide them with policies and treatments that they like. Under a government system, politicians and bureaucrats have the power. A secondary consideration is many Americans believe that the government is not likely to be more efficient than a private system, even a FUBAR one.

After a promising start, the healthcare reforms proposed by Bill and Hillary Clinton in 1993 and 1994 fizzled and died because of powerful special interests and the fact that many Americans met them with incredulity. If the government botched Medicare and Medicaid, they wondered, how could it be expected to efficiently run the nation's entire healthcare system? The insurance lobby caught the mood perfectly with an advertisement featuring Harry and Louise, two middle-aged Americans who called the Clinton proposals a medical Leviathan.[31] That Medicare came to bite proponents of national healthcare in the posterior was ironic since some saw the program as a backdoor mechanism for slowly sliding into socialized medicine. Americans are generous to a fault when they believe the recipient is worthy of aid. If they have the slightest doubt, however, they typically refuse to give a dime. That attitude is due to the widespread belief that anybody with half a brain and a little gumption can at least get along in this land of opportunity. Handouts therefore hurt the recipients by preventing them from achieving their independent destiny. This belief may partly explain some of the recent hysteria over the Obama plan, as may agitation by lobbyists and other interested parties. Americans relax this belief a bit when it comes to old folks. (I speak generally here. A few of us, including myself, think the aged are the least worthy of aid on both moral and practical grounds.) It was therefore easier to enact Medicare than a national healthcare program for workers.[32]

Signed into law in 1965 as part of President Lyndon B. Johnson's Great Society program, Medicare began with two parts, A and B. To this day, Part A provides hospital insurance to virtually all Americans over age sixty-five and is funded by a flat payroll tax with no income cap. Part B provides physicians' care and nonhospital services. Funded one quarter by premiums paid by seniors and three quarters by general tax revenues, Part B is technically voluntary, but given the large subsidy, most senior citizens opt into it. Funding Medicare has become increasingly difficult because people are living longer, receiving more medical treatment, and receiving more expensive medical treatment than the government expected when it enacted the program—the existence of which itself increased each of those variables by large amounts. The for-profits had avoided the senior market out of a keen understanding of just such an eventuality, not venality.[33]

Medicare is very costly, yet it does not meet all of the healthcare needs of seniors, many of whom find it prudent to purchase private "Medigap" insurance covering Medicare co-payments, coinsurance, deductibles, excess charges not covered under Medicare, foreign travel emergency, preventive care, and, perhaps most interestingly, the first three pints of blood.[34] Filling the gaping holes in coverage, however, only further exacerbates the funding problem. For example, in 2003 the George W. Bush administration won passage of a prescription drug benefit, Medicare Part D, that helps seniors to buy their pills while simultaneously putting untold additional burdens on future taxpayers. For all those reasons, instead of crediting Medicare for happy and healthy grandparents, most Americans associate it with higher taxes, red tape, and burgeoning bureaucracy.[35]

And it doesn't help that Medicare sounds a lot like Medicaid, a government healthcare program for the poor, including the aged poor. Medicaid is notoriously costly and inefficient in part because, although a federal program, its administration varies greatly from state to state. In many states, the program induces poor people to use emergency room doctors as primary-care physicians, a very wasteful use of expensive ER resources. For example, researchers recently discovered that nine drug addicts cost taxpayers some $3 million by visiting Austin, Texas, emergency rooms 2,678 times between 2003 and 2008.[36]

The specter of government healthcare still looms, even after the reforms passage of 2010, because earlier reform attempts like managed care—HMOs (health maintenance organizations), PPOs (preferred provider organizations), EPOs (exclusive provider organizations), and sundry hybrid forms—failed to stem rising healthcare costs or to provide millions of Americans with affordable insurance. They failed, I contend, because they, like Obama's new law, maintained the employer-provision model. If individuals bore the costs of the healthcare system more directly, the long-running inflationary cost spiral would slow, maybe stop, and possibly even reverse to some extent.[37]

The best evidence of this comes from Switzerland, a federal republic composed of twenty-six different cantons or states whose 7.5 million or so citizens enjoy perhaps the best health insurance and healthcare system on the planet. A well-established nation with a stable government, little poverty, and a standard of living comparable to that of the United States,[38] Switzerland possesses a healthcare system that tops the world in most measures of user satisfaction.[39] "In Switzerland," a recent study concluded, "expectations of choice and involvement are high and people are relatively satisfied with their healthcare system in this regard." Of the eight affluent Western European countries studied, Switzerland scored second highest to the question "How often did the doctor listen carefully to you?" first to "How often did the doctor give you time to ask questions?" first to "How often did the doctor explain things in a way you could understand?" and first to "Overall how would you rate how well healthcare providers communicated with you?"[40]

The structure of the Swiss system requires that most people pay for a significant part of their own medical care and ensures that information asymmetry is minimized.[41] Moral hazard is reduced by the fact that the Swiss pay almost a third of their medical expenses out of pocket. (Americans, by contrast, pay only about 13 percent of their healthcare costs out of pocket.) The Swiss apparently like it that way, as providing insurance for out-of-pocket expenses is not just frowned upon, it is illegal.[42] Coverage exclusions for common, expected medical expenses also serve to keep costs in check. (Think about it. Why does anyone need insurance for an *annual* physical examination?)

The Swiss government reduces the adverse selection problem inherent in individual policies by mandating that everyone obtain at least a basic health insurance policy. The cantons subsidize those who cannot afford one. Through that mechanism almost exactly one quarter of health expenses are paid for by the cantons. The government takes the sting out of forcing young, healthy people to pay for something they probably won't need by allowing so-called bonus plans, five-year policies that refund some premiums to insureds who suffered no health problems over the policy term. Swiss healthcare is therefore universal but completely private and not intertwined with politics or large government bureaucracies. (By the way, that is why many people prefer not to call government-sponsored healthcare proposals in the US "universal"—as Switzerland shows, universality can be achieved without government providers or insurance.)

All health insurance in Switzerland is private and individual. Employer-provided plans are not allowed and coverage is extended to individuals, not to families or groups. Insurers offering basic policies must be nonprofits. They cannot deny coverage, but a mandatory risk-adjustment pool attempts to reduce selection biases, with companies with riskier policyholders taking from the pool and those with safer ones contributing to it. About one-third of all healthcare expenditures in Switzerland are paid for by basic insurers. In addition, individuals in Switzerland, if so inclined, can buy unsubsidized supplemental insurance, the providers of which may be for-profit entities. Supplemental insurers also have wider latitude in setting premium rates—within parameters established by regulators they can adjust premiums for risk factors like location, gender, and age—and may deny coverage outright if they think fit. About one-tenth of all healthcare payments in Switzerland stem from supplemental insurance policies.[43]

All those features were designed to provide Swiss individuals and insurers with some incentives to control costs by obtaining the best available medical value, which is to say the best combination of cost and quality. For all its advantages, however, the system, which has been in place since the mid-1990s, is imperfect because regulation of policy terms and prices is excessive. (Price regulation cannot make anything affordable and freely available. If the regulated price is set too low, below the cost of production, quality will suffer or the regulated good will not be provided at all.) Moreover, technical problems mar the proper functioning of the risk-adjustment pool, allowing some insurers to skim the best risks, which, in turn, reduces their incentive to control costs.[44]

Most important of all, it remains difficult for patients to tell the difference between Dr. House and Dr. Scrub, so the latter persists. A better system would pay doctors for curing patients rather than just seeing them, an incentive misalignment that goes a long way toward explaining why House doesn't get his diagnoses right the first time. Nonetheless, Switzerland presents a model upon which a non-FUBAR US health system could be built. In short, neither the Left nor the Right has the correct answer, the Center does—the center of Europe that is.[45] (Others suggest emulating Holland or Germany, but Switzerland's program seems like the best fit for the United States, another geographically isolated federal republic.[46] The United States is geographically larger than Switzerland and has a much larger and more ethnically diverse population. But those factors are relatively unimportant in this context and would also apply to Holland, Germany, and, frankly, every other country on the planet.[47])

But getting the right answer is not really what it's about, at least not from the standpoint of politicians and their partisans. Many on the Left want national health "insurance" not because it is efficient but because they believe that it is morally superior. They deprecate consumer-directed healthcare because it is actuarially sound, because it provides actual risk-pooling or indemnity against loss paid for by members of the pool based on the risks they pose to the pool. Rather than redistributing resources from rich to poor, in other words, insurance shares risks within relatively small groups of people (or companies) with similar risk profiles. Instead of insurance, many on the Left want community rating writ large, "where risks are pooled broadly and costs distributed widely" in order to guarantee protection to everyone, "regardless of income or health status."[48] It would be far more efficient to allow actuaries to determine premiums in a free-market setting and then, as the Swiss do, assist those who cannot afford their premiums. Otherwise, income policy and health policy become conflated and public discourse focuses on the wealth redistribution effects of policy proposals instead of the most efficient ways of providing insurance and healthcare.

Partisan politics aside, it is likely that additional healthcare policy reforms will be necessary, and soon. Given that healthcare costs have been rising much faster than inflation and apparently will continue to do so, Medicare, Medicaid, and the recently enacted entitlements loom large, rendering even Social Security's trillions a mere drop in a very large bucket of fiscal slop. Meanwhile, employer-provided insurance is an increasingly large drag on the competitiveness of US firms in globalized markets. The employer-based system is dying and probably will continue to do so. The only question is what will replace it?[49]

The government cannot stop people from aging or getting sick, but it can stop medical costs from rising while simultaneously ensuring that America continues to produce top-notch medical research. It is going to take some politically tough decisions, however. Consider, for example, insurance regulation. While not the direct cause of the healthcare industry's woes, regulators do prevent the creation of better health insurance policies by keeping insurers' costs high and by stifling, nay, in many cases outlawing, policy innovations. A major problem is that each state has its own set of insurance regulators and regulations. That increases insurers' costs and the overall level of uncertainty, especially in states that regulate premiums. Even more important, however, regulators often stymie innovation by prescribing policy forms and even regulating prices.[50] Combining annuities and life insurance, or life insurance and health insurance policies, is also verboten in most jurisdictions.

Were it not for regulatory barriers, for example, it would be possible to combine health and life insurance (and probability disability too) into a single long-term contract that would induce people to make rational decisions about life and death by tying their death benefits to their healthcare expenditures. Confronted with clear trade-offs, people might voluntarily forgo expensive treatments with a low probability of success in order to maintain the value of their estate. That is a clear benefit over the current situation, where the sick willingly spend vast gobs of other people's money for a small chance of continued life. Insurers would also face an explicit trade-off. Under the current system, macabre as it is, insurers benefit if a gravely ill insured dies, so unsurprisingly they often deny coverage. Under a joint policy, they would have to weigh the costs of current and expected future treatment against an immediate death benefit payout. The bigger the face value of the policy, the more likely the insurer would pay for treatment, all else constant.

Joint policies would also give insurers even stronger incentives to keep insureds as healthy as possible. Indeed, life insurers have expended considerable sums on general medical research and hygiene programs in addition to policyholder-specific programs. By the 1920s, most life insurers had launched health services programs that educated policyholders and also ensured that they had access to basic healthcare, including routine physical examinations. Such programs faded after the ascension of employer-provided group health following World War II. For a variety of tax, regulatory, and economic reasons, health insurers rarely try to improve the health of their transient policyholders prophylactically. In fact, *health* insurers would like nothing better than for their policyholders to keel over dead immediately after paying their premiums.[51] (*Life* insurers, by contrast, would like it if policyholders were healthy enough to never die.)

Joint policies would also encourage the creation of a desperately needed market for cadaveric transplant organs. For decades, far more people have stood in need of organ transplants than have received them. Each year thousands of people die prematurely and thousands of others suffer untold physical and psychological pain because most potential donors simply refuse to authorize the use of their organs after death. If they knew that their estates (and hence their children, grandchildren, siblings, and other close family members) would benefit, however, many more people would offer their organs for transplant. Insurers could handle the payments discretely through increases in death benefits, easing people's natural aversion to the monetization of life. Even if priced, markets for eyes, kidneys, hearts, and other body parts might not work as regular markets do because the supply would be extremely inelastic. In other words, once everyone had been induced to become a donor, increasing the price further would not increase the supply, which is largely a function of automobile accidents. But paying people's estates could maximize the number of available organs, which could then be rationed by the nonprice mechanisms already in use relating to the patient's age, postoperative viability, and the like.[52] (Another good proposal might work, too, invoking a "no give, no take" rule. In other words, you can only receive an organ if you have previously pledged yours to the common pool.[53] Other nudges, like those implemented in Illinois, might also work wonders without raising anyone's hackles.[54] Will Smith's approach in *Seven Pounds*, by contrast, is not likely to catch on, admirable as it was.[55])

Regulators also block the creation of synthetic long-term policies built on self-enforcing short-term contracts and severance payments. Many economists believe that markets cannot create long-term health insurance contracts due to adverse selection, to wit, the withdrawal of healthier people and the retention of sickly ones. One way to mitigate the problem, short of the politically unlikely one of forcing healthy people to honor long-term healthcare contracts, is to require condition-contingent severance payments. At the end of the contract term, sickly people would receive a lump sum, offsetting their higher premiums under the next contract, while healthy ones would make a payment to the insurer, offsetting the premium deduction they will receive over the course of the next contract. In other words, such policies would be the ultimate in experience testing, much like two-sided mutual insurance policies that paid dividends when experience was better than expected and charged assessments when reality turned out worse than forecasted. Such policies would not require payment of more premium dollars but rather would simply rearrange the legal rights those payments create. They would also solve one of the paradoxes of health insurance, the fact that larger pools experience less adverse selection but also create less competition, variety, and so forth, which if taken to the extreme is the national health system or socialized medicine that so many Americans rightly fear.[56]

If allowed by regulators, rapid advances in genetics will help insurers to charge more appropriate premiums than they currently do. That will be good news (lower premiums) for people with "good" genes but double bad news for others, who will find themselves saddled with both "bad" genes and higher premiums. Consumers, however, should not fight gene rating. Those at higher risk for contracting expensive diseases should pay more than safer risks, just like bad drivers should pay higher automobile insurance than safe ones. At first glance, it may seem that bad drivers have a choice in their driving habits whereas sick people are victims of bad genes.

In reality, the situation is much more complex. A bad driver may simply be a victim of bad luck or the circumstance in which he or she has to drive (e.g., late at night on dangerous roads) while sickly people may bring on ailments themselves by engaging in extreme sports or other physically risky activities, not washing their hands, and eating, drinking, and/or smoking too much, and so forth. Moreover, genes are rarely destiny. Knowledge of bad genes can help individuals to make better-informed lifestyle decisions. Those predisposed to diabetes, for example, would do well to stay away from sweets and generally keep their weight in check. If allowed, insurers could reward those who stay within weight parameters with lower premiums. Those more genetically prone to lung cancer should pay much higher premiums if they choose to smoke, and so forth. In those rare instances where genes determine outcomes, bad gene insurance, purchased before testing, should be available.[57]

The sorry plight of America's pharmaceutical giants also demands attention. For decades, they have turned research and development dollars into breakthrough technologies that have made people's lives worldwide longer and better. Today, however, some consumers and populist politicians malign the industry as "a Goliath with a wanton abuse of power," particularly the market power provided by their patents.[58] The fact is, however, that without the profits that high pill prices provide, pharmaceutical companies would not have invested in the R & D that gave people more effective means of battling diabetes, high cholesterol counts, influenza, and, yes, impotence.

8

3RD ROCK FROM THE SUN
Agency Problems in Higher Education

Self-examination is salutary, just and necessary, especially in those who censure the conduct of others.[1]

I love John Lithgow. I mean, I love his acting. I don't want to marry him or anything. In fact, I know his wife, business historian and college professor Mary Yeager Lithgow. In one of his funnier roles, as a kooky alien named Dick Solomon, John portrayed a college professor, actually an alien "high commander" pretending to be a professor of physics. He was smitten with Mary Albright, an anthropology prof played by Jane Curtin (of "Jane, you ignorant slut" fame/infamy).[2] One of the many allures of the show, called *3rd Rock from the Sun*, was its hilarious treatment of American higher education. The couple's employer, Pendleton State University, was a thinly cloaked fictionalized version of Kent State, the alma mater of the show's creators. Mary and her colleagues were far too neurotic and underpaid to teach effectively, while Dick, fake credentials and all, knew far too much advanced physics to be an effective undergraduate instructor. Students and faculty alike found themselves at Pendleton, which was built on a reclaimed uranium mine, because none of them could make it elsewhere.

The library was appalling, but the school still sported a football team, and a dreadful one at that. One professor (played by Harry Morgan of *M*A*S*H* fame) was still on the payroll despite the fact he had not taught a class in four years. Unsurprisingly, the student body was dismally demoralized, with comedic results.

***

The state of America's real colleges and universities is, however, no laughing matter.[3] Unfortunately, they have not prepared Americans for the massive economic transformations likely to rock the twenty-first century's world. Simply put, US higher education does not, and as currently constituted cannot, produce enough quality graduates to ensure the continued success of the American economy. Our educational system is simply too FUBAR to keep pace with the rapidly changing modern world. Current professorial pedagogical technique, which usually entails little more than blabbing away at undergraduates, is as old as the hills (and hence almost as old as the professors themselves). It doesn't teach students how to think for themselves, how to be what *New York Times* columnist Thomas Friedman calls "really adaptable."[4]

The proximate cause of the problem is that professors do not spend much, if any, time discussing important problems with students one-on-one or in small groups. Many classes are grotesquely obese, with hundreds and in some cases thousands of students. Exacerbating that problem, most of those huge classes are taught by the young, inexperienced professors. As a general rule, celebrity professors, arguably the best and the brightest of the lot, hardly teach at all. This chapter explores the reasons why classes are so large and lecture oriented and why the best professors typically teach only a few advanced graduate students.

As with construction and healthcare, the US system of higher education is far better than most, or perhaps all, others in the world. Students the world over flock to it, although not in as large numbers as they did before the 9/11 attacks. Unfortunately, however, nobody knows how to accurately measure learning, so we do not know if American higher education effectively transforms minds or if it is simply popular. Derek Bok, the erstwhile president of Harvard University, concurs. "No one can confidently assert," he argues, "that colleges today are helping students write better, speak more eloquently, think more rigorously, or reason quantitatively more proficiently than they did in the 1950s."[5] Yet in inflation-adjusted terms, tuition is far higher today than then. Many students are already wondering whether college is worth the cost. That is a warning sign that policymakers would do well to heed.

Past performance is no indication of future results. History is littered with the corpses of previously dominant industries. In 1960, for instance, the American steel industry led the world, but just twenty years later it resembled a train wreck. On the eve of World War I, America's railroad industry was the most efficient in the world, but today it is far from being world class. Once seemingly invincible people, companies, industries, sectors, regions, and, yes, entire national economies are now moribund. In most instances, monumental resistance to change and dizzying degrees of hubris precipitated the plummet. Consider the poem "Ozymandias":

> "My name is Ozymandias, king of kings:
> Look on my works, ye Mighty, and despair!"
> Nothing beside remains: round the decay
> Of that colossal wreck, boundless and bare,
> The lone and level sands stretch far away.[6]

Like the empire in Shelley's sonnet, many mighty empires have fallen, some quite recently. In the late 1980s and early 1990s, many Americans thought the Japanese were going to buy up the whole United States, lock, stock, and barrel. Instead, the Japanese economy fell off the wall and the Japanese are still trying to put their Humpty Dumpty back together again. Economists purport to know why the Japanese economy tumbled—too much regulation, too much coddling of zombie banks, overly rigid labor markets, and ineffective monetary policy.[7] But the real questions are *why* was the Japanese economy overregulated, why weren't the banks allowed to fail, why did they cling to lifetime employment, and why couldn't their monetary policymakers adapt to changed circumstances? Clearly, I argue, the Japanese education system did not prepare the Japanese workforce for globalization or the information revolution because it placed far too much emphasis on rote memorization.[8] "We will learn to be independent thinkers," students chanted as they cleaned their own school. Japanese students learned discipline and frugality, which was great when Japan churned out commodities and consumer electronics. But most did not achieve independence or creativity of mind, the sine qua non of the postmodern workplace.

The service sector rules modern economies. Only 20 to 25 percent of the labor force in the world's richest economies still engage in manufacturing and, at most, 5 percent of it grows food. Most wealth production stems from services, which encompass low-skilled, low-value activities like flipping burgers and high-skilled, high-value activities like consulting, design, and other professional work.[9] The latter require an education that fosters independent thought, even creativity. Japan's economy ran into trouble when not enough people could be found to fill those important jobs. A similar problem could strike the US economy, especially if political forces pinch off immigration as they long have in Japan. Strong US productivity growth is not a foregone conclusion. Some observers, including Bill Lewis of the McKinsey Global Institute, see trouble ahead.[10] The truly idiotic subprime mortgage mess detailed in chapter 2 suggests the critics may be right. Ominously, many signs of the rot that infected the Japanese educational system, like the tacit acceptance of widespread cheating, and frequently shortened or canceled classes, also dog US higher education. Tellingly, Japan is now turning to educational reform to help pull its economy back together.[11]

Economic growth necessitates change. Competitive markets induce growth by forcing inefficient persons, firms, and entire sectors to change their pursuits. When horsewhip manufacturers discovered that the automobile made their main products obsolete, some went out of business, but many switched to the production of fan belts and other automotive products. When American television manufacturers discovered that they could not compete against foreign firms, they stopped production and furloughed their workers. The media typically portrays such news negatively. It is difficult to watch people who've just been let go. In a dynamic capitalist economy, however, the failure of an inefficient industry is good news because it frees up resources (human, financial, and physical capital) for more efficient uses.[12] Economist Joseph Schumpeter called this process "creative destruction" because new industries arise out of the ashes of old ones.[13] "Progress" is another apt term.

Throughout its two-plus-century history, the US economy has shown remarkable resilience. To date, the destruction of antiquated or inefficient industries has always spurred the creation of new and often better ones.

Agriculture is a prime example. To feed one hundred people, the economy now needs only two farmers, not the ninety it required in 1790. Yet mass unemployment of farmers is not a problem because would-be farmers instead became engineers, mechanics, pilots, editors, and teachers. That same process of creative destruction currently reshapes the US manufacturing sector and even parts of the service sector.

Today, three out of every five working Americans are "knowledge workers" who rely on sophisticated numeracy and literacy skills to perform their jobs.[14] According to the Census Bureau, the percentage of jobs requiring a college education rose from 42 percent in 1987 to 75 percent in 2000. Those figures are even higher today and will likely continue to increase, albeit more slowly, in the future. American higher education can definitely award all those people diplomas, but it remains to be seen if it can help sufficient numbers of them to learn to think for themselves—the one crucial skill they will need to be successful in the third millennium labor market. Graduates need to know how to teach themselves, how to come to independent judgments, and how to put disparate ideas together in new combinations, to think creatively inside, outside, and *through* the proverbial box.

"Liberal education," Duke University president Nannerl Keohane once wrote, "teaches people how to learn rather than to master a technical skill that may someday become obsolete."[15] To date, however, US higher education has failed to produce enough independent thinkers. Recent experiments show just how few people actually think for themselves. Put in a group setting, three out of four individuals will knowingly give the wrong answers to very simple questions that they had easily answered correctly when not influenced by the answers of others. Americans show no more independence of mind in such experiments than do denizens of Europe, Japan, or even Kuwait. Extreme views find a significant number of adherents only when group dynamics are at play, suggesting that Americans easily cave in to peer pressure.[16] (Where, then, is their competitive advantage? How will they be able to compete against lower-wage, foreign workers?) That's pretty FUBAR, but it gets worse.

***

US higher education is extremely diverse, so none of the generalizations proffered here hold in all instances. However, this should not present a problem because the goal of this chapter is to characterize overall trends, not to document every aspect of the industry. So it doesn't matter if students at school X are sober or if professors at college Y work hard or if administrators at university Z are not selfish morons. Exceptions abound. But exceptions often prove the rule. No school should take umbrage simply because I mention it in the pages that follow because the entire system is at fault. Problems at a particular school are effects, not causes— in short, manifestations of FUBAR. By necessity, this chapter focuses on the FUBAR aspects of American higher education. I purposefully ignore the few bright spots, the professors, schools, and students who still believe in the importance of a liberal education and self-actualization.

Evidence that US higher education is in trouble is undeniable. I could not possibly discuss all of the signs in a single chapter. Let's take a minute, though, to cover ten of the more troubling facts:

1. The United States spends more on education in per capita terms than almost every other nation on earth but gets relatively little for it.
2. Governments are not very good at producing education themselves, but there are few signs that they are prepared to turn it over to private producers, even at the crucial primary and secondary levels.
3. Many Americans are therefore educating their children at home. (In 2003, the figure was about 1.1 million. In a survey conducted in 1999, 38 percent of parents cited religious reasons for home schooling their children while the other 72 percent pointed to the low quality of available public schools.)[17]
4. At college, most students do not talk to faculty members outside of class.
5. Grade compression (aka inflation) is rampant.
6. Tuition inflation far outpaces general inflation.
7. Many employers fret that US colleges seem incapable of providing them with quality workers, thereby accelerating the trend toward outsourcing. (Increasingly, American students cannot justify their relatively higher pay with higher levels of productivity. A business is indifferent to hiring ten people who can each do $5 worth of work in an hour and work for $1 per hour each [in some foreign country] and someone who can do $50 worth and work for $10 per hour [say, in the USA]. Increasingly, however, the US worker can

do only $40 or even $30 per hour of work and still demands $10 per hour, thereby making hiring the ten foreign workers more attractive.)

8. Thousands of employers have responded to weak entry-level workers by creating their own "universities" and training centers.

9. America's long-standing lead in graduate education is in danger of evaporating in the next decade.

10. Globalization is here to stay, so American workers will continue to come under intense competitive pressure from foreign workers.

Increasingly, employers realize that the "sheepskin effect" has weakened. Mere attainment of a degree, especially from a weaker school, no longer automatically signals worker quality. Degree inflation is therefore taking place as workers try to signal their value to employers by obtaining graduate degrees. A related problem is that graduates who did not really learn much in college often find promotion, or even retaining their first job, difficult. This does not bode well in today's global economy, where there is no longer any place to hide.

Around the turn of the twentieth century, only about 1 percent of Americans received bachelor's degrees and only 5 percent received a high school diploma. When the economy demanded more highly educated workers, people simply attended school for more years. First, high school graduation rates increased, then bachelor's degree rates. The economy is now in the era of the master's degree with about 380,000 awarded annually, about a third of the number of bachelor's degrees awarded each year. The emphasis on quantity rather than quality means that many people are now in their late twenties or early thirties before they begin their careers. If longevity continues to increase, that might not be a problem, provided that the retirement age also increases, a point taken up in the concluding chapter. As matters stand now, however, people want to educate themselves for thirty years, work for thirty years, and chill out retired in Florida for thirty years.[18] That probably is not sustainable. Instead of tacking on more years of formal schooling, Americans should make better use of the many years already devoted to education.

***

After teaching at a local university, San Antonio IT systems architect Mike Arguello neatly summarized the deficit of independent thought that is currently threatening to Ozymandiasize the American economy: "Of the students I taught over six semesters, I'd only consider hiring two of them. The rest lacked the creativity, problem-solving abilities and passion for learning."[19] Many other observers echo Arguello's judgment. Colleges and universities are not getting the job done, and neither are their students.

America wastes higher education on its youth. About 65 percent of new undergraduates are traditional ones who go to college directly from high school. About half of them, however, eventually drop out, and many of those who stay really shouldn't. Studies show that only about 10 percent of our traditional undergraduates are serious about scholarship. Over 25 percent have been characterized as "disengaged" or "recreators," and another 15 percent as strategic students who "grind" their way through school with little enjoyment. The rest are more interested in having fun than in taxing their gray matter.[20]

For most students, college is a form of entertainment. Some fall in love with learning, but most remain oblivious to the benefits of research and reflection. The biggest single indicator of their performance is the quality of their randomly chosen roommates, not their parents' education level, the depth of their preparation for college, or the skill of their professors.[21] (In other words, if a student's roommate is studious, the student will be more likely to be studious. If the roomie is a drug-taking, TV-watching moron, his or her influence will, statistically speaking, trump the effects of other variables.) Rather than an opportunity to enrich their understanding of a complex world, many view college as an *obstacle* to their dreams, a hoop that must be jumped through to attain material success in life. They see education as a right, not a privilege, so when they bother to attend class, they sit as far in the back as they can, hats on, heads down, praying that they won't be called upon to think. If pressed, most think of the university as little more than an entertaining diploma mill. Students pony up the bread and the school is supposed to reciprocate by showing them a good time and then by handing them a valuable degree. They don't seem to think of the university as a place of learning. The troubling thing is that their analysis is not far off the mark.

Some schools claim that up to twenty hours of work per week puts students under a little time pressure that gets them to focus the rest of their time on school. More likely, schools want to maintain a cheap source of labor, the student worker, and hence argue that a vice is actually a virtue. (An important exception is students who work ten or fewer hours per week *in jobs related to their studies*, as in internships, externships, or research.) Students ought to spend sixty hours per week in class and studying, fifty-six sleeping, and the other fifty-two eating, cleaning, exercising, and enjoying recreation. The reality is that any time spent working comes out of sleep or study, not recreation. Either way, education suffers.

Colleges and universities also encourage students to work so that they will be able to pay their ever-increasing tuition bills. According to one survey, 63 percent of college students could not afford college if they did not work.[22] As a result of these cost pressures, students are spending more time working and less time studying than ever before. One study places traditional full-time undergraduate working rates at 80 percent of the time![23] Nontraditional or returning students are even more likely to work.

Working students can be wonderful additions to college classrooms because they have real-world experience upon which to draw. They are particularly useful in business and technical classes, and they can also add to public policy debates over taxation and minimum wages and the like, too. Most of the time, however, working students are simply a pain in the proverbial posterior. They show up late or leave early; they miss examinations and deadlines. Worst of all, they use work as a convenient excuse for everything. Work has become the perfect excuse to which professors have no effective retort. By allowing students to use work as an excuse, professors and staff implicitly agree that work is more important than education. By accommodating the working student, institutions of higher education have basically admitted that work is necessary and college is secondary and need only be attended to when it is as the *Saturday Night Live* Church Chat Lady would say, "conveeeeeeeeeeeeeenient."

That stance is counterproductive because working impairs the student's ability to focus on his schoolwork. More than half of students who work twenty-five or more hours per week *self-report* that work negatively affects their studies. Four out of ten report that working limits their class schedule and decreases their grades. One in three admits that it limits their class choices. One in four claims that it limits their library access. Working is also associated with higher dropout rates.

When American undergraduates are not working, or participating in loud, drug- and rum-soaked orgies, they can often be found carrying on at their respective school's ubiquitous sporting events. Although most are underage, traditional college students consume "mass quantities" of alcohol that would make the Coneheads (the French/aliens of early *Saturday Night Live* lore) blush. According to one study, college students drink over $6 billion of alcohol annually and almost half of all college students admit to binge drinking. In other words, they do not drink every day, but when they do, they drink till they drop. (If readers wonder how that is possible, they should Google the string "drinking games," and they'll get an idea.) Every year, a few students manage to "play" themselves to death while untold others impair their mental capabilities. And these days the females are as prone to binge on booze as the frat boys were in the smash smashed movie hit *Animal House*.[24]

Sad as it is, a good number of students leave college dumber than when they arrived. That is unsurprising, given that many of them waste four nights a week in bars instead of in libraries and spend more time drinking than writing. You know you are in America when "calculus" is not a challenging mathematics course but the name that the frat boys give to the dried puke on the rims of their toilets. Schools rarely condone such activities, of course, but it is rarer still that they succeed in doing anything about them, and most refuse to touch the "Greek" system of frats and sororities, a major fount of crazed, *Animal House*–style behaviors.[25] At least the government has a Web site, College Drinking—Changing the Culture, http://www.collegedrinkingprevention.gov/. Unfortunately, the guide to drinking games, Webtender: Bartender's Handbook, http://www.web tender.com/handbook/games/ receives far more hits.

Speaking of hits, were college students only pounding beers and shots, we might pass it off as preparation for their adult lives. But they are also pounding drugs and each other with a frequency and alacrity that is unhealthy. Some abuse prescription drugs, from various "happy" pills to sundry brain and body performance enhancers. Moreover, college students are more likely to use illicit drugs than non–college students in the same age bracket. The drug of choice varies from school to school and time to time, probably due to underlying supplies and prices. Acid (LSD) has been a steady favorite. Cocaine is queen at some affluent schools, ice (crystal methamphetamine) at many poorer ones. Marijuana is ubiquitous. From 1991 to 2001, about one out of every three college students admitted to smoking pot in the last year. They also smoke, eat, drink, inhale, inject, or otherwise ingest a host of crap new to nonconnoisseurs. One of these relative newcomers, Ecstasy, has become notorious due to its use as a date rape drug. "X" is now so popular in many places that the running joke is that the only reason that students still take chemistry is to learn how to concoct the stuff in their dorm rooms. Ecstasy meshes nicely with students' other major pastime, casual sex. STDs, especially gonorrhea, Chlamydia, genital warts, and herpes, are rampant on most college campuses. According to one study, fully half of all sexually active college students contract a STD by age twenty-five. (If that seems a little old for an undergraduate, consider this: hardly anyone graduates in four years anymore and many students take a year or more off between high school and college or during their college experience, which often involves transferring to at least one new school.)

***

Many, if not most, college students these days think nothing of lying, cheating, or stealing their way through college. I am not talking about the occasional cheater of yore. I am talking about a repeated pattern of systematic deception. According to one study, many students repeatedly lie, even to their own mothers. Students have long been known to fabricate stories to avoid the punishments that teachers dole out for slacking. The old standby, "the dog ate my homework," no longer quite cuts it, so students have had to become better liars. Dead and dying relatives, automobile accidents, computer hardware failures, and crazed roommates abound. Professors know they are often lied to, or at least they should, because for the last fifteen years or so a parody of a scholarly article that purports to explain why deaths, maladies, accidents, and other misfortunes seem to occur only during examination week has enjoyed a wide circulation. But professors need to worry about their evaluations, so they generally just shrug off the excuses and accommodate the distressed student so as not to appear a "hard ass." That used to be a compliment. Today, it is the kiss of death.

A few schools have retaliated against disingenuous students by hiring people whose sole or major function it is to verify student excuses, to call doctors and body shops, look up obituaries, ask for police reports, and so on. Once word gets out that excuses will be vigorously investigated, the spurious or fictional ones tend to dissipate. Of course one effect of clamping down on lying is simply to make students more desperate during examination and term paper periods. The frightening thing about the current epidemic of cheating is that many of the cheaters no longer feel remorse. Forty years ago, even cheaters themselves considered cheating sinful. Today, no opprobrium is attached to it. Because school is supposed to be entertaining, not taxing, because it is supposed to be fun, not stressful, many of today's students cheat on examinations without compunction. As with drugs and cheap sex, everybody seems to be doing it, and that is a compelling incentive to join the sordid game when professors, as they often do, employ "curves," even if the curve is a "gut." (Curves limit the percentage of students in a class who can receive an A, a B, and so on. A gut curve is generous with As and stingy with Cs, Ds, and Fs.) With curves in place, even students with some ethical sense feel pressured to cheat, just to maintain their rank in the distribution. Students know that grades are important if they want to land a good job, so they do everything they can to maximize them, learning be damned.

Technology has made cheating easier too. Cell phones, pagers, wristwatches, graphing calculators, handheld computers, and a variety of other electronic gadgets can easily hold or access enough information to turn an F performance into an A. Meanwhile, aging and computer-illiterate professors confidently assign grades and write glowing letters of recommendation for some people who are devoid of a moral compass and good at little other than drinking and carousing. Those too dumb to even cheat effectively—and they are becoming increasingly common—can hire a professional test taker to complete their exams for them.[26] How could a nonstudent take an exam? Very easily, it turns out. Many classes, especially introductory classes at big universities, have huge enrollments. We're talking two hundred fifty, five hundred, even one thousand students per class. Even with aid from assistants, professors cannot track that many people. So on exam day, the mercenary test taker simply comes into class, takes the exam, and signs the other student's name and ID number. It's just that easy. And in some ways it is difficult to blame students for taking a shortcut because it must be difficult for them to believe that an institution that would cram hundreds of students into a single class gives a damn about educational quality.

Plagiarism, using another's ideas or words without quotation or attribution, is also rampant. Technological asymmetry is a major culprit here, but not the only reason for its rise. In the 1990s, many students knew how to use search engines while many professors did not. Today, most profs know about Google and many have access to Turninit.com, a service that checks submitted papers for "originality" by comparing them to public Web sites, proprietary databases, and all papers ever submitted to Turninit.com. But plagiarism remains a plague. Turninit.com cannot tell if a student has purchased an original paper from a professional paper writer or obtained it from a friend, spouse, or lover. More important, the service is ineffective if professors do not use it because they have no incentive to catch plagiarists and many reasons not to. Turninit.com also cannot force administrators to take action once a case of plagiarism comes to their attention.

The sad fact of the matter is that many professors have neither the time nor the patience to prevent or punish plagiarism because they must publish or perish. Some are even trying to make plagiarism acceptable![27] The ploy might just work because most professors appear to have given up on undergraduate education. Higher education is in a nasty, downward cycle. Some students lie, cheat, and steal, so professors no longer care about teaching. Other students see low professor morale and high professor apathy as signals that they, too, might as well cheat. That, in turn, reinforces professorial views that students do not want to learn, further decreasing their interest level. I fear we are just one or two more spins away from the drainpipe. But maybe I am being overly optimistic. Some professors, and apparently most students, think that US higher education has already entered the sewer system.

You know things are bad when professors become the brunt of harsh jokes that are usually reserved for lawyers, like this one:

Five surgeons are discussing who makes the best patients to operate on.

The first surgeon says, "I like to see accountants on my operating table because when you open them up, everything inside is numbered."

The second responds, "Yeah, but you should try electricians! Everything inside them is color coded."

The third surgeon says, "No, I really think librarians are the best; Everything inside is in alphabetical order."

The fourth surgeon chimes in: "You know, I like construction workers. Those guys always understand when you have a few parts left over at the end and when the job takes longer than you said it would."

But the fifth surgeon shut them all up when he observed: "You're all wrong! Professors are the easiest to operate on. There's no guts, no heart, no balls, no brains, and no spine, and the head and the ass are interchangeable."

And this one:

News Bulletin: Breakthrough medical technology makes brain transplants a reality! (*New York Times*, December 31, 2015)

Guy goes to a brainshow at the Javits center. He arrives at a table marked "Professional Brains for Sale." Five jars containing lumps of gray matter pickled in formaldehyde are on display, priced as marked.
    Civil Engineer $17,500 per ounce
    Pharmacist $16,250 per ounce
    Physician $18,000 per ounce
    Surveyor $12,800 per ounce (special this month!)
    Professor $1,840,000 per ounce.

"Why," asks the guy of the exhibitor, "are professors' brains so expensive?" "Labor costs," replies the exhibitor. "Do you have any idea how many professors we have to dig up to get an ounce of brain?"

The second joke, by the way, shows what an awful job we are doing with economics education in this country. If professors were truly that dumb, nobody would pay $1.84 million for an ounce of their brains, so nobody would bother to incur the labor costs. Price is a function of supply and demand, not just costs. In any event, the effect of group pressure also exacerbates higher education's downward spiral. As the number of spineless, gutless, brainless faculty members increases, it becomes increasingly difficult for the remaining professors to hold the line. What faculty member wants to be the only one working the little scoundrels? After a while, it starts to look like the faculty member is a maverick, or worse yet, a freak bent on destroying students' lives. Other professors who know what is going on but who choose to look the other way will empathize with the holdout, but administrators will not.[28] What do they care about an institution's long-term reputation?

***

Students are not to blame for the FUBAR aspects of higher education, a massive hybrid failure is. Their attitudes and behaviors are consequences, not causes, and I have to give them credit for seeing straight through higher education's hypocrisy. It is supposed to create a vibrant meritocracy, a society where people are judged by what they do and not from whose loins they emerged. But college faculty and administrators are elitist to the core. Color doesn't matter much anymore, but other signals of elite status count more than ever. Politics suffuse higher education; professors are often judged not by their merit but by the prevailing politics of the school. Furthermore, most administrators, and even many professors, now talk of students as "consumers" and "customers" with a straight face. Students do likewise, which affects their performance and acquisition of knowledge. "College is a business, classes are a service and we are the customers," a student at a liberal arts college in South Dakota recently argued in an op-ed run in the school's paper. "Choosing to go or not to go to class," he concluded, "should be at our discretion."[29]

Students, I counter, are just that, students. If one wants to discuss their relationship with their schools in a broader context, "clients" would be a much more apt term. The student-as-customer model, however, fits nicely with academe's unbelievably snobbish elitism. How dare a mere undergraduate deign to consider himself a client of *moi*, the mighty Professor Fuglipuss, PhD, EdD, JD, CPA, JERK, MA, MS, BA, and above all, BS, graduate of such incredible institutions as Penneton and Harvanell?

"Words like 'arrogant' and 'self-serving,'" admits higher education professor Arthur Levine, "are commonly used in statehouses to describe colleges and universities."[30] It is not at all clear why most academics are so high about themselves. Most of them know an incredible amount of information about an unbelievably narrow, unimportant subject, be it science, the arts, or business. Too much scholarship has become self-referential and inward looking, which is to say more about scholarly "discourse" than about reality.[31] Ideas become widely accepted not because of their intrinsic merit but because friends cite their buddies, creating the illusion of substance and replication where dwells only a political or career agenda.

Ask academics to step outside of their little intellectual world and most of them founder, perhaps after floundering a bit. Since the 1970s they have spewed a tremendous amount of verbiage about interdisciplinary this and multidisciplinary that, but when push comes to shove, the vast majority cannot think outside of their discipline, or increasingly even their subdiscipline, let alone put together a decent paragraph. (That may be difficult for outsiders to believe or test, but keep in mind that you see the words of only the small percentage of professors who publish regularly.) This is a problem because research is most fruitful at the interstices of existing disciplines. Rather than probing those boundaries, most scholars stay smack dab in the middle of their fields of study, churning out, at best, reams of production-line scholarship, trivial minutia detached from the real world.

Many tenured academics are lazy and inefficient. "Advertised office hours," admits erstwhile Cornell president Frank Rhodes, "are not always faithfully kept by faculty members. Faculty advisers are sometimes absent for the whole period of freshman registration."[32] "Light-to-nonexistent teaching loads, substantial research and travel budgets, frequent time off," and other perks abound, Penn State English professor Christopher Clausen claims.[33] Tenured professors are lazy partly due to their incentive structure. Guaranteed lifetime employment has a way of making matters seem less urgent. Moreover, lazy and inefficient people are naturally drawn to higher education. At many schools, much of the actual teaching is done by graduate students and adjuncts, people paid a pittance and devoid of job security. The existence of so many oppressed adjuncts, who now out-number the full-time professoriate, is truly frightening. These disfran-chised members of the intelligentsia are extremely bright, articulate, and educated individuals. They are angry because despite its mission higher education is not meritocratic. With few exceptions, the well-born and well-bred, rather than the best researchers and teachers, acquire the choice jobs.

From a policy standpoint, tenure is a double-edged sword. On the one hand, it protects professors with unpopular views from retaliation by students, parents, and administrators. In other words, tenure provides professors with "academic freedom," a degree of freedom of speech unparalleled in our society. Although the First Amendment protects people's speech from government sanction, it does not protect people or their ideas from their employers, who can fire employees who do not toe the organization's line. The World Bank, for example, fired Bill Easterly after he argued in his book *The Elusive Quest for Growth* that the World Bank sucks. Soon after, Easterly became a tenured professor at New York University, where he is free to expose the suckiness of anything that he wishes without having to worry about finding a new job. (That was the chronology. Readers can discern cause and effect for themselves.) To the extent that our society needs disinterested people who are unafraid to speak their minds to remind us that the emperor is naked, academic freedom is of paramount importance.

On the other hand, tenure allows institutions of higher education to get fat and inefficient. Most academic organizations are run like Athenian direct democracies. Everyone gets a say; everyone gets a vote. Anyone can hold up a decision as long as she wants. It's like being married, to scores or even hundreds of other people! Arthur Levine's hilarious parody of the situation is, unfortunately, only slightly exaggerated:

> The usual mechanism has been to create an 87-member strategic planning committee that after two years of weekly meetings manages to select for cutting one program, one with no new students in three years. This recommendation triggers a faculty no-confidence vote in the president. A new president is hired, who says the institution can get out of this situation by raising more money.[34]

This rule-by-committee-of-the-whole, this wholesale reversion to the failed precepts of the Articles of Confederation, is, of course, very cumbersome. Apparently, the proliferation of what one English professor in Colorado called "mind-numbing committee discussions" is the whole point.[35] Professors get to do what they do best, guffaw, procrastinate, and profess, while not actually implementing any change at all. So higher education has long faced what pundits call a "chronic crisis of stagnation."[36]

Many a professor has found tenure a form of quasi-retirement, a sinecure, an easy monthly check. Some tenured professors continue to be productive throughout their careers. They get accustomed to working hard and teaching well, and their schools and students benefit from it. As they age, however, many naturally slow down, even as their salaries continue skyward. The obligatory raise that puts nine hundred dollars into the pockets of new hires brings the dinosaurs three or four thousand dollars. Too many cling to their jobs even though they must realize that no matter how experienced and wise they may be, they are not worth three or four of their younger colleagues. But their pay and benefits say otherwise. They finally bow out at age seventy-five or eighty, *bona fide* millionaires.[37]

The other major problem with tenure is that it turns our citadels of higher learning into what Professor Eric Gould calls "a place of Machiavellian intrigue, self-serving negotiation, passive aggression, [and] devious alliances."[38] That lends itself to hyperpoliticization, which, in turn, allows ideological cliques to gain permanent control over departments, divisions, colleges, and even entire universities. The technique is simple: stealthily build a majority, dominate search committees, and hire your own without mercy or apology. Tell disappointed applicants that they simply did not "fit" with the department. Universities are supposed to be places where people of every political and religious persuasion can air their views, bring forth their evidence, and discuss the strengths and weaknesses of their arguments. They no longer are such places. In the words of education guru Frank Rhodes:

> The fundamental reason for the existence of the university is the benefit of shared dialogue. Without it, the claim to be a university or a collegium is groundless. If dialogue is not restored, universities will be cooperating in a pretense. They will have become an elaborate hoax, an expensive sham. They will have shortchanged the society that supports them.[39]

Tenure does not provide true academic freedom because the schools in general have political biases and hire accordingly.

***

But not even biased administrators are to blame for what is FUBAR in US higher education. In a competitive environment, tenure and hiring decisions based on anything other than merit would have been long since eradicated. In fact, the new breed of for-profit, corporate universities will not touch tenure with a ten-foot pole. But most of higher education is not competitive. Sure, schools fight over the "best" students and the "best" professors.[40] The "best," however, are usually not defined by their merit. Schools also compete for grants. That process is a little less politicized, but not by much because all the old elitist biases in favor of certain fancy schools get magnified many times over.

Most schools do not compete as businesses do, on the basis of overall institutional efficiency, because there is no reason for them to do so. The strange fact is that most US colleges and universities have no owners. Run as nonprofit institutions, they are, if part of state systems, controlled by state legislatures and state education bureaucracies. If private, they are controlled by boards of trustees. Since neither the states nor the trustees can extract much in the way of profits from their schools, they allow them to become inefficient. Tenure allegedly protects academic freedom, so it stays. Sports programs allegedly add to the educational experience, so they stay, too. Buildings that have become inadequate are torn down and replaced, although renovation of the existing structure would have been more cost efficient. A "star" professor (one who publishes up a storm in the "right" way) threatens to leave unless she gets a big raise, so she gets it and two new faculty hires are forgone instead. Such examples of inefficiency go on and on and on. They persist because the added costs are simply passed on to taxpayers and students, in the form of higher taxes, tuition bills, and fees. Tuition increases have long outpaced inflation as measured by the Consumer Price Index, so college costs take an increasing number of days of work to pay. Students therefore groan under an enormous load of work and debt.

Like rising medical costs, the current rate of tuition increases is simply unsustainable for much longer. We cannot spend our entire net incomes to pay off our hospital and college bills. We might need some money for food, shelter, and clothing, for instance! Why has tuition spiked so high? The ultimate cause, I believe, is that nobody owns most institutions of higher education, so there is no real competition between producers. Nobody, nobody in a position to do something about it anyway, cares if there are cost overruns. In addition, those with the greatest stake in higher education, tenured professors and well-ensconced administrators, often push for bigger budgets rather than cost-cutting, efficient ones. The professors want more services, like student workers to get books out of the library for them, clerical staff to answer phones and write e-mails for them, and complex webs of administrators to deal with students for them. The administrators seek bigger salaries for themselves, bigger budgets for their departments, and more direct reports. This sort of "empire building" is common in non-profit organizations as well as in poorly governed for-profit corporations. But in the latter case, corporate raiders, like that portrayed by Danny DeVito in *Other People's Money*, step in, buy out, takeover, and implement reforms. Nobody can take over and rationalize a nonprofit and, more important, nobody has the incentive to do so. So, like my waistline, the nonprofits tend to bloat and bloat and bloat.

There are diminishing returns to scale at play here, too. In other words, at some point the bigger an administrative bureaucracy gets, the less efficient, not the more efficient, it becomes. Soon, millions of student and taxpayer dollars go toward nothing at all except perpetuating the administrative monster. "It is not that it never changes," higher education consultant Frank Rhodes argues, "but that it never shrinks; it always grows."[41] "When faced with new situations," education guru Philip Altbach admits, "the traditional institutions either adjust by adding functions without changing their basic character or create entirely new divisions or institutes."[42] "Growth and progress," Arthur Levine notes, "were treated as synonyms."[43] (I protest only his use of the past tense.) "Bowen's Law of Higher Education" asserts that schools "try to increase their resources without limit."[44] In other words, colleges and universities follow the path of least resistance and get bigger, but not necessarily better. Worst of all, many within higher education conflate efficiency, which most if pressed would find palatable, with profitability, which most see as a dirty word. Little wonder, then, that most of our colleges and universities are almost in perpetual financial crisis.

If we allowed nonprofits to produce chewing gum, a pack would cost $117 and would taste like sawdust. Why, then, do we allow, nay, almost insist, that nonprofits produce education? I say "almost insist" because corporate universities are having a hard time of it. Often, state regulators harass them, forcing them to produce far more documentation than required of nonprofits. Worse, some snobby academics look down their noses at faculty who deign to teach at for-profit universities. Professors at such schools might as well have red, glowing noses because they often get excluded from professor reindeer games, like conferences and grants, simply because they happen to teach at a for-profit institution.

I worked for a for-profit, joint-stock university for only a short period, so I cannot say much about the industry that stems from personal experience. The public record is pretty clear, though. By the early third millennium CE some forty publicly traded corporations concentrated on the production of higher education. The for-profits are one of the few growth segments of the higher education industry in the United States. Traditionally, academe pooh-poohed for-profit schools, but in recent years it has begun to take notice as increasing numbers of them gain regional accreditation. It appears that the quality of education offered by the for-profits is not lower than that offered by most nonprofit institutions. The for-profits tend to stress outcomes, particularly job placement rates, while the non-profits tend to stress the stringency of entrance requirements. That gives the for-profits the high ground in many ways because they can, to some extent, demonstrate that their instructional practices facilitate learning or at least enhance student employability. The most that many nonprofits can say is that they are highly selective. (Little wonder then that their students see the actual course of their education as relatively unimportant. The main things are to *get in* and then to *get out*.)

For-profit higher education still makes many folks queasy because the potential for fraud seems perilously high. Much of this sentiment probably stems from the fact that well-endowed schools that charge thirty-five thousand dollars per year in tuition and pay no taxes barely break even. People cannot understand how endowment-less for-profits can earn 40 percent gross profits on eight thousand dollars per year in tuition without cutting corners, many corners. Avoiding the expense of a campus is not necessarily one of those cost savings. Some of the for-profits are online only, but most offer face-to-face, hybrid, and online courses, which are by no means cheap. They save by leasing rather than owning their classroom spaces and computer services and avoiding high-cost extras, such as fancy student unions and sports teams. The answer to the conundrum is that the for-profits need to be efficient, so they are, and the nonprofits do not have to be, so they aren't.

But those who worry about corporate universities have a point. A joint-stock corporation might skimp on student services, or entice people to sign up who have no business in the college classroom, or hire cheap, unqualified instructors, simply to meet profitability targets. I am not asserting that any for-profit has done any of those things, merely that the threat exists because the interests of the faculty (long term), the students (intermediate term), and the stockholders (short term) are not aligned. And, of course, there are gray areas. At one time, for example, one of the for-profits had been seen to invest precious little in library books. Under pressure from its accreditor, it has since beefed up its holdings, but it will never own a first- or even second-class collection.[45] Is its stingy library cost efficient, or is it simply the tip of a greedy iceberg? That is a difficult call. Why should an institution buy a book that will be used once, or perhaps never at all? Why should students who read fewer books subsidize those who read more books? Why not let students simply buy the books that they need? Professors ask them to buy required textbooks, for example. Why not also have them buy books that they might need to write papers or to complete other projects? The answer is clear. If students had to purchase all of the books that they might want to read, the law of demand predicts that they would read less. (And they read very little already!) Moreover, one of the great things about a library is that it helps students to find materials that they probably did not even know existed in the first place. As with everything else in life, a trade-off exists. Some of the schools with smaller libraries will buy any book that a professor says is needed for a class and also purchase major, recent books across the Library of Congress call number spectrum. But together they do not come close to buying all new academic titles. Some may think that this cheats students, but others may find its lean, mean library the very essence of efficiency.

Similarly, the techniques used by admissions officials at for-profits resemble those used by life insurance salesmen. The analogy is a close one. Life insurance and higher education are both difficult products to price, so it is easy to think that purchasers are getting a raw deal. On the other hand, both life insurance and higher education are crucial products for most people, but products that they may not buy if not properly guided. Many a person tried to slam the door in the face of the insurance agent, only in later years to appreciate the peace of mind and other benefits that a policy provided. Similarly, many people would not have given college a try (or a second or third try in many cases) unless persuaded to do so by a skilled admissions counselor. In both cases, the for-profit provider can be seen as greedy. But, as Adam Smith pointed out long ago, private greed often leads to great public good. As noted earlier, a college degree gives an individual a step over those without degrees; education appears to create large positive spillover effects for the rest of society.

That said, I think that the risk of corporate defalcation is high, especially once the for-profit education segment matures and the inevitable shakeouts begin. Skeptics correctly point out that simply because for-profits have kept their noses clean so far does not mean that they will continue to do so in the future. The possibility of a corporate buyout is especially problematic. What if an acquisition were to take place? Could the acquired school be completely shuttered? Could some campuses be sold or spun off? Could degree programs be sliced? What would happen to the students and faculty in those programs? What would happen to the faculty's terms of employment (teaching and research responsibilities, benefits, pay, parking spaces)? Are regulatory safeguards in place to ensure that there would be no wrongdoing, no breaches of contract? After all, state education regulators are not exactly prepared to deal with Larry the Liquidator. We are in uncharted waters here, so little can be said other than the possibility for malfeasance exists. Due to the principal-agent problem inherent in large, joint-stock corporations, one of the for-profit universities could turn out to be the next Enron.[46]

***

Is there a solution to the higher education ownership problem? Is there an organizational form that, like the corporation, gives educators incentives to produce high-quality education but that, like the nonprofits, does not expose students to the whims of stockholders? There is a solution, I believe, but one that becomes obvious only after we realize that students are clients, not mere customers, as most administrators and many professors now believe. Unfortunately, college officials seem to mean the term customer literally and narrowly, not as a synonym for sensitivity to the needs of students and the marketplace. How this sad state of affairs came to be, I know not, but I can attest to the utter ludicrousness of the doctrine. A "customer" is an individual who buys mass-produced goods or services. Thus you play the role of customer when you buy a pack of gum, a haircut, or an automobile. A customer buys the good or service more or less as is. A customer might be able to make a few, basic choices—sugar-free gum, take a little more off the top, no antilock braking system—but customers have no direct say in the design of the product. Where competitive markets rule, the "customer is always right," so producers will take consumer preferences into consideration, but only over time, and only if enough other customers express similar preferences.

In other situations, people expect much more personal attention. When you need to sue somebody, for example, you want an attorney who will work with you to create a compelling case. Similarly, your tax accountant had better pay close attention to your individual circumstances. And when you hire an architect or an interior designer, you also expect the product to be closely tailored to your needs and desires. When the suppliers provide highly individualized goods or services in which the purchaser has significant input, we have a professional-client relationship, not a seller-customer relationship.

The professional-client relationship is much deeper, much more intense, and much more personal than the seller-customer relationship. Most important, unlike the customer, the client is not always right. The client purchases advice so complex from the professional that the client may not be able to readily ascertain its value. This does not mean that the client is enslaved to the professional. Clients can and do change professional service providers. But it does mean that clients ultimately must trust their professionals. This insight helps to explain why professionals regularly form associations or other self-regulatory bodies that seek to define the ethical standards of their respective professions.

Some professional-client relationships are, or should be, so important or so intimate that English provides specialized words to characterize them. One obvious specialized word is "patient," which we reserve for the relationship between healthcare providers and their clients. One now not-so-obvious specialized word is "student," which at one time signified the professional relationship between educators and their clients. But many institutions of higher education in this country seem eager to degrade students, to reduce them from clients to mere customers. The implications of this change are truly frightening.

US higher education has been McDonaldized. To be sure, some of the restaurants are more upscale than others, but almost all institutions serve up the same menu of homogenized crap. In response to the student riots of the 1960s, during the Vietnam War when young men were drafted into the armed services, many schools began to allow students to choose electives. This quelled discontent by expanding the menu, by giving students a greater variety of crap to choose from. But each new menu item, each new elective, was simply another mass-produced commodity. At larger schools it might be possible to "hold the onions" by choosing a professor wisely, but any way you slice it, most of our schools serve up mass-consumption pabulum. After all, treating students as customers makes life easier for everybody in the short run. Administrators can pack classrooms, professors need not bother learning anything about their students, even their names, and students can slip, slide, and slack their way through school without having to think too much or to take control of their own educational destinies.

The student-as-customer model is a race to the bottom. Students soon learn that they can punish professors simply by complaining about them to the chair or dean, the same way that they might obtain satisfaction by asking to speak to a customer service representative's supervisor. Since the customer is always right, the professor's supervisor comes down on the prof. Professors quickly learn not to do anything that might antagonize their students. That spells easy assignments, high grades, frequently cancelled classes, and truncated discussions. Where student customers rule, there can be no academic freedom, only the tyranny of student misconceptions. Heaven forbid that a professor should ever "dis" a student by suggesting that his or her work is not up to par. Professors can no longer write on a paper "this is wrong because of X, Y, and Z." Rather, she must blandly suggest that "this could use some improvement." Or better yet, she should offer nothing at all, except "A–" or, if daring, a "B+."

That's right, grade inflation and the student-as-customer model are two peas of a pod. Remember, customers are always right. So how can they get low grades? They can't and, in fact, don't. Although some observers contend that grade inflation does not exist, most educators believe that it is out of control. It is difficult to believe otherwise when the *Chronicle of Higher Education* runs stories in which professors openly admit that they trade grades for good evaluations. Under tenure pressure, one recently admitted, she "approached the pile of papers with a new attitude, giving only As and Bs. I felt a little polluted," she admitted, "but I also felt the need to receive better marks myself on those cursed computerized forms. I need these students on my side. I need them to like me."[47]

In the 1950s, 42 percent of the grades assigned at Rutgers University were As or Bs. Today, those two letters account for 67 percent of the grades assigned at that school. At Princeton, As increased from 31 percent in the mid-1970s to almost half in recent years. To its credit, Princeton announced that in the future no more than 35 percent of its grades would be As or A–s. At Duke, the average GPA jumped from 2.7 in 1969 to 3.3 in 1996. Students at the University of Pennsylvania regularly challenge their grades and win. At Harvard, where the average grade a quarter century ago was a B–, the average grade is now a B+. That means that half of all grades are A or A– and that 90 percent of students graduate with honors. Things are so bad at Harvard that one professor provides students with two grades, the official high one that goes on the transcript and a second, lower one deflated to remove the effects of inflation. Harvard has recently trimmed its honors roll to about 50 percent, but grade inflation continues.

Grade inflation is not a victimless crime because it destroys student morale. Imagine how students at Yale felt when they learned that one of their fellow classmates pulled a B average even though he had nearly flunked out of a community college. He used a fake transcript to get into Yale and his deception went undetected for two years. (Perhaps Yale motivated him to do better in his studies. More likely, though, Yale professors were less demanding than those at the student's erstwhile community college. That is not to say that the community college professors are better or smarter than those at major research universities, merely that they have more incentive to attend to students' needs than do professors who must publish or perish.) Moreover, better students resent getting only slightly higher grades than weaker students. They learn not to work as hard. So do the weaker students, who soon realize than any old thing will get them a B, or maybe even an A–. Grade inflation rewards students for behaving strategically, for cramming into the easiest classes and eschewing the demanding ones, where professors use words like eschew.

Worst of all, grade inflation prevents professors from turning wayward students into gems. Students need to hear that their lab results are wrong, that their political views are immature, that their economic analyses are weak. This need not be done harshly, but the message must be clear if students are to improve and thrive. When administrators and even just a few professors begin to believe the student-as-customer model, an institution is not on a slippery slope, it is on an Olympic bobsled with nobody working the brakes. Quickly, students begin to make demands that lead to destruction of the curriculum. Professors who cave in make it more difficult for their hardier colleagues to continue under the student-as-client model because they embolden students to make derogatory comments like the following:

"Professor X doesn't give us homework. Why do you have to be such a hard ass?"
"Professor Y lets us use notes [textbooks, calculators, Cray supercomputers, the Internet, cell phones, etc.] on examinations."
"Mary [!!!!] says that we are entitled to our opinions so everything and anything we say is correct."

"Our math [English, history, economics, physics] class meets only once a week for an hour. Why do we have to come to this class twice a week for almost two hours?"

If the old-fashioned professor doesn't cave in, she finds nice comments like the following on her evaluations:

"I didn't learn anything this semester because this professor is too hard."

"I hate this prick."

"This professor is terrible. She tried to teach us things that we don't already know."

"I paid good money for this course but I am not even going to get an A."

"This professor discriminates in favor of the brighter, harder-working students."

"We had to write a paper AND give an oral presentation. Does this ogre think that the only class we are taking is hers?"

"We had to talk in class or lose points. That is wrong. I paid to listen to the professor talk, not my classmates."

"You'd have to be like a nerd or something to do well in this class."

In the student-as-customer model, comments like these will quickly put even a tenured faculty member in a pot of boiling water. Any sane person would jump out before the lid comes down and even the most obstinately professional professor eventually capitulates and lowers standards. Even the best professors come under pressure because students have become so self-centered, such good "customers" of education, that they can no longer tell the good professors from the bad ones. All that matters then is level of difficulty, and here lower is better. If the professor wises up and dumbs down, evaluations start to contain niceties like:

"This is a very good professor because she is really easy."

"The professor cancelled class a lot, so the course wasn't too bad."

"I really liked the professor because she reminded me of all the stuff that I learned in high school."

"The professor was really funny and entertaining so the class wasn't too boring."

"We watched a movie in almost every class, which was great. I like to watch TV and this class wasn't much different."

"I was reelly wurried bout this class cause my freind who took it a couple of years ago said the professor was a reel beatch. She seemed reelly nice in this class and only had good things to say about every body alltime. She made me feel reelly gud bout myself. Im sur to git a great job."

Seriously, standards are now so low that literary agents have difficulty hiring competent manuscript readers and university presses cannot find enough good monographs to publish. Employers more generally report a decline in the ability of their employees to express ideas in writing, even short memoranda. Conditions have deteriorated so much that one disgusted professor established a "Society for the Return to Academic Standards." It hasn't done much because it can't do much. Too many economic incentives are set against it.

9

FIGHTING FUBAR
Pareto Proposals

"Laws should not be made as if society was wholly composed of knaves and dupes," a nineteenth-century jurist argued. "The mass of the community is well disposed, and will act fairly under equitable laws."[1] That's a good point, but unfortunately it takes only a few knaves and dupes well placed in government to lead the economy seriously astray. Marx was closest to the mark when he noted that "politics is the art of looking for trouble, finding it everywhere, diagnosing it incorrectly, and applying the wrong remedies."[2] That was Groucho, not Karl, by the way. Governments throughout time and place have shown a predilection for turning relatively minor market failures into nearly intractable hybrid failures of epic proportions.[3] That suggests that the ultimate solution for the economy's ills is to create a new form of government, or at least a new Constitution. I don't want to go there, not here. If you do, I recommend Larry Sabato's *A More Perfect Constitution*.[4]

My goal here is much more modest. I think our current politicians and bureaucracies are capable of implementing FUBAR-reducing, "Pareto-improving" policies. A Pareto improvement, in economists' jingoistic lingo, is a policy or reform that makes at least one person better off without making anyone worse off. Some types of tax reforms could be Pareto.

Everyone would be better served, for example, if taxes were based on negative externalities, such as pollution, and consumption rather than on income. Policies that improve efficiency are almost always Pareto, or close to it. For example, my town recently implemented a Pareto policy when it moved to a more capital-intensive way of collecting garbage and recyclables, using fancy trucks with extendable arms that pick up and dump huge, covered, wheeled garbage cans. By cutting labor costs, decreasing the weight of garbage (covered cans means no water-logged trash) taken to the regional landfill, and increasing the amount of recycling, the township was able to cut its annual tax collection fee. Nobody lost their job (workers who left voluntarily were not replaced) and many fewer get hurt on the job (the truck does most of the work).

While "win–not lose" is not as good as trade, which is "win-win," Pareto policies are far better than most policy reforms, which at best are redistributive or "win-lose." Too many policies, like those that lull investors into complacency by tricking them into believing that government regulators are superior monitors of their property, are actually "lose-lose." Taxpayers bleed through the nose for the regulatory bureaucracy, but consumers are not well served by it. Rationally, no one should oppose a Pareto policy because by definition no one is injured by it.[5] Of course humans are not entirely rational, yielding frequently to base emotions like jealousy. Others, imbued with religious or socialist notions of distributional equity, insist that the worst off must be helped *before* others are aided, even if the worst off are not injured by the policy. That said, all else constant, it should be easier to enact a Pareto-improving reform than a merely redistributive one.

Acclaimed Baltimore writer and social critic Henry Louis Mencken (1880–1956) was only half right when he wrote that "for every problem there is a solution that is simple, direct, and wrong."[6] For every problem there are many solutions that are wrong but surely at least one that is "right," or at least Pareto improving. In this chapter, I propose policy reforms designed to fix every major FUBAR area of the American economy discussed in this book. Each reform is a Pareto improvement, or darn close to it, because the economic gains that would be unleashed would be so large that even vested interests would do at least as well under the proposed system as they currently do. Therefore, passage should be politically plausible if, alas, far from inevitable.

The Financial System

Fixing the complex mess created by the financial crisis that started in 2007 will not be easy. Neither will trying to prevent a repeat, politically that is. Economically, however, the correct path is pretty clear. In October 2008, Jacob Weisberg, the editor-in-chief of *Slate* magazine, proclaimed the end of libertarianism. "Any competent forensic work," he wrote, "has to put the libertarian theory of self-regulating financial markets at the scene of the crime."[7] Meanwhile, Republican congressman and 2008 presidential candidate Ron Paul believes that "it is not the market that has failed. It is intervention into the market that has failed."[8] Isn't it clearly both? Why do we have to think in terms of markets or government? Why not both? I agree with Paul, whom I voted for in the Pennsylvania primaries, that more government intervention is likely to worsen the crisis and render the financial system shakier than ever. I disagree, however, with his worship of Austrian economics, the ultralibertarian faction of economic theory. FUBAR runs much deeper than the Fed.

First and foremost, the government needs to stop backdoor redistribution. It's easier politically than a direct handout but very inefficient because of the sundry distortions it creates. If the government decides, through constitutional mechanisms, that it needs to promote homeownership, then it should give Americans money for down payments. Such a policy will work better than the current hodgepodge approach because it is directly linked to the ultimate goal. It's also more transparent and will have fewer side effects. All other policies that purport to foster homeownership should be abolished: the mortgage interest deduction, the Community Reinvestment Act, the GSEs, and whatever other monsters lurk in our laws. The government should also allow people to use pretax money to pay down their mortgage balances up to the current retirement account limits per year. Reducing a dollar of debt in a long-lived asset like a house is a form of investment, one with a guaranteed return equal to the interest that will no longer have to be paid.

What about securitization, the process of lumping mortgages (or other loans or bonds) together for resale? Throughout world history, such schemes have worked only when the government was heavily involved, as when Fannie was a federal agency instead of the hybrid abomination of nature it became in 1968.[9] So maybe the government can safely fold Fannie and Freddie back into itself, where they can work to keep mortgage rates low by providing securitization services.[10] Or maybe we should just go with the Danish model. The Danes got through the subprime mess relatively unscathed because borrowers could buy their mortgages at their market value. They therefore did not experience the whopping losses that occurred elsewhere, where borrowers could only "buy" their mortgages at par (the full principal owed at any given moment) while everyone else could buy them for less![11]

Instead of carping on details, government regulators ought to work to reduce asymmetric information and incentive misalignments. They should encourage mortgage originators to receive their commissions over five or ten years, or to keep a significant equity stake in the mortgages they are originating. If they do not take the hint, tell investors the assets they are buying could be much riskier than they think! Hire experts to study and report on relevant historical episodes or comparable cross-country cases.

Regulators also need to examine the incentives that they themselves create. If you announce that you will come to the aid of companies that you consider "too big to fail" and don't charge an appropriate price for that protection well, heck, even my then twelve-year-old-daughter could predict the results: you'll create lots of big companies with a penchant for playing subprime poker, derivative blackjack, and other crazy craps. The government should tax companies that are Too Big to Fail (TBTF—or, as argued below, it should not offer to bail them out at all), just like it should tax polluters, cigarette smokers, and others who create negative externalities. Similarly, if regulators cajole lenders into making loans to risky borrowers, they will eventually do so, especially if serious agency problems within the lenders already exist. Such agency problems are market failures but ones exacerbated by decades of regulator meddling that chipped away at the safeguards market participants had constructed over the eighteenth and nineteenth centuries.

Regulators should take the equivalent of the Hippocratic Oath: do no harm to the patient, which in this case is the American economy. Regulators should look upon themselves as interior designers rather than as police officers. Instead of monitoring and punishing, they should arrange the room, the market, so that visitors can police themselves. It isn't even that difficult to do, especially once corporate governance reforms have restored the balance of power to stockholders. Markets for instruments like subordinated debt will tell regulators how risky banks are relative to their peers. If regulators tax the riskiest ones, banks will pull back for the sake of their profits. Private companies are already offering automatic forensic accounting software that will help investors to spot the next Bernie Madoff well before he makes off with billions. But what if some of the software doesn't work? If no independent private party emerges to rate the software or stamp it with its Good Housekeeping Seal of Approval, regulators should monitor the performance of the software carefully and publish it to the world. Prudent self-interest will take care of the rest.

Construction

Information creation and dissemination would also help to iron out the many wrinkles in the custom construction industry. So-called cost planning is one very promising avenue of approach. With cost planning, owners pay contractors, construction managers, and architects to develop full, realistic planning documents. The documents are then used to solicit sealed bids and/or serve as the basis for a contract with an immutable price. Cognizant that change orders are not possible, contractors will bid their expected costs plus profits rather than bid strategically. In other words, with cost planning, owners pay up front to reduce asymmetric information and to greatly reduce bid gaming and change-order artistry.[12]

Another way of decreasing asymmetric information is to induce someone to create information and share it. As the nation's largest purchaser of custom construction projects, the government (all three levels) is in the best position to begin collecting and disseminating information about construction firms. It should create a mechanism (probably a Web site) where businesses and individuals could also post information. Unlike the Better Business Bureau, which essentially collects and tries to resolve complaints, the Web site would include just the main facts: who, what, when, where, and how much? The Web site would track individuals as well as construction firms to prevent people from erasing a bad record by merely changing a company name. If the site is comprehensive, it would give owners much better information than they currently have, which often is limited to a few usually highly unrepresentative references and samples.

Lawsuits filed by angry contractors would not be a problem because the site would be government run and sanctioned and would strive to include all projects, good and bad. People are more prone to complain rather than to praise, but contractors would induce customers on projects that went well to submit a post. To avoid bad press, they might pay off customers who they have wronged, but that seems to be a nice summary form of punishment to me. If the data is skewed, the government could implement a clever mechanism, like the carrot of a tax refund and the stick of a fine, to ensure that every construction project is included. It would also, of course, have to ensure that spurious entries are not made. Random checks, heavy fines, jail time, and a permanent note in the contractor's record should be sufficient deterrents to minimize such behavior.

The point of the database would be to allow owners to accept the *best* bid, not the lowest bid. Suppose Firm A bid $500,000, Firm B $550,000, and Firm C $600,000 to build a house with certain specifications. In today's market, clouded as it is with asymmetric information, most owners would choose Firm A. But what if the database showed that A's projects always ended up 20 to 25 percent over budget? It suddenly would not look so good. B was usually on budget and on time, but what if the Web site revealed that owners started complaining of leaky roofs, high utility bills, and other signs of shoddy workmanship? C, by contrast, had a sterling reputation for quality and staying on budget and on time. Most owners would go with C, which would eventually drive A and B to shape up or ship out to another line of work. The state of Hawaii currently uses just such a database to hire roofing contractors, and it has worked wonders.

Other reform policies have also been suggested. Some are better than others. In 1999, the authors of *Producing Affordable Housing* made two broad suggestions for making the title of their book a reality. They suggested that "soft second loans" and more flexibility in mortgage underwriting would help. As we learned in chapter 2, such policies did help—nevertheless—to create a massive housing bubble that exploded, crashing the financial system! The authors also suggested reducing contractors' costs "and passing savings on to buyers."[13] That looks like another overly simplistic recipe for disaster because it does not specify how those costs would come down or why contractors would willingly pass them on to owners.

Once we realize that asymmetric information and postcontractual monopoly power are the key culprits in construction project rip-offs, the solution becomes easy and direct. Better information! Once construction contractors have an incentive to compete on cost, time, and quality, they will do so. That may very well lead to industry consolidation, the emer-gence of intermediaries, better control of workers, and the like. But poli-cies that try to induce consolidation, intermediation, and better labor rela-tions directly, without overcoming the information problem at the root of the issue, will not help and may actually make matters worse. Fixing FUBAR means finding and alleviating causes, not symptoms, and letting nature take over from there.

Slavery

Slavery sullied our past and haunts our present but does not have to be part of our future. What will deter potential future slaveholders are incentives to use other forms of labor, not moralizing speeches. Evil governments, like that of the Nazis, and criminals, especially those allowed to operate in plain sight, cannot be easily stopped from enslaving the weak and vulnerable. Wide-spread peacetime chattel slavery, however, can be discouraged in a variety of ways. Promoting economic development worldwide, disrupting slave mar-kets wherever possible, ensuring that no society subsidizes slaveholders' costs, and keeping the costs of hypocrisy high by constantly reinforcing the value of human life and freedom are good places to start.

This book has focused mostly on the United States, but let me take this opportunity to sketch a way of helping poor countries to grow rich (and hence decrease the allure of slavery). It is finally no longer a secret that aid doesn't work. That goes for IMF loans, outright cash payments, and in-kind aid like medicines, condoms, and even entire factories—most of which get expropriated by crooks, often wearing military or police uni-forms. Ultimately, poor countries are poor for one reason: their govern-ments are predatory. In other words, instead of protecting life, liberty, and property, they take one or more, often all three, from the people they are supposed to protect. It is the ultimate principal-agent problem, just as John Locke theorized three centuries ago. With a predatory government in place, people have no incentives to form financial systems, to create startup companies, or frankly to do much of anything. Sometimes they try to oust their evil leaders, but they usually either fail or end up with an even worse bastard in power.

The United States has a very long history of trying to oust predatory leaders, but it has rarely succeeded. It defeated the Southern slavocracy only to allow the emergence of Jim Crow soon after. It forcibly removed Spain from the Philippines and Cuba, but the former is still a basket case and the latter is Communist. During World War I, it helped Britain and France to overthrow the German and Austro-Hungarian empires, and World War II was the direct result! A hundred million or so deaths and untold billions of dollars later, two major success stories occurred with the ouster of Hitler and Tojo from Germany and Japan, respectively. In the postwar period, America failed to remove tyrants from North Korea and Vietnam, but through the arms race helped to liberate the satellite states of the Soviet Empire. Some of the newly independent nations are thriving, but others remain mired in predation. More recently, the United States tried to replace the predatory Taliban in mountainous Afghanistan but still faces an *uphill* struggle there, bad as that pun is. Iraq has shown signs of improvement recently, but the elimination of Saddam Hussein has already been extremely costly in terms of blood and black gold, Iraqi tea.

An incentive-compatible market approach would likely prove much more cost effective and certainly less bloody than the traditional blazing-guns technique. The core cause of continued poverty is not that the leaders of poor countries cannot implement wealth-enabling policies but rather that they will not do so because the personal profits they earn through repression are greater than what they expect to earn through liberalization. Occasionally, a country reforms itself from within, as China did in the late 1970s, when its government went from being outright murderous to merely very repressive. In most instances, however, tyrants reign even when superpowers and international bodies attempt to intercede. What is needed is what I call *terraforming*, or literally "Earth-shaping." The term is appropriated here as shorthand for a process of business-led changes in the political economy of poor nations that entails paying (in careful, incentive-compatible ways) the leaders of poor countries to implement liberal growth policies followed by a well-coordinated infusion of foreign direct investment.

The process of politically and economically transforming poor countries into rich(er) ones could work this way or in a similar way:

1. A large and broad consortium of international businesses would identify a terraform target.
2. The consortium would negotiate the terms of payment and policies

with the target nation's leaders. The contract should stipulate payments to be made by the consortium (and aid agencies, if applicable) to the country's leadership in exchange for the enactment (de jure), implementation (de facto), and retention (long term) of a specific set of policies (generally, to reduce corruption, increase transparency and accountability, ease entry, and reduce the time and cost of turning mere property into collateralizable capital) on a detailed time table. Well-understood techniques for limiting opportunistic behavior, like holding a large percentage of the payments in escrow, should of course be utilized. Partial payment in the form of equity stakes in consortium businesses might also help to align the interests of the country's leaders with those of the consortium.

3. If the leaders implement the required policies, the consortium would make a predetermined set of direct investments in the target country. Details would vary depending on each country's most basic and urgent needs. In some countries, microfinance, microirrigation pump, distributed water purification, white light–emitting diode, and cell phone companies might move in first. In others, perhaps agribusinesses might work to increase crop yields in the countryside while textile manufactures would set up shop in the cities, and industrial life insurers would help to change incentives. Maslow's hierarchy of needs (water, food, and shelter must be adequate before "belonging" needs can be met, etc.), history, and context-sensitive logic provide rough guidelines regarding what types of businesses would be most appropriate.

4. As the target nation becomes politically and economically terraformed, some sort of representative government would likely evolve without prompting from the consortium or other outside groups. Once wealthy enough, the citizens might find it expedient to pay their once tyrannical leaders to "retire."

Obviously, terraforming would do much more for the world than reduce the prevalence of slavery. But those who question the wisdom of trying to stimulate further economic growth would do well to consider the ramifications of economic stagnation on human freedom.

Depressions and Bailouts

The Great Depression is a thing of the past. There is nothing we can do to help the millions of victims who inspired Steinbeck's depiction of the Joads. But we can, indeed *must*, stop the current and future recessions from degenerating into a similar debacle. If depression returns, the worst-case scenario would be that slavery experiences a resurgence, if not in the United States, then in the many economies worldwide that depend upon its tremendous purchasing power. The best-case scenario would be that the world is a poorer and sadder place than it would have been if depression had been averted. As noted in chapter 5, governments are just as culpable as markets when it comes to depressions, to long and sustained downturns in real per capita economic growth. Economies cycle between periods of growth and retrenchment, with an upward trend in countries, like the United States, that have good institutions, including nonpredatory governments, modern financial systems, and open-access entrepreneurship, in place. That means that the natural tendency is for the economy to rebound from recessions automatically. Once labor, land, and other factors of production get cheap enough, companies begin to invest in productive capacity again and another period of expansion commences. Mild downturns are good because they serve to cleanse the economy of inefficient firms and other forms of waste.

Instead of educating people about this, politicians often do whatever they can to prevent anyone from losing any money on their watch. That helps them to get reelected in the short run, but in the long term it puts the economy at risk. It's sort of like the FUBAR firefighting policies the government put in place in the arid West. For decades, the government stamped out wildfires as quickly as its firefighters could do so. That saved property and made the government seem very proactive and even brave. Over time, however, the policy had the catastrophic effect of turning naturally mild wildfires into virtually unstoppable cyclones of fire. It turns out that a little fire now and again keeps forests healthier by removing underbrush. (In fact, Amerindians deliberately set small fires for that very purpose.) With lots of forest-floor fuel to burn, fires now rage uncontrollably.[14]

Our economy suffers from the same sort of unnatural tampering. Interventions have therefore become increasingly enormous. In 1987, Greenspan more or less waved his hand and the stock market corrected. In

1997–1998, he had to break a sweat but still managed to avoid the fallout from the Southeast Asian, Russian, and Long-Term Capital Management crises. The softness that began with the deflation of the stock market bubble in 2000 and the terrorist attacks on 9/11 required yet more intervention, in the form of massive monetary stimulus and low interest rates. To stop the crisis of 2008, which was fueled by a lot of risky-banker underbrush that should have burned itself out over the previous several decades, the government had to implement multitrillion-dollar bailouts. So far, those bailouts have been successful—at angering Americans who perceive, largely correctly, that government policy has been rewarding those whom it should be punishing. Wait until they find out that taxpayer-funded bailouts are far from sure bets. In other words, they may not help the economy to revive any faster than it would have on its own. To be fair, bailouts may stop the economic situation from deteriorating further, but, that said, they may also make matters worse, as they probably did during the Great Depression. They almost certainly plant the seeds for the next crisis either by increasing moral hazard, inducing inflation, or introducing new distortions.[15]

Governments that want to try to stop the spread of financial panic can do no better than adopt Hamilton's rule, that is, lend freely at a penalty rate to all who can post good collateral. Such a policy saves safe firms while allowing risky ones to fail. That minimizes moral hazard and frees up poorly utilized human and physical resources for other, hopefully more productive, outlets.[16] Moreover, Hamilton's rule does not entail the massive redistribution of resources from taxpayers to risk takers because the government lends only on good collateral. Finally, due to the imposition of the above market rate, only those companies that need to borrow from the government will do so. Hamilton's rule would limit the government to being a lender of last resort, not the seemingly bottomless till of (almost) free money that it has become.

Retirement Savings

As we learned in chapter 6, the Social Security program was created, continued, and expanded for complex political reasons. But when we get right down to it, Social Security succeeded politically because it paid large windfalls at first—very high returns based on the incipient sweat of gen-

erations unborn—and because of the elaborate ruse that people had contributed to some sort of insurance or investment policy.[17] "With those
taxes in there," FDR once said, "no damn politician can ever scrap my
social security program."[18] So it would seem. Touching Social Security can
be deadly for politicians. Just as some LCFI are "too big to fail," the SSA is
"too big to be messed with."[19] The program is over seventy-five years old,
however, and shows signs of its age. Maybe it is high time that Social Security retired. That is not to say that we should return to what economist
Jared Bernstein calls a YOYO economy (You are On Your Own).[20] What it
means is that we can find a better way, one based on private security with
government income guarantees.

"There is no such thing," House Ways and Means Committee
chairman Al Ullman said in 1977, "as an easy way out of the social security dilemma."[21] If we fixed everything else FUBAR in the economy, we
might then get the productivity growth we need to keep the system afloat
without crushing the next generation. In case that does not happen, we
need a backup plan.[22] Finding more people to join the system would work.
Instead of spending billions to try to keep Mexicans out of an economy
that desperately needs them, we could allow them in as guest workers who
pay Social Security taxes but never receive any benefits.[23] That might
sound unfair at first, but if immigrants were informed of the conditions
and still came, the policy would simply be a revised form of the large
immigration fees that many other countries already impose. Of course,
that would be a political nonstarter because most on the Right do not want
to let immigrants in on any grounds and some on the Left would overreact
and consider the policy inhumane and not far from slavery.

Another approach is simply to raise the retirement age, indexing it to
increases in longevity and the nature of work. That may sound cruel, but
Social Security was not meant to provide people with an end-of-life vacation perk. It was meant to help people who were superannuated, to wit, too
old to work.[24] For eons, most people died before their economic value was
extinguished. In marginal areas, like the Arctic, the aged and disabled
ended their lives rather than burden their families, while in more forgiving
climes they simply shifted into tasks, such as childcare and food preparation, that they could physically handle. Over the nineteenth century, due
to the demise of family-owned firms (including but not limited to farms),
the highly physical nature of most paid work, increases in longevity, and

modestly improved healthcare, increasing numbers of people entered the frightening netherworld between work and death that we now call retirement. They responded rationally, by increasing savings in homes, in savings accounts, and in life insurance, and in living with kin or, if necessary, unrelated boarders. We know that those strategies worked tolerably well until the Great Depression, because while the number of indigent aged increased, their percentage of the total population did not. Social Security "fixed" arrangements that only seemed broken due to the general economic distress of the 1930s.[25]

Today, people can work much longer than they used to because they are living longer and because jobs have become less physically demanding. In 1940, the average sixty-five-year-old man had 11.9 years left to live and the average women 13.4 years. Those same figures today are over fifteen years for men and about twenty for women.[26] Today, most jobs are in the service sector and are not physically demanding, allowing people to work comfortably well past the current retirement age.[27] (Dementia can still force people out of the workplace, but, of course, is much less common than the many types of debilitating physical ailments, and medical advances are increasingly staving off their worst effects.) As far back as the 1950s, few professionals retired at sixty-five. Professional and semiprofessional occupations compose an increasingly large percentage of the workforce and will continue to grow in the future.[28] Moreover, even factory and transportation jobs are no longer as demanding as they once were due to computer automation, motorized forklifts, and the like. Even the military can now use older hands. Combat pilots used to be young men in top physical condition, like Tom Cruise in *Top Gun*. Today, an octogenarian manipulating a joystick connected to a drone can take out a gaggle of terrorists. Technological advances will only extend such trends. Some people who have accumulated significant assets will always choose to stop working, but retirement for all may be a historical anomaly largely confined to the twentieth century. Already one out of every seven Americans aged sixty-five or older still works,[29] and their disability rates have fallen significantly.[30]

It is important to note that seniors will not have to take potentially demeaning jobs like doing paper routes or flipping burgers at McDonald's, a melancholy fate that has befallen too many recent retirees.[31] Rather, I think seniors will retire from their regular career jobs later in life, if at all.[32] Of course, many people hate their jobs and hence want to retire as soon as possible.[33] The solution to that problem is easily stated—make jobs less sucky—but that is harder to implement. To some extent, economic growth has made jobs less onerous over time and will likely continue to do so. (It will also ensure that there are enough jobs for everyone who wants one, recessions and frictional unemployment excepted, of course.) Employees are more likely to see the virtue of taking extended vacations when they can be more fully enjoyed (with their children rather than their grandchildren) and pushing employers to accept the same. (Let's not emulate the French and take all of our vacations at the same time, however!) But again, the key point here is that Social Security or other social care for the aged should go to those who *can't* work, not to those who *won't*. If you don't like your job, help to change it—don't tax our progeny so you can lounge about in Florida.[34]

Another not mutually exclusive option is to reprivatize Social Security. Robert Eisner suggests supplementing Social Security with voluntary extra contributions that the government would invest on contributors' behalf in "passive, indexed stock or bond funds."[35] Contributions would be tax free going in and taxable going out, like private retirement accounts, but without the "high administrative costs or the commissions and profits that figure in privatized programs."[36] Of course, that raises the question of why Social Security is needed at all. Why not nudge people into saving enough for their retirement and give cash supplements to those who become disabled or demented before they have saved enough? That is much more honest than running a multigenerational quasi-Ponzi scheme and also rewards people for saving more and investing wisely. That would be a far cry better than the current system, which rewards them for muddling through their lives until age sixty-something.

By nudge, by the way, I mean subtle persuasion techniques like those advocated by Richard Thaler and Cass Sunstein in their book *Nudge*.[37] Like me, they profess to be *"not for bigger government, just for better governance"* [emphasis original].[38] Their story hinges on the fact that human thought is biased in various ways, some of which are very well understood. Their natural aberrant thought patterns lead people to make irrational decisions like eating too much or not saving enough. Just as children can be gently induced to eat more carrots and fewer cupcakes simply by rearranging their choices, so too can adults be nudged into saving more and more intelligently simply by having them opt *out* of the best choices instead of *into* them. Because people usually accept and stick with default options, if a government or employer strongly suspects that one choice is better than another, it should make that choice the default but allow those who wish to make another choice to do so. For example, it is far better for twenty-somethings to invest in risky stocks than in Treasury bills because their portfolios have a long time to recover. Employers should therefore automatically enroll their young employees in risky stock mutual funds but allow them to switch to another type of fund, or not to invest at all, if they so choose.

Keep in mind that reprivatization does not and should not refer only to investing in the stock market, as critics of Social Security reform often claim.[39] A rational private security strategy would start with the accumulation of a savings account large enough to handle typical contingencies like job loss or temporary illness. The acquisition of disability insurance, of the "any occ" (a term of art short for "any occupation") variety for unskilled workers and "own occ" (a term of art for "own occupation") for skilled ones, should come next. Upon marriage, term life policies should be purchased. Only when a good cash buffer and insurance screen is in place should people begin to think about investing in real estate, stocks, bonds, annuities, or whole-life insurance. Finally, investors must change the mix of their investments over time, toward ever-safer instruments as their desired retirement age approaches. Apparently many people just a few years from expected retirement learned that the hard way during the great bear market that awakened from its slumber following the financial panic of 2008. Many retirement investment companies now offer funds that automatically shift sector weights (from risky toward cash) over time. As the worker nears retirement, she or he should, of course, shift into less volatile assets. Many do not, so the company would arrange to do it for them, automatically.[40]

The government need not provide investment products, as Eisner suggests, but it should clean up the retail investment sector, which is rife with inefficiencies. Fees are much too high, research is often tainted by conflicts of interest, and brokers often give advice designed to maximize their commissions, not investor returns.[41] As argued above, the government should also again encourage people to invest in their homes by eliminating the tax bias in favor of retirement accounts, ideally by allowing homeowners to pay down their mortgages with pretax dollars. The government should also work harder to ensure that all Americans know the basics of investing.

Implementing the educational reforms described in chapter 8 would be a great starting place. Salespersons are currently doing too much investor education. When the investor knows little or nothing about investment principles, sales agents find it too easy and tempting to provide them with self-serving advice. If education proves insufficient, government should prepare to give people a good nudge or two ... or twelve.[42]

Retirees also need to have good postretirement investment strategies if they are to outlive their savings.[43] One approach is to ladder ten-year insured certificates of deposit so that 10 percent of the principal comes due every year to be reinvested at the current market rate. With such a ladder, default risk would be negligible and the retiree would receive the average interest rate over the previous decade. Tying a life annuity to a life insurance policy is another option, where it is allowed. A life annuity pays the investor a predetermined sum each year (now typically monthly) for as long as he or she lives. A life insurance policy pays a lump sum upon the insured's death. In the first case, the insurer has a pecuniary interest in the policyholder's death, in the latter in the policyholder's continued life. When the policies are tied together, the face value of the insurance policy decreases the longer the retiree lives, rendering the insurer indifferent as to the policyholder's longevity. It will either pay a larger death benefit or make more annuity payments. Such policies protect both the insurer (who need not worry about a large life insurance policyholder dying young or an annuitant dying very old) and the policyholder—and his or her heirs—(who need not fear outliving his or her income or dying soon after retirement without leaving a legacy to heirs).

People would have the funds to buy private security products once the regressive Social Security payroll tax was abolished. That does not mean abolishing Social Security payments. Recall that to keep policies politically palatable, they must be Pareto. No one should be rendered worse off, in other words, and that especially includes members of powerful political lobbies! Under my proposal, everyone born before January 1, 1969 (my birthdate, by the way), would receive everything Social Security has promised them, except that ridiculous two-hundred-fifty-dollar death benefit, out of general revenues. By shifting the burden to a progressive income tax, the system would be fairer for people with lower life expectancies, fewer children, and so forth. General taxes would have to increase, but hopefully the shift would induce taxpayers to make it clear to their elected officials that they need to hold the line on other spending. There is probably enough fat in the federal budget to fund half the increase.

People, like me, born on or after January 1, 1969, would be on our own, after a few years of grace to obtain sufficient life and disability insurance. If the economy does well and we invest intelligently, we would be able to retire around age seventy or so, if we wished. Those of us who did not save enough, or save wisely enough, would have to work until we became disabled, at which time we would receive direct income assistance out of general revenue. The proportion of such people would decrease as the pernicious effects of Social Security began to wear off. The poor would again look forward to receiving an inheritance that would help them to obtain their own private security. People rich and poor would know basic investment strategies and not fall easy victim to shysters. Most important, the government would stop surreptitiously robbing poor minority men to support middle-class white women because annuities and life and disability insurance would be priced properly, by actuaries competing in free markets. Similar gains would also be possible in healthcare and insurance.

Healthcare and Insurance

America must get healthcare costs under control while simultaneously providing basic coverage to all.[44] That task is not as daunting as it may at first seem. As with retirement, America could do so much more with what it already spends.[45] The basic coverage part is easy. As in Switzerland, the government could simply mandate, as it has in recent legislation, that everyone obtain insurance and, if need be, give the poor money to buy it. Government mandates are rarely a good idea, but sometimes they are crucial. Mandates work well for immunizations and automobile insurance and seem to make sense for health insurance because universal coverage would reduce the adverse selection problem that caused the initial market failure. The most direct route is often the cheapest and, crucially, the least distortionary.

Good nudge policies here would get people to eat better, drink and smoke less, get more exercise, and get appropriate medical tests. A major problem, however, is that it isn't always clear which behaviors are healthier than others. Allegedly "healthy" foods one week are unhealthy the next, and vice versa. Some nutritionists deride the Atkins diet (low carb) while others note that it helps some people. I've shown elsewhere that too often politics overrides science, as in the creation of the so-called Food Pyramid.[46] Before the government nudges, it should make damn sure that it is doing so in the right direction. Of course, by its very nature a misdirected nudge will cause less damage than more intrusive policy implementation.

Perhaps, though, nudging is best left to insurers or medical care providers who have proper incentives to point people in the right direction. As matters stand now, healthcare incentives are backward because patients pay medical providers for seeing them, not for fixing them. That means the providers have incentives *not* to heal the sick but merely to evaluate them. If regulators didn't stand in the way, insurers and/or healthcare providers could create prepaid programs whereby people would pay a monthly fee when they are well. When they are sick, payments would cease until they are better. Such a system would reward providers for fixing people up and quickly doing it. Regulators would be needed mostly to adjudicate disputes that would arise when providers and patients would disagree over states of illness and to ensure that providers did not renege if the cost of a patient's illness or injury exceeded the discounted present value of her future payments. A market mechanism for ensuring the same would be to unite health and life insurance into a single policy, so the company would compare paying the life benefit to the healthcare expenses. In a combined policy, the life insurance benefit would be reduced for those who received expensive medical care and augmented for those who used relatively little healthcare. That would reward healthy people and perhaps even induce them to obtain insurance.[47] In addition, under a combined policy, individuals would be forced to decide whether or not they want to greatly reduce the value of their estates to undertake costly and risky procedures. That may sound heartless to some, but keep in mind that the problem is not with the policy but with the opportunity costs imposed upon humanity by nature. The resources necessary to extend every individual's life indefinitely simply do not exist, so they must be rationed, and better by the market than by politicians.

Higher Education

US higher education is terribly inefficient, unfair, and elitist. A major problem is that traditional schools, public and private, are too cloistered from competition because nobody owns them. The usual solution to such problems, the introduction of ownership via joint-stock corporate structures, however, is rife with incentive alignment problems. In short, stockholders and managers may expropriate resources from students and faculty in order to achieve their own short-term financial goals. Because administrators and faculty tend to think of students as mere customers, we are stuck in a seemingly unsolvable dilemma or paradox—both nonprofit and for-profit schools are bad for students' education!

Once people realize that students are more than customers, that they are best described as clients, the paradox at once disappears. US colleges and universities should be for-profit institutions, but not joint-stock corporations. They should be organized as professional partnerships, like law firms, with professors as the owner-operators.[48] (Most professionals are not allowed to form joint-stock corporations because stockholders might pressure them to take advantage of their clients in hopes of short-term gains. For example, stockholders might beseech lawyers to advise their clients to settle a court case simply so the firm can make its quarterly numbers.)[49]

Unfortunately, professor-partnerships are not currently recognized by law, and entry costs, mostly in the form of state education boards, are prohibitive. At this point, those in their right mind would not form a professional partnership and try to establish a college. It would simply cost too much and return too little. They would be crushed like bugs, not by competitive pressures but by the bigotry of big schools grown fat on government subsidies. Many students would opt to attend where they can party and watch football and basketball. With two minor changes, however, the playing field could be leveled. First, government subsidies should go to students, not to schools. Otherwise, the schools compete at begging for scraps from the government instead of in attracting, retaining, and teaching students. This fits perfectly with former Democratic New York governor Mario Cuomo's adage that "it is not the government's obligation to provide services, but to see that they're provided."[50] (Foreign students would still be welcome at US colleges, of course, but it would remain up to their respective home governments to decide what, if any, subsidies they would receive.) Second, colleges need to start with better raw material. In too many places, our primary and secondary teachers are not helping enough students to learn the basic reading, writing, and thinking skills they need to thrive in the semiskilled workplace, much less college. Those schools could also be improved by turning their ownership over to teachers and providing subsidies to students, not to schools. The government doesn't need to provide schooling for everyone, it merely needs to ensure that it is provided for all, and the more efficiently, the better.

Another way to improve the quality of students before they enter college is to make them work a little for their government subsidies. People always treat things they have worked for better than they do gifts. A couple of years in the military or four cleaning national parks or building houses for the poor would do wonders for the country and the young people, who often need to grow up a little away from home. After a stint of such service, subsidies could be quite generous, enough for most students to attend the school of their choice for four years without having to work. And as the money would be earned and paid to students, rather than to schools, subsidies could not be slashed every time the economy staggers a little.[51] The GI Bill worked wonders and so could an expanded version open, *voluntarily* of course, to every American high school graduate.[52]

Finally, any group of PhDs should be able to launch a school with the same ease that any group of MDs or JDs could open their own medical or legal offices. Instead of bureaucratic government certification of minimal acceptable levels of inputs (student-teacher and student-computer ratios, number of contact hours, number of courses offered, and so forth), schools should be judged on their students' scores on standardized exit examinations. That would make direct comparison between schools easier and also end the peculiar conflict of interest inherent in having professors both teach and grade their students. That conflict is best exemplified in the joke: "I know I am a great professor... I gave all of my students As."

Once those reforms are in place, some young professors would opt to form partnerships instead of joining the publish-or-perish culture of ivoried academia. Undoubtedly, some would fail. But others would succeed spectacularly. They would never drive Harvard out of business, unless it loses its endowment in a Ponzi scheme, but they would attract ever-larger numbers of students. Over a generation or two, the face of US higher education would change for the better. Some current college professors and administrators would not be better off, but neither would they be made worse off. The same goes for taxpayers. America already devotes a higher percentage of its resources to education than almost every other nation on earth. The reforms suggested here would not increase those subsidies and could even reduce them through the increases in efficiency almost certain to occur with the rise of professor-owned colleges. If we could get the incentives right, good results would follow, in our hallowed halls as well as in our homes because American students would be able to think independently and hence compete internationally once again.

Concluding Thoughts

When it comes to the hyperdysfunctional or FUBAR parts of the economy, neither the government nor the market is wholly to blame. They both are, to different degrees and in different ways. The next time you hear a Republican blame the government and a Democrat blame the market for some economic fiasco, you'll know the true score. Each is only partially correct. Combine their stories in a historically accurate narrative, and you'll expose the hybrid failure at the root of the problem.

We need both governments and markets. With no government, there could be no economy of any size. We would be too busy trying to steal from each other to get much work done. With no market, there could be no government of any significance. Although both governments and markets are crucial to our happiness, the simple fact of the matter is that the government has to initiate reforms if our educational, financial, construction, employment, and healthcare institutions are to improve. Market forces constantly flummox government's efforts, rendering regulators ridiculous. Nevertheless, markets can seldom trump enforced governmental rules and regulations. The government is just too big and powerful. Too many policies use a construction worker's sledgehammer where an archeologist's brush would be more appropriate. Before any policy becomes law (or a regulation), the government should have to prove that the policy goal is necessary and that the policy tool is the best way of achieving that goal. Too often, policy goals are not even clearly stated, much less justified. And almost always politicians pick the politically easiest plausible implementation route instead of the optimal one, or at least one resembling the optimal one. Too often that leads to the massive distortion of incentives underlying the FUBAR components of the economy.

A good place to start would be to require Congress to give appropriate labels to bills. Too many bills sound like "An Act for Increasing Happiness for Everyone All the Time" when they should have titles like "An Act for Increasing Red Tape and Little Else," "An Omnibus Bill for Passing Crap

That Would Never Make It on Its Own," and even "A Law That Will Hurt Almost Everyone but Make Our Campaign Donors Really Happy." FUBAR-creating policies must end or something must give. Change will happen. It is simply a matter of whether it will be slow, rational change or the uncontrollable type of change that occurs during crises.

NOTES

CHAPTER 1: FUBAR, FUBAR EVERYWHERE

1. Rick Brooks and Ruth Simon, "Subprime Debacle Traps Even Very Credit-Worthy," *Wall Street Journal*, December 3, 2007, p. A1.

2. William Baumol, Robert Litan, and Carl Schramm, *Good Capitalism, Bad Capitalism, and the Economics of Growth and Prosperity* (New Haven, CT: Yale University Press, 2007), p. 231.

3. Ibid., p. 229.

4. John Wilke, "How Lawmaker Rebuilt Hometown on Earmarks," *Wall Street Journal*, October 30, 2007, p. A1.

5. Shailagh Murray, "For a Senate Foe of Pork Barrel Spending, Two Bridges Too Far," *Washington Post*, October 21, 2005, p. A8.

6. Such views find ample support in the public choice literature, including Gordon Tullock, Arthur Seldon, and Gordon Brady, *Government Failure: A Primer in Public Choice* (Washington, DC: Cato Institute, 2002) and Clifford Winston, *Government Failure versus Market Failure: Microeconomics Policy Research and Government Performance* (Washington, DC: AEI-Brookings Joint Center for Regulatory Studies, 2006).

7. Theodore Sedgwick, *What Is a Monopoly? or, Some Considerations Upon the Subject of Corporations and Currency* (New York: George P. Scott & Co., 1835), p. 27.

8. Price Van Meter Fishback et al., *Government and the American Economy: A New History* (Chicago: University of Chicago Press, 2007), pp. 403 and 462.

9. Saturday Night Live, "*Saturday Night Live* Transcripts, Season 17, Episode 19," http://snltranscripts.jt.org/91/91sperot.phtml (accessed August 27, 2009).

10. Readers who want to know more about markets, asymmetric information, the financial system, and such are urged to visit flatworldknowledge.com, which offers free college-level texts. The author of this book coauthored Flat World Knowledge's *Money and Banking*, which is available at: http://www.flatworld knowledge.com/printed-book/1634 (accessed August 27, 2009).

11. Robert Clark Seger, *The Fire Down Below*, Hideout Records/Distributors.

12. Lawrence J. White, "The Residential Real Estate Brokerage Industry: What Would More Vigorous Competition Look Like?" *Real Estate Law Journal* 35, no. 1 (Summer 2006): 11–35.

13. Joseph W. Eaton and David Eaton, *The American Title Insurance Industry: How a Cartel Fleeces the American Consumer* (New York: New York University Press, 2007).

14. Barry LePatner, Timothy Jacobson, and Robert E. Wright, *Broken Buildings, Busted Budgets: How to Fix America's Trillion-Dollar Construction Industry* (Chicago: University of Chicago Press, 2007).

15. Ibid., pp. 94–98.

16. Fishback et al., *Government and the American Economy*, p. 400.

17. Robert E. Wright, "The College as Partnership," *Forbes.com* (December 29, 2005), http://www.forbes.com/columnists/2005/12/29/higher-education -partnerships-cx_rw_1230college.html (accessed August 27, 2009); Adam Smith, *An Inquiry into the Nature and Causes of the Wealth of Nations* (New York: Modern Library, 1937), pp. 716–40; Milton Friedman and Rose Friedman, *Free to Choose: A Personal Statement* (New York: Harcourt, 1990), pp. 175–87.

CHAPTER 2: DEATH OF A SALESMAN

1. Mick Jagger and Keith Richards, "You Can't Always Get What You Want," performed by the Rolling Stones, ABXCO Music, 1969.

2. Kenneth Snowden, "Mortgage Securitization in the United States: Twentieth Century Developments in Historical Perspective," in *Anglo-American Financial Systems: Institutions and Markets in the Twentieth Century*, ed. Michael Bordo and Richard Sylla (Burr Ridge, IL: Irwin Professional Publishing, 1995), pp. 261–98.

3. Except where otherwise noted, this section is based on Donald Kemmerer, "The Colonial Loan-Office System in New Jersey," *Journal of Political Economy* 47 (December 1939): 867–74; John Frederick Koffler, *A Letter from a Tradesman in Lancaster to the Merchants of the Cities of Philadelphia, New York, and Boston* (Philadelphia: n.p., 1760); Leonard Labaree et al., eds., *Papers of Benjamin Franklin* (New Haven,

CT: Yale University Press, 1959); Bruce H. Mann, *Republic of Debtors: Bankruptcy in the Age of American Independence* (Cambridge, MA: Harvard University Press, 2002); Ron Michener and Robert E. Wright, *Control of the Purse: Money, Politics, and the Imperial Crisis in New York* [tentative title] (New Haven, CT: Yale University Press, forthcoming); Ron Michener and Robert E. Wright, "Farley Grubb's Noisy Evasions on Colonial Money: A Rejoinder," *Econ Journal Watch* (May 2006): 251–74; Ron Michener and Robert E. Wright, "Development of the US Monetary Union," *Financial History Review* 13, no. 1 (2006): 19–41; Ron Michener and Robert E. Wright, "Miscounting Money of Colonial America," *Econ Journal Watch* (January 2006): 4–44; Ron Michener and Robert E. Wright, "State 'Currencies' and the Transition to the US Dollar: Clarifying Some Confusions," *American Economic Review* (June 2005): 682–703; "New Jersey Currency Question," Record Group 23, Box 4, New Jersey Historical Society, Newark, NJ; Mary Schweitzer, *Custom and Contract: Household, Government, and the Economy in Colonial Pennsylvania* (New York: Columbia University Press, 1987); J. W., *An Address to the Freeholders of New-Jersey, on the Subject of Public Salaries* (Philadelphia: n.p., 1763); Robert E. Wright, *Hamilton Unbound: Finance and the Creation of the American Republic* (New York: Praeger, 2002).

4. "New Jersey Currency Question."

5. *New Jersey Gazette*, January 30, 1786.

6. Koffler, *Letter from a Tradesman*, pp. 10–11.

7. Philip L. White, ed., *The Beekman Mercantile Papers, 1746–1799*, 3 vols. (New York: New York Historical Society, 1956), 1:461.

8. Labaree et al., *Papers of Benjamin Franklin*, 10:209.

9. As quoted in Leslie V. Brock, *Currency of the American Colonies, 1700–1764: A Study in Colonial Finance and Imperial Relations* (New York: Arno Press, 1975), p. ix.

10. J. W., *Address to the Freeholders of New-Jersey*, pp. 13–14.

11. Labaree et al., *Papers of Benjamin Franklin*, 18:134–36.

12. Ibid., 19:191–92.

13. "New Jersey Currency Question."

14. Koffler, *Letter from a Tradesman*, pp. 7–10.

15. Ibid., pp. 13–14.

16. "New Jersey Currency Question."

17. Koffler, *Letter from a Tradesman*, pp. 9–13.

18. Dorothy C. Barck, ed., *Letter Book of John Watts, Merchant and Councillor of New York, January 1, 1762–December 22, 1765* (New York: John Watts De Peyster Publication Fund Series, 1928), pp. 163, 176.

19. White, *Beekman Mercantile Papers, 1746–1799*, 1:461.

20. Barck, *Letter Book of John Watts*, p. 254.

21. Quoted in Virginia Harrington, *The New York Merchant on the Eve of the Revolution* (New York: Columbia University Press, 1935), p. 323.

22. Barck, *Letter Book of John Watts*, p. 368.

23. Ibid.

24. "New Jersey Currency Question."

25. J. W., *Address to the Freeholders of New-Jersey*, pp. 142–43, 149, 157, 162.

26. Wright, *Hamilton Unbound.*

27. As quoted in Donald Kemmerer, "A History of Paper Money in Colonial New Jersey, 1668–1775," *Proceedings of the New Jersey Historical Society* 74 (1956): 137.

28. William B. Reed, *The Life of Esther De Berdt, afterwards Esther Reed, of Pennsylvania* (Philadelphia: C. Sherman, 1853), pp. 99, 114.

29. Labaree et al., *Papers of Benjamin Franklin*, 13:475.

30. David Vanhorne to Nicholas Browne and Co., October 3, 1766, Brown Papers, John Carter Brown Library, Providence, RI.

31. As quoted in Kemmerer, "History of Paper Money," p. 137.

32. Paul L. Ford, ed., *The Writings of John Dickinson* (Philadelphia: Historical Society of Pennsylvania, 1895), pp. 227–28.

33. Ibid.

34. *Publications of the Colonial Society of Massachusetts, Vol. 13, 1910–1911* (Boston: Colonial Society of Massachusetts, 1912), p. 441.

35. White, *Beekman Mercantile Papers*, p. 708.

36. John Mitchell, *The Present State of Great Britain and North America* (London: T. Becket and P. A. De Hondt, 1767), p. 311.

37. Labaree et al., *Papers of Benjamin Franklin*, 14:330–331.

38. Stephen Sayre, *The Englishman Deceived* (New York: John Holt, 1768), p. 10.

39. Mann, *Republic of Debtors*, pp. 85–86.

40. Ibid.

41. "Alexander Mackraby to Sir Philip Francis," *Pennsylvania Magazine of History and Biography* 11 (1887): 282.

42. White, *Beekman Mercantile Papers*, p. 469.

43. The American Papers of the Second Earl of Dartmouth, Staffordshire Record Office, Staffordshire, UK, D(W) 1778/II/119.

44. Ibid.

45. "New Jersey Currency Question."

46. Robert Fairlane to Walter Rutherford, January 1, 1765, March 28, 1767, Walter Rutherford Papers, Reel 3, New York Historical Society, New York, NY.

47. Ibid.

48. William Smith, *Historical Memoirs from 16 March 1763 to 25 July 1778 of William Smith* (New York: Arno Press, 1969), p. 29.

49. Labaree et al., *Papers of Benjamin Franklin*, 10:209.

50. Mark Skousen, ed., *The Compleated Autobiography by Benjamin Franklin* (Washington, DC: Regnery, 2006), pp. 74–75.

51. Richard H. Thaler and Cass R. Sunstein, *Nudge: Improving Decisions about Health, Wealth, and Happiness* (New Haven, CT: Yale University Press, 2008), pp. 53–54.

52. Dilip Abreu and Markus Brunnermeier, "Bubbles and Crashes," *Econometrica* 71 (2003): 173–204; Viral Acharya and Matthew Richardson, eds., *Restoring Financial Stability: How to Repair a Failed System* (Hoboken, NJ: John Wiley and Sons, 2009); Franklin Allen, Stephen Morris, and Andrew Postlewaite, "Finite Bubbles with Short Sale Constraints and Asymmetric Information," *Journal of Economic Theory* 61 (1993): 206–229; Gadi Barlevy, "Economic Theory and Asset Bubbles," *Economic Perspectives: Federal Reserve Bank of Chicago*, no. 3 (2007): 44–59; Efraim Benmelech, Eugene Kandel, and Pietro Veronesi, "Stock-Based Compensation and CEO (Dis)incentives" (NBER working paper no. 13732, 2008); Utpal Bhattacharya and Xiaoyun Yu, "The Causes and Consequences of Recent Financial Market Bubbles: An Introduction," *Review of Financial Studies* 21 (2008): 3–10; Markus Brunnermeier, "Bubbles," in *The New Palgrave Dictionary of Economics* (New York: Oxford University Press, 2007); Markus Brunnermeier and Christian Julliard, "Money Illusion and Housing Frenzies," *Review of Financial Studies* 21 (2008): 135–80; Nishant Dass, Massimo Massa, and Rajdeep Patgiri, "Mutual Funds and Bubbles: The Surprising Role of Contractual Incentives," *Review of Financial Studies* 21 (2008): 51–99; Robin Greenwood and Stefan Nagel, "Inexperienced Investors and Bubbles" (NBER working paper no. 14111, 2008); Refet Gurkaynak, "Econometric Tests of Asset Price Bubbles: Taking Stock," *Journal of Economic Surveys* 22 (2008): 166–86; Robert Hetzel, "Government Intervention in Financial Markets: Stabilizing or Destabilizing?" (working paper, Federal Reserve Bank of Richmond, 2009); Sidney Homer and Richard Sylla, *A History of Interest Rates*, 4th ed. (Hoboken, NJ: John Wiley and Sons, 2005); Charles Kindleberger, *Manias, Panics, and Crashes: A History of Financial Crises*, 4th ed. (Hoboken, NJ: Wiley and Sons, 2000); Stephen LeRoy, "Rational Exuberance," *Journal of Economic Literature* 42 (2004): 783–804; Ronald McKinnon, "Bagehot's Lessons for the Fed," *Wall Street Journal*, April 25, 2008; Gianni Nicolo, Luc Laeven, and Kenichi Ueda, "Corporate Governance Quality: Trends and Real Effects," *Journal of Financial Intermediation* 17 (2008): 198–228; Maureen O'Hara, "Bubbles: Some Perspectives (and Loose Talk) from History," *Review of Financial Studies* 21 (2008): 11–17; Frank Partnoy, "The Siskel and Ebert of Financial Markets? Two Thumbs Down for the Credit Rating Agencies," *Washington University Law Quarterly* 77 (1999): 619–714; David Porter and Vernon Smith, "Stock Market Bubbles in the Laboratory," *Journal of Behavioral Finance* 4 (2003): 7–20; J. Patrick Raines, J. Ashley McLeod, and Charles Leathers, "Theories of Stock Prices and the Greenspan-Bernanke Doctrine on Stock Market Bubbles," *Journal of Post-Keynesian Economics* 29 (2007): 393–408; Carmen Reinhart and Ken-

neth Rogoff, "Banking Crises: An Equal Opportunity Menace" (NBER working paper no. 14587, 2008); Carmen Reinhart and Kenneth Rogoff, "This Time Is Different: A Panoramic View of Eight Centuries of Financial Crises" (NBER working paper no. W13882, April 2008); Tina Saitone and Richard Sexton, "Alpaca Lies? Speculative Bubbles in Agriculture: Whey They Happen and How to Recognize Them," *Review of Agricultural Economics* 29 (2007): 286–305; Robert J. Shiller, *New Financial Order: Risk in the 21st Century* (Princeton, NJ: Princeton University Press, 2003); Jean Tirole, "On the Possibility of Speculation Under Rational Expectations," *Econometrica* 50 (1982): 1163–81; Eugene White, "The Great American Real Estate Bubble of the 1920s: Causes and Consequences" (working paper, Rutgers University, October 2008); Robert E. Wright, ed., *Bailouts: Public Money, Private Profit* (New York: Columbia University Press, 2010).

53. Vincent P. Carosso, *Investment Banking in America: A History* (Cambridge, MA: Harvard University Press, 1970).

54. Joe Nocera, "Risk Management," *New York Times,* January 2, 2009, http://www.nytimes.com/2009/01/04/magazine/04risk-t.html (accessed August 27, 2009).

55. Jonathan Michael Kerr and Thomas Morgan Robertson, *She Blinded Me with Science,* performed by Thomas Dolby, Bienstock Publishing, 1983.

56. Felix Salmon, "Recipe for Disaster: The Formula That Killed Wall Street," *Wired,* February 23, 2009; "Did Math Formula Cause Financial Crisis?" Marketplace, NPR, February 4, 2009, http://marketplace.publicradio.org/display/web/2009/02/24/pm_stock_formula_q/ (accessed August 27, 2009).

57. Kristin Roberts and Emily Kaiser, "AIG CEO Defends Bonuses as Public Fury Mounts," Thomson Reuters, March 18, 2009; Thomas E. Woods, *Meltdown: A Free-Market Look at Why the Stock Market Collapsed, the Economy Tanked, and Government Bailouts Will Make Things Worse* (Washington, DC: Regnery Publishing, 2009), p. 151.

58. Jane W. D'Arista, *The Evolution of Finance, Volume II: Restructuring Institutions and Markets* (Armonk, NY: M. E. Sharpe, 1994), pp. 300–301.

59. As quoted in Michael Simkovic, "Secret Liens and the Financial Crisis of 2008" (working paper, January 4, 2009).

60. *SEC Annual Report,* 2000.

61. Ibid., 2001.

62. Ibid.

63. Ibid.

64. Ibid., 2002.

65. Ibid.

66. Ibid.

67. Economist Intelligence Unit, "Country Finance: Japan" (New York: EIU, April 2004), pp. 23–24.

68. *SEC Annual Report,* 2003.

69. Ibid.

70. SEC Litigation Release no. 18854, August 26, 2004.

71. *SEC Annual Report*, 2003.

72. SEC Litigation Release no. 18985, November 30, 2004.

73. SEC Litigation Release no. 18958, November 4, 2004.

74. "BoA, Fleet in $675M fund settlement," *CNN Money*, March 15, 2004, http://money.cnn.com/2004/03/15/funds/fundsfire_sec/ (accessed August 27, 2009).

75. Brian Carroll, "The Mutual Fund Trading Scandals," *Journal of Accountancy* 198 (2004): 32–36; James B. McCallum, "Mutual Fund Market Timing: A Tale of Systematic Abuse and Executive Malfeasance," *Journal of Financial Regulation and Compliance* 12 (2004): 170–77.

76. The SEC recently encouraged more competition in ratings creation, but the Fed continues to favor the big three. "Wages of Sin: The Fed Is Perpetuating a Discredited Oligopoly," *Economist*, April 25, 2009, p. 80.

77. "David Einhorn on the Financial Crisis," *Mapping Strategy*, April 29, 2008, http://cartegic.typepad.com/mapping_strategy/2008/04/david-einhorn-o.html (accessed September 2, 2009).

78. Julie Satow, "Madoff Whistleblower Markopolos to Speak to *60 Minutes*," *Huffington Post*, March 2, 2009, http://www.huffingtonpost.com/2009/03/02/madoff-whistleblower-mark_n_171120.html (accessed September 2, 2009); "Madoff Whistleblower Went Unheeded for Years," *MSNBC*, December 19, 2008, http://www.msnbc.msn.com/id/28310980/ (accessed September 2, 2009).

79. "Con of the Century," *Economist*, December 20, 2008, pp. 119–20.

80. David Einhorn, *Fooling Some of the People All of the Time: A Long Short Story* (Hoboken, NJ: John Wiley and Sons, 2008).

81. Gwendolyn Wright, *Building the Dream: A Social History of Housing in America* (New York: Pantheon Books, 1981), p. 101.

82. "Labour Mobility: The Road Not Taken," *Economist*, March 21, 2009, pp. 31–32.

83. Harold Wolman, *Housing and Housing Policy in the US and the UK* (Lexington, MA: D. C. Heath, 1975).

84. Cushing Dolbeare, *Federal Housing Assistance: Who Needs It? Who Gets It?* (Washington, DC: National League of Cities, 1985).

85. Michael Stegman, *Housing Finance and Public Policy: Cases and Supplementary Readings* (New York: Van Nostrand Reinhold, 1986); Dennis Rourke, *The American Home Builder and the Housing Industry* (Rockville, MD: Management Practice Press, 1994), pp. 66–67; Edwin Mills, "Urban Land-Use Controls and the Subprime Mortgage Crisis," *Independent Review* 13, no. 4 (Spring 2009): 559–65.

86. Ned Eichler, *The Merchant Builders* (Cambridge, MA: MIT Press, 1982), pp. xvii, 6–9.

87. As quoted in Gary Gershman, *The Legislative Branch of Federal Government* (New York: ABC-CLIO, 2008), p. 303.

88. Woods, *Meltdown*, pp. 148–49.

89. Robert E. Wright et al., eds., *History of Corporate Governance: The Importance of Stakeholder Activism* (London: Pickering & Chatto, 2004).

90. As quoted in Mark Roe, "A Political Theory of American Corporate Finance," *Columbia Law Review* 91, no. 1 (1991): 34–35.

91. Ibid., pp. 11, 19–31.

92. Horace Robbins, "'Bigness,' the Sherman Act, and Antitrust Policy," *Virginia Law Review* 39, no. 7 (1953): 941. See also Edwin J. Perkins, *Wall Street to Main Street: Charles Merrill and Middle-Class Investors* (New York: Cambridge University Press, 1999), p. 137.

93. See, for example, Randall Kroszner and Raghuram Rajan, "Is the Glass-Steagall Act Justified? A Study of the US Experience with Universal Banking Before 1933," *American Economic Review* 84 (1994): 810–32.

94. Mark Roe, *Strong Managers, Weak Owners: The Political Roots of American Corporate Finance* (Princeton, NJ: Princeton University Press, 1996).

95. Wolman, *Housing and Housing Policy*; Eichler, *Merchant Builders*, p. vii.

96. Wright, *Building the Dream*, pp. 262–63.

97. Woods, *Meltdown*, p. 156.

98. Glen Ballard and Alanis Nadine Morissette, "Ironic," performed by Alanis Nadine Morissette, Aerostation, 1995.

99. *Title Insurance: Actions Needed to Improve Oversight of the Title Industry and Better Protect Consumers* (Washington, DC: GAO, 2007).

100. White, "Residential Real Estate Brokerage," pp. 11–32.

101. As quoted in ibid., p. 12.

CHAPTER 3: BOB THE BUILDER

1. Except where otherwise noted, this chapter is based on Barry B. LePatner, Timothy C. Jacobson, and Robert E. Wright, *Broken Buildings, Busted Budgets: How to Fix America's Trillion-Dollar Construction Industry* (Chicago: University of Chicago Press, 2007).

2. Theodore Sedgwick, *What Is a Monopoly? or, Some Considerations upon the Subject of Corporations and Currency* (New York: G. P. Scott, 1835), p. 27.

3. Robert E. Wright, *One Nation Under Debt: Hamilton, Jefferson, and the History of What We Owe* (New York: McGraw-Hill, 2008).

4. LePatner, Jacobson, and Wright, *Broken Buildings*.

5. Ibid.

6. Julian Lange and Daniel Mills, eds., *The Construction Industry: Balance Wheel of the Economy* (Lexington, MA: D. C. Heath, 1979), pp. 11–18.

7. Dennis Rourke, *The American Home Builder and the Housing Industry* (Rockville, MD: Management Practice Press, 1994), p. 47.

8. LePatner, Jacobson, and Wright, *Broken Buildings.*

9. Ibid.

10. Ned Eichler, *The Merchant Builders* (Cambridge, MA: MIT Press, 1982), p. 78.

11. John Kenneth Galbraith, *The Age of Uncertainty* (New York: Houghton Mifflin, 1979).

12. Lange and Mills, *Construction Industry*, pp. 6–7.

13. Martin Mayer, *The Builders: Houses, People, Neighborhoods, Governments, Money* (New York: W. W. Norton, 1978), p. 242.

14. Robert Sharoff, "Drawing a Line on Drugs," *Builder* 20 (March 1997): 154–57.

15. Lange and Mills, *Construction Industry*, p. 7.

16. John McMahan, *Property Development*, 2nd ed. (New York: McGraw Hill, 1989), p. 387.

17. Business Roundtable, *More Construction for the Money: Summary Report of the Construction Industry Cost Effectiveness Project* (January 1983), p. 13.

18. Rourke, *American Home Builder*, p. 159.

19. Lange and Mills, *Construction Industry.*

20. US Census Bureau, *Industry Summary: Construction, 1997 Economic Census*, tables 5, 12, http://www.census2010.gov/prod/ec97/97c23-is.pdf (accessed September 3, 2009).

21. Eichler, *Merchant Builders*, pp. xiii–xiv.

22. Ibid., p. 187.

23. McMahan, *Property Development*, p. 379.

24. Lange and Mills, *Construction Industry*, pp. 13–14, 29–30.

25. Ibid., p. 15.

26. David Gerstel, *Running a Successful Construction Company* (Newtown, CT: Taunton Press, 2002), p. 31.

27. William D. Booth, *Marketing Strategies for Design-Build Contracting* (New York: Chapman and Hall, 1995), p. 115.

28. Ibid.

29. Mark Federle and Steven Pigneri, "Predictive Model of Cost Overruns," *Transactions of the AACE International* (1993).

30. Lange and Mills, *Construction Industry*, p. 15.

31. Mayer, *Builders*, p. 38.

32. Rourke, *American Home Builder*, pp. 316–17.

33. Ibid., p. xi.

34. Leo Grebler, *Large-Scale Housing and Real Estate Firms: Analysis of a New Business Enterprise* (New York: Praeger, 1973), pp. 157–60.

35. Peter Philips, "The United States: Dual Worlds: The Two Growth Paths in US Construction," in *Building Chaos: An International Comparison of Deregulation in the Construction Industry*, ed. Gerhard Bosch and Peter Philips (New York: Routledge, 2003), p. 184.

36. Mayer, *Builders*, p. 73.

37. Ibid., p. 349.

38. Robert Hetzel, *The Monetary Policy of the Federal Reserve: A History* (New York: Cambridge University Press, 2008).

39. *Letters to the People of New Jersey on the Frauds, Extortions, and Oppressions of the Railroad Monopoly* (Philadelphia: Carey and Hart, 1848), p. 15.

40. Eichler, *Merchant Builders*.

41. As quoted in NAHB Economics, Mortgage Finance and Housing Policy Division, *Producing Affordable Housing: Partnerships for Profit* (Washington, DC: Home Builder Press, 1999), p. x.

42. Eichler, *Merchant Builders*, pp. 27–32, 70–77.

43. William Bragg Ewald, *Trammell Crow: A Legacy of Real Estate Business Innovation* (Washington, DC: Urban Land Institute, 2005).

44. Eichler, *Merchant Builders*, pp. 184, 200–210.

CHAPTER 4: UNCLE TOM'S CABIN

1. Merle Travis, "Sixteen Tons," Unichappell Music, 1947.

2. William Francis Allen, Charles Pikard Ware, and Lucy McKim Garrison, *Slave Songs of the United States* (New York: A. Simpson, 1867), p. 7.

3. Ibid., p. 20.

4. Harriet Beecher Stowe, *Uncle Tom's Cabin* (Mineola, NY: Dover Thrift Edition, 2005), pp. 306–307.

5. Ibid., p. 349.

6. Alan Houston, *Benjamin Franklin and the Politics of Improvement* (New Haven, CT: Yale University Press, 2008), p. 216.

7. Robert Fogel, *Without Consent or Contract: The Rise and Fall of American Slavery* (New York: W. W. Norton, 1989), p. 17.

8. B. F. Stairley to Henry C. Carey, May 6, 1855, Edward Carey Gardiner Collection, Historical Society of Pennsylvania, Philadelphia, PA.

9. Robert Fogel, *Without Consent or Contract: The Rise and Fall of American Slavery* (New York: W. W. Norton, 1989), pp. 17, 84–86; St. George Tucker, *A Dis-*

sertation on Slavery: With a Proposal for the Gradual Abolition of It, in the State of Virginia (Philadelphia: Mathew Carey, 1796), p. 40; Donald R. Wright, *African Americans in the Early Republic, 1789–1831* (Arlington Heights, IL: Harlan Davidson, 1993), pp. 25, 27; Gary Nash, *Forging Freedom: The Formation of Philadelphia's Black Community, 1720–1840* (Cambridge, MA: Harvard University Press, 1988), p. 4; Paul David et al., *Reckoning with Slavery: A Critical Study in the Quantitative History of American Negro Slavery* (New York: Oxford University Press, 1976), pp. 304, 332–33; James Huston, *Calculating the Value of the Union: Slavery, Property Rights, and the Economic Origins of the Civil War* (Chapel Hill: University of North Carolina Press, 2003), pp. 30–31. See also H. S. Bodley (Lexington) to William S. Bodley (Vicksburg), March 15, 1837, Bodley Family Papers, Filson Historical Society, Louisville, KY.

10. Alexis de Tocqueville, *Democracy in America* (Chicago: University of Chicago Press, 2000), pp. 331–32; Huston, *Calculating the Value*, p. 19; Joseph John Gurney, *A Journey in North America* (Norwich: n. p., 1841), pp. 188–89.

11. Nathaniel Appleton, *Considerations on Slavery: In a Letter to a Friend* (Boston: Edes and Gill, 1767), p. 12; Benjamin Franklin, *The Interest of Great Britain Considered* (Boston: B. Mecom, 1760), pp. 54–55; Tocqueville, *Democracy in America*, p. 337; Frederick Law Olmsted, *A Journey in the Seaboard Slave States, with Remarks on Their Economy* (New York: Negro Universities Press, 1968), p. 197.

12. Tocqueville, *Democracy in America*, p. 336; Tench Coxe, *A View of the United States of America* (Philadelphia: William Hall and Wrigley & Berriman, 1794), p. 488; Thomas F. Lynch, "Foundations of Radicalism," in *Understanding International Relations: The Value of Alternative Lenses*, 4th ed., ed. Daniel Kaufman, Jay Parker, and Kimberly Field (New York: McGraw-Hill, 1999), pp. 503–19.

13. For a lengthier overview of slavery and servitude in mainland North America up to 1800, see Kenneth Morgan, *Slavery and Servitude in Colonial North America: A Short History* (New York: New York University Press, 2000).

14. From today's perspective, it is interesting that Franklin said this, since it was the slave's life that was stolen. From the perspective of Franklin's time, slaves were commodities with no claims to their masters' other property.

15. Franklin, *Interest of Great Britain*, pp. 53–54.

16. Richard Nisbet, *Slavery Not Forbidden by Scripture; or, a Defence of the West-India Planters, from the Aspersions Thrown Out against Them* (Philadelphia: John Sparhawk, 1773), p. 8.

17. Slaves were insurable, although many companies, including Guardian, refused to insure them. Robert E. Wright and George D. Smith, *Mutually Beneficial: The Guardian and Life Insurance in America* (New York: New York University Press, 2004), p. 3.

18. This model is adapted from models and ideas found in Alfred Conrad and John Meyer, *The Economics of Slavery and Other Studies in Econometric History* (Chicago:

Aldine Publishing, 1964), pp. 46–73; Fogel, *Without Consent*, pp. 69, 108; Huston, *Calculating the Value*, p. 66; Tocqueville, *Democracy in America*, pp. 326–48. At some margins, sexual intercourse may have played a role in firm decision making. As early as 1773, people knew that slaveholders often took sexual advantage of their female slaves. Benjamin Rush, *An Address to the Inhabitants of the British Settlements in America, Upon Slave-Keeping* (New York: Hodge and Shober, 1773), p. 18.

19. Before 1830, and especially before 1800, firms also compared the costs and benefits of indentured servants (I) as well. In that case, $W_{prod} + W_{liq} - W_{hyp} - W_{con} \equiv S_{prod} + S_{liq} - S_{hyp} - S_{con} \equiv I_{prod} + I_{liq} - I_{hyp} - I_{con}$. Any number of other types of labor, including convicts, redemptioners, contractors, and family members, could be added to the comparison. Morgan, *Slavery and Servitude*, pp. 45–58, 72. For a good, recent overview of the literature on the decision of firms to "make or buy" and to "own or lease," see Oliver E. Williams and Sidney G. Winter, eds., *The Nature of the Firm: Origins, Evolution, and Development* (New York: Oxford University Press, 1993).

20. John Schulz, *The Financial Crisis of Abolition* (New Haven, CT: Yale University Press, 2008), pp. xi–xii, 56.

21. Economists will recognize the model as an application of Markowitz's portfolio selection model. A readable introduction to that theory can be found in Frederic Mishkin, *The Economics of Money, Banking, and Financial Markets*, 5th ed. (New York: Addison-Wesley, 1997), pp. 94–103. For a more sophisticated treatment, see Charles P. Jones, *Investments: Analysis and Management*, 8th ed. (New York: John Wiley and Sons, 2002).

22. B. F. Stairley to Henry C. Carey, May 6, 1855, Edward Carey Gardiner Collection, Historical Society of Pennsylvania, Philadelphia, PA.

23. Fogel, *Without Consent*, pp. 201; Huston, *Calculating the Value*, p. 6.

24. James Oliver Horton and Lois E. Horton, *In Hope of Liberty: Culture, Community and Protest among Northern Free Blacks, 1700–1860* (New York: Oxford University Press, 1997), p. 6; Winthrop Jordan, *White over Black: American Attitudes towards the Negro, 1550–1812* (Chapel Hill: University of North Carolina Press, 1968); Olaudah Equiano, "The Horrors of the Middle Passage," in *Afro-American History: Primary Sources*, 2nd ed., ed. Thomas Frazier (Belmont, CA: Wadsworth Publishing, 1988), p. 15.

25. Tucker, *Dissertation on Slavery*, pp. 36–37; Jared Diamond, *Guns, Germs, and Steel: The Fates of Human Societies* (New York: W. W. Norton, 1997), pp. 77–78, 197–212, 357, 373–74; Brett Rushford, "'A Little Flesh We Offer You': The Origins of Indian Slavery in New France," *William and Mary Quarterly* 60 (2003): 777–808; Rush, *Address to the Inhabitants*, pp. 5, 17–18; Tocqueville, *Democracy in America*, p. 326.

26. Huston, *Calculating the Value*, pp. 4–5, 9; Appleton, *Considerations on Slavery*, p. 4; Juvenis, *Observations on the Slavery of the Negroes, in the Southern States, Particu-*

larly Intended for the Citizens of Virginia (New York: W. Ross, 1785), p. 10; Horton and Horton, *Hope of Liberty*, p. 40; Olmsted, *Journey in the Seaboard Slave States*, p. 226; Tocqueville, *Democracy in America*, p. 327; Nash, *Forging Freedom*, p. 12; Morgan, *Slavery and Servitude*, pp. 94–100.

27. Huston, *Calculating the Value*, p. 3.

28. William Pollard to Mark Byrne, May 22, 1772, William Pollard Letterbook, Historical Society of Pennsylvania, Philadelphia, PA. All quotations from Pollard within this paragraph are derived from the above source.

29. Huston, *Calculating the Value*, p. 98; Olmsted, *Journey in the Seaboard Slave States*, p. 228; Rush, *Address to the Inhabitants*, p. 6; Horton and Horton, *Hope of Liberty*, p. 11; Adam Smith, *An Inquiry into the Nature and Causes of the Wealth of Nations* (New York: Modern Library, 1937), p. 553; Nash, *Forging Freedom*, pp. 10, 72; Tucker, *Dissertation on Slavery*, pp. 13–14; Tocqueville, *Democracy in America*, p. 338; Jonathan Dickinson to Isaac Norris, April 10, 1703, Maria Dickinson Logan Papers, Historical Society of Pennsylvania, Philadelphia, PA.

30. Sharon V. Salinger, *"To Serve Well and Faithfully": Labor and Indentured Servants in Pennsylvania, 1682–1800* (Cambridge: Cambridge University Press, 1987).

31. Robert Pindyck and Daniel Rubinfeld, *Microeconomics*, 3rd ed. (Englewood Cliffs, NJ: Prentice Hall, 1995), pp. 198–212. All the information at the beginning of this paragraph is derived from this source.

32. Martin Finkelstein, "Understanding the American Academic Profession," in *In Defense of American Higher Education*, ed. Philip Altbach, Patricia Gumport, and D. Bruce Johnstone (Baltimore, MD: Johns Hopkins University Press, 2001), p. 336.

33. *National Era*, March 16, 1848, as excerpted in *Northern Labor and Antislavery: A Documentary History*, ed. Philip Foner and Herbert Shapiro (Westport, CT: Greenwood Press, 1994), p. 57.

34. Olmsted, *Journey in the Seaboard Slave States*, pp. 82–83; Horton and Horton, *Hope of Liberty*, p. 14; Nash, *Forging Freedom*, p. 11; Morgan, *Slavery and Servitude*, p. 68; Fogel, *Without Consent*, p. 109; Joseph Richardson account book, 1733–1739, Historical Society of Pennsylvania, Philadelphia, PA.

35. Fogel, *Without Consent*, p. 110.

36. Nisbet, *Slavery Not Forbidden*, p. 12; Tocqueville, *Democracy in America*, p. 338; Nash, *Forging Freedom*, p. 72; Horton and Horton, *Hope of Liberty*, p. 11; *Pennsylvania Gazette*, December 22, 1768, July 13, 1769.

37. Nisbet, *Slavery Not Forbidden*, p. 11; Tocqueville, *Democracy in America*, pp. 338–39; Fogel, *Without Consent*, pp. 26, 34–40, 74–80, 162.

38. Appleton, *Considerations on Slavery*, p. 13; William Dilwyn, *Brief Considerations on Slavery, and the Expediency of Its Abolition* (Burlington, NJ: Isaac Collins, 1773), p. 7; Tucker, *Dissertation on Slavery*, pp. 80–81.

39. Rush, *Address to the Inhabitants*, p. 4.

40. Smith, *Wealth of Nations*, p. 365.

41. John Hammond Moore, ed., *A Plantation Mistress on the Eve of the Civil War: The Diary of Keziah Goodwyn Hopkins Brevard, 1860–1861* (Columbia: University of South Carolina Press, 1993), pp. 33, 34, 42, 49, 95, 111; Rush, *Address to the Inhabitants*, pp. 26–27; John Ashworth, *Slavery, Capitalism, and Politics in the Antebellum Republic* (New York: Cambridge University Press, 1995), p. 9; Nisbet, *Slavery Not Forbidden*, pp. 15–17; John Wesley, *Thoughts upon Slavery* (London: n.p., 1774), pp. 46, 60; Charles Crawford, *Observations upon Negro-Slavery* (Philadelphia: Joseph Crukshank, 1784), pp. 9–11; Huston, *Calculating the Value*, pp. 20, 84; Nash, *Forging Freedom*, pp. 8–9; Olmsted, *Journey in the Seaboard Slave States*, pp. 44–45; Eugene Genovese, *Roll, Jordan, Roll: The World the Slaves Made* (New York: Random House, 1972), pp. 295–324; Mary Reynolds, "Life as a Slave: A Narrative," in *Afro-American History: Primary Sources*, 2nd ed., ed. Thomas Frazier (Belmont, CA: Wadsworth Publishing, 1988), pp. 67–68.

42. Horton and Horton, *Hope of Liberty*, p. 22; Fogel, *Without Consent*, p. 197; Morgan, *Slavery and Servitude*, pp. 99–100; Jonathan Dickinson to Isaac Norris, April 10, 1703, Maria Dickinson Logan Papers, Historical Society of Pennsylvania, Philadelphia, PA.

43. Fogel, *Without Consent*, pp. 192–94; Reynolds, "Life," pp. 65–66; Horton and Horton, *Hope of Liberty*, p. 15; Rush, *Address to the Inhabitants*, p. 22; Tocqueville, *Democracy in America*, p. 341; Crawford, *Observations upon Negro-Slavery*, pp. 5–7.

44. *National Era*, March 16, 1848, as excerpted in Foner and Shapiro, *Northern Labor*, p. 57; Smith, *Wealth of Nations*, pp. 365–66; Rush, *Address to the Inhabitants*, pp. 7–8.

45. David et al., *Reckoning with Slavery*, p. 18; Smith, *Wealth of Nations*, p. 81.

46. Tucker, *Dissertation on Slavery*, pp. 14–15, 22.

47. Wright, *African Americans*, p. 31; Horton and Horton, *Hope of Liberty*, p. 26; Dilwyn, *Brief Considerations*, p. 10.

48. Nash, *Forging Freedom*, pp. 9–10; James Logan to John Penn, November 10, 1740, James Logan Letterbook; Horton and Horton, *Hope of Liberty*, p. 13; Philadelphia Yearly Meeting, *An Epistle of Caution and Advice, concerning the Buying and Keeping of Slaves* (Philadelphia: James Chattin, 1754), p. 2.

49. Juvenis, *Observations on the Slavery*, p. 19.

50. Charles Royster, *A Revolutionary People at War: The Continental Army and American Character, 1775–1783* (Chapel Hill: University of North Carolina Press, 1979); Charles H. Lesser, ed., *The Sinews of Independence: Monthly Strength Reports of the Continental Army* (Chicago: University of Chicago Press, 1976). Eighteenth- and nineteenth-century European economists accustomed to thinking about the effects of a growing labor force and a fixed amount of arable land developed and obsessed about the "law," which had little application to the American economy

because, as noted, slaveholders could simply purchase more land or sell excess slaves. In other words, they could increase all inputs, not just labor. Modern economists recognize three possibilities in that case: diminishing, constant, or increasing returns to scale. Pindyck and Rubinfeld, *Microeconomics*, p. 187; William Bernstein, *The Birth of Plenty: How the Prosperity of the Modern World Was Created* (New York: McGraw-Hill, 2004), p. 42, no. 1.

51. Isaac Foster, *A Discourse upon Extortion* (Hartford, CT: n.p., 1777); David Cooper, *A Serious Address to the Rulers of America on the Inconsistency of Their Conduct Respecting Slavery: Forming a Contrast between the Encroachments of England on American Liberty, and American Injustice in Tolerating Slavery* (Trenton, NJ: Isaac Collins, 1783); Appleton, *Considerations on Slavery*, pp. 4, 7, 19; A Lover of Constitutional Liberty, *The Appendix; or, Some Observations on the Expediency of the Petition of the Africans, Living in Boston, &c. Lately Presented to the General Assembly of this Province* (Boston: E. Russell, 1773), pp. 13–15; Rush, *Address to the Inhabitants*, pp. 20, 21, 29; *Observations on the Slaves and the Indented Servants, Inlisted in the Army, and in the Navy of the United States* (Philadelphia: n.p., 1777), p. 1; Morgan, *Slavery and Servitude*, pp. 88, 98–99, 102–108; Horton and Horton, *Hope of Liberty*, pp. 55–58; Fogel, *Without Consent*, pp. 194–95, 242–44; Huston, *Calculating the Value*, p. 15; David et al., *Reckoning with Slavery*, p. 344; Nisbet, *Slavery Not Forbidden*, pp. 19–20; Reynolds, "Life as a Slave," p. 65; Elizur Wright to H. M. Darlington, March 8, 1839, Gratz—Inventors, Historical Society of Pennsylvania, Philadelphia, PA.

52. Philadelphia Yearly Meeting, *Epistle*, p. 1.

53. Nash, *Forging Freedom*, pp. 8, 24–26; Horton and Horton, *Hope of Liberty*, p. 57.

54. Alice Hanson Jones, *Wealth of a Nation to Be: The American Colonies on the Eve of the Revolution* (New York: Columbia University Press, 1980), p. 51; Huston, *Calculating the Value*, p. 15; Wright, *African Americans*, p. 46; Nash, *Forging Freedom*, p. 63; Horton and Horton, *Hope of Liberty*, pp. 74, 80–82; Tocqueville, *Democracy in America*.

55. Register of Slaves, 1783–1830, Office of the Prothonotary, Bucks County, PA.

56. Tench Coxe, *A View of the United States of America* (Philadelphia: William Hall and Wrigley & Berriman, 1794), p. 488.

57. Craig Horle et al., eds., *Lawmaking and Legislators in Pennsylvania* (Harrisburg: Pennsylvania House of Representatives, 2005); US Census, 1790, Historical Census Browser, http://fisher.lib.virginia.edu/collections/stats/hist census/ (accessed September 3, 2009); Timothy Pitkin, *A Statistical View of the Commerce of the United States* (New York: Augustus Kelley, 1967), pp. 377–78.

58. Dilwyn, *Brief Considerations*, p. 6.

59. Horton and Horton, *Hope of Liberty*, p. 5; Eli Faber, *Jews, Slaves, and the Slave Trade: Setting the Record Straight* (New York: New York University Press, 1998), pp. 131–42; Fogel, *Without Consent*, p. 32.

60. George Washington to John Sinclair, December 11, 1796, in *The Writings*

of George Washington from the Original Manuscript Sources, 1754–1799, ed. John C. Fitzpatrick (Washington, DC: Government Printing Office, 1931).

61. Robert E. Wright, *The Origins of Commercial Banking in America, 1750–1800* (Lanham, MD: Rowman and Littlefield, 2001); Robert E. Wright, *The Wealth of Nations Rediscovered: Integration and Expansion in American Financial Markets, 1780–1850* (New York: Cambridge University Press, 2002); Robert E. Wright, *Hamilton Unbound: Finance and the Creation of the American Republic* (New York: Praeger, 2002); Robert E. Wright, *The First Wall Street: Chestnut Street, Philadelphia, and the Birth of American Finance* (Chicago: University of Chicago Press, 2005); Robert E. Wright and David J. Cowen, *Financial Founding Fathers: The Men Who Made America Rich* (Chicago: University of Chicago Press, 2006).

62. Patrick White, ed., *Lord Selkirk's Diary, 1803–1804: A Journal of His Travels in British North America and the Northeastern United States* (Toronto: Champlain Society, 1958), pp. 262–63.

63. David Galenson, "The Rise and Fall of Indentured Servitude in the Americas: An Economic Analysis," *Journal of Economic History* 44 (March 1984): 1, 13; Morgan, *Slavery and Servitude*, p. 124; Huston, *Calculating the Value*, pp. 25–26; Fogel, *Without Consent*, pp. 309–12; Farley Grubb, "The End of European Servitude in the United States: An Economic Analysis of Market Collapse, 1772–1835," *Journal of Economic History* 54, no. 4 (1994): 794–824. On p. 806 Grubb notes the essential point here: "Alternative sources of unbound labor were readily available. ... By the nineteenth century, immigrant servitude was a marginal appendage to the [Philadelphia] region's labor market."

64. As quoted in Huston, *Calculating the Value*, p. 67.

65. Ibid.

66. Olmsted, *Journey in the Seaboard Slave States*, pp. 82–84.

67. Tocqueville, *Democracy in America*, p. 332; Huston, *Calculating the Value*, pp. 67, 88; Olmsted, *Journey in the Seaboard Slave States*, pp. 187–88; Fogel, *Without Consent*, pp. 91–92.

68. Hinton Helper, *The Impending Crisis of the South: How to Meet It* (New York: Burdick Brothers, 1857), pp. 42–43.

69. Fogel, *Without Consent*, p. 238; Reynolds, "Life as a Slave," p. 68; Tucker, *Dissertation on Slavery*, pp. 50–52; Tocqueville, *Democracy in America*, p. 611.

70. Tucker, *Dissertation on Slavery*, p. 81; Huston, *Calculating the Value*, pp. 28–29.

71. As quoted in Helper, *Impending Crisis*, pp. 87–88.

72. Wright, *African Americans*, p. 58; Helper, *Impending Crisis*, pp. 87–88; Huston, *Calculating the Value*, p. 36; Conrad and Meyer, *Economics of Slavery*, pp. 69–72, 83; David et al., *Reckoning with Slavery*, p. 169; Fogel, *Without Consent*, pp. 32–34.

73. Ashworth, *Slavery, Capitalism, and Politics*, p. 97.

74. Ibid., p. 92.

75. Olmsted, *Journey in the Seaboard Slave States*, pp. 192–93.

76. Ibid., p. 100.

77. Ashworth, *Slavery, Capitalism, and Politics*, pp. 95–96; Nisbet, *Slavery Not Forbidden*, p. 17; Olmsted, *Journey in the Seaboard Slave States*, pp. 192–93; Robert Starobin, *Industrial Slavery in the Old South* (New York: Oxford University Press, 1970), p. 78.

78. The best recent study of slave hiring that I have seen is Jonathan D. Martin, *Divided Mastery: Slave Hiring in the American South* (Cambridge, MA: Harvard University Press, 2004).

79. Ashworth, *Slavery, Capitalism, and Politics*, pp. 102–110; *An Act to Empower Certain Commissioners Herein Appointed to Regulate the Hire of Porters and Labour of Slaves in the Town of Savannah* (Savannah, GA: James Johnston, 1783).

80. From the *National Anti-Slavery Standard*, August 5, 1847, as excerpted in Foner and Shapiro, *Northern Labor*, p. 25.

81. Harriet H. Robinson, *Loom and Spindle; or, Life among the Early Mill Girls* (New York: n.p. 1898), pp. 196–98.

82. Huston, *Calculating the Value*, p. 38.

83. Tucker, *Dissertation on Slavery*, pp. 72–73; Olmsted, *Journey in the Seaboard Slave States*, p. 94.

84. Dilwyn, *Brief Considerations*, p. 12; Tocqueville, *Democracy in America*, p. 347; Horton and Horton, *Hope of Liberty*, pp. 74, 115–18.

85. In 1800, enslaved blacksmith Gabriel Prosser laid plans for a large slave rebellion in the vicinity of Richmond. Several other slaves betrayed his cause, however. After his capture by Virginia state militiamen, Gabriel was hanged, as were over two dozen other coconspirators. Although the planned insurrection never took place, the episode created tremendous anxiety among slaveholders.

86. Olmsted, *Journey in the Seaboard Slave States*, pp. 20–21; Morgan, *Slavery and Servitude*, pp. 92–94.

87. Ashworth, *Slavery, Capitalism, and Politics*, p. 100; *National Era*, July 24, 1851, as excerpted in Foner and Shapiro, *Northern Labor*, p. 86.

88. As quoted in Huston, *Calculating the Value*, p. 207.

89. Ashworth, *Slavery, Capitalism, and Politics*, pp. 101, 107.

90. Fred Bateman and Thomas Weiss, *A Deplorable Scarcity: The Failure of Industrialization in the Slave Economy* (Chapel Hill: University of North Carolina Press, 1981), p. 158.

91. Olmsted, *Journey in the Seaboard Slave States*, pp. 212–15; Tocqueville, *Democracy in America*, pp. 333–34; Peter Bernstein, *Wedding of the Waters: The Erie Canal and the Making of a Great Nation* (New York: W. W. Norton, 2005); Fogel, *Without Consent*, p. 304.

92. Ronald Coase, "The Problem of Social Cost," *Journal of Law and Economics* 3 (1960): 1–44; Pindyck and Rubinfeld, *Microeconomics*, pp. 624–26.

93. Armen A. Alchian, *Economic Forces at Work* (Indianapolis: Liberty Fund, 1977), pp. 205, 210; Pindyck and Rubinfeld, *Microeconomics*, pp. 626–27.

94. John Majewski, *A House Dividing: Economic Development in Pennsylvania and Virginia before the Civil War* (New York: Cambridge University Press, 2000).

95. Richard H. Kilbourne Jr., *Debt, Investment, Slaves: Credit Relations in East Feliciana Parish, Louisiana, 1825–1885* (Tuscaloosa: University of Alabama Press, 1995); Tucker, *Dissertation on Slavery*, p. 82; Ashworth, *Slavery, Capitalism, and Politics*, p. 102; Helper, *Crisis*, pp. 32, 147; Fogel, *Without Consent*, p. 109; Wright, *Wealth of Nations Rediscovered*, pp. 88–89.

96. Winifred Rothenberg, *From Marketplaces to a Market Economy: The Transformation of Rural Massachusetts, 1750–1850* (Chicago: University of Chicago Press, 1992).

97. Smith, *Wealth of Nations*, p. 648.

98. Olmsted, *Journey in the Seaboard Slave States*, pp. 194, 196.

99. *The Liberator*, January 12, 1844, as excerpted in Foner and Shapiro, *Northern Labor*, p. 66.

100. Ibid., p. 58; *National Era*, March 16, 1848; Huston, *Calculating the Value*, pp. 45–47; Helper, *Crisis*, p. 43.

101. Juvenis, *Observations*, p. 20.

102. Ibid.

103. Helper, *Crisis*, pp. 11–122.

104. David et al., *Reckoning with Slavery*, p. 351; Fogel, *Without Consent*, p. 106; Ashworth, *Slavery, Capitalism, and Politics*, pp. 89–90.

105. Helper, *Crisis*, p. 77.

106. Ashworth, *Slavery, Capitalism, and Politics*, p. 80; Olmsted, *Journey in the Seaboard Slave States*, p. 208; Fogel, *Without Consent*, pp. 60, 352–69.

107. Fogel, *Without Consent*, pp. 82–83; Olmsted, *Journey in the Seaboard Slave States*, pp. 204–208; David et al., *Reckoning with Slavery*, pp. 27–28.

108. B. F. Stairley to Henry C. Carey, June 12, August 10, and September 18, 1856, Edward Carey Gardiner Collection.

109. Ibid.

110. Olmsted, *Journey in the Seaboard Slave States*, pp. 98, 588–89.

111. David et al., *Reckoning with Slavery*, pp. 327, 354.

112. Alexander Garden, *Six Letters to the Rev. Mr. George Whitefield* (Boston: T. Fleet, 1740), pp. 50–53.

113. Moore, *Plantation Mistress*, p. 70.

114. Olmsted, *Journey in the Seaboard Slave States*, pp. 208–209; Wright, *African Americans*, pp. 26–31; Huston, *Calculating the Value*, p. 49; David et al., *Reckoning with Slavery*, p. 308.

115. Moore, *Plantation Mistress*, p. 33.

116. Schulz, *Financial Crisis*.

117. Aldo Musacchio, *Experiments in Financial Democracy: Corporate Governance and Financial Development in Brazil, 1882–1950* (New York: Cambridge University Press, 2009).

CHAPTER 5: THE GRAPES OF WRATH

1. Grace Abbott, *From Relief to Social Security: The Development of the New Public Welfare Service* (Chicago: University of Chicago Press, 1941), pp. 49–68.

2. Ibid., pp. 79–112.

3. As quoted in Mark Skousen, *The Big Three in Economics: Adam Smith, Karl Marx, and John Maynard Keynes* (New York: M. E. Sharpe, 2007), p. 211.

4. National Bureau of Economic Research, "Business Cycle Expansions and Contractions," http://www.nber.org/cycles.html (accessed September 4, 2009).

5. Robert Sobel, *Panic on Wall Street: A History of America's Financial Disasters* (New York: Macmillan, 1968), p. 352.

6. For a similar analysis built on the foundations of Austrian economics, see Thomas E. Woods, *Meltdown: A Free-Market Look at Why the Stock Market Collapsed, the Economy Tanked, and Government Bailouts Will Make Things Worse* (Washington, DC: Regnery Publishing, 2009), pp. 96–98.

7. Sidney Homer and Richard Sylla, *A History of Interest Rates* (New Brunswick, NJ: Rutgers University Press, 1996), pp. 347–52; John Kenneth Galbraith, *The Great Crash 1929* (New York: Time, 1962), pp. 15–16.

8. *Historical Statistics of the United States*, table Cj251–265, "Commercial Banks—Number and Assets, 1834–1980," available at http://hsus.cambridge.org/HSUSWeb/HSUSEntryServlet (accessed April 6, 2010).

9. Galbraith, *Great Crash*, pp. 9–12; William Frazer and John J. Guthrie Jr., *The Florida Land Boom: Speculation, Money, and the Banks* (Westport, CT: Quorum Books, 1995).

10. Eugene White, "Great American Real Estate Bubble" (working paper, Rutgers University, October 2008).

11. Galbraith, *Great Crash*, pp. 13–16.

12. White, "Great American Real Estate Bubble."

13. Sobel, *Panic on Wall Street*, pp. 355–56.

14. Edith Sparks, *Capital Intentions: Female Proprietors in San Francisco, 1850–1920* (Chapel Hill: University of North Carolina Press, 2006), pp. 148–82.

15. *New York Sun* as quoted in Janice Traflet, "Courting Women Stockholders: The NYSE, Brokers' Marketing Practices, and the Democratization of the Stock Market" (working paper, Bucknell University, 2008).

16. Galbraith, *Great Crash*, pp. 79–80; Sobel, *Panic on Wall Street*, p. 367.

17. As quoted in Sobel, *Panic on Wall Street*, p. 371.

18. Ibid., pp. 364–65.

19. Galbraith, *Great Crash*, pp. 23–27.

20. Ibid., p. 21.

21. As quoted in ibid., p. 7.

22. Ibid., p. 39.

23. Ibid., p. 21.

24. Sobel, *Panic on Wall Street*, p. 367.

25. As quoted in ibid., p. 353.

26. Ibid., p. 354.

27. John J. Raskob, "Everybody Ought to Be Rich," *Ladies' Home Journal*, August 1929, p. 9.

28. Sobel, *Panic on Wall Street*, pp. 367–68.

29. Ibid., p. 354.

30. Ibid., p. 366.

31. Galbraith, *Great Crash*, p. x.

32. Sobel, *Panic on Wall Street*, pp. 383–84.

33. All quotations from the Harvard Economic Society are derived from Galbraith, *Great Crash*, p. 148.

34. Charles Calomiris and Eugene White, "The Origins of Federal Deposit Insurance," in *The Regulated Economy: A Historical Approach to Political Economy*, ed. Claudia Goldin and Gary Libecap (Chicago: University of Chicago Press, 1994), pp. 145–88.

35. Alfred Marshall, *Money, Credit, and Commerce* (New York: Augustus M. Kelley, 1960), p. 305.

36. Amity Shlaes, *The Forgotten Man: A New History of the Great Depression* (New York: Harper Perennial, 2007), p. 111.

37. Information in this paragraph is derived from Benjamin Bernanke, *Essays on the Great Depression* (Princeton, NJ: Princeton University Press, 2000).

38. Federal Reserve, "Concentration of Banking in the United States," in *Staff Report of the Board of Governors of the Federal Reserve System* (Washington, DC: Government Printing Office, 1952).

39. John Chapman, *Concentration of Banking: The Changing Structure and Control of Banking in the United States* (New York: Columbia University Press, 1934); Lawrence J. White, "The Partial Deregulation of Banks and Other Depository Institutions," in *Regulatory Reform: What Actually Happened*, ed. Leonard W. Weiss and Michael W. Klass (Boston: Little, Brown, 1986), p. 174; Joseph Stagg Lawrence, *Banking Concentration in the United States: A Critical Analysis* (New York: Bankers Publishing, 1930), pp. 2–3; Galbraith, *Great Crash*, p. 181; Joseph Haubrich, "Nonmon-

etary Effects of Financial Crises: Lessons from the Great Depression in Canada," *Journal of Monetary Economics* 25 (1990): 223–52; Eugene White, *The Regulation and Reform of the American Banking System, 1900–1929* (Princeton, NJ: Princeton University Press, 1983), pp. 205–207, 219–20; Howard Preston, "Branch Banking with Special Reference to California Conditions," *Journal of Political Economy* 30, no. 4 (1922): 512.

40. As quoted in Arthur M. Schlesinger Jr. *The Age of Jackson* (Boston: Little, Brown, 1945), p. 81.

41. For econometric evidence of bankers' market power, see Miguel Cantillo Simon, "The Rise and Fall of Bank Control in the United States: 1890–1939," *American Economic Review* 88 (1998): 1077–93.

42. Louis Brandeis, *Other People's Money and How the Bankers Use It* (New York: Frederick A. Stokes, 1932), p. 18; Vincent Carosso, "The Wall Street Money Trust from Pujo through Medina," *Business History Review* 47 (1973): 421–37.

43. As quoted in White, *Regulation and Reform*, p. 86.

44. Simon, "Rise and Fall of Bank Control."

45. White, "Partial Deregulation," p. 174.

46. White, *Regulation and Reform*, pp. 14–23.

47. Ibid., pp. 23–25.

48. Ibid., pp. 25–33.

49. Ibid., pp. 33–35.

50. Galbraith, *Great Crash*, p. 32.

51. Shlaes, *Forgotten Man*, pp. 106, 138.

52. Bernanke, *Essays.*

53. For a variety of more partisan views, from both the Right and the Left, on Hoover and his administration, see the essays in J. Joseph Huthmacher and Warren I. Susman, eds., *Herbert Hoover and the Crisis of American Capitalism* (Cambridge, MA: Schenkman Publishing, 1973).

54. William Barber, *From New Era to New Deal: Herbert Hoover, the Economists, and American Economic Policy, 1921–1933* (New York: Cambridge University Press, 1985), p. 79.

55. Rexford G. Tugwell, *Mr. Hoover's Economic Policy* (New York: John Day, 1932), pp. 9–10.

56. As quoted in Woods, *Meltdown*, p. 99.

57. Barber, *From New Era to New Deal*, pp. 80–86.

58. Shlaes, *Forgotten Man*, p. 99.

59. Barber, *From New Era to New Deal*, p. 91.

60. As quoted in Shlaes, *Forgotten Man*, p. 97.

61. The information and the quotation from Hoover in this paragraph are derived from Barber, *From New Era to New Deal*, pp. 104–111.

62. Ibid., pp. 128–29.

63. Calomiris and White, "Origins of Federal Deposit Insurance," pp. 145–88; Joseph Mason, "The Evolution of the Reconstruction Finance Corporation as a Lender of Last Resort in the Great Depression," in *Bailouts: Public Money, Private Profit*, ed. Robert E. Wright (New York: Columbia University Press, 2010).

64. Tugwell, *Mr. Hoover's Economic Policy*, pp. 15–16, 24.

65. Barber, *From New Era to New Deal*, pp. 139–45, 169–88.

66. Tugwell, *Mr. Hoover's Economic Policy*, p. 5.

67. Ibid., p. 10.

68. Ibid., p. 14.

69. Bernanke, *Essays*. For a different view of why the government's bailouts did not work, see Woods, *Meltdown*, pp. 98–106.

70. Brian Doherty, "Yesterday Is Tomorrow: Revisiting Annie as a New New Deal Dawns," *Reason Online* (May 2009), http://www.reason.com/news/show/132661.html (accessed September 5, 2009).

71. Burt Folsom, *New Deal or Raw Deal?* (New York: Threshold, 2008).

72. Blanche Coll, *Safety Net: Welfare and Social Security, 1929–1979* (New Brunswick, NJ: Rutgers University Press, 1995).

73. Calomiris and White, "Origins of Federal Deposit Insurance."

74. Ibid.

75. Franklin Edwards, "Banks and Securities Activities: Legal and Economic Perspectives on the Glass-Steagall Act," in *The Deregulation of the Banking and Securities Industries*, ed. Lawrence Goldberg and Lawrence J. White (Boston: D. C. Heath, 1979), pp. 273–91.

76. James Barth, Gerard Caprio, and Ross Levine, *Rethinking Bank Regulation: Till Angels Govern* (New York: Cambridge University Press, 2005).

77. Edwards, "Banks and Securities Activities."

78. Goulin Jiang, Paul Mahoney, and Jianping Mei, "Market Manipulation: A Comprehensive Study of Stock Pools," *Journal of Financial Economics* 77, no. 1 (2005): 147–70.

79. This and the following quotation are derived from Joseph de La Vega, *Confusion de Confusiones* (Hoboken, NJ: John Wiley and Sons, 1995).

80. Thomas Mortimer, *Every Man His Own Broker; or, A Guide to Exchange-Alley*, 3rd ed. (London: S. Hooper, 1761), p. 63.

81. J. S., *A Dialogue Between a Gentleman and a Broker* (London: T. Cooper, 1736), p. 18.

82. Adam Smith, *An Inquiry into the Nature and Causes of the Wealth of Nations* (New York: Modern Library, 1937), pp. 452–53.

83. Paul Harrison, "The More Things Change the More They Stay the Same:

Analysis of the Past 200 Years of Stock Market Evolution" (PhD diss., Duke University, 1994).

84. *Wall Street Journal*, "Protecting the Investor," October 24, 1912, p. 1.

85. Clifton Wooldridge, *The Grafters of America* (Chicago: Monarch Book, 1906), pp. 48–49, 172–77.

86. Ibid., pp. 125–34.

87. Ibid., pp. 87–92.

88. Jonathan Macey and Geoffrey Miller, "Origin of the Blue Sky Laws," *Texas Law Review* 70, no. 2 (December 1991): 355.

89. Wooldridge, *Grafters of America*, p. 134.

90. Paul Mahoney, "The Origins of the Blue Sky Laws: A Test of Competing Hypotheses," *Journal of Law and Economics* 46 (April 2003): 229–51.

91. Stephen Axilrod, *Inside the Fed: Monetary Policy and Its Management, Martin through Greenspan to Bernanke* (Cambridge, MA: MIT Press, 2009), p. 5.

92. Stuart Banner, *Anglo-America Securities Regulation: Cultural and Political Roots, 1690–1860* (New York: Cambridge University Press, 2002).

93. Douglass C. North, *Understanding the Process of Economic Change* (Princeton, NJ: Princeton University Press, 2005), p. 63.

94. Paul Rubin, *Darwinian Politics: The Evolutionary Origin of Freedom* (New Brunswick, NJ: Rutgers University Press, 2002).

95. Sobel, *Panic on Wall Street*, pp. 392–96.

96. Alan Gart, *Regulation, Deregulation, Reregulation: The Future of the Banking, Insurance, and Securities Industries* (New York: John Wiley and Sons, 1994), pp. 42–44; Jane W. D'Arista, *The Evolution of Finance, Volume II: Restructuring Institutions and Markets* (Armonk, NY: M. E. Sharpe, 1994), p. 335.

97. Paul Mahoney and Jianping Mei, "Mandatory vs. Contractual Disclosure in Securities Markets: Evidence from the 1930s" (working paper, University of Virginia Law, 2006).

98. Paul Mahoney, "The Political Economy of the Securities Act of 1933," *Journal of Legal Studies* 30 (January 2001): 1–31.

99. John Woolsey, "The Capital Problem of Small and Medium-Sized Businesses," *Southern Economic Journal* 7 (1941): 461–74; Vincent Carosso, "Washington and Wall Street: The New Deal and Investment Bankers, 1933–1940," *Business History Review* 44 (1970): 425–44; Donald Kemmerer, "American Financial Institutions: The Marketing of Securities, 1930–1952," *Journal of Economic History* 12 (1952): 454–68.

100. Robert E. Wright, "Reforming the US IPO Market: Lessons from History and Theory," *Accounting, Business, and Financial History* 12, no. 3 (2002): 419–37.

101. Sobel, *Panic on Wall Street*, pp. 362–63.

102. Ibid., p. 367.

103. Ibid., p. 370.

104. Sylvester Schieber and John Shoven, *The Real Deal: The History and Future of Social Security* (New Haven, CT: Yale University Press, 1999), p. 21.

105. Veronique de Rugy, "Stimulating Ourselves to Death," *Reason Online* (April 2009), http://www.reason.com/news/show/131968.html (accessed September 5, 2009); Shlaes, *Forgotten Man*, p. 168.

106. Elizabeth Hoffman and Gary Libecap, "Political Bargaining and Cartelization in the New Deal: Orange Marketing Orders," in *The Regulated Economy: A Historical Approach to Political Economy*, ed. Claudia Goldin and Gary Libecap (Chicago: University of Chicago Press, 1994), pp. 189–221.

107. This and similar letters are available all over the Internet, including "Not Raising Hogs," February 6, 2003, http://www.rangebiome.org/editorials/not raisinghogs.html (accessed September 4, 2009).

108. Franklin D. Roosevelt, speech, July 24, 1933, as cited in Jason E. Taylor, "Buy Now! Buy Here!: The Rise and Fall of the Patriotic Blue Eagle Emblem 1933–1935," *Essays in Economic & Business History: The Journal of the Economic & Business Historical Society* 25 (2007): 117–30.

109. Ibid.

110. As quoted in Shlaes, *Forgotten Man*, p. 94.

111. Taylor, "Buy Now! Buy Here! The Rise and Fall of the Patriotic Blue Eagle Emblem, 1933–1935." For an alternative view of the administration's thoughtlessness, see Woods, *Meltdown*, p. 100.

112. As quoted in David Lewis, *The Public Image of Henry Ford: An American Folk Hero and His Company* (Detroit: Wayne State University Press, 1976), p. 243.

113. Shlaes, *Forgotten Man*, pp. 214–45.

114. Ibid., pp. 263, 347–48.

115. Gart, *Regulation, Deregulation, Regulation*, p. 55.

116. For a similar view that differs in emphasis, see Woods, *Meltdown*, pp. 102–106.

117. Adam Smith, *Lectures on Jurisprudence* (New York: Oxford University Press, 1976).

CHAPTER 6: SACRED HOAX

1. Mitchell A. Orenstein, ed., *Pensions, Social Security, and the Privatization of Risk* (New York: Columbia University Press/SSRC, 2009), p. 3.

2. Sheryl Tynes, *Turning Points in Social Security: From "Cruel Hoax" to "Sacred Entitlement"* (Stanford: Stanford University Press, 1996), p. 4; Sylvester Schieber and John Shoven, *The Real Deal: The History and Future of Social Security* (New Haven, CT: Yale University Press, 1999), p. 53.

3. Edwin Amenta, *When Movements Matter: The Townsend Plan and the Rise of Social Security* (Princeton, NJ: Princeton University Press, 2006), p. vii; Schieber and Shoven, *Real Deal*, p. 242.

4. Michael Graetz and Jerry Mashaw, *True Security: Rethinking American Social Insurance* (New Haven, CT: Yale University Press, 1999), p. 10.

5. Elizabeth Caucutt, Thomas Cooley, and Nezih Guner, "The Farm, the City, and the Emergence of Social Security" (working paper, May 2007).

6. Orenstein, *Pensions*, p. 11.

7. Schieber and Shoven, *Real Deal*, pp. 18–19.

8. Orenstein, *Pensions*, p. 11.

9. Joseph Stiglitz, *Globalization and Its Discontents* (New York: W. W. Norton, 2003), p. 55.

10. Dominick Pratico, *Eisenhower and Social Security: The Origins of the Disability Program* (New York: Writers Club Press, 2001), pp. 30, 38; Graetz and Mashaw, *True Security*, pp. 17–18.

11. Grace Abbott, *From Relief to Social Security: The Development of the New Public Welfare Service* (Chicago: University of Chicago Press, 1941), pp. 230–39.

12. Schieber and Shoven, *Real Deal*, p. 115.

13. Amenta, *When Movements Matter*, pp. 62–64; Blanche Coll, *Safety Net: Welfare and Social Security, 1929–1979* (New Brunswick, NJ: Rutgers University Press, 1995), pp. 4–6; Schieber and Shoven, *Real Deal*, p. 18.

14. Tynes, *Turning Points*, p. 41; Graetz and Mashaw, *True Security*, p. 24; Coll, *Safety Net*, p. 41.

15. Alan Olmstead, *New York City Mutual Savings Banks, 1819–1861* (Chapel Hill: University of North Carolina Press, 1976); Peter Payne and Lance Davis, *The Savings Bank of Baltimore, 1818–1886* (Baltimore: Johns Hopkins University Press, 1956); Weldon Welfling, *Savings Banking in New York State: A Study of Changes in Savings Bank Practice and Policy Occasioned by Important Economic Changes* (Durham, NC: Duke University Press, 1939); David Mason, *From Buildings and Loans to Bail Outs: A History of the American Savings and Loan Industry, 1831–1995* (New York: Cambridge University Press, 2004).

16. Robert E. Wright and George D. Smith, *Mutually Beneficial: The Guardian and Life Insurance in America* (New York: New York University Press, 2004); Miles Dawson, "Fraternal Life Insurance," *Annals of the American Academy of Political and Social Science* 26 (1905): 128–36.

17. Tynes, *Turning Points*, pp. 41–43; Schieber and Shoven, *Real Deal*, p. 19; Orenstein, *Pensions*, p. 13.

18. Wright and Smith, *Mutually Beneficial*, pp. 40–50; Miles Dawson, "Mutualization of Life Insurance Companies," *Annals of the American Academy of Political and Social Science* 70 (1917): 62–76.

19. Tynes, *Turning Points*, p. 42.

20. Wright and Smith, *Mutually Beneficial*, pp. 146–49.

21. Vincent Carosso, "The Wall Street Money Trust from Pujo through Medina," *Business History Review* 47 (1973): 421–37; Perkins, *Wall Street to Main Street*, p. 136.

22. This quotation also appears in Edward Chancellor, *Devil Take the Hindmost: A History of Financial Speculation* (New York: Plume, 1999), p. 220.

23. Franklin Delano Roosevelt, first inaugural address, March 4, 1933.

24. Amity Shlaes, *The Forgotten Man: A New History of the Great Depression* (New York: Harper Perennial, 2007), p. 338.

25. As quoted in Tynes, *Turning Points*, p. 55.

26. Graetz and Mashaw, *True Security*, p. 10.

27. Abbott, *From Relief to Social Security*, p. 260.

28. Robert Eisner, *Social Security: More, Not Less* (New York: Century Foundation Press, 1998), p. v.

29. Using the unskilled wage comparison from MeasuringWorth, "Six Ways to Compute the Relative Value of a US Dollar Amount, 1774 to Present," http://www.measuringworth.com/uscompare/ (accessed September 4, 2009).

30. Except where otherwise noted, this section is based on Amenta, *When Movements Matter*.

31. Shlaes, *Forgotten Man*.

32. Amenta, *When Movements Matter*, p. 48.

33. Abbott, *From Relief to Social Security*, p. 230; Schieber and Shoven, *Real Deal*, p. 26.

34. Tynes, *Turning Points*, pp. 66, 80, 87; Schieber and Shoven, *Real Deal*, pp. 41–42, 64.

35. Schieber and Shoven, *Real Deal*, pp. 49–50.

36. As quoted in Coll, *Safety Net*, pp. 92–93.

37. Tynes, *Turning Points*, pp. 65, 78–79.

38. Pratico, *Eisenhower and Social Security*, pp. 12–13; Tynes, *Turning Points*, pp. 65, 80–88; Coll, *Safety Net*, pp. 93–94; Schieber and Shoven, *Real Deal*, pp. 58–59.

39. Tynes, *Turning Points*, pp. 27, 32, 88, 155; Martin Feldstein and Jeffrey Liebman, eds., *The Distributional Aspects of Social Security and Social Security Reform* (Chicago: University of Chicago Pres, 2002), p. 15; Coll, *Safety Net*, p. 278; Schieber and Shoven, *Real Deal*, pp. 107–111; Andrew Yarrow, *Forgive Us Our Debts: The Intergenerational Dangers of Fiscal Irresponsibility* (New Haven, CT: Yale University Press, 2008), p. 25.

40. Tynes, *Turning Points*, p. 89.

41. Ibid., p. 202.

42. Feldstein and Liebman, *Distributional Aspects of Social Security*, pp. 30, 207–208; Schieber and Shoven, *Real Deal*, pp. 71–74, 92–96, 100–107, 210–13.

43. As quoted in Tynes, *Turning Points*, p. 99.

44. Schieber and Shoven, *Real Deal*, pp. 51–52; Yarrow, *Forgive Us Our Debts*, p. 25.

45. Geoffry Kollmann and Carmen Solomon-Fears, *Social Security: Major Decisions in the House and Senate: 1935–2000* (New York: Novinka Books, 2002), p. 21.

46. Tynes, *Turning Points*, p. 100.

47. Amenta, *When Movements Matter*, p. 213.

48. Pratico, *Eisenhower and Social Security*, pp. 42, 94.

49. Tynes, *Turning Points*, pp. 106–107, 113–14.

50. Ibid., p. 120.

51. Eisner, *Social Security*, p. vi; Social Security Online, "Social Security & Medicare Tax Rates," http://www.ssa.gov/OACT/ProgData/taxRates.html (accessed September 4, 2009).

52. Tynes, *Turning Points*, pp., 32, 195.

53. Ibid., pp. 131–42.

54. Ibid., pp. 143–47.

55. Ibid., pp. 55–92; Kollmann and Solomon-Fears, *Social Security*, pp. 2–3, 83–84, 181–83.

56. Eisner, *Social Security*, pp. 16–17; Schieber and Shoven, *Real Deal*, pp. 1–14, 197–99.

57. A Brazil rating agency has already said that it will begin rating US Treasuries at AA, a step below the AAA status they have held de facto for several centuries. "Is America Still AAA?" *Economist*, May 23, 2009, p. 80. See also "Not So Risk-Free," *Economist*, May 30, 2009, p. 76.

58. Yarrow, *Forgive Us Our Debts*, pp. 12, 25–27, 71, 77.

59. Tynes, *Turning Points*, pp. 178–80; Coll, *Safety Net*, p. 278.

60. Eisner, *Social Security*, p. 1.

61. Ibid., p. 5.

62. Ibid., p. 12; Schieber and Shoven, *Real Deal*, pp. 214–16.

63. Feldstein and Liebman, *Distributional Aspects of Social Security*, pp. 1–2; Schieber and Shoven, *Real Deal*, p. 73; Orenstein, *Pensions*, p. 84.

64. Eisner, *Social Security*, pp. 7–10.

65. Schieber and Shoven, *Real Deal*, p. 213.

66. Tynes, *Turning Points*, p. 202; Feldstein and Liebman, *Distributional Aspects of Social Security*, p. 30.

67. Schieber and Shoven, *Real Deal*, pp. 237–39.

68. Tynes, *Turning Points*, p. 113.

69. Ibid., p. 141; Coll, *Safety Net*, p. 279.

70. Eisner, *Social Security*, pp. 19–20.

71. Tynes, *Turning Points*, pp. 109–14; Orenstein, *Pensions*, p. 14.

72. Orenstein, *Pensions*, p. 15.

73. Stephanie Aaronson and Julia Coronado, "Are Firms or Workers behind the Shift Away from DB Pension Plans?" *Finance and Economic Discussion Series, Federal Reserve Board*, no. 17 (February 2005); Accountants International Study Group, *Accounting for Pension Costs: Current Practices in Canada, the United Kingdom and the United States* (New York: Accountants International Study Group, 1977); Robin Blackburn, *Banking on Death; or, Investing in Life: The History and Future of Pensions* (London: Verso, 2002); William E. Even and David A. MacPherson, "Improving Pension Coverage at Small Firms," in *Overcoming Barriers to Entrepreneurship in the United States*, ed. Diana Furchtgott-Roth (Lanham, MD: Lexington Books, 2008), pp. 123–56; Leora Friedberg and Michael Owyang, "Explaining the Evolution of Pension Structure and Job Tenure" (NBER working paper no. 10714, 2004); William D. Hall and David Landsittel, *A New Look at Accounting for Pension Costs* (Homewood, IL: Pension Research Council, 1977); Steven Sass, *The Promise of Private Pensions: The First Hundred Years* (Cambridge, MA: Harvard University Press, 1997).

74. Orenstein, *Pensions*, pp. 61–63.

75. Peter M. Lencsis, *Insurance Regulation in the United States: An Overview for Business and Government* (Westport, CT: Quorum Books, 1997).

76. Joseph Belth, "Discussion," in *The Financial Condition and Regulation of Insurance Companies*, ed. Richard E. Randall and Richard W. Kopcke (Boston: Federal Reserve Bank of Boston, 1991), pp. 218–21.

77. Richard Butler, Yijing Cui, and Andrew Whitman, "Insurers' Demutualization Decisions," *Risk Management and Insurance Review* 3 (2000): 135–54; Otgo Erhemjamts and Richard Phillips, "What Drives Life Insurer Demutualizations" (working paper, 2005).

78. Kenneth J. Meier, *The Political Economy of Regulation: The Case of Insurance* (Albany: State University of New York Press, 1988).

79. Richard E. Randall and Richard W. Kopcke, "The Financial Condition and Regulation of Insurance Companies: An Overview," in Randall and Kopcke, *Financial Condition*, pp. 1–18; Gerard M. Brannon, "Public Policy and Life Insurance," in Randall and Kopcke, *Financial Condition*, pp. 199–217.

80. Vanishing premium policies promised that dividends would grow so quickly that they would soon be greater than premiums, relieving the policyholder of the need to make any further payments. Such promises were possible only with high levels of inflation, which would have rendered the real value of the policy negligible anyway. Policy twisting entailed enticing policyholders to cash in older policies for newer ones. Because most whole-life policies are priced based on the age at which the insurance is taken out, policyholders rarely gained from the switch, but the agent pocketed a nice commission. Investment churning also benefited the agent by increasing his or her commissions but rarely benefited policyholders.

81. Robert E. Wright, "Insuring America: Market, Intermediated, and Government Risk Management Since 1790" (working paper, 2008).

82. Schieber and Shoven, *Real Deal*, pp. 239–40.

83. Robert J. Shiller, *New Financial Order: Risk in the 21st Century* (Princeton, NJ: Princeton University Press, 2003).

84. Schieber and Shoven, *Real Deal*, p. 216.

85. Amenta, *When Movements Matter*, p. 167; Tynes, *Turning Points*, p. 208; Eisner, *Social Security*, p. 2; Graetz and Mashaw, *True Security*, p. 7.

86. Schieber and Shoven, *Real Deal*, p. 209; Yarrow, *Forgive Us Our Debts*, p. 76.

87. Yarrow, *Forgive Us Our Debts*, p. 24.

88. Tynes, *Turning Points*, p. 3; Orenstein, *Pensions*, p. 4.

89. Eisner, *Social Security*, p. vii.

90. Feldstein and Liebman, *Distributional Aspects of Social Security*, p. 5.

91. Schieber and Shoven, *Real Deal*, pp. 228, 241.

92. Pratico, *Eisenhower and Social Security*, p. 104; Eisner, *Social Security*, pp. vi, 10.

93. Eisner, *Social Security*, p. 10; Orenstein, *Pensions*, p. 25.

94. Orenstein, *Pensions*, p. 19.

95. Tynes, *Turning Points*, pp. 2–3.

96. Pratico, *Eisenhower and Social Security*, pp. 58–80.

97. Wright and Smith, *Mutually Beneficial*, pp. 149–52.

98. Pratico, *Eisenhower and Social Security*, pp. 81–82, 105; Wright and Smith, *Mutually Beneficial*, p. 150.

99. Kollmann and Solomon-Fears, *Social Security*, pp. 43, 75; Tynes, *Turning Points*, p. 177.

100. Kollmann and Solomon-Fears, *Social Security*, pp. 56.

101. "Social Security & Medicare Tax Rates"; Social Security Online, "Contribution and Benefit Base," http://www.ssa.gov/OACT/COLA/cbb.html#Series (accessed September 5, 2009).

102. Tynes, *Turning Points*, pp. 74–75; Schieber and Shoven, *Real Deal*, p. 129.

103. Feldstein and Liebman, *Distributional Aspects of Social Security*, pp. 4–5, 85, 106.

104. Ibid., p. 208.

105. Graetz and Mashaw, *True Security*, p. 6; Feldstein and Liebman, *Distributional Aspects of Social Security*, pp. 11–41; Schieber and Shoven, *Real Deal*, pp. 223–27.

106. Feldstein and Liebman, *Distributional Aspects of Social Security*, pp. 41–42; Schieber and Shoven, *Real Deal*, pp. 111–13; Yarrow, *Forgive Us Our Debts*, p. 76.

107. Eisner, *Social Security*, p. 10.

108. Graetz and Mashaw, *True Security*, pp. 43, 45.

109. Schieber and Shoven, *Real Deal*, pp. 63–64.

CHAPTER 7: HOUSE SCRUBS

1. Elizabeth McGlynn, David Meltzer, and Jacob S. Hacker, "Just How Good *Is* American Medical Care?" in *Health at Risk: America's Ailing Health System— and How to Heal It*, ed. Jacob S. Hacker (New York: Columbia University Press/ SSRC, 2008), p. 91.

2. Michael Graetz and Jerry Mashaw, *True Security: Rethinking American Social Insurance* (New Haven, CT: Yale University Press, 1999), pp. 163–64; McGlynn, Meltzer, and Hacker, "Just How Good?" pp. 88–105.

3. Ronald Bailey, "Hips Abroad: Medical Outsourcing," *Reason Online*, http://www.reason.com/news/show/132610.html (accessed September 5, 2009); "Lessons from a Frugal Innovator," *Economist*, April 18, 2009, pp. 67–68.

4. As quoted in John E. Murray, *Origins of American Health Insurance: A History of Industrial Sickness Funds* (New Haven, CT: Yale University Press, 2007), p. 108.

5. Grace Abbott, *From Relief to Social Security: The Development of the New Public Welfare Service* (Chicago: University of Chicago Press, 1941), p. 291.

6. Sheryl Tynes, *Turning Points in Social Security: From "Cruel Hoax" to "Sacred Entitlement"* (Stanford: Stanford University Press, 1996), pp. 88–89, 109.

7. McGlynn, Meltzer, and Hacker, "Just How Good?" pp. 88–105.

8. Katherine Swartz, "Uninsured in America: New Realities, New Risks," in Hacker, *Health at Risk*, p. 41.

9. Deborah Thorne and Elizabeth Warren, "Get Sick, Go Broke," in Hacker, *Health at Risk*, pp. 66–87.

10. Andrew Yarrow, *Forgive Us Our Debts: The Intergenerational Dangers of Fiscal Irresponsibility* (New Haven, CT: Yale University Press, 2008), pp. 21–23; Graetz and Mashaw, *True Security*, pp. 127–28; Hacker, *Health at Risk*, p. 1.

11. Gerald Morgan, *Public Relief of Sickness* (New York: Macmillan Company, 1922).

12. Except where otherwise noted, this section is based on Murray, *Origins of American Health Insurance.*

13. Katherine Swartz, "Uninsured in America," Hacker, *Health at Risk*, pp. 34–41.

14. Robert Whaples and David Buffum, "Fraternalism, Paternalism, the Family, and the Market: Insurance a Century Ago," *Social Science History* 15 (1991): 97–122.

15. *Present Status of Mutual Benefit Associations* (New York: National Industrial Conference Board, 1931), p. v.

16. Ibid., p. 3.

17. McGlynn, Meltzer, and Hacker, "Just How Good?" pp. 96–99; Richard H.

Thaler and Cass R. Sunstein, *Nudge: Improving Decisions about Health, Wealth, and Happiness* (New Haven, CT: Yale University Press, 2008), p. 98.

18. Thaler and Sunstein, *Nudge*, pp. 99–100.

19. "Lessons from a Frugal Innovator"; Thaler and Sunstein, *Nudge*, pp. 207–14.

20. Noel Whiteside, "Insurance: Health and Accident," in *The Oxford Encyclopedia of Economic History*, ed. Joel Mokyr (New York: Oxford University Press, 2003), 3:94–98.

21. Robert Cunningham III and Robert M. Cunningham Jr., *The Blues: A History of the Blue Cross and Blue Shield System* (Dekalb: Northern Illinois University, 1997); Melissa Thomasson, "Health Insurance in the United States," in *EH.Net Encyclopedia*, ed. Robert Whaples, http://eh.net/encyclopedia/article/thomasson .insurance.health.us (accessed September 4, 2009).

22. David M. Cutler and Jonathan Gruber, "Does Public Insurance Crowd Out Private Insurance?" *Quarterly Journal of Economics* 111 (1996): 391–430.

23. McGlynn, Meltzer, and Hacker, "Just How Good?" pp. 92–94.

24. For a similar analysis, see Swartz, "Uninsured in America," p. 56.

25. Tynes, *Turning Points*, p. 30.

26. Hacker, *Health at Risk*, pp. 1–7, 106–36.

27. Graetz and Mashaw, *True Security*, pp. 128–31; Hacker, *Health at Risk*, p. 1; Jacob S. Hacker, "The New Push for American Health Security," in Hacker, *Health at Risk*, pp. 106–36.

28. The initial push, just after World War I, also suffered from an ill-timed recession, perceived ideological association with Germany, opposition from fraternals and unions, and reports that Britain reeled under its national healthcare system.

29. As quoted in Abbott, *From Relief to Social Security*, pp. 291–92.

30. Ibid., pp. 297–301.

31. "Harry and Louise Ride Again," *Economist*, April 4, 2009, pp. 36–37.

32. Graetz and Mashaw, *True Security*, pp. 131–32; Hacker, "New Push," pp. 115–17, 119, 124.

33. Graetz and Mashaw, *True Security*, pp. 132–33.

34. Centers for Medicare and Medicaid Services, *Choosing a Medigap Policy 2009: A Guide to Health Insurance for People with Medicare* (Washington, DC: Department of Health and Human Services, 2009), p. 10.

35. Graetz and Mashaw, *True Security*, p. 134.

36. Ibid., pp. 134–35; Associated Press, "9 Patients Made Nearly 2,700 ER Visits in Texas," April 1, 2009.

37. Loftin Graham and Xiaoying Xie, "The United States Insurance Market: Characteristics and Trends," in *Handbook of International Insurance: Between Global*

Dynamics and Local Contingencies, ed. J. David Cummins and Bertrand Venard (New York: Springer, 2007), pp. 25–146; Theda Skocpol, *The Time Is Never Ripe: The Repeated Defeat of Universal Health Insurance in the 20th Century United States* (Dublin, Ireland: Economic and Social Research Institute, 1995); Harry A. Millis, *Sickness and Insurance: A Study of the Sickness Problem and Health Insurance* (Chicago: University of Chicago Press, 1937); Beatrix Hoffman, *The Wages of Sickness: The Politics of Health Insurance in Progressive America* (Chapel Hill: University of North Carolina Press, 2001); "Signed, Sealed, Delivered," *Economist*, March 27, 2010, pp. 31–32; "Miracle or Monstrosity?" *Economist*, March 27, 2010, pp. 32–33.

38. Central Intelligence Agency, *The World Factbook*, "Switzerland," https://www.cia.gov/library/publications/the-world-factbook/geos/sz.html (accessed September 4, 2009).

39. Nelson Schwartz, "Swiss Health Care Thrives without Public Option," *New York Times*, September 30, 2009.

40. Angela Coulter and Crispin Jenkinson, "European Patients' Views on the Responsiveness of Health Systems and Healthcare Providers," *European Journal of Public Health* 15 (2005): 355–60.

41. "Do the Swiss Have the Answer to America's Health Care Dilemma?" *PR Newswire*, July 31, 2009.

42. Yarrow, *Forgive Us Our Debts*, p. 23.

43. Richard Frank and Karine Lamiraud, "Choice, Price Competition and Complexity in Markets for Health Insurance" (NBER working paper no. 13817, February 2008); Robert E. Leu and Martin Schellhorn, "The Evolution of Income-Related Inequalities in Health Care Utilization in Switzerland Over Time" (IZA discussion paper no. 1316, September 2004).

44. Konstantin Beck, "Growing Importance of Capitation in Switzerland," *Health Care Management Sciences* 3 (2000): 111–19.

45. Regina Herzlinger, "Foreign Health Affairs," *Wall Street Journal*, November 19, 2007; Yarrow, *Forgive Us Our Debts*, pp. 112–23.

46. Swartz, "Uninsured in America," pp. 111–12.

47. For additional discussion, see Rowena Jacobs and Maria Goddard, "Trade-Offs in Social Health Insurance Systems," *International Journal of Social Economics* (2002): 861–75.

48. Jill Quadagno and J. Brandon McKelvey, "The Transformation of American Health Insurance," in Hacker, *Health at Risk*, pp. 10–11; "Harry and Louise Ride Again."

49. Swartz, "Uninsured in America," p. 58.

50. Robert E. Wright and George D. Smith, *Mutually Beneficial: The Guardian and Life Insurance in America* (New York: New York University Press, 2004), pp. 152–57, 283–95.

51. Ibid., pp. 76, 237.

52. Andy H. Barnett, Roger D. Blair, and David L. Kaserman, "A Market for Organs," in *Entrepreneurial Economics: Bright Ideas from the Dismal Science*, ed. Alexander Tabarrok (New York: Oxford University Press, 2002), pp. 89–105.

53. Alexander Tabarrok, "The Organ Shortage: A Tragedy of the Commons?" in Tabarrok, *Entrepreneurial Economics* (New York: Oxford University Press, 2002), pp. 107–11.

54. Thaler and Sunstein, *Nudge*, pp. 175–82.

55. Internet Movie Database, *Seven Pounds*, http://www.imdb.com/title/tt0814314/ (accessed September 4, 2009).

56. John H. Cochrane, "Time-Consistent Health Insurance," in Tabarrok, *Entrepreneurial Economics*, pp. 53–76.

57. Alexander Tabarrok, "Gene Insurance," in Tabarrok, *Entrepreneurial Economics*, pp. 47–51.

58. Richard Epstein, *Overdose: How Excessive Government Regulation Stifles Pharmaceutical Innovation* (New Haven, CT: Yale University Press, 2006), p. 238.

CHAPTER 8: 3RD ROCK FROM THE SUN

1. Anonymous, *Cause of, and Cure for, Hard Times* (New York: n.p., 1818), p. 73.

2. Saturday Night Live, "*Saturday Night Live* Transcripts, Season 4, Episode 5," http://snltranscripts.jt.org/78/78eupdate.phtml (accessed September 5, 2009).

3. Except where otherwise noted, this chapter is based on Robert E. Wright, *Higher Education and the Common Weal: Protecting Economic Growth and Political Stability with Professional Partnerships* (Hyderabad, India: ICFAI, 2010).

4. Thomas L. Friedman, *The World Is Flat: A Brief History of the Twenty-first Century* (New York: Farrar, Straus, and Giroux, 2005), p. 239.

5. Derek Bok, "The New 'U,'" *Forbes*, April 18, 2006, http://www.forbes .com/2006/04/15/derek-bok-university_cx_db_06slate_0418bok.html (accessed September 5, 2009).

6. Percy Bysshe Shelley, "Ozymandias," lines 10–14.

7. William W. Lewis, *The Power of Productivity: Wealth, Poverty, and the Threat to Global Stability* (Chicago: University of Chicago Press, 2004), pp. 23–49.

8. US-Japan Twenty-first Century Committee, "Summary Discussions on 'Education in the 21st Century,'" (Kyoto, Japan, May 18, 1998).

9. Lewis, *Power of Productivity*, p. 10; Richard Lanham, *The Economics of Attention: Style and Substance in the Age of Information* (Chicago: University of Chicago Press, 2006), pp. 5, 8, 11.

10. Lewis, *Power of Productivity*, pp. 80–104.

11. Jane Barnes Mack-Cozzo, "If You Think We Have Problems...Japan's Inferior University System," *American Enterprise* 13, no. 6 (2002): 46–47.

12. A great, readable introduction to this idea is Russell Roberts, *The Choice: A Fable of Free Trade and Protectionism* (Upper Saddle River, NJ: Prentice Hall, 2001).

13. Joseph Schumpeter, *Capitalism, Socialism, and Democracy* (New York: Harper, 1942).

14. Frank H. T. Rhodes, *The Creation of the Future: The Role of the American University* (Ithaca, NY: Cornell University Press, 2001), pp. 98, 208.

15. Nannerl Keohane, "The Liberal Arts and the Role of Elite Higher Education," in *In Defense of American Higher Education*, ed. Philip Altbach, Patricia Gumport, and D. Bruce Johnstone (Baltimore: Johns Hopkins University Press, 2001), p. 184.

16. Richard H. Thaler and Cass R. Sunstein, *Nudge: Improving Decisions about Health, Wealth, and Happiness* (New Haven, CT: Yale University Press, 2008), pp. 56–59.

17. S. Bielick, K. Chandler, and S. P. Broughman, *Homeschooling in the United States: 1999* (Washington, DC: National Center for Education Statistics, 2001).

18. Mitchell A. Orenstein, ed., *Pensions, Social Security, and the Privatization of Risk* (New York: Columbia University Press/SSRC, 2009), p. 4.

19. Friedman, *World Is Flat*, p. 261.

20. Wright, *Higher Education and the Common Weal*, p. 26

21. Thaler and Sunstein, *Nudge*, p. 55.

22. Jonathan M. Orszag, Peter R. Orszag, and Diane M. Whitmore, "Learning and Earning: Working in College" (working paper commissioned by Upromise, Inc., 2001), http://www.brockport.edu/career01/upromise.htm (accessed April 8, 2010).

23. Nancy Fitzgerald, "Students at Work," *Careers and Colleges* (November 2000), http://articles.findarticles.com/p/articles/mi_m0BTR/is_2_21/ai_7857 3946.

24. Koren Zailckas, *Smashed: Story of a Drunken Girlhood* (New York: Viking, 2005).

25. George Kuh, "College Students Today: Why We Can't Leave Serendipity to Chance," in Altbach, Gumport, and Johnstone, *In Defense of American Higher Education*, pp. 297–98.

26. "Full Service Fakery: Inside the Life of a Professional Essay Writer and Test Taker," *ABC News, Primetime Thursday*, April 29, 2004.

27. See, for example, Malcolm Gladwell, "The Picture Problem: Should a Charge of Plagiarism Ruin Your Life?" *New Yorker*, November 22, 2004. For a hilarious spoof, see Emrys Westacott, "The Future of Plagiarism," *Chronicle of Higher Education*, May 13, 2008.

28. A. L. Herman, "College Cheating: A Plea for Leniency," *Journal of Higher Education* 37 (1966): 260–66.

29. Dirk Tedmon, "Students Penalized Unfairly by Mandatory Attendance Regulation," *Augustana Mirror*, April 8, 2009, http://www.augustanamirror.com/forum/students-penalized-unfairly-by-mandatory-attendance-regulation-1.1648782 (accessed September 5, 2009).

30. Arthur Levine, "Higher Education as a Mature Industry," in Altbach, Gumport, and Johnstone, *In Defense of American Higher Education*, p. 42.

31. Rhodes, *Creation of the Future*, pp. 21, 54.

32. Ibid., p. 77.

33. Christopher Clausen, "The New Ivory Tower," *Wilson Quarterly* 30, no. 4 (2006): 35.

34. Levine, "Higher Education as a Mature Industry," p. 42.

35. Eric Gould, *The University in a Corporate Culture* (New Haven, CT: Yale University Press, 2003), p. xvii.

36. Robert Birnbaum and Frank Shushok Jr., "The 'Crisis' Crisis in Higher Education: Is That a Wolf or a Pussycat at the Academy's Door?" in Altbach, Gumport, and Johnstone, *In Defense of American Higher Education*, pp. 68–69.

37. Michael McPherson and Morton Schapiro, "Tenure Issues in Higher Education," *Journal of Economic Perspectives* 13 (1999): 85–98.

38. Gould, *University in a Corporate Culture*, p. xvii.

39. Rhodes, *Creation of the Future*, p. 54.

40. Gould, *University in a Corporate Culture*, p. xi.

41. Rhodes, *Creation of the Future*, p. 93.

42. Philip G. Altbach, "The American Academic Model in Comparative Perspective," in Altbach, Gumport, and Johnstone, *In Defense of American Higher Education*, pp. 31–32.

43. Levine, "Higher Education as a Mature Industry," p. 40.

44. Birnbaum and Shushok, "The 'Crisis' Crisis," p. 72.

45. Richard S. Ruch, *Higher Ed, Inc.: The Rise of the For-Profit University* (Baltimore: Johns Hopkins University Press, 2001), pp. 41, 96.

46. Robert E. Wright et al., eds., *History of Corporate Governance: The Importance of Stakeholder Activism* (London: Pickering & Chatto, 2004).

47. Louise Churchill, "Professor Goodgrade," *Chronicle of Higher Education*, February 24, 2006.

CHAPTER 9: FIGHTING FUBAR

1. "Manufacturing Corporations," *American Jurist* (July 1829): 109.

2. As quoted in Andrew Yarrow, *Forgive Us Our Debts: The Intergenerational Dangers of Fiscal Irresponsibility* (New Haven, CT: Yale University Press, 2008), p. 81.

3. Pavel Chalupnicek and Lukas Dvorak, "Health Insurance before the Welfare State: The Destruction of Self-Help by State Intervention," *Independent Review* 13 (Winter 2009): 367–87.

4. Larry J. Sabato, *A More Perfect Constitution: 23 Proposals to Revitalize Our Constitution and Make America a Fairer Country* (New York: Walker, 2007).

5. Robert E. Wright, "Could an Italian Economist Born in the 19th Century Offer an Answer to Our Political Prayers?" *History News Network*, September 1, 2008, http://hnn.us/articles/51848.html (accessed September 5, 2009).

6. As quoted in Graham Hancock, *Lords of Poverty: The Power, Prestige, and Corruption of the International Aid Business* (New York: Atlantic Monthly Press, 1989), p. 35.

7. Jacob Weisberg, "The End of Libertarianism: The Financial Collapse Proves That Its Ideology Makes No Sense," *Slate*, October 18, 2008, http://www.slate.com/id/2202489/ (accessed September 5, 2009).

8. Thomas E. Woods, *Meltdown: A Free-Market Look at Why the Stock Market Collasped, the Economy Tanked, and Government Bailouts Will Make Things Worse* (Washington, DC: Regnery Publishing, 2009), pp. ix.

9. Kenneth Snowden, "Mortgage Securitization in the United States: Twentieth-Century Developments in Historical Perspective," in *Anglo-American Financial Systems: Institutions and Markets in the Twentieth Century*, ed. Michael Bordo and Richard Sylla (Burr Ridge, IL: Irwin Professional Publishing, 1995).

10. Viral Acharya and Matthew Richardson, eds., *Restoring Financial Stability: How to Repair a Failed System* (Hoboken, NJ: John Wiley and Sons, 2009).

11. "Slice of Danish," *Economist,* January 3, 2009, p. 55.

12. Barry LePatner, Timothy Jacobson, and Robert E. Wright, *Broken Buildings, Busted Budgets: How to Fix America's Trillion-Dollar Construction Industry* (Chicago: University of Chicago Press, 2007).

13. NAHB Economics, Mortgage Finance and Housing Policy Division, *Producing Affordable Housing: Partnerships for Profit* (Washington, DC: Home Builder Press, 1999), p. x.

14. Alison Berry Cronon, "Forest Policy Up in Smoke: Fire Suppression in the United States" (Searle Center on Law, Regulation, and Economic Growth, Research Symposium on Bad Public Goods, working paper, September 15–16, 2008).

15. Robert E. Wright, ed., *Bailouts: Public Money, Private Profit* (New York: Columbia University Press, 2010).

16. Woods, *Meltdown*, pp. 147–48.

17. Sylvester Schieber and John Shoven, *The Real Deal: The History and Future of Social Security* (New Haven, CT: Yale University Press, 1999), pp. 128–29.

18. As quoted in Sheryl Tynes, *Turning Points in Social Security: From "Cruel Hoax" to "Sacred Entitlement"* (Stanford: Stanford University Press, 1996), p. 64.

19. Ibid., p. 198.

20. Yarrow, *Forgive Us Our Debts*, p. 94.

21. As quoted in Tynes, *Turning Points*, p. 155.

22. Richard H. Thaler and Cass R. Sunstein, *Nudge: Improving Decisions about Health, Wealth, and Happiness* (New Haven, CT: Yale University Press, 2008), p. 103; Mitchell A. Orenstein, ed., *Pensions, Social Security, and the Privatization of Risk* (New York: Columbia University Press/SSRC, 2009), p. 5.

23. Schieber and Shoven, *Real Deal*, p. 234.

24. Dora Costa assumes otherwise when she argues that the trend toward ever-earlier retirements is unlikely to reverse. Of course it will not reverse, except following a major bear market. Who could turn down so much free time coupled with an adequate income? The government needs to do a better job of publicizing the distinction between attainment of a nominal age and superannuation. Costa's work is otherwise highly recommended. Dora Costa, *The Evolution of Retirement: An American Economic History, 1880–1990* (Chicago: University of Chicago Press, 1998). For a more realistic view of the situation as it stands today, see "The End of Retirement," *Economist*, June 27, 2009, p. 18.

25. Carole Haber and Brian Gratton, *Old Age and the Search for Security: An American Social History* (Bloomington: Indiana University Press, 1994).

26. Schieber and Shoven, *Real Deal*, p. 298; Orenstein, *Pensions*, p. 4.

27. Schieber and Shoven, *Real Deal*, pp. 298–300.

28. Tynes, *Turning Points*, p. 116.

29. Orenstein, *Pensions*, p. 47.

30. "World of Methuselahs," *Economist*, June 27, 2009, p. SR 7.

31. Tynes, *Turning Points*, p. 204.

32. Yarrow, *Forgive Us Our Debts*, pp. 100–106.

33. Schieber and Shoven, *Real Deal*, pp. 232–33.

34. Some one-third of the population over age 62 may be unable to continue employment for health or productivity reasons. Orenstein, *Pensions*, p. 23.

35. Robert Eisner, *Social Security: More, Not Less* (New York: Century Foundation Press, 1998), pp. 2, 19–22.

36. Ibid.

37. Thaler and Sunstein, *Nudge*.

38. Ibid., p. 14.

39. Eisner, *Social Security*, p. 8.

40. Orenstein, *Pensions*, pp. 27, 67.

41. Ibid., pp. 92–103, 122–26.

42. Numerous examples can be found sprinkled throughout Thaler and Sunstein, *Nudge*.

43. Orenstein, *Pensions*, p. 33.

44. Yarrow, *Forgive Us Our Debts*, p. 113.

45. Graetz and Mashaw, *True Security*, p. 10.

46. Robert E. Wright, "Are Dietary Guidelines a Public Good?" *Freeman: Ideas on Liberty* (November 2002): 16–19.

47. This idea is similar to that recently put forth by Tom Baker and Peter Siegelman, "Enticing Low Risks into the Health Insurance Pool: Tontines for the Invincibles, An Idea from Insurance History and Behavioral Economics" (working paper 09-07, University of Pennsylvania Institute for Law and Economic Research, July 28, 2009).

48. This is much different than the "family-owned, mom and pop, storefront proprietary schools" of yore. Richard S. Ruch, *Higher Ed, Inc.: The Rise of the For-Profit University* (Baltimore: Johns Hopkins University Press, 2001), p. 51. For a fuller discussion and framework, albeit one focused on K–12, see Richard K. Vedder, *Can Teachers Own Their Own Schools? New Strategies for Educational Excellence* (Oakland: Independent Institute, 2000).

49. Jack L. Carr and G. F. Mathewson, "Unlimited Liability as a Barrier to Entry," *Journal of Political Economy* 96 (1988): 766–84.

50. Northern Illinois Building Contractors Association, "Build-Operate-Transfer (Lease-Back)," http://www.nibca.net/usersbuild.asp (accessed September 5, 2009).

51. Keith Miller, "The Furlough Blues," *Chronicle of Higher Education* (April 10, 2009); David Shieh, "Princeton Slashes Its Budget Again and Freezes Salaries," *Chronicle of Higher Education*, April 10, 2009.

52. For a similar vision, see Saul Cornell, *A Well-Regulated Militia: The Founding Fathers and the Origins of Gun Control in America* (New York: Oxford University Press, 2006).

BIBLIOGRAPHY

Aaronson, Stephanie, and Julia Coronado. "Are Firms or Workers behind the Shift Away from DB Pension Plans?" *Finance and Economic Discussion Series, Federal Reserve Board*, no. 17 (February 2005).

Abbott, Grace. *From Relief to Social Security: The Development of the New Public Welfare Service.* Chicago: University of Chicago Press, 1941.

ABC News, Primetime Thursday, "Full Service Fakery: Inside the Life of a Professional Essay Writer and Test Taker," April 29, 2004.

Abreu, Dilip, and Markus Brunnermeier. "Bubbles and Crashes." *Econometrica* 71 (2003): 173–204.

Accountants International Study Group. *Accounting for Pension Costs: Current Practices in Canada, the United Kingdom, and the United States.* New York: Accountants International Study Group, 1977.

Acharya, Viral, and Matthew Richardson, eds. *Restoring Financial Stability: How to Repair a Failed System.* Hoboken, NJ: John Wiley and Sons, 2009.

Alchian, Armen A. *Economic Forces at Work.* Indianapolis: Liberty Fund, 1977.

"Alexander Mackraby to Sir Philip Francis." *Pennsylvania Magazine of History and Biography* 11 (1887): 282.

Allen, Franklin, Stephen Morris, and Andrew Postlewaite. "Finite Bubbles with Short Sale Constraints and Asymmetric Information." *Journal of Economic Theory* 61 (1993): 206–29.

Altbach, Philip G. "The American Academic Model in Comparative Perspective." In *In Defense of American Higher Education,* edited by Philip Altbach, Patricia

Gumport, and D. Bruce Johnstone. Baltimore: Johns Hopkins University Press, 2001.

Amenta, Edwin. *When Movements Matter: The Townsend Plan and the Rise of Social Security.* Princeton, NJ: Princeton University Press, 2006.

American Jurist, "Manufacturing Corporations," July 1829.

Anonymous. *Act to Empower Certain Commissioners Herein Appointed to Regulate the Hire of Porters and Labour of Slaves in the Town of Savannah.* Savannah, GA: James Johnston, 1783.

Anonymous. *Address to the Freeholders of New-Jersey, on the Subject of Public Salaries.* Philadelphia: Steuart, 1763.

Anonymous. *Cause of, and Cure for, Hard Times.* New York: n.p., 1818.

Anonymous. *Observations on the Slaves and the Indented Servants, Inlisted in the Army, and in the Navy of the United States.* Philadelphia: n.p., 1777.

Appleton, Nathaniel. *Considerations on Slavery: In a Letter to a Friend.* Boston: Edes and Gill, 1767.

Ashworth, John. *Slavery, Capitalism, and Politics in the Antebellum Republic.* New York: Cambridge University Press, 1995.

Associated Press. "9 Patients Made Nearly 2,700 ER Visits in Texas," April 1, 2009.

Axilrod, Stephen. *Inside the Fed: Monetary Policy and Its Management, Martin through Greenspan to Bernanke.* Cambridge, MA: MIT Press, 2009.

Bailey, Ronald. "Hips Abroad: Medical Outsourcing." *Reason Online* (May 2009). http://www.reason.com/news/show/132610.html (accessed September 5, 2009).

Baker, Tom, and Peter Siegelman. "Enticing Low Risks into the Health Insurance Pool: Tontines for the Invincibles, An Idea from Insurance History and Behavioral Economics." Working Paper, University of Pennsylvania Institute for Law and Economic Research, July 28, 2009.

Banner, Stuart. *Anglo-America Securities Regulation: Cultural and Political Roots, 1690–1860.* New York: Cambridge University Press, 2002.

Barber, William. *From New Era to New Deal: Herbert Hoover, the Economists, and American Economic Policy, 1921–1933.* New York: Cambridge University Press, 1985.

Barck, Dorothy C., ed. *Letter Book of John Watts, Merchant and Councillor of New York, January 1, 1762–December 22, 1765.* New York: John Watts De Peyster Publication Fund Series, 1928.

Barlevy, Gadi. "Economic Theory and Asset Bubbles." *Economic Perspectives: Federal Reserve Bank of Chicago*, no. 3 (2007): 44–59.

Barnett, Andy H., Roger D. Blair, and David L. Kaserman. "A Market for Organs." In *Entrepreneurial Economics: Bright Ideas from the Dismal Science*, edited by Alexander Tabarrok. New York: Oxford University Press, 2002.

Bateman, Fred, and Thomas Weiss. *A Deplorable Scarcity: The Failure of Industrial-*

ization in the Slave Economy. Chapel Hill: University of North Carolina Press, 1981.

Baumol, William, Robert Litan, and Carl Schramm. *Good Capitalism, Bad Capitalism, and the Economics of Growth and Prosperity.* New Haven, CT: Yale University Press, 2007.

Beck, Konstantin. "Growing Importance of Capitation in Switzerland." *Health Care Management Sciences* 3 (2000): 111–19.

Belth, Joseph. "Discussion." In *The Financial Condition and Regulation of Insurance Companies,* edited by Richard E. Randall and Richard W. Kopcke. Boston: Federal Reserve Bank of Boston, 1991.

Benmelech, Efraim, Eugene Kandel, and Pietro Veronesi. "Stock-Based Compensation and CEO (Dis)incentives." NBER Working Paper no. 13732, 2008.

Bernanke, Benjamin. *Essays on the Great Depression.* Princeton, NJ: Princeton University Press, 2000.

Bernstein, Peter. *Wedding of the Waters: The Erie Canal and the Making of a Great Nation.* New York: W. W. Norton, 2005.

Bernstein, William. *The Birth of Plenty: How the Prosperity of the Modern World Was Created.* New York: McGraw-Hill, 2004.

Bhattacharya, Utpal, and Xiaoyun Yu. "The Causes and Consequences of Recent Financial Market Bubbles: An Introduction." *Review of Financial Studies* 21 (2008): 3–10.

Bielick, S., K. Chandler, and S. P. Broughman. *Homeschooling in the United States: 1999.* Washington, DC: National Center for Education Statistics, 2001.

Birnbaum, Robert, and Frank Shushok Jr. "The 'Crisis' Crisis in Higher Education: Is That a Wolf or a Pussycat at the Academy's Door?" In *In Defense of American Higher Education,* edited by Philip Altbach, Patricia Gumport, and D. Bruce Johnstone. Baltimore: Johns Hopkins University Press, 2001.

Blackburn, Robin. *Banking on Death; or, Investing in Life: The History and Future of Pensions.* London: Verso, 2002.

Bodley Family Papers, Filson Historical Society, Louisville, KY.

Bok, Derek. "The New 'U.'" *Forbes.com,* April 18, 2006. http://www.forbes.com/2006/04/15/derek-bok-university_cx_db_06slate_0418bok.html (accessed September 5, 2009).

Booth, William D. *Marketing Strategies for Design-Build Contracting.* New York: Chapman and Hall, 1995.

Brandeis, Louis. *Other People's Money and How the Bankers Use It.* New York: Frederick A. Stokes, 1932.

Brannon, Gerard M. "Public Policy and Life Insurance." In *The Financial Condition and Regulation of Insurance Companies,* edited by Richard E. Randall and Richard W. Kopcke. Boston: Federal Reserve Bank of Boston, 1991.

Brock, Leslie V. *Currency of the American Colonies, 1700–1764: A Study in Colonial Finance and Imperial Relations.* New York: Arno Press, 1975.

Brooks, Rick, and Ruth Simon. "Subprime Debacle Traps Even Very Credit-Worthy." *Wall Street Journal,* December 3, 2007.

Brown Papers, John Carter Brown Library, Providence, RI.

Brunnermeier, Markus. "Bubbles." In *The New Palgrave Dictionary of Economics.* New York: Oxford University Press, 2007.

Brunnermeier, Markus, and Christian Julliard. "Money Illusion and Housing Frenzies." *Review of Financial Studies* 21 (2008): 135–80.

Butler, Richard, Yijing Cui, and Andrew Whitman. "Insurers' Demutualization Decisions." *Risk Management and Insurance Review* 3 (2000): 135–54.

Calomiris, Charles, and Eugene White. "The Origins of Federal Deposit Insurance." In *The Regulated Economy: A Historical Approach to Political Economy,* edited by Claudia Goldin and Gary Libecap. Chicago: University of Chicago Press, 1994.

Carosso, Vincent P. *Investment Banking in America: A History.* Cambridge, MA: Harvard University Press, 1970.

———. "The Wall Street Money Trust from Pujo through Medina." *Business History Review* 47 (1973): 421–37.

———. "Washington and Wall Street: The New Deal and Investment Bankers, 1933–1940." *Business History Review* 44 (1970): 425–44.

Carr, Jack L., and G. F. Mathewson. "Unlimited Liability as a Barrier to Entry." *Journal of Political Economy* 96 (1988): 766–84.

Carroll, Brian. "The Mutual-Fund Trading Scandals." *Journal of Accountancy* 198 (2004): 32–36.

Caucutt, Elizabeth, Thomas Cooley, and Nezih Guner. "The Farm, the City, and the Emergence of Social Security." Working Paper, May 2007.

Centers for Medicare and Medicaid Services. *Choosing a Medigap Policy 2009: A Guide to Health Insurance for People with Medicare.* Washington, DC: Department of Health and Human Services, 2009.

Central Intelligence Agency. "Switzerland." *The World Factbook.* https://www.cia .gov/library/publications/the-world-factbook/geos/sz.html (accessed September 4, 2009).

Chalupnicek, Pavel, and Lukas Dvorak. "Health Insurance before the Welfare State: The Destruction of Self-Help by State Intervention." *Independent Review* 13 (Winter 2009): 367–87.

Chancellor, Edward. *Devil Take the Hindmost: A History of Financial Speculation.* New York: Plume, 1999.

Chapman, John. *Concentration of Banking: The Changing Structure and Control of Banking in the United States.* New York: Columbia University Press, 1934.

Churchill, Louise. "Professor Goodgrade." *Chronicle of Higher Education*, February 24, 2006.

Clausen, Christopher. "The New Ivory Tower." *Wilson Quarterly* 30, no. 4 (2006): 31–36.

CNN Money, "BoA, Fleet in $675M fund settlement," March 15, 2004. http://money.cnn.com/2004/03/15/funds/fundsfire_sec/ (accessed August 27, 2009).

Coase, Ronald. "The Problem of Social Cost." *Journal of Law and Economics* 3 (1960): 1–44.

Cochrane, John H. "Time-Consistent Health Insurance." In *Entrepreneurial Economics: Bright Ideas from the Dismal Science*, edited by Alexander Tabarrok. New York: Oxford University Press, 2002.

Coll, Blanche. *Safety Net: Welfare and Social Security, 1929–1979*. New Brunswick, NJ: Rutgers University Press, 1995.

Colonial Society of Massachusetts. *Publications of the Colonial Society of Massachusetts, vol. 13, 1910–1911*. Boston: Colonial Society of Massachusetts, 1912.

Conrad, Alfred, and John Meyer. *The Economics of Slavery and Other Studies in Econometric History*. Chicago: Aldine Publishing, 1964.

Cooper, David. *A Serious Address to the Rulers of America on the Inconsistency of Their Conduct Respecting Slavery: Forming a Contrast between the Encroachments of England on American Liberty, and American Injustice in Tolerating Slavery*. Trenton, NJ: Isaac Collins, 1783.

Cornell, Saul. *A Well-Regulated Militia: The Founding Fathers and the Origins of Gun Control in America*. New York: Oxford University Press, 2006.

Costa, Dora. *The Evolution of Retirement: An American Economic History, 1880–1990*. Chicago: University of Chicago Press, 1998.

Coulter, Angela, and Crispin Jenkinson. "European Patients' Views on the Responsiveness of Health Systems and Healthcare Providers." *European Journal of Public Health* 15 (2005): 355–60.

Coxe, Tench. *A View of the United States of America*. Philadelphia: William Hall and Wrigley & Berriman, 1794.

Crawford, Charles. *Observations upon Negro-Slavery*. Philadelphia: Joseph Crukshank, 1784.

Cronon, Alison Berry. "Forest Policy Up in Smoke: Fire Suppression in the United States." Working Paper, Searle Center on Law, Regulation, and Economic Growth, Research Symposium on Bad Public Goods, September 15–16, 2008.

Cunningham, Robert III, and Robert M. Cunningham Jr. *The Blues: A History of the Blue Cross and Blue Shield System*. Dekalb: Northern Illinois University, 1997.

Cutler, David M., and Jonathan Gruber. "Does Public Insurance Crowd Out Private Insurance?" *Quarterly Journal of Economics* 111 (1996): 391–430.

D'Arista, Jane W. *The Evolution of Finance, Volume II: Restructuring Institutions and Markets*. Armonk, NY: M. E. Sharpe, 1994.

Dass, Nishant, Massimo Massa, and Rajdeep Patgiri. "Mutual Funds and Bubbles: The Surprising Role of Contractual Incentives." *Review of Financial Studies* 21 (2008): 51–99.

David, Paul, Herbert Gutman, Richard Sutch, Peter Temin, and Gavin Wright. *Reckoning with Slavery: A Critical Study in the Quantitative History of American Negro Slavery*. New York: Oxford University Press, 1976.

Dawson, Miles. "Fraternal Life Insurance." *Annals of the American Academy of Political and Social Science* 26 (1905): 128–36.

———. "Mutualization of Life Insurance Companies." *Annals of the American Academy of Political and Social Science* 70 (1917): 62–76.

De La Vega, Joseph. *Confusion de Confusiones*. Hoboken, NJ: John Wiley and Sons, 1995.

De Rugy, Veronique. "Stimulating Ourselves to Death." *Reason Online* (April 2009), http://www.reason.com/news/show/131968.html (accessed September 5, 2009).

De Tocqueville, Alexis. *Democracy in America*. Chicago: University of Chicago Press, 2000.

Diamond, Jared. *Guns, Germs, and Steel: The Fates of Human Societies*. New York: W. W. Norton, 1997.

Dilwyn, William. *Brief Considerations on Slavery, and the Expediency of Its Abolition*. Burlington, NJ: Isaac Collins, 1773.

Doherty, Brian. "Yesterday Is Tomorrow: Revisiting Annie as a New New Deal Dawns." *Reason Online* (May 2009). http://www.reason.com/news/show/132661.html (accessed September 5, 2009).

Dolbeare, Cushing. *Federal Housing Assistance: Who Needs It? Who Gets It?* Washington, DC: National League of Cities, 1985.

Eaton, Joseph W., and David Eaton. *The American Title Insurance Industry: How a Cartel Fleeces the American Consumer*. New York: New York University Press, 2007.

Economist, "Con of the Century," December 20, 2008.

———, "End of Retirement," June 27, 2009.

———, "Harry and Louise Ride Again," April 4, 2009.

———, "Is America Still AAA?" May 23, 2009.

———, "Labour Mobility: The Road Not Taken," March 21, 2009.

———, "Lessons from a Frugal Innovator," April 18, 2009.

———, "Not So Risk-Free," May 30, 2009.

———, "A Slice of Danish," January 3, 2009.

———, "Wages of Sin: The Fed Is Perpetuating a Discredited Oligopoly," April 25, 2009.

————, "World of Methuselahs," June 27, 2009.

Economist Intelligence Unit. "Country Finance: Japan." New York: EIU, April 2004.

Edward Carey Gardiner Collection, Historical Society of Pennsylvania, Philadelphia, PA.

Edwards, Franklin. "Banks and Securities Activities: Legal and Economic Perspectives on the Glass-Steagall Act." In *The Deregulation of the Banking and Securities Industries*, edited by Lawrence Goldberg and Lawrence J. White. Boston: D. C. Heath, 1979.

Eichler, Ned. *The Merchant Builders*. Cambridge, MA: MIT Press, 1982.

Einhorn, David. *Fooling Some of the People All of the Time: A Long Short Story*. Hoboken, NJ: John Wiley and Sons, 2008.

Eisner, Robert. *Social Security: More, Not Less*. New York: Century Foundation Press, 1998.

Epstein, Richard. *Overdose: How Excessive Government Regulation Stifles Pharmaceutical Innovation*. New Haven, CT: Yale University Press, 2006.

Equiano, Olaudah. "The Horrors of the Middle Passage." In *Afro-American History: Primary Sources*. 2nd ed., edited by Thomas Frazier. Belmont, CA: Wadsworth Publishing, 1988.

Erhemjamts, Otgo, and Richard Phillips. "What Drives Life Insurer Demutualizations?" Working Paper, 2005.

Even, William E., and David A. MacPherson. "Improving Pension Coverage at Small Firms." In *Overcoming Barriers to Entrepreneurship in the United States*, edited by Diana Furchtgott-Roth. Lanham, MD: Lexington Books, 2008.

Ewald, William Bragg. *Trammell Crow: A Legacy of Real Estate Business Innovation*. Washington, DC: Urban Land Institute, 2005.

Faber, Eli. *Jews, Slaves, and the Slave Trade: Setting the Record Straight*. New York: New York University Press, 1998.

Federal Reserve. "Concentration of Banking in the United States." *Staff Report of the Board of Governors of the Federal Reserve System*. Washington, DC: Government Printing Office, 1952.

Federle, Mark, and Steven Pigneri. "Predictive Model of Cost Overruns." *Transactions of the AACE International* (1993).

Feldstein, Martin, and Jeffrey Liebman, eds. *The Distributional Aspects of Social Security and Social Security Reform*. Chicago: University of Chicago Press, 2002.

Finkelstein, Martin. "Understanding the American Academic Profession." In *In Defense of American Higher Education*, edited by Philip Altbach, Patricia Gumport, and D. Bruce Johnstone. Baltimore: Johns Hopkins University Press, 2001.

Fishback, Price Van Meter, et al. *Government and the American Economy: A New History*. Chicago: University of Chicago Press, 2007.

Fitzpatrick, John C., ed. *The Writings of George Washington from the Original Manuscript Sources, 1754–1799.* Washington, DC: Government Printing Office, 1931.

Fogel, Robert. *Without Consent or Contract: The Rise and Fall of American Slavery.* New York: W. W. Norton, 1989.

Folsom, Burt. *New Deal or Raw Deal?* New York: Threshold, 2008.

Foner, Philip, and Herbert Shapiro, eds. *Northern Labor and Antislavery: A Documentary History.* Westport, CT: Greenwood Press, 1994.

Ford, Paul L., ed. *The Writings of John Dickinson.* Philadelphia: Historical Society of Pennsylvania, 1895.

Foster, Isaac. *A Discourse upon Extortion.* Hartford, CT: n.p., 1777.

Frank, Richard, and Karine Lamiraud. "Choice, Price Competition and Complexity in Markets for Health Insurance." NBER Working Paper no. 13817, February 2008.

Franklin, Benjamin. *The Interest of Great Britain Considered.* Boston: B. Mecom, 1760.

Frazer, William, and John J. Guthrie Jr. *The Florida Land Boom: Speculation, Money, and the Banks.* Westport, CT: Quorum Books, 1995.

Friedberg, Leora, and Michael Owyang. "Explaining the Evolution of Pension Structure and Job Tenure." NBER Working Paper no. 10714, 2004.

Friedman, Milton, and Rose Friedman. *Free to Choose: A Personal Statement.* New York: Harcourt, 1990.

Friedman, Thomas L. *The World Is Flat: A Brief History of the Twenty-first Century.* New York: Farrar, Straus, and Giroux, 2005.

Galbraith, John Kenneth. *The Age of Uncertainty.* New York: Houghton Mifflin, 1979.

———. *The Great Crash 1929.* New York: Time, 1962.

Galenson, David. "The Rise and Fall of Indentured Servitude in the Americas: An Economic Analysis." *Journal of Economic History* 44 (March 1984): 1–13.

Garden, Alexander. *Six Letters to the Rev. Mr. George Whitefield.* Boston: T. Fleet, 1740.

Gart, Alan. *Regulation, Deregulation, Reregulation: The Future of the Banking, Insurance, and Securities Industries.* New York: John Wiley and Sons, 1994.

Genovese, Eugene. *Roll, Jordan, Roll: The World the Slaves Made.* New York: Random House, 1972.

Gershman, Gary. *The Legislative Branch of Federal Government.* New York: ABC-CLIO, 2008.

Gerstel, David. *Running a Successful Construction Company.* Newtown, CT: Taunton Press, 2002.

Gladwell, Malcolm. "The Picture Problem: Should a Charge of Plagiarism Ruin Your Life?" *New Yorker,* November 22, 2004.

Gould, Eric. *The University in a Corporate Culture.* New Haven, CT: Yale University Press, 2003.

Graetz, Michael, and Jerry Mashaw. *True Security: Rethinking American Social Insurance*. New Haven, CT: Yale University Press, 1999.

Graham, Loftin, and Xiaoying Xie. "The United States Insurance Market: Characteristics and Trends." In *Handbook of International Insurance: Between Global Dynamics and Local Contingencies*, edited by J. David Cummins and Bertrand Venard. New York: Springer, 2007.

Gratz—Inventors, Historical Society of Pennsylvania, Philadelphia, PA.

Grebler, Leo. *Large-Scale Housing and Real Estate Firms: Analysis of a New Business Enterprise*. New York: Praeger, 1973.

Greenwood, Robin, and Stefan Nagel. "Inexperienced Investors and Bubbles." NBER Working Paper no. 14111, 2008.

Grubb, Farley. "The End of European Servitude in the United States: An Economic Analysis of Market Collapse, 1772–1835." *Journal of Economic History* 54, no. 4 (1994): 794–824.

Gurkaynak, Refet. "Econometric Tests of Asset Price Bubbles: Taking Stock." *Journal of Economic Surveys* 22 (2008): 166–86.

Gurney, Joseph John. *A Journey in North America*. Norwich: n.p., 1841.

Haber, Carole, and Brian Gratton. *Old Age and the Search for Security: An American Social History*. Bloomington: Indiana University Press, 1994.

Hacker, Jacob S. "The New Push for American Health Security." In *Health at Risk: America's Ailing Health System—and How to Heal It*, edited by Jacob S. Hacker. New York: Columbia University Press/SSRC, 2008.

Hall, William D., and David Landsittel. *A New Look at Accounting for Pension Costs*. Homewood, IL: Pension Research Council, 1977.

Harrington, Virginia. *The New York Merchant on the Eve of the Revolution*. New York: Columbia University Press, 1935.

Harrison, Paul. "The More Things Change the More They Stay the Same: Analysis of the Past 200 Years of Stock Market Evolution." PhD diss., Duke University, 1994.

Haubrich, Joseph. "Nonmonetary Effects of Financial Crises: Lessons from the Great Depression in Canada." *Journal of Monetary Economics* 25 (1990): 223–52.

Helper, Hinton. *The Impending Crisis of the South: How to Meet It*. New York: Burdick Brothers, 1857.

Herman, A. L. "College Cheating: A Plea for Leniency." *Journal of Higher Education* 37 (1966): 260–66.

Herzlinger, Regina. "Foreign Health Affairs." *Wall Street Journal*, November 19, 2007.

Hetzel, Robert. "Government Intervention in Financial Markets: Stabilizing or Destabilizing?" Working Paper, Federal Reserve Bank of Richmond, 2009.

———. *The Monetary Policy of the Federal Reserve: A History*. New York: Cambridge University Press, 2008.

Historical Statistics of the United States. "Commercial Banks—Number and Assets, 1834–1980," table Cj251–65.

Hoffman, Beatrix. *The Wages of Sickness: The Politics of Health Insurance in Progressive America.* Chapel Hill: University of North Carolina Press, 2001.

Hoffman, Elizabeth, and Gary Libecap. "Political Bargaining and Cartelization in the New Deal: Orange Marketing Orders." In *The Regulated Economy: A Historical Approach to Political Economy,* edited by Claudia Goldin and Gary Libecap. Chicago: University of Chicago Press, 1994.

Homer, Sidney, and Richard Sylla. *A History of Interest Rates.* 4th ed. Hoboken, NJ: John Wiley and Sons, 2005.

Horle, Craig, et al., eds. *Lawmaking and Legislators in Pennsylvania.* Harrisburg: Pennsylvania House of Representatives, 2005.

Horton, James Oliver, and Lois E. Horton. *In Hope of Liberty: Culture, Community and Protest among Northern Free Blacks, 1700–1860.* New York: Oxford University Press, 1997.

Houston, Alan. *Benjamin Franklin and the Politics of Improvement.* New Haven, CT: Yale University Press, 2008.

Huston, James. *Calculating the Value of the Union: Slavery, Property Rights, and the Economic Origins of the Civil War.* Chapel Hill: University of North Carolina Press, 2003.

Huthmacher, J. Joseph, and Warren I. Susman, eds. *Herbert Hoover and the Crisis of American Capitalism.* Cambridge, MA: Schenkman Publishing, 1973.

Internet Movie Database. *Seven Pounds.* http://www.imdb.com/title/tt0814314/ (accessed September 4, 2009).

Jacobs, Rowena, and Maria Goddard. "Trade-Offs in Social Health Insurance Systems." *International Journal of Social Economics* (2002): 861–75.

Jiang, Goulin, Paul Mahoney, and Jianping Mei. "Market Manipulation: A Comprehensive Study of Stock Pools." *Journal of Financial Economics* 77, no. 1 (2005): 147–70.

Jones, Alice Hanson. *Wealth of a Nation to Be: The American Colonies on the Eve of the Revolution.* New York: Columbia University Press, 1980.

Jones, Charles P. *Investments: Analysis and Management.* 8th ed. New York: John Wiley and Sons, 2002.

Jordan, Winthrop. *White over Black: American Attitudes towards the Negro, 1550–1812.* Chapel Hill: University of North Carolina Press, 1968.

Joseph Richardson Account Book, 1733–1739. Historical Society of Pennsylvania, Philadelphia, PA.

J. S. *A Dialogue between a Gentleman and a Broker.* London: T. Cooper, 1736.

Juvenis. *Observations on the Slavery of the Negroes, in the Southern States, Particularly Intended for the Citizens of Virginia.* New York: W. Ross, 1785.

J. W. *An Address to the Freeholders of New-Jersey, on the Subject of Public Salaries.* Philadelphia: n.p., 1763.

Kemmerer, Donald. "American Financial Institutions: The Marketing of Securities, 1930–1952." *Journal of Economic History* 12 (1952): 454–68.

———. "The Colonial Loan-Office System in New Jersey." *Journal of Political Economy* 47 (December 1939): 867–74.

———. "A History of Paper Money in Colonial New Jersey, 1668–1775." *Proceedings of the NJ Historical Society* 74 (1956): 107–44.

Keohane, Nannerl. "The Liberal Arts and the Role of Elite Higher Education." In *In Defense of American Higher Education,* edited by Philip Altbach, Patricia Gumport, and D. Bruce Johnstone. Baltimore: Johns Hopkins University Press, 2001.

Kilbourne, Richard H., Jr. *Debt, Investment, Slaves: Credit Relations in East Feliciana Parish, Louisiana, 1825–1885.* Tuscaloosa: University of Alabama Press, 1995.

Kindleberger, Charles. *Manias, Panics, and Crashes: A History of Financial Crises.* 4th ed. Hoboken, NJ: John Wiley and Sons, 2000.

Koffler, John Frederick. *A Letter from a Tradesman in Lancaster to the Merchants of the Cities of Philadelphia, New York, and Boston.* Philadelphia: n.p., 1760.

Kollmann, Geoffry, and Carmen Solomon-Fears. *Social Security: Major Decisions in the House and Senate: 1935–2000.* New York: Novinka Books, 2002.

Kroszner, Randall, and Raghuram Rajan. "Is the Glass-Steagall Act Justified? A Study of the US Experience with Universal Banking before 1933." *American Economic Review* 84 (1994): 810–32.

Kuh, George. "College Students Today: Why We Can't Leave Serendipity to Chance." In *In Defense of American Higher Education,* edited by Philip Altbach, Patricia Gumport, and D. Bruce Johnstone. Baltimore: Johns Hopkins University Press, 2001.

Labaree, Leonard, et al., eds. *Papers of Benjamin Franklin.* New Haven, CT: Yale University Press, 1959.

Lange, Julian, and Daniel Mills, eds. *The Construction Industry: Balance Wheel of the Economy.* Lexington, MA: D. C. Heath, 1979.

Lanham, Richard. *The Economics of Attention: Style and Substance in the Age of Information.* Chicago: University of Chicago Press, 2006.

Lawrence, Joseph Stagg. *Banking Concentration in the United States: A Critical Analysis.* New York: Bankers Publishing, 1930.

Lencsis, Peter M. *Insurance Regulation in the United States: An Overview for Business and Government.* Westport, CT: Quorum Books, 1997.

LePatner, Barry, Timothy Jacobson, and Robert E. Wright. *Broken Buildings, Busted Budgets: How to Fix America's Trillion-Dollar Construction Industry.* Chicago: University of Chicago Press, 2007.

LeRoy, Stephen. "Rational Exuberance." *Journal of Economic Literature* 42 (2004): 783–804.

Lesser, Charles H., ed. *The Sinews of Independence: Monthly Strength Reports of the Continental Army.* Chicago: University of Chicago Press, 1976.

Letters to the People of New Jersey on the Frauds, Extortions, and Oppressions of the Railroad Monopoly. Philadelphia: Carey and Hart, 1848.

Leu, Robert E., and Martin Schellhorn. "The Evolution of Income-Related Inequalities in Health Care Utilization in Switzerland over Time." IZA Discussion Paper no. 1316, September 2004.

Levine, Arthur. "Higher Education as a Mature Industry." In *In Defense of American Higher Education,* edited by Philip Altbach, Patricia Gumport, and D. Bruce Johnstone. Baltimore: Johns Hopkins University Press, 2001.

Lewis, William W. *The Power of Productivity: Wealth, Poverty, and the Threat to Global Stability.* Chicago: University of Chicago Press, 2004.

A Lover of Constitutional Liberty. *The Appendix; or, Some Observations on the Expediency of the Petition of the Africans, Living in Boston, &c. Lately Presented to the General Assembly of This Province.* Boston: E. Russell, 1773.

Lynch, Thomas F. "Foundations of Radicalism." In *Understanding International Relations: The Value of Alternative Lenses.* 4th ed., edited by Daniel Kaufman, Jay Parker, and Kimberly Field. New York: McGraw-Hill, 1999.

Macey, Jonathan, and Geoffrey Miller. "Origin of the Blue Sky Laws." *Texas Law Review* 70, no. 2 (December 1991): 347–98.

Mack-Cozzo, Jane Barnes. "If You Think We Have Problems...Japan's Inferior University System." *American Enterprise* 13, no. 6 (2002): 46–47.

Mahoney, Paul. "The Origins of the Blue Sky Laws: A Test of Competing Hypotheses." *Journal of Law and Economics* 46 (April 2003): 229–51.

———. "The Political Economy of the Securities Act of 1933." *Journal of Legal Studies* 30 (January 2001): 1–31.

Mahoney, Paul, and Jianping Mei. "Mandatory vs. Contractual Disclosure in Securities Markets: Evidence from the 1930s." Working Paper, University of Virginia, 2006.

Majewski, John. *A House Dividing: Economic Development in Pennsylvania and Virginia before the Civil War.* New York: Cambridge University Press, 2000.

Mann, Bruce H. *Republic of Debtors: Bankruptcy in the Age of American Independence.* Cambridge, MA: Harvard University Press, 2002.

Mapping Strategy, "David Einhorn on the Financial Crisis," April 29, 2008. http://cartegic.typepad.com/mapping_strategy/2008/04/david-einhorn-o.html (accessed September 2, 2009).

Maria Dickinson Logan Papers, Historical Society of Pennsylvania, Philadelphia, PA.

Marshall, Alfred. *Money, Credit, and Commerce*. New York: Augustus M. Kelley, 1960.

Martin, Jonathan D. *Divided Mastery: Slave Hiring in the American South*. Cambridge, MA: Harvard University Press, 2004.

Mason, David. *From Buildings and Loans to Bail Outs: A History of the American Savings and Loan Industry, 1831–1995*. New York: Cambridge University Press, 2004.

Mason, Joseph. "The Evolution of the Reconstruction Finance Corporation as a Lender of Last Resort in the Great Depression." In *Bailouts: Public Money, Private Profit*, edited by Robert E. Wright. New York: Columbia University Press, 2010.

Mayer, Martin. *The Builders: Houses, People, Neighborhoods, Governments, Money*. New York: W. W. Norton, 1978.

McCallum, James B. "Mutual-Fund Market Timing: A Tale of Systematic Abuse and Executive Malfeasance." *Journal of Financial Regulation and Compliance* 12 (2004): 170–77.

McGlynn, Elizabeth, David Meltzer, and Jacob S. Hacker. "Just How Good *Is* American Medical Care?" In *Health at Risk: America's Ailing Health System—and How to Heal It*, edited by Jacob S. Hacker. New York: Columbia University Press/SSRC, 2008.

McKinnon, Ronald. "Bagehot's Lessons for the Fed." *Wall Street Journal*, April 25, 2008.

McMahan, John. *Property Development*. 2nd ed. New York: McGraw Hill, 1989.

McPherson, Michael, and Morton Schapiro. "Tenure Issues in Higher Education." *Journal of Economic Perspectives* 13 (1999): 85–98.

Meier, Kenneth J. *The Political Economy of Regulation: The Case of Insurance*. Albany: State University of New York Press, 1988.

Michener, Ron, and Robert E. Wright. *Control of the Purse: Money, Politics, and the Imperial Crisis in New York* [tentative title]. New Haven, CT: Yale University Press, forthcoming.

———. "Development of the US Monetary Union." *Financial History Review* 13, no. 1 (2006): 19–41.

———. "Farley Grubb's Noisy Evasions on Colonial Money: A Rejoinder." *Econ Journal Watch* (May 2006): 251–74.

———. "Miscounting Money of Colonial America." *Econ Journal Watch* (January 2006): 4–44.

———. "State 'Currencies' and the Transition to the US Dollar: Clarifying Some Confusions." *American Economic Review* (June 2005): 682–703.

Miller, Keith. "The Furlough Blues." *Chronicle of Higher Education*, April 10, 2009.

Millis, Harry A. *Sickness and Insurance: A Study of the Sickness Problem and Health Insurance*. Chicago: University of Chicago Press, 1937.

Mills, Edwin. "Urban Land-Use Controls and the Subprime Mortgage Crisis." *Independent Review* 13 (Spring 2009): 559–65.

Mishkin, Frederic. *The Economics of Money, Banking, and Financial Markets*. 5th ed. New York: Addison-Wesley, 1997.

Mitchell, John. *The Present State of Great Britain and North America*. London: T. Becket and P. A. De Hondt, 1767.

Moore, John Hammond, ed. *A Plantation Mistress on the Eve of the Civil War: The Diary of Keziah Goodwyn Hopkins Brevard, 1860–1861*. Columbia: University of South Carolina Press, 1993.

Morgan, Gerald. *Public Relief of Sickness*. New York: Macmillan, 1922.

Morgan, Kenneth. *Slavery and Servitude in Colonial North America: A Short History*. New York: New York University Press, 2000.

Mortimer, Thomas. *Every Man His Own Broker; or, A Guide to Exchange-Alley*. 3rd ed. London: S. Hooper, 1761.

MSNBC, "Madoff Whistleblower Went Unheeded for Years," December 19, 2008. http://www.msnbc.msn.com/id/28310980/ (accessed September 2, 2009).

Murray, John E. *Origins of American Health Insurance: A History of Industrial Sickness Funds*. New Haven, CT: Yale University Press, 2007.

NAHB Economics, Mortgage Finance and Housing Policy Division. *Producing Affordable Housing: Partnerships for Profit*. Washington, DC: Home Builder Press, 1999.

Nash, Gary. *Forging Freedom: The Formation of Philadelphia's Black Community, 1720–1840*. Cambridge, MA: Harvard University Press, 1988.

National Bureau of Economic Research. "Business Cycle Expansions and Contractions." http://www.nber.org/cycles.html (accessed September 4, 2009).

"New Jersey Currency Question." Record Group 23, Box 4. New Jersey Historical Society, Newark, NJ.

Nicolo, Gianni, Luc Laeven, and Kenichi Ueda. "Corporate Governance Quality: Trends and Real Effects." *Journal of Financial Intermediation* 17 (2008): 198–228.

Nisbet, Richard. *Slavery Not Forbidden by Scripture; or, a Defence of the West-India Planters, from the Aspersions Thrown Out Against Them*. Philadelphia: John Sparhawk, 1773.

Nocera, Joe. "Risk Management." *New York Times*, January 2, 2009. http://www.nytimes.com/2009/01/04/magazine/04risk-t.html (accessed August 27, 2009).

North, Douglass C. *Understanding the Process of Economic Change*. Princeton, NJ: Princeton University Press, 2005.

Northern Illinois Building Contractors Association. "Build-Operate-Transfer (Lease-Back)." http://www.nibca.net/usersbuild.asp (accessed September 5, 2009).

NPR, Marketplace, "Did Math Formula Cause Financial Crisis?" February 4, 2009. http://marketplace.publicradio.org/display/web/2009/02/24/pm_stock_formula_q/. (accessed August 27, 2009).

O'Hara, Maureen. "Bubbles: Some Perspectives (and Loose Talk) from History." *Review of Financial Studies* 21 (2008): 11–17.

Olmstead, Alan. *New York City Mutual Savings Banks, 1819–1861.* Chapel Hill: University of North Carolina Press, 1976.

Olmsted, Frederick Law. *A Journey in the Seaboard Slave States, with Remarks on Their Economy.* New York: Negro Universities Press, 1968.

Orenstein, Mitchell A., ed. *Pensions, Social Security, and the Privatization of Risk.* New York: Columbia University Press/SSRC, 2009.

Partnoy, Frank. "The Siskel and Ebert of Financial Markets? Two Thumbs Down for the Credit Rating Agencies." *Washington University Law Quarterly* 77 (1999): 619–714.

Payne, Peter, and Lance Davis. *The Savings Bank of Baltimore, 1818–1886.* Baltimore: Johns Hopkins University Press, 1956.

Perkins, Edwin J. *Wall Street to Main Street: Charles Merrill and Middle-Class Investors.* New York: Cambridge University Press, 1999.

Philadelphia Yearly Meeting. *An Epistle of Caution and Advice, concerning the Buying and Keeping of Slaves.* Philadelphia: James Chattin, 1754.

Philips, Peter. "The United States: Dual Worlds: The Two Growth Paths in US Construction." In *Building Chaos: An International Comparison of Deregulation in the Construction Industry,* edited by Gerhard Bosch and Peter Philips. New York: Routledge, 2003.

Pindyck, Robert, and Daniel Rubinfeld. *Microeconomics.* 3rd ed. Englewood Cliffs, NJ: Prentice Hall, 1995.

Pitkin, Timothy. *A Statistical View of the Commerce of the United States.* New York: Augustus Kelley, 1967.

Porter, David, and Vernon Smith. "Stock Market Bubbles in the Laboratory." *Journal of Behavioral Finance* 4 (2003): 7–20.

Pratico, Dominick. *Eisenhower and Social Security: The Origins of the Disability Program.* New York: Writers Club Press, 2001.

Present Status of Mutual Benefit Associations. New York: National Industrial Conference Board, 1931.

Preston, Howard. "Branch Banking with Special Reference to California Conditions." *Journal of Political Economy* 30, no. 4 (1922): 494–517.

PR Newswire, "Do the Swiss Have the Answer to America's Health Care Dilemma?" July 31, 2009.

Quadagno, Jill, and J. Brandon McKelvey. "The Transformation of American Health Insurance." In *Health at Risk: America's Ailing Health System—and How to Heal It,* edited by Jacob S. Hacker. New York: Columbia University Press/SSRC, 2008.

Raines, J. Patrick, J. Ashley McLeod, and Charles Leathers. "Theories of Stock

Prices and the Greenspan-Bernanke Doctrine on Stock Market Bubbles."
Journal of Post-Keynesian Economics 29 (2007): 393–408.

Randall, Richard E., and Richard W. Kopcke. "The Financial Condition and Regulation of Insurance Companies: An Overview." In *The Financial Condition and Regulation of Insurance Companies*, edited by Richard E. Randall and Richard W. Kopcke. Boston: Federal Reserve Bank of Boston, 1991.

Raskob, John J. "Everybody Ought to Be Rich." *Ladies' Home Journal*, August 1929.

Reed, William B. *The Life of Esther De Berdt, afterwards Esther Reed, of Pennsylvania.* Philadelphia: C. Sherman, 1853.

Register of Slaves, 1783–1830. Office of the Prothonotary, Bucks County, PA.

Reinhart, Carmen, and Kenneth Rogoff. "Banking Crises: An Equal Opportunity Menace." NBER Working Paper no. 14587, 2008.

———. "This Time Is Different: A Panoramic View of Eight Centuries of Financial Crises." Working Paper, April 2008.

Reynolds, Mary. "Life as a Slave: A Narrative." In *Afro-American History: Primary Sources.* 2nd ed., edited by Thomas Frazier. Belmont, CA: Wadsworth Publishing, 1988.

Rhodes, Frank H. T. *The Creation of the Future: The Role of the American University.* Ithaca, NY: Cornell University Press, 2001.

Robbins, Horace. "'Bigness,' the Sherman Act, and Antitrust Policy." *Virginia Law Review* 39, no. 7 (1953): 907–48.

Roberts, Kristin, and Emily Kaiser. "AIG CEO Defends Bonuses as Public Fury Mounts." Thomson Reuters, March 18, 2009.

Roberts, Russell. *The Choice: A Fable of Free Trade and Protectionism.* Upper Saddle River, NJ: Prentice Hall, 2001.

Robinson, Harriet H. *Loom and Spindle; or, Life among the Early Mill Girls.* New York: n.p., 1898.

Roe, Mark. "A Political Theory of American Corporate Finance." *Columbia Law Review* 91, no. 1 (1991): 10–67.

———. *Strong Managers, Weak Owners: The Political Roots of American Corporate Finance.* Princeton, NJ: Princeton University Press, 1996.

Roosevelt, Franklin Delano. First Inaugural Address. March 4, 1933.

Rothenberg, Winifred. *From Marketplaces to a Market Economy: The Transformation of Rural Massachusetts, 1750–1850.* Chicago: University of Chicago Press, 1992.

Rourke, Dennis. *The American Home Builder and the Housing Industry.* Rockville, MD: Management Practice Press, 1994.

Royster, Charles. *A Revolutionary People at War: The Continental Army and American Character, 1775–1783.* Chapel Hill: University of North Carolina Press, 1979.

Rubin, Paul. *Darwinian Politics: The Evolutionary Origin of Freedom.* New Brunswick, NJ: Rutgers University Press, 2002.

Ruch, Richard S. *Higher Ed, Inc.: The Rise of the For-Profit University.* Baltimore: Johns Hopkins University Press, 2001.

Rush, Benjamin. *An Address to the Inhabitants of the British Settlements in America, upon Slave-Keeping.* New York: Hodge and Shober, 1773.

Rushford, Brett. "'A Little Flesh We Offer You': The Origins of Indian Slavery in New France." *William and Mary Quarterly* 60 (2003): 777–808.

Sabato, Larry J. *A More Perfect Constitution: 23 Proposals to Revitalize Our Constitution and Make America a Fairer Country.* New York: Walker, 2007.

Saitone, Tina, and Richard Sexton. "Alpaca Lies? Speculative Bubbles in Agriculture: Why They Happen and How to Recognize Them." *Review of Agricultural Economics* 29 (2007): 286–305.

Salinger, Sharon V. *"To Serve Well and Faithfully": Labor and Indentured Servants in Pennsylvania, 1682–1800.* Cambridge: Cambridge University Press, 1987.

Salmon, Felix. "Recipe for Disaster: The Formula That Killed Wall Street." *Wired,* February 23, 2009.

Sass, Steven. *The Promise of Private Pensions: The First Hundred Years.* Cambridge, MA: Harvard University Press, 1997.

Satow, Julie. "Madoff Whistleblower Markopolos to Speak to *60 Minutes.*" *Huffington Post,* March 2, 2009. http://www.huffingtonpost.com/2009/03/02/madoff-whistleblower-mark_n_171120.html (accessed September 2, 2009).

Saturday Night Live. "Buck Henry/The Grateful Dead." *Saturday Night Live* Transcripts. Season 4, Episode 5. http://snltranscripts.jt.org/78/78eupdate.phtml (accessed September 5, 2009).

Sayre, Stephen. *The Englishman Deceived.* New York: John Holt, 1768.

Schieber, Sylvester, and John Shoven. *The Real Deal: The History and Future of Social Security.* New Haven, CT: Yale University Press, 1999.

Schlesinger, Arthur M., Jr. *The Age of Jackson.* Boston: Little, Brown, 1945.

Schulz, John. *The Financial Crisis of Abolition.* New Haven, CT: Yale University Press, 2008.

Schumpeter, Joseph. *Capitalism, Socialism, and Democracy.* New York: Harper, 1942.

Schwartz, Nelson. "Swiss Health Care Thrives without Public Option." *New York Times,* September 30, 2009.

Schweitzer, Mary. *Custom and Contract: Household, Government, and the Economy in Colonial Pennsylvania.* New York: Columbia University Press, 1987.

Securities and Exchange Commission. *SEC Annual Report,* various years.

Sharoff, Robert. "Drawing a Line on Drugs." *Builder* 20 (March 1997): 154–57.

Shelley, Percy Bysshe. "Ozymandias." 1818.

Shieh, David. "Princeton Slashes Its Budget Again and Freezes Salaries." *Chronicle of Higher Education,* April 10, 2009.

Shiller, Robert J. *New Financial Order: Risk in the 21st Century.* Princeton, NJ: Princeton University Press, 2003.

Shlaes, Amity. *The Forgotten Man: A New History of the Great Depression.* New York: Harper Perennial, 2007.

Simkovic, Michael. "Secret Liens and the Financial Crisis of 2008." Working Paper, January 4, 2009.

Simon, Miguel Cantillo. "The Rise and Fall of Bank Control in the United States: 1890–1939." *American Economic Review* 88 (1998): 1077–93.

"Six Ways to Compute the Relative Value of a US Dollar Amount, 1774 to Present." *MeasuringWorth.* http://www.measuringworth.com/uscompare/ (accessed September 4, 2009).

Skocpol, Theda. *The Time Is Never Ripe: The Repeated Defeat of Universal Health Insurance in the 20th Century United States.* Dublin, Ireland: Economic and Social Research Institute, 1995.

Skousen, Mark, ed. *The Big Three in Economics: Adam Smith, Karl Marx, and John Maynard Keynes.* New York: M. E. Sharpe, 2007.

———. *The Compleated Autobiography by Benjamin Franklin.* Washington, DC: Regnery, 2006.

Slave Songs of the United States. New York: A. Simpson, 1867.

Smith, Adam. *An Inquiry into the Nature and Causes of the Wealth of Nations.* New York: Modern Library, 1937.

———. *Lectures on Jurisprudence.* New York: Oxford University Press, 1976.

Smith, William. *Historical Memoirs from 16 March 1763 to 25 July 1778 of William Smith.* New York: Arno Press, 1969.

Snowden, Kenneth. "Mortgage Securitization in the United States: Twentieth-Century Developments in Historical Perspective." In *Anglo-American Financial Systems: Institutions and Markets in the Twentieth Century,* edited by Michael Bordo and Richard Sylla. Burr Ridge, IL: Irwin Professional Publishing, 1995.

Sobel, Robert. *Panic on Wall Street: A History of America's Financial Disasters.* New York: Macmillan, 1968.

Social Security Online. "Contribution and Benefit Base." *Social Security Online.* http://www.ssa.gov/OACT/COLA/cbb.html#Series (accessed September 5, 2009).

———. "Social Security & Medicare Tax Rates." *Social Security Online.* http://www.ssa.gov/OACT/ProgData/taxRates.html (accessed September 4, 2009).

Sparks, Edith. *Capital Intentions: Female Proprietors in San Francisco, 1850–1920.* Chapel Hill: University of North Carolina Press, 2006.

Starobin, Robert. *Industrial Slavery in the Old South.* New York: Oxford University Press, 1970.

Stegman, Michael. *Housing Finance and Public Policy: Cases and Supplementary Readings.* New York: Van Nostrand Reinhold, 1986.

Stiglitz, Joseph. *Globalization and Its Discontents.* New York: W. W. Norton, 2003.

Stowe, Harriet Beecher. *Uncle Tom's Cabin.* Mineola, NY: Dover Thrift Edition, 2005.

Swartz, Katherine. "Uninsured in America: New Realities, New Risks." In *Health at Risk: America's Ailing Health System—and How to Heal It,* edited by Jacob S. Hacker. New York: Columbia University Press/SSRC, 2008.

Tabarrok, Alexander. "Gene Insurance." In *Entrepreneurial Economics: Bright Ideas from the Dismal Science,* edited by Alexander Tabarrok. New York: Oxford University Press, 2002.

———. "The Organ Shortage: A Tragedy of the Commons?" In *Entrepreneurial Economics: Bright Ideas from the Dismal Science,* edited by Alexander Tabarrok. New York: Oxford University Press, 2002.

Taylor, Jason E. "Buy Now! Buy Here!: The Rise and Fall of the Patriotic Blue Eagle Emblem, 1933–1935." *Essays in Economic and Business History* 25 (2007): 117–30.

Tedmon, Dirk. "Students Penalized Unfairly by Mandatory Attendance Regulation." *Augustana Mirror,* April 8, 2009. http://www.augustanamirror.com/forum/students-penalized-unfairly-by-mandatory-attendance-regulation -1.1648782 (accessed September 5, 2009).

Thaler, Richard H., and Cass R. Sunstein. *Nudge: Improving Decisions about Health, Wealth, and Happiness.* New Haven, CT: Yale University Press, 2008.

Thomasson, Melissa. "Health Insurance in the United States." In *EH.Net Encyclopedia,* edited by Robert Whaples. http://eh.net/encyclopedia/article/thomasson.insurance.health.us (accessed September 4, 2009).

Thorne, Deborah, and Elizabeth Warren. "Get Sick, Go Broke." In *Health at Risk: America's Ailing Health System—and How to Heal It,* edited by Jacob S. Hacker. New York: Columbia University Press/SSRC, 2008.

Tirole, Jean. "On the Possibility of Speculation under Rational Expectations." *Econometrica* 50 (1982): 1163–81.

Title Insurance: Actions Needed to Improve Oversight of the Title Industry and Better Protect Consumers. Washington, DC: GAO, 2007.

Traflet, Janice. "Courting Women Stockholders: The NYSE, Brokers' Marketing Practices, and the Democratization of the Stock Market." Working Paper, Bucknell University, 2008.

Tucker, St. George. *A Dissertation on Slavery: With a Proposal for the Gradual Abolition of It, in the State of Virginia.* Philadelphia: Mathew Carey, 1796.

Tugwell, Rexford G. *Mr. Hoover's Economic Policy.* New York: John Day, 1932.

Tullock, Gordon, Arthur Seldon, and Gordon Brady. *Government Failure: A Primer in Public Choice.* Washington, DC: Cato Institute, 2002.

Tynes, Sheryl. *Turning Points in Social Security: From "Cruel Hoax" to "Sacred Entitlement."* Stanford: Stanford University Press, 1996.

United Kingdom. Staffordshire Record Office. American Papers of the Second Earl of Dartmouth.

US Bureau of the Census. Historical Census Browser. http://fisher.lib .virginia.edu/collections/stats/histcensus/ (accessed September 3, 2009).

———. *Industry Summary: Construction, 1997 Economic Census*, tables 5, 12. http:// www.census2010.gov/prod/ec97/97c23-is.pdf (accessed September 3, 2009).

US-Japan 21st Century Committee. "Summary Discussions on 'Education in the 21st Century.'" Kyoto, Japan, May 18, 1998.

Van Cortland, John. John van Cortland Letter Book. New York Historical Society, New York.

Vedder, Richard K. *Can Teachers Own Their Own Schools? New Strategies for Educational Excellence*. Oakland: Independent Institute, 2000.

Wall Street Journal, "Protecting the Investor," October 24, 1912.

Walter Rutherford Papers, New York Historical Society, New York.

Weisberg, Jacob. "The End of Libertarianism: The Financial Collapse Proves That Its Ideology Makes No Sense." *Slate*, October 18, 2008. http://www.slate .com/id/2202489/ (accessed September 5, 2009).

Welfling, Weldon. *Savings Banking in New York State: A Study of Changes in Savings Bank Practice and Policy Occasioned by Important Economic Changes*. Durham, NC: Duke University Press, 1939.

Wesley, John. *Thoughts upon Slavery*. London: n.p., 1774.

Westacott, Emrys. "The Future of Plagiarism." *Chronicle of Higher Education*, May 13, 2008.

Whaples, Robert, and David Buffum. "Fraternalism, Paternalism, the Family, and the Market: Insurance a Century Ago." *Social Science History* 15 (1991): 97–122.

What Is a Monopoly? or, Some Considerations upon the Subject of Corporations and Currency. New York: George P. Scott, 1835.

White, Eugene. "The Great American Real Estate Bubble of the 1920s: Causes and Consequences." Working Paper, Rutgers University, October 2008.

———. *The Regulation and Reform of the American Banking System, 1900–1929*. Princeton, NJ: Princeton University Press, 1983.

White, Lawrence J. "The Partial Deregulation of Banks and Other Depository Institutions." In *Regulatory Reform: What Actually Happened*, edited by Leonard W. Weiss and Michael W. Klass. Boston: Little, Brown, 1986.

———. "The Residential Real Estate Brokerage Industry: What Would More Vigorous Competition Look Like?" *Real Estate Law Journal* 35, no. 1 (Summer 2006): 11–35.

White, Patrick, ed. *Lord Selkirk's Diary, 1803–1804: A Journal of His Travels in British North America and the Northeastern United States*. Toronto: Champlain Society, 1958.

White, Philip L., ed. *The Beekman Mercantile Papers, 1746–1799.* New York: New York Historical Society, 1956.

Whiteside, Noel. "Insurance: Health and Accident." In *The Oxford Encyclopedia of Economic History.* Vol. 3, edited by Joel Mokyr. New York: Oxford University Press, 2003.

Wilke, John. "How Lawmaker Rebuilt Hometown on Earmarks." *Wall Street Journal*, October 30, 2007.

William Pollard Letterbook, Historical Society of Pennsylvania, Philadelphia, PA.

Williams, Oliver E., and Sidney G. Winter, eds. *The Nature of the Firm: Origins, Evolution, and Development.* New York: Oxford University Press, 1993.

Winston, Clifford. *Government Failure versus Market Failure: Microeconomics Policy Research and Government Performance.* Washington, DC: AEI-Brookings Joint Center for Regulatory Studies, 2006.

Wolman, Harold. *Housing and Housing Policy in the US and the UK.* Lexington, MA: D. C. Heath, 1975.

Woods, Thomas E. *Meltdown: A Free-Market Look at Why the Stock Market Collapsed, the Economy Tanked, and Government Bailouts Will Make Things Worse.* Washington, DC: Regnery Publishing, 2009.

Wooldridge, Clifton. *The Grafters of America.* Chicago: Monarch Book, 1906.

Woolsey, John. "The Capital Problem of Small and Medium-Sized Businesses." *Southern Economic Journal* 7 (1941): 461–74.

Wright, Donald R. *African Americans in the Early Republic, 1789–1831.* Arlington Heights, IL: Harlan Davidson, 1993.

Wright, Gwendolyn. *Building the Dream: A Social History of Housing in America.* New York: Pantheon Books, 1981.

Wright, Robert E. "Are Dietary Guidelines a Public Good?" *Freeman: Ideas on Liberty* (November 2002): 16–19.

———, ed. *Bailouts: Public Money, Private Profit.* New York: Columbia University Press, 2010.

———. "The College as Partnership." *Forbes.com*, December 29, 2005, http://www.forbes.com/columnists/2005/12/29/higher-education-partnerships -cx_rw_1230college.html (accessed August 27, 2009).

———. "Could an Italian Economist Born in the 19th Century Offer an Answer to Our Political Prayers?" *History News Network*, September 1, 2008. http://hnn.us/articles/51848.html (accessed September 5, 2009).

———. *The First Wall Street: Chestnut Street, Philadelphia, and the Birth of American Finance.* Chicago: University of Chicago Press, 2005.

———. *Hamilton Unbound: Finance and the Creation of the American Republic.* New York: Praeger, 2002.

————. *Higher Education and the Common Weal: Protecting Economic Growth and Political Stability with Professional Partnerships.* Hyderabad, India: ICFAI, 2010.

————. "Insuring America: Market, Intermediated, and Government Risk Management Since 1790." Working Paper, 2008.

————. *The Origins of Commercial Banking in America, 1750–1800.* Lanham, MD: Rowman and Littlefield, 2001.

————. "Reforming the US IPO Market: Lessons from History and Theory." *Accounting, Business, and Financial History* 12, no. 3 (2002): 419–37.

————.*The Wealth of Nations Rediscovered: Integration and Expansion in American Financial Markets, 1780–Dragonfly fall1850.* New York: Cambridge University Press, 2002.

Wright, Robert E., Wray Barber, Matthew Crafton, and Anand Jain, eds. *History of Corporate Governance: The Importance of Stakeholder Activism.* London: Pickering & Chatto, 2004.

Wright, Robert E., and David J. Cowen. *Financial Founding Fathers: The Men Who Made America Rich.* Chicago: University of Chicago Press, 2006.

Wright, Robert E., and George D. Smith. *Mutually Beneficial: The Guardian and Life Insurance in America.* New York: New York University Press, 2004.

Yarrow, Andrew. *Forgive Us Our Debts: The Intergenerational Dangers of Fiscal Irresponsibility.* New Haven, CT: Yale University Press, 2008.

Zailckas, Koren. *Smashed: Story of a Drunken Girlhood.* New York: Viking, 2005.

INDEX

AAA (Agricultural Adjustment Administration), 143
Abbott, Grace, 156
Abington, PA, 228
ABN Ambro, 58
abolitionism, 107, 113. *See also* slavery; South (US region)
academic freedom, 214, 216–17. *See also* tenure
actuarial data, 184, 193–94
adverse selection, 15–16, 172, 181–86, 192, 196–97. *See also* asymmetric information
Aetna Express Company, 138
AFDC (Aid to Families with Dependent Children), 160
Afghanistan, 234
AFL (American Federation of Labor), 161
Africa, 91–92
aggregate output (Y), 9, 13, 26, 75, 86, 119, 121, 126, 130, 133, 145, 147, 166, 181, 202

Agricultural Adjustment Administration. *See* AAA
agriculture: bubbles in, 52; policies concerning, 12–13, 143; productivity of, 203; sector of economy, 119
AIDS, 178
Aid to Families with Dependent Children. *See* AFDC
AIG (American International Group), 50, 53, 58
Alabama, 136
Alaska, 10
Albany, NY, 46
Albright, Mary, 199
Alexander, William (Lord Stirling), 38
Algiers, Algeria, 85
Allen, William, 41
Allied Capital, 60
al Qaeda, 12
Altbach, Philip, 218
Altmeyer, Arthur, 173
AMA (American Medical Association), 180, 189